W9-AAC-131

JavaScript for Absolute Beginners

Terry McNavage

Apress®

JavaScript for Absolute Beginners

Copyright © 2010 by Terry McNavage

All rights reserved. No part of this work may be reproduced or transmitted in any form or by any means, electronic or mechanical, including photocopying, recording, or by any information storage or retrieval system, without the prior written permission of the copyright owner and the publisher.

ISBN-13 (pbk): 978-1-4302-7219-9

ISBN-13 (electronic): 978-1-4302-7218-2

Printed and bound in the United States of America 9 8 7 6 5 4 3 2 1

Trademarked names, logos, and images may appear in this book. Rather than use a trademark symbol with every occurrence of a trademarked name, logo, or image we use the names, logos, and images only in an editorial fashion and to the benefit of the trademark owner, with no intention of infringement of the trademark.

The use in this publication of trade names, trademarks, service marks, and similar terms, even if they are not identified as such, is not to be taken as an expression of opinion as to whether or not they are subject to proprietary rights.

President and Publisher: Paul Manning
Lead Editors: Ben Renow-Clarke, Matthew Moodie
Technical Reviewers: Kristian Besley, Rob Drimmie, Tom Barker
Editorial Board: Steve Anglin, Mark Beckner, Ewan Buckingham, Gary Cornell, Jonathan Gennick, Jonathan Hassell, Michelle Lowman, Matthew Moodie, Duncan Parkes, Jeffrey Pepper, Frank Pohlmann, Douglas Pundick, Ben Renow-Clarke, Dominic Shakeshaft, Matt Wade, Tom Welsh
Coordinating Editor: Mary Tobin
Copy Editor: Kim Wimpsett
Compositor: MacPS, LLC
Indexer: Toma Mulligan
Cover Designer: Anna Ishchenko

Distributed to the book trade worldwide by Springer Science+Business Media, LLC., 233 Spring Street, 6th Floor, New York, NY 10013. Phone 1-800-SPRINGER, fax (201) 348-4505, e-mail orders-ny@springer-sbm.com, or visit www.springeronline.com.

For information on translations, please e-mail rights@apress.com, or visit www.apress.com.

Apress and friends of ED books may be purchased in bulk for academic, corporate, or promotional use. eBook versions and licenses are also available for most titles. For more information, reference our Special Bulk Sales–eBook Licensing web page at www.apress.com/info/bulksales.

The information in this book is distributed on an "as is" basis, without warranty. Although every precaution has been taken in the preparation of this work, neither the author(s) nor Apress shall have any liability to any person or entity with respect to any loss or damage caused or alleged to be caused directly or indirectly by the information contained in this work.

To the Little Flower, St. Thérèse de Lisieux, for sending me this rose.

Contents at a Glance

Contents

About the Author

■ **Terry McNavage**, www.popwebdesign.com, has been hand-coding JavaScript for 12 years. In addition to being a JavaScript wizard, he has expertise in creative design, XHTML, CSS, PHP, Perl, and MySQL. Terry is an elite runner, too. For the past 14 years he has run 100 or more miles per week over the hilly terrain of Pittsburgh. He is also a bit of a foodie. Though his Pirates have had 18 losing seasons in a row, Terry remains hopeful they'll raise the Jolly Roger more often than the white flag in 2011.

About the Technical Reviewers

 **Kristian Besley** (pictured center) is a lead developer at Beetroot Design (www.beetrootdesign.co.uk) where he develops web applications, web sites, educational interactions, and games written mainly in various combinations of PHP, Flash, and JavaScript.

He has been working with computers and the Web for far too long.

He also spends far too much time hacking and developing for open source applications—including Moodle—so that they work just so. Health warning: he has an unhealthy obsession with making his applications super-RSS compatible and overly configurable.

His past and current clients include the BBC, Pearson Education, Welsh Assembly Government, and loads of clients with acronyms such as JISC, BECTA, MAWWFIRE, and—possibly his favorite of all (well, just try saying it out loud)—SWWETN.

When he isn't working, he's working elsewhere lecturing in interactive media (at Gower College–Swansea) or providing geeky technical assistance to a whole gamut of institutions or individuals in an effort to save them time and money (at his own expense!).

He has authored and coauthored a large number of books for friends of ED and Apress including the Foundation Flash series, *Flash MX Video*, *Flash ActionScript for Flash* (with the wonderful David Powers), and *Flash MX Creativity*. His words have also graced the pages of *Computer Arts* a few times too.

Kristian currently resides with his family in Swansea, Wales, and is a proud fluent Welsh speaker with a passion for pushing the language on the Web and in bilingual web applications where humanly possible.

 **Rob Drimmie** is lucky. He has an amazing wife, two awesome kids, and a new keyboard. Rob's creative urges tend to manifest in the form of web applications, and he prefers they be fuelled by pho and hamburgers—the creative urges, that is.

 **Tom Barker** is a software engineer, solutions architect, and technical manager with more than a decade of experience working with ActionScript, JavaScript, Perl, PHP, and the Microsoft .NET Framework. Currently, he is the manager of web development at Comcast Interactive Media where he leads the group of developers responsible for www.comcast.net and www.xfinity.com. He is also an adjunct professor at Philadelphia University where he has been teaching undergrad and graduate courses on web development since 2003, as well as a regular contributor to www.insideRIA.com. When not working, teaching, or writing, Tom likes to spend time with his family, read, and play video games until very early in the morning.

Acknowledgments

I wish to thank my family—Mom, Dad, John, and Ryan—for their love and support. I wish to also thank everyone at Apress, especially Ben Renow-Clarke, Matthew Moodie, Kristian Besley, Dominic Shakeshaft, and Mary Tobin, for their diligence, patience, and encouragement.

—Terry McNavage

Preface

In the 2005 film adaptation of *The Hitchhiker's Guide to the Galaxy* by Douglas Adams, aliens demolish the earth to make way for a hyperspace expressway. Our demise could have been averted insofar as the demolition proposal had been on file at local planning offices worldwide for some time. However, no one complained during the public comment period.

Like construction proposals, no one ever bothers to read the preface to a programming book. Typically, that's mostly harmless, but not for this book. Though you won't be vaporized into star dust for jumping to Chapter 1 or later, you'll be befuddled for not having downloaded and familiarized yourself with Firebug, our tool for learning JavaScript.

JavaScript is a beginner-friendly programming language available in browsers such as Internet Explorer, Firefox, Safari, Opera, and Chrome. Those browsers contain a JavaScript interpreter to parse and run your JavaScript programs, which you write in plain text with a text editor. So, you can use the same text editor that you code your XHTML and CSS with.

JavaScript derives its syntax, which is to say its grammar, from the ECMAScript standard and its features for manipulating XHTML, CSS, and HTTP from the DOM standard. Typically, JavaScript interpreters implement ECMAScript and DOM in separate libraries. So, just as your brain has left and right lobes, a browser's JavaScript brain has ECMAScript and DOM lobes.

In the first six chapters, we'll converse with the ECMAScript lobe. Then we'll converse with the DOM lobe for a couple of chapters. I guess you could say we'll be picking a JavaScript's brain one lobe at a time—ECMAScript and then DOM, with Firebug. Finally, in the last two chapters, we'll hand-code an uber-cool JavaScript program with our preferred text editors. But we'll never make it through Chapters 1–8 without Firebug. So, our first order of business will be to have you download and familiarize yourself with Firebug, a free add-on to Firefox for Windows, Mac, or Linux.

Obviously, prior to installing a Firefox add-on like Firebug, you need to have Firefox. Note that Firefox is a free web browser for Windows, Mac OS X, or Linux. To download Firefox, go to www.mozilla.com, and click the Download Firefox – Free button, as displayed in Figure 1. Then follow the wizard to install Firefox on your computer.

Open Firefox, and then download the Firebug add-on from www.getfirebug.com. Simply click Install Firebug for Firefox button in the top-right corner, as shown in Figure 2. Then follow the wizard, granting permission to install the add-on if prompted by Firefox.

Figure 1. *Downloading Firefox for Windows, Mac OS X, or Linux*

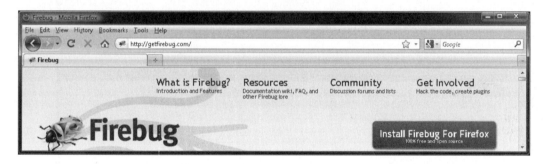

Figure 2. *Downloading the Firebug add-on*

Now that you have Firefox and Firebug installed, let's run through how to work with Firebug. Firebug runs JavaScript code relative to whatever HTML document is loaded in Firefox. In other words, you need to have an HTML document open in Firefox for Firebug to work.

Insofar as ECMAScript provides no way to manipulate HTML or CSS, in Chapters 1–6 we will simply load the following blank HTML document, `firebug.html` in the downloads at `www.apress.com`, in Firefox:

```
<html>
<head>
<meta http-equiv="Content-Type" content="text/html; charset=utf-8">
<title>Firebug</title>
</head>
<body>
</body>
</html>
```

Opening Firebug

Load firebug.html in Firefox, and then press F12 to open Firebug, as in Figure 3. Note that pressing F12 does the inverse, too. In other words, pressing F12 toggles Firebug from closed to open or from open to closed. Note that if F12 is a shortcut for something else on your computer, you can open Firebug by choosing Tools ➤ Firebug ➤ Open Firebug in the menu bar of Firefox, as illustrated in Figure 4.

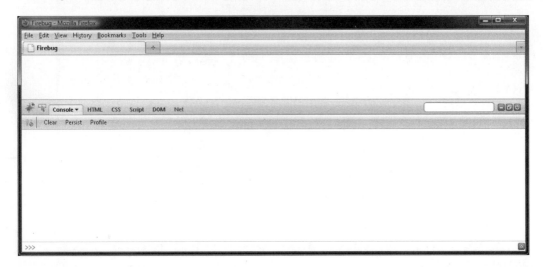

Figure 3. Press F12 to open or close Firebug.

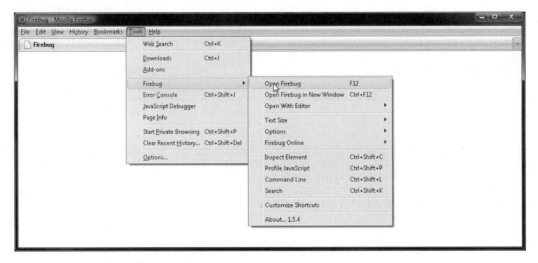

Figure 4. Manually opening Firebug if F12 is a shortcut for something else on your computer

Enabling Firebug

The first time you open Firebug, you may have to enable it by choosing Enabled from the Console menu, as shown in Figure 5.

Figure 5. Enabling Firebug from the Console menu

Command Line

Firebug has a command line for running a single line of JavaScript with. This runs along the bottom of Firebug and is prefaced by >>>. Type the following sample on the command line, as in Figure 6:

```
alert("Don't Panic");
```

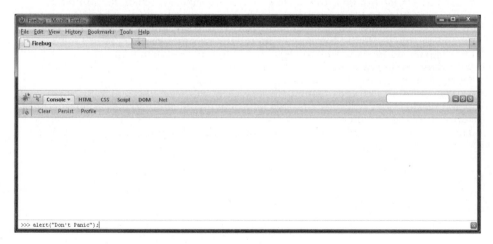

Figure 6. Keying in a one-liner on the command line

Now press Return on your keyboard to have JavaScript run the sample. As Figure 7 displays, this tells Firefox to open an alert dialog box.

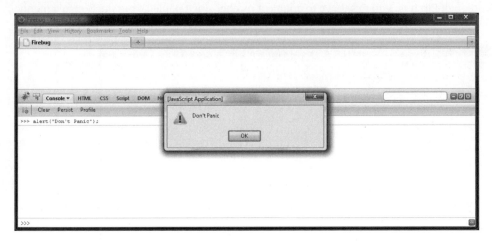

Figure 7. Pressing Return on your keyboard tells Firefox to open an alert dialog box.

Command Editor

Nearly all the JavaScript samples we will run in Firebug are more than one line of code. So, the command line won't do. Instead, we'll toggle the console from the command line to the command editor by clicking the upward-facing arrow icon in the bottom-right corner of Firebug. As Figure 8 displays, this divides Firebug into two panels. The one on the right is the command editor. This is where you will type all the code samples in this book.

Note that there are three menu options, Run, Clear, and Copy, on the bottom of the command editor. Clicking Run will run whatever code you typed into the command editor. Note that the keyboard shortcut for clicking Run is Ctrl+Return (Command+Return). That is to say, pressing Return runs your sample in the command line but not in the command editor. If it were otherwise and Return was for running code in the command editor, you wouldn't be able to enter more than one line of code. In other words, the command editor would run the first line of code you typed, because you'd hit Return after entering it; you'd never get a chance to enter a second line!

The other two, Clear and Copy, are aptly named. Clicking Clear will clear any code from the command editor, while clicking Copy will copy any code in the command editor to the clipboard. Note that to clear the left panel of Firebug, you must click Clear in its menu. So, there is a Clear option in both the left and right panels. Oftentimes in this book I will say "double-clear Firebug," which is your clue to click Clear in both menus.

Figure 8. The command editor has a separate menu with Run, Clear, and Copy options.

OK, type in the previous sample in the command editor, and then click Run or press Ctrl+Return (Command+Return) to have JavaScript execute it:

```
alert("Don't Panic");
```

As Figure 9 displays, Firefox will open an alert dialog box, same as before.

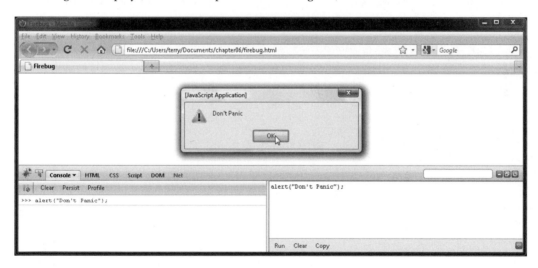

Figure 9. Clicking Run tells Firefox to open an alert dialog box.

One thing to note is that the command editor and command line are under the Console tab in Firebug. So if you inadvertently toggle to the HTML, CSS, Script, DOM, or Net tab, the command editor will disappear. So, you will have to click the Console tab in the top-left corner to make the command editor reappear. Note that the keyboard shortcut for toggling to the Console tab is Ctrl+Shift+L (Command+Shift+L). Table 1 lists vital keyboard shortcuts for Firebug.

Table 1. Firebug Keyboard Shortcuts

Shortcut Description	Windows or Linux	Mac
Open Firebug	F12	F12
Close Firebug	F12	F12
Toggle to Console tab	Ctrl+Shift+L	Command+Shift+L
Run code in command editor	Ctrl+Return	Command+Return

If you are a fallible typist, inevitably you will mistype a code sample. Consequently, when you click Run, JavaScript will print an error in the left panel of Firebug. Those are simply JavaScript's way of calling you a dummy.

Syntax and reference errors are the most common. JavaScript names those SyntaxError and ReferenceError, respectively. So, let's screw up in both ways now to get you off the schneid with errors. In Firebug, mistype alert as alrt in order to make a reference error, which is to say you mistyped the name of something:

```
alrt("Don't Panic");
```

As Figure 10 displays, JavaScript prints a ReferenceError containing the message "alrt is not defined":

Figure 10. Oops—JavaScript returns a ReferenceError saying "alrt is not defined".

OK, fix that typo, reverting `alrt` to `alert`, and then delete the closing parentheses like so:

```
alert("Don't Panic";
```

Now click Run. As Figure 11 displays, JavaScript prints a `SyntaxError` containing the message `"missing ) after argument list"`. Note that a syntax error in programming is like a grammar error in writing.

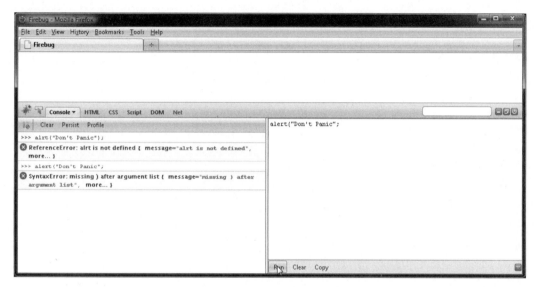

Figure 11. Oops—JavaScript returns a SyntaxError saying `"missing ) after argument list"`.

Don't panic if you get an error. It probably just means you need to fix a typo or two.

Now that you have installed and gained familiarity with Firebug, let's begin exploring ECMAScript!

CHAPTER 1

■ ■ ■

Representing Data with Values

When you walk into my childhood home in Pittsburgh, it's evident a fellow with a lively mind lives there. Photos from trips to some thirty-one countries on six continents line the walls. Intermingling those are Aborigine and Aleut art, prints by Klimt and Degas, tapestries from Egypt and Peru, and Greek sculptures. Notable literary works fill the library.

Though conversations with my dad are interesting, they tend to be interspersed with what my mom would call "the comment from nowhere," an unpredicated excerpt from whatever he is thinking about. For example, I was over there for a Steelers game on a damp November day. I think they were playing the Ravens, their blood rival. So, the carnage was fairly medieval. Moreover, Heinz Field was a mess. It was more like a muddy cow pasture than a football field.

On a third and long with the Steelers nearly within field goal range, Roethlisberger dropped back to pass. But Hines Ward, his intended receiver, slipped and fell on a timing pattern, sprawling face down in the mud. So, the ball sailed over the first down marker, incomplete.

As the Steelers prepared to punt, I probably muttered something unprintable. Dad, on the other hand, peered at me overtop his reading glasses and queried, "Did you know that the French may have lost to the English at Agincourt due to the depth of the mud?" Though I didn't say, "No, and why are you telling me that?" I sure was thinking it.

If you are new to JavaScript and programming, some of the things I say in the first few chapters may bewilder you like Dad's query did me. Just know that, although I've been hand-coding JavaScript for 12 years, I've not forgotten how tough it can be at the very beginning. So, this book is written conversational style, covering only things that matter.

It's kind of like the knee-deep mud in a rain-soaked, newly plowed field bordering the woods of Agincourt did on October 25, 1415. That proved very tiring for French knights to wade through wearing some 50 to 60 pounds of full-plate armor. Those who later fell in the deep mud during the mêlée had difficulty regaining their feet, leaving them still targets for English longbowmen. Some trampled French knights even drowned in their armor. Within a few hours, the French army had been crushed by an English army one-fifth its size. Historians put the French dead at 10,000 compared to 112 for the English, attributing the slaughter to the muddy terrain.

Dad told me those details over dinner following the game, noting that he had been prepping a lecture on *Henry V*, a Shakespeare play featuring the battle of Agincourt, for a course he was giving at Penn State University. So, the comment from nowhere came from somewhere, too!

So, hang in there during early going while the mud is deep. Things will fall into place for you later in the book just like they did for me later in the day.

What Are Value Types?

In JavaScript, data is represented with values. There are four value types to convey data with: string, number, boolean, and object. Additionally, there are two value types to convey no data with: undefined and null. Two ways to convey "nothing there" won't seem so strange in Chapter 3.

The simplest way to create a string, number, boolean, or object value in JavaScript is to literally type it into your script. Doing so creates a literal value, or, more plainly, a literal.

Creating a String Literal

Plain text like my favorite ice cream, Ben & Jerry's Chocolate Fudge Brownie, is represented with a string value in JavaScript. Just wrap some text in a pair of double or single quotation marks, and you have yourself a string.

Alright, open `firebug.html` in Firefox, and then press F12 to enable Firebug. If you're just joining us, flip back to the Preface for details on how to do this. Type the following string in the right panel of Firebug, and click Run. As Figure 1–1 displays, JavaScript will echo the string value, printing it in the left panel of Firebug:

```
"Ben & Jerry's Chocolate Fudge Brownie";
```

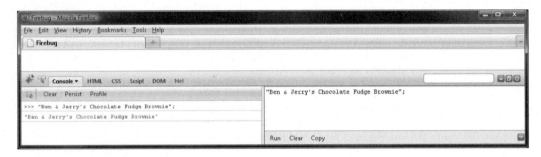

Figure 1–1. *JavaScript parrots the string literal back to us.*

JavaScript interpreters for Firefox and other browsers return a string value in double quotes. So, we'll go with double quotes in this book. But it doesn't matter. The only thing I would say is choose one style or the other and stick with it.

Note that the previous string is followed by a semicolon. Every statement, which is simply something you tell JavaScript to do, ends with a semicolon. Our simple statement shown earlier tells JavaScript to create a string literal in memory. We'll explore statements more fully in Chapter 4.

Commenting Code

Just like CSS or XHTML, JavaScript permits you to comment your code and format it with whitespace. Single-line comments begin with a //. JavaScript disregards anything following the // until the end of the line. In this book, code samples I want you to enter and run are followed by a comment listing the return value JavaScript will print in Firebug. So, to let you know JavaScript will echo the string literals, I'd write this:

```
"Ben & Jerry's";
// "Ben & Jerry's"
"Chocolate Fudge Brownie";
// "Chocolate Fudge Brownie"
```

But you would just enter and run the following:

```
"Ben & Jerry's";
"Chocolate Fudge Brownie";
```

If a code sample has two or more comments, that is your clue to stop and click Run to verify a return value before keying in the remainder of the sample.

Gluing Strings Together with the + Operator

To glue two strings together, separate them with the + concatenation operator. We'll explore + and a slew of other operators, listed here, in Chapter 3. Note that the values you give an operator to work with are referred to as *operands*.

```
[]
.
()
new
++
--
!
delete
typeof
void
*
/
%
+
-
<
<=
>
>=
instanceof
in
===
!===
==
!=
&&
||
?:
=
*=
/=
%=
+=
-=
,
```

Click Clear in both Firebug panels, and then cobble together a larger string from five smaller ones.

```
"Ben & Jerry's" + " " + "Chocolate Fudge Brownie" + " is my favorite icecream.";
// "Ben &  Jerry's Chocolate Fudge Brownie is my favorite icecream."
```

Verify your work with Figure 1–2.

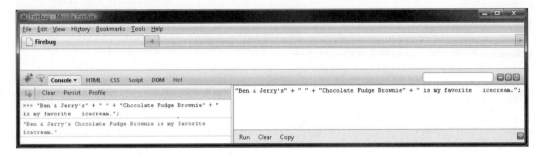

Figure 1–2. Gluing five strings together with the + operator

Note that "Ben & Jerry's" + " " + "Chocolate Fudge Brownie" + " is my favorite icecream." is referred to as an expression for a value. In JavaScript, those are any phrases of code that create a value. You might think of an expression as a recipe for a value. We'll explore that analogy in Chapter 3.

Creating a Number Literal

Scripts typically do a lot of math. So, JavaScript, of course, has a number value type. Click Clear in Firebug, and let's have JavaScript do some math.

Chocolate Fudge Brownie has 4 servings per pint and 260 calories per serving. So, we could have JavaScript calculate the calories per pint with the * operator, which multiplies its operands:

```
4 * 260;
// 1040
```

I'm an avid runner, taking daily runs of some 14 miles Monday through Saturday. On Sundays I go for 21. We could have JavaScript calculate yearly miles with the following expression. Note that / does division and + does addition. Note too that JavaScript evaluates anything in parentheses first.

```
(6 * 14 + 21) / 7 * 365;
// 5475
```

It takes roughly 100 calories to run a mile, so, if I were to fuel my running entirely with Chocolate Fudge Brownie, how many pints would I need per year? Note that Math.round() rounds a decimal number to an integer. So, in our case, it rounds 526.4423076923077 to 526. Math.round() is one of the features for manipulating numbers that we'll explore in Chapter 5. Note too that + does addition if both its operands are numbers but concatenation if either operand is a string. For that to work, JavaScript converts the number 526 to the string "526" before gluing it to "pints of Chocolate Fudge Brownie". Verify your work with Figure 1–3.

```
Math.round((6 * 14 + 21) / 7 * 365 * 100 / (4 * 260)) + " pints of Chocolate Fudge Brownie";
// "526 pints of Chocolate Fudge Brownie"
```

I think I'll stay with an organic, whole-foods diet for now. But, if I'm still running when I'm 90, maybe I'll give that a try!

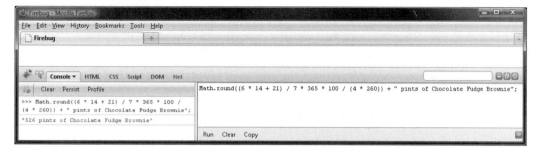

Figure 1–3. Doing some math with numbers

■ **Note** JavaScript's value type conversion feature is covered more fully in Chapter 2.

Creating a Boolean Literal

Sometimes you will want a simple yes or no answer from JavaScript. In those circumstances, the return value for an expression will be `true` for yes and `false` for no.

Click Clear in both Firebug panels, and let's ask JavaScript whether Chocolate Fudge Brownie is just chocolate ice cream. Note that the `===` operator tells you whether two values are identical:

```
"Chocolate Fudge Brownie" === "chocolate icecream";
// false
```

That's an understatement. Alright, now let's compare the previous calculation to its return value, before verifying our work with Figure 1–4:

```
Math.round((6 * 14 + 21) / 7 * 365 * 100 / (4 * 260)) + " pints of Chocolate Fudge Brownie"
===
   "526 pints of Chocolate Fudge Brownie";
// true
```

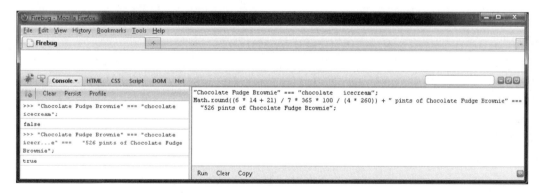

Figure 1–4. The === operator always returns a boolean.

■ **Note** Comparison operators such as === all return booleans. Moreover, JavaScript can convert any string, number, object, null, or undefined value to a boolean. We'll explore value type conversion in Chapter 2. For those reasons, booleans are vital for controlling flow, something we'll explore in Chapter 4.

Naming a Value with an Identifier

Insofar as the literals we have created thus far are anonymous, we have no way to query or manipulate their values later. To fix this, we need to name them with an identifier. Doing so creates a variable, which of course is a named value.

OK, click Clear in both Firebug panels. Then type the keyword var followed by the identifier iceCream and a semicolon. Doing so declares a variable named iceCream to JavaScript. However, iceCream contains undefined, a literal conveying no value.

```
var iceCream;
```

Let's put the string literal "Chocolate Fudge Brownie" in iceCream with the = operator:

```
var iceCream;
iceCream = "Chocolate Fudge Brownie";
```

To query the value contained by a variable, type its identifier. Type iceCream, and click Run. JavaScript will then return the string literal:

```
var iceCream;
iceCream = "Chocolate Fudge Brownie";
iceCream;
// "Chocolate Fudge Brownie"
```

To put a new value in iceCream, do another = operation. So, let's replace "Chocolate Fudge Brownie" with "New York Super Fudge Chunk" like so:

```
var iceCream;
iceCream = "Chocolate Fudge Brownie";
iceCream = "New York Super Fudge Chunk";
iceCream;
// "New York Super Fudge Chunk"
```

Can I Name a Variable Anything I Want?

Sorry, no. JavaScript identifiers may only contain letters, numbers, and the _ underscore character. It can't begin with a number, though. Insofar as identifiers may not contain whitespace, ones containing two or more words are written in camel case. That is to say, spaces are deleted, and the first letter in every word but the first is capitalized. So, newYorkSuperFudgeChunk is camel case for "New York Super Fudge Chunk".

Though you may not name a variable anything you want, you may put any expression in it. So, you're not limited to literals. Click Clear in both Firebug panels, and then enter and run the following, before verifying this and the previous few samples with Figure 1–5.

```
var newYorkSuperFudgeChunk = 4 * 300 + " calories per pint";
newYorkSuperFudgeChunk;
// "1200 calories per pint"
```

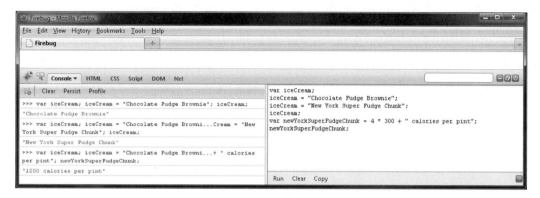

***Figure 1–5.** Creating validly named variables*

The reason this works is that = has very low precedence compared to * and +. In Chapter 3, we'll explore precedence, which determines the pecking order of operators more fully.

Some Valid Identifiers Are Already Taken

JavaScript syntax, as defined by the ECMAScript standard, reserves the following identifiers, referred to as *keywords*. Those are JavaScript's key to do something for you. So, the term is apt. Naming a variable with a keyword returns a syntax error:

```
break
case
catch
continue
default
delete
do
else
finally
for
function
if
in
instanceof
new
return
switch
this
throw
try
typeof
var
void
while
with
```

By the end of this book, you will know what all these keywords tell JavaScript to do. So, by then, it will be obvious not to name a variable with a keyword.

On the other hand, future versions of ECMAScript may add the following keywords. Those still won't mean anything to you by the end of the book. But don't feel bad; they still don't mean anything to JavaScript either. Anyway, don't name a variable with one of the following reserved words:

```
abstract
boolean
byte
char
class
const
debugger
double
enum
export
extends
final
float
goto
implements
import
int
interface
long
native
package
private
protected
public
short
static
super
synchronized
throws
transient
volatile
```

In addition to keywords and reserved words, JavaScript has some predefined variables, too. So, the following identifiers are already taken:

```
arguments
Array
Boolean
Date
decodeURI
decodeURIComponent
encodeURI
Error
escape
eval
EvalError
Function
Infinity
isFinite
```

```
isNaN
Math
NaN
Number
Object
parseFloat
parseInt
RangeError
ReferenceError
RegExp
String
SyntaxError
TypeError
undefined
unescape
URIError
```

■ **Note** If you are curious about the ECMAScript standard, visit http://www.ecmascript.org.

Creating an Object Literal

The object value type provides a way for you to create a place in memory for related values, which may be named with an identifier or string. Those related values are referred to as *members*. So, we say an object contains members.

Alright, click Clear in both Firebug panels. Then create an empty object literal named iceCream by keying in a pair of curly braces, followed of course by a semicolon.

```
var iceCream = {
};
```

Now add a member named "Chocolate Fudge Brownie" followed by an expression with the number of calories per pint. Just like variables, members may contain a literal value or an expression for a value. Note that the name of the member is separated from the value by a colon.

```
var iceCream = {
  "Chocolate Fudge Brownie": 4 * 260
};
```

OK, now members are separated by a comma. So to add a second member, follow the first one with a comma, like so:

```
var iceCream = {
  "Chocolate Fudge Brownie": 4 * 260,
  "Half Baked": 4 * 250
};
```

Now there are several more members so that we have ten in all. Just remember to separate them with a comma. But don't follow the final member—"Mission to Marzipan"—with a comma.

```
var iceCream = {
  "Chocolate Fudge Brownie": 4 * 260,
  "Half Baked": 4 * 250,
  "New York Super Fudge Chunk": 4 * 300,
  "Coffee Heath Bar Crunch": 4 * 280,
  "Cherry Garcia": 4 * 240,
  "Mud Pie": 4 * 270,
  "Milk & Cookies": 4 * 270,
  "Cinnamon Buns": 4 * 290,
  "Chocolate Chip Cookie Dough": 4 * 270,
  "Mission to Marzipan": 4 * 260
};
```

To query a member in iceCream, type iceCream, and then put the member name within the [ ] operator. Let's query "Chocolate Fudge Brownie", my favorite Ben & Jerry's, then verify our work with Figure 1–6.

```
var iceCream = {
  "Chocolate Fudge Brownie": 4 * 260,
  "Half Baked": 4 * 250,
  "New York Super Fudge Chunk": 4 * 300,
  "Coffee Heath Bar Crunch": 4 * 280,
  "Cherry Garcia": 4 * 240,
  "Mud Pie": 4 * 270,
  "Milk & Cookies": 4 * 270,
  "Cinnamon Buns": 4 * 290,
  "Chocolate Chip Cookie Dough": 4 * 270,
  "Mission to Marzipan": 4 * 260
};
iceCream["Chocolate Fudge Brownie"] + " calories per pint";
// "1040 calories per pint"
```

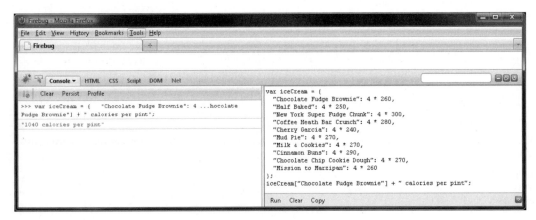

Figure 1–6. Querying a member in iceCream

Hmm. It think I mismarked "Half Baked". It ought to be 270 per serving, not 250. So, how would we write a new value to the "Half Baked" member?

Yup, with the = operator. Writing a member is like writing a variable. Let's do so in Firebug, verifying our work with Figure 1–7:

```
var iceCream = {
  "Chocolate Fudge Brownie": 4 * 260,
  "Half Baked": 4 * 250,
  "New York Super Fudge Chunk": 4 * 300,
  "Coffee Heath Bar Crunch": 4 * 280,
  "Cherry Garcia": 4 * 240,
  "Mud Pie": 4 * 270,
  "Milk & Cookies": 4 * 270,
  "Cinnamon Buns": 4 * 290,
  "Chocolate Chip Cookie Dough": 4 * 270,
  "Mission to Marzipan": 4 * 260
};
iceCream["Half Baked"] = 4 * 270;
iceCream["Half Baked"] + " calories per pint";
// "1080 calories per pint"
```

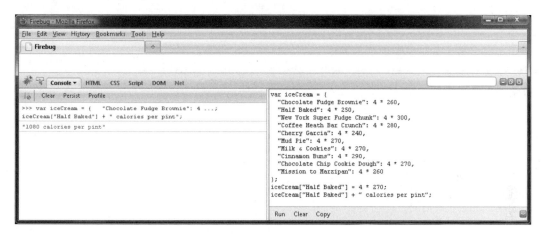

Figure 1–7. Writing a new value to a member

Now what if I want to add a new flavor, say "Peanut Butter Cup" to iceCream? That works the same way as changing the value of a member. So, = changes the value of a member or adds a new one. It just depends on whether the member you query is defined already.

In Firebug, let's add a member named "Peanut Butter Cup" like so. Then query its value, verifying our work with Figure 1–8:

```
var iceCream = {
  "Chocolate Fudge Brownie": 4 * 260,
  "Half Baked": 4 * 270,
  "New York Super Fudge Chunk": 4 * 300,
  "Coffee Heath Bar Crunch": 4 * 280,
  "Cherry Garcia": 4 * 240,
  "Mud Pie": 4 * 270,
  "Milk & Cookies": 4 * 270,
  "Cinnamon Buns": 4 * 290,
```

```
  "Chocolate Chip Cookie Dough": 4 * 270,
  "Mission to Marzipan": 4 * 260
};
iceCream["Peanut Butter Cup"] = 4 * 360;
iceCream["Peanut Butter Cup"] + " calories per pint";
// "1440 calories per pint"
```

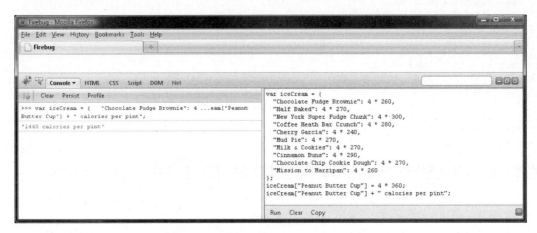

Figure 1–8. Adding a new member to an object

Yipes, 1440 calories! On second thoughts, I'd like to remove that from iceCream. To do so, pass the "Peanut Butter Cup" member to the delete operator, which as its name implies deletes a member from an object. Consequently, when we query iceCream["Peanut Butter Cup"] following its demolition, JavaScript returns undefined to convey no value. We can't glue undefined to a string, though. So, JavaScript converts it to "undefined" first.

```
var iceCream = {
  "Chocolate Fudge Brownie": 4 * 260,
  "Half Baked": 4 * 270,
  "New York Super Fudge Chunk": 4 * 300,
  "Coffee Heath Bar Crunch": 4 * 280,
  "Cherry Garcia": 4 * 240,
  "Mud Pie": 4 * 270,
  "Milk & Cookies": 4 * 270,
  "Cinnamon Buns": 4 * 290,
  "Chocolate Chip Cookie Dough": 4 * 270,
  "Mission to Marzipan": 4 * 260
};
iceCream["Peanut Butter Cup"] = 4 * 360;
delete iceCream["Peanut Butter Cup"];
iceCream["Peanut Butter Cup"] + " calories per pint";
// "undefined calories per pint"
```

Naming Members with Identifiers

Naming iceCream members with strings enabled us to use whitespace, which is forbidden for identifiers. But we could have gone with camel case identifiers like so:

```
var iceCream = {
  chocolateFudgeBrownie: 4 * 260,
  halfBaked: 4 * 270,
  newYorkSuperFudgeChunk: 4 * 300,
  coffeeHeathBarCrunch: 4 * 280,
  cherryGarcia: 4 * 240,
  mudPie: 4 * 270,
  milkCookies: 4 * 270,
  cinnamonBuns: 4 * 290,
  chocolateChipCookieDough: 4 * 270,
  missionToMarzipan: 4 * 260
};
```

Having done so, we can now query members with the . operator followed by an identifier. Try doing so in Firebug by entering and running the following sample, verifying your work with Figure 1–9.

```
var iceCream = {
  chocolateFudgeBrownie: 4 * 260,
  halfBaked: 4 * 270,
  newYorkSuperFudgeChunk: 4 * 300,
  coffeeHeathBarCrunch: 4 * 280,
  cherryGarcia: 4 * 240,
  mudPie: 4 * 270,
  milkCookies: 4 * 270,
  cinnamonBuns: 4 * 290,
  chocolateChipCookieDough: 4 * 270,
  missionToMarzipan: 4 * 260
};
iceCream.newYorkSuperFudgeChunk + " calories per pint";
// "1200 calories per pint"
```

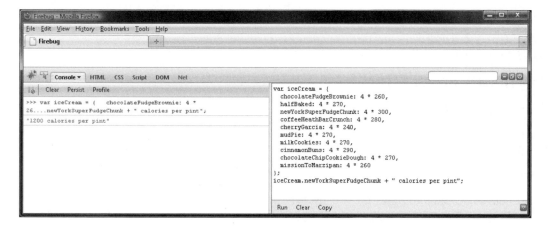

Figure 1–9. Querying a member with an identifier rather than with a string

To update the value of a member or to add a new member, you would use the = operator, same as before. Let's add a bostonCreamPie member to iceCream. Then query its value, verifying our work with Figure 1–10:

```
var iceCream = {
  chocolateFudgeBrownie: 4 * 260,
  halfBaked: 4 * 270,
  newYorkSuperFudgeChunk: 4 * 300,
  coffeeHeathBarCrunch: 4 * 280,
  cherryGarcia: 4 * 240,
  mudPie: 4 * 270,
  milkCookies: 4 * 270,
  cinnamonBuns: 4 * 290,
  chocolateChipCookieDough: 4 * 270,
  missionToMarzipan: 4 * 260
};
iceCream.bostonCreamPie = 4 * 250;
iceCream.bostonCreamPie + " calories per pint";
// "1000 calories per pint"
```

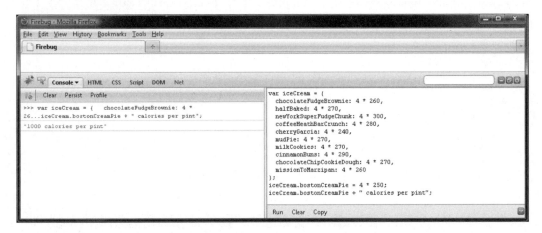

Figure 1–10. Writing a new value to a member named with an identifier

Creating an Array Literal

The members in iceCream are coded like a top-ten list. However, there's no way to have JavaScript query them that way. We couldn't ask, "What's my third favorite flavor?" for example. Plus, we have to name members and give them a value.

So, if we wanted to simply create a top-ten list of flavors, omitting the depressing calorie details, an object wouldn't do. For that we'd need an array, which is a subtype of the object value type. That is to say, an array is still an object; it just has some additional features.

One of those features is ordering values numerically with non-negative integers beginning at 0. JavaScript does so behind the scenes. So, you just list values in an array from first to last; JavaScript takes care of the numbering. Note that numbered values are referred to as *elements* rather than members.

Next click Clear in both Firebug panels. Then create an empty array literal named `iceCream` by typing a pair of square braces, followed of course by a semicolon.

```
var iceCream = [
];
```

Now add an element to `iceCream` like so:

```
var iceCream = [
  "Chocolate Fudge Brownie"
];
```

Just as object members are separated by commas, so too are array elements. We would add my second favorite flavor like so:

```
var iceCream = [
  "Chocolate Fudge Brownie",
  "Half Baked"
];
```

Then continue separating elements with commas to fill in the rest of my top ten. Note that final element, `"Mission to Marzipan"`, is not followed by a comma. Note too that JavaScript numbers flavors from 0 to 9. Although `"New York Super Fudge Chunk"` is 3 in my heart, it's 2 to JavaScript:

```
var iceCream = [
  "Chocolate Fudge Brownie",
  "Half Baked",
  "New York Super Fudge Chunk",
  "Coffee Heath Bar Crunch",
  "Cherry Garcia",
  "Mud Pie",
  "Milk & Cookies",
  "Cinnamon Buns",
  "Chocolate Chip Cookie Dough",
  "Mission to Marzipan"
];
```

To query an element in `iceCream`, put its number in the [ ] operator. Note that an element's number is referred to as its *index*. Therefore, in Firebug, query a few elements in `iceCream` like so. Remember to stop and click Run prior to each comment.

```
var iceCream = [
  "Chocolate Fudge Brownie",
  "Half Baked",
  "New York Super Fudge Chunk",
  "Coffee Heath Bar Crunch",
  "Cherry Garcia",
  "Mud Pie",
  "Milk & Cookies",
  "Cinnamon Buns",
  "Chocolate Chip Cookie Dough",
  "Mission to Marzipan"
];
iceCream[0];
// "Chocolate Fudge Brownie"
iceCream[3];
// "Coffee Heath Bar Crunch"
```

```
iceCream[6];
// "Milk & Cookies"
```

Verify your work with Figure 1–11.

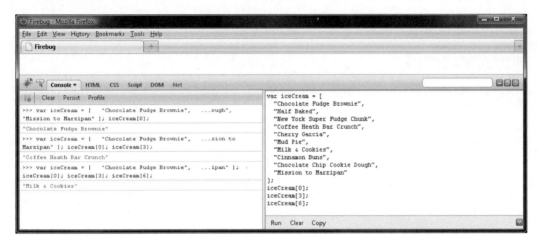

Figure 1–11. Creating an array and querying elements

Now what if I try a new flavor and want to add it to the top 10. Say swap "Mission to Marzipan" for "Boston Cream Pie". How would you do that?

Yup, with the = operator. So, = writes a new value to an element or member. Try doing so in Firebug. Then query the new number 10, before verifying your work with Figure 1–12:

```
var iceCream = [
  "Chocolate Fudge Brownie",
  "Half Baked",
  "New York Super Fudge Chunk",
  "Coffee Heath Bar Crunch",
  "Cherry Garcia",
  "Mud Pie",
  "Milk & Cookies",
  "Cinnamon Buns",
  "Chocolate Chip Cookie Dough",
  "Mission to Marzipan"
];
iceCream[9] = "Boston Cream Pie";
iceCream[9];
// "Boston Cream Pie"
```

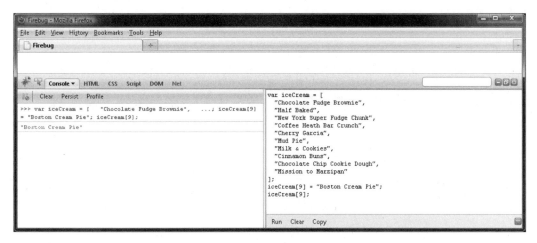

Figure 1–12. Writing a new value to an element in an array

Admit it, you're skeptical that an array is of the object value type. Members are named with strings or identifiers, while elements are named with numbers. Or are they?

No. JavaScript names elements with strings, too. They're numeric ones but strings nonetheless. So, our array is like the following object:

```
var iceCream = {
  "0": "Chocolate Fudge Brownie",
  "1": "Half Baked",
  "2": "New York Super Fudge Chunk",
  "3": "Coffee Heath Bar Crunch",
  "4": "Cherry Garcia",
  "5": "Mud Pie",
  "6": "Milk & Cookies",
  "7": "Cinnamon Buns",
  "8": "Chocolate Chip Cookie Dough",
  "9": "Boston Cream Pie"
};
```

OK, so if array elements are not named with numbers, how come we read and write their values by number, not by string?

Sorry, JavaScript tricked you again. The [ ] operator converts the number you put in there to a string. If you give it a 3 to work with, it will return the value of the element named 3. To illustrate the point, query an element in iceCream with a string in Firebug:

```
var iceCream = [
  "Chocolate Fudge Brownie",
  "Half Baked",
  "New York Super Fudge Chunk",
  "Coffee Heath Bar Crunch",
  "Cherry Garcia",
  "Mud Pie",
  "Milk & Cookies",
  "Cinnamon Buns",
  "Chocolate Chip Cookie Dough",
```

```
    "Mission to Marzipan"
];
iceCream["7"];
// "Cinnamon Buns"
```

Verify your work with Figure 1–13.

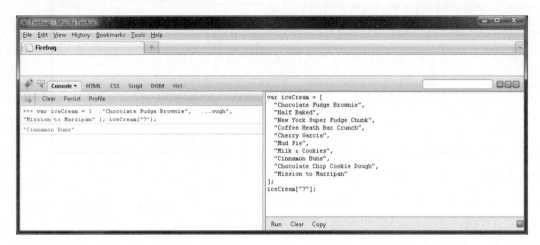

Figure 1–13. Querying an element with a string rather than with a number

Similarly, we could query a member in an equivalent object literal with a number. Try it in Firebug, verifying your work with Figure 1–14:

```
var iceCream = {
    "0": "Chocolate Fudge Brownie",
    "1": "Half Baked",
    "2": "New York Super Fudge Chunk",
    "3": "Coffee Heath Bar Crunch",
    "4": "Cherry Garcia",
    "5": "Mud Pie",
    "6": "Milk & Cookies",
    "7": "Cinnamon Buns",
    "8": "Chocolate Chip Cookie Dough",
    "9": "Mission to Marzipan"
};
iceCream[5];
// "Mud Pie"
```

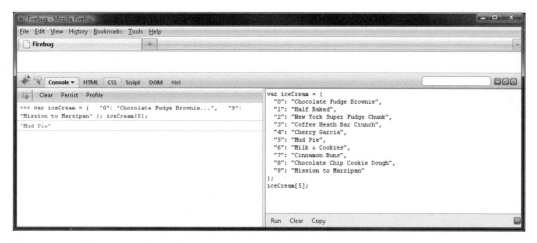

Figure 1–14. *Objects may have elements, too.*

In Chapter 5, we'll explore some array-only features for manipulating elements. Those make elements in array magical compared to those in an object. It's sort of like how putting on the spidey suit turns ordinary Peter Parker into Spiderman.

Creating a Function Literal

Alright, it's trivial to query our ice cream array for what flavor I'd rank eighth:

```
var iceCream = [
  "Chocolate Fudge Brownie",
  "Half Baked",
  "New York Super Fudge Chunk",
  "Coffee Heath Bar Crunch",
  "Cherry Garcia",
  "Mud Pie",
  "Milk & Cookies",
  "Cinnamon Buns",
  "Chocolate Chip Cookie Dough",
  "Mission to Marzipan"
];
iceCream[7];
// "Cinnamon Buns"
```

But it's quite another to query whether a flavor like "Cinnamon Buns" is among my top ten, as the following sample and Figure 1–15 illustrate:

```
var iceCream = [
  "Chocolate Fudge Brownie",
  "Half Baked",
  "New York Super Fudge Chunk",
  "Coffee Heath Bar Crunch",
  "Cherry Garcia",
```

```
      "Mud Pie",
      "Milk & Cookies",
      "Cinnamon Buns",
      "Chocolate Chip Cookie Dough",
      "Mission to Marzipan"
];
"Cinnamon Buns" === iceCream[0];
// false
"Cinnamon Buns" === iceCream[1];
// false
"Cinnamon Buns" === iceCream[2];
// false
"Cinnamon Buns" === iceCream[3];
// false
"Cinnamon Buns" === iceCream[4];
// false
"Cinnamon Buns" === iceCream[5];
// false
"Cinnamon Buns" === iceCream[6];
// false
"Cinnamon Buns" === iceCream[7];
// true
```

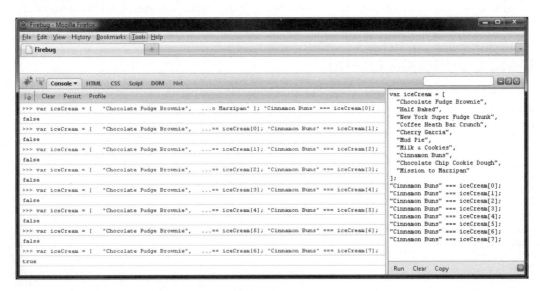

Figure 1–15. Determining whether a flavor is among the top ten, a real bear

We wouldn't want to do that for a bunch of flavors. For eliminating this kind of drudgery, JavaScript provides a second object subtype named `function`. In addition to being able to contain members or elements, functions can also contain statements. Remember, those are commands you give to JavaScript.

Functions provide a way to save snippets of frequently run code to a place in memory, that is to say, for code reuse.

One of those would come in handy for determining whether a flavor is among my top ten. In Firebug, let's save a function literal to a variable named `rankFlavor`. To do so, type the keyword `function`, a pair of parentheses, and a pair of curly braces. Note that the parentheses contain a comma-separated list of identifiers, referred to as *parameters* or *arguments*. Those contain the values you pass to a function when you invoke it. Let's define a `flavor` parameter. Then if we pass our function `"Cherry Garcia"`, JavaScript will assign that to `flavor`.

```
var iceCream = [
  "Chocolate Fudge Brownie",
  "Half Baked",
  "New York Super Fudge Chunk",
  "Coffee Heath Bar Crunch",
  "Cherry Garcia",
  "Mud Pie",
  "Milk & Cookies",
  "Cinnamon Buns",
  "Chocolate Chip Cookie Dough",
  "Mission to Marzipan"
];
var rankFlavor = function(flavor) {
};
```

In an object literal, the curly braces contain members, but in a function literal, the curly braces contain statements. Just type in the following `for`, `if`, and `return` statements for now. We'll explore `if` and `for` in Chapter 4 and `return` in Chapter 6. In a nutshell, this snippet of code compares the value of `flavor` to each element in `iceCream`. If `flavor` is among my top ten, JavaScript returns the value of the expression:

```
flavor + " is number " + (i + 1) + ".";
```

Note that `i` is the element's index in `iceCream`. Otherwise, JavaScript returns this expression:

```
flavor + " is not among my top 10.";
```

Let's pass `rankFlavor()` `"Coffee Heath Bar Crunch"` and then `"Dublin Mudslide"` like so, verifying our work with Figure 1–16:

```
var iceCream = [
  "Chocolate Fudge Brownie",
  "Half Baked",
  "New York Super Fudge Chunk",
  "Coffee Heath Bar Crunch",
  "Everything but the...",
  "Mud Pie",
  "Karamel Sutra",
  "Cinnamon Buns",
  "Milk & Cookies",
  "Mission to Marzipan"
];
var rankFlavor = function(flavor) {
  for (var i = iceCream.length; i --; ) {
    if (iceCream[i] === flavor) {
        return flavor + " is number " + (i + 1) + ".";
    }
  }
  return flavor + " is not among my top 10.";
```

```
};
rankFlavor("Coffee Heath Bar Crunch");
// "Coffee Heath Bar Crunch is number 4."
rankFlavor("Dublin Mudslide");
// "Dublin Mudslide is not among my top 10."
```

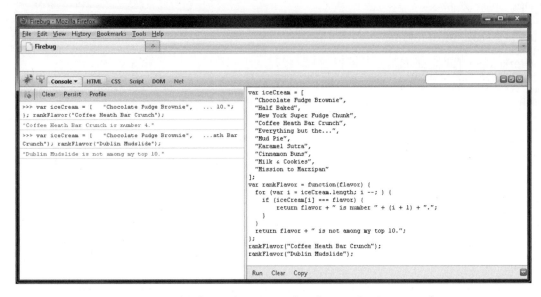

Figure 1–16. Saving a snippet of code to a function rather than typing it over and over

Though a function may seem very different from an object or array, it is quite similar. The following sample illustrates the point. Here, we add the elements from the iceCream array to the rankFlavor function. Therefore, rankFlavor() now contains ten elements in addition to a snippet of code. If we then modify the code snippet so that it iterates over the elements in rankFlavor() rather than those in iceCream, it works just as well, as Figure 1–17 displays:

```
var rankFlavor = function(flavor) {
  for (var i = rankFlavor.len; i --; ) {
    if (rankFlavor[i] === flavor) {
        return flavor + " is number " + (i + 1) + ".";
    }
  }
  return flavor + " is not among my top 10.";
};
rankFlavor[0] = "Chocolate Fudge Brownie";
rankFlavor[1] = "Half Baked";
rankFlavor[2] = "New York Super Fudge Chunk";
rankFlavor[3] = "Coffee Heath Bar Crunch";
rankFlavor[4] = "Everything but the...";
rankFlavor[5] = "Mud Pie";
rankFlavor[6] = "Karamel Sutra";
rankFlavor[7] = "Cinnamon Buns";
rankFlavor[8] = "Milk & Cookies";
```

```
rankFlavor[9] = "Mission to Marzipan";
rankFlavor.len = 10;
rankFlavor("New York Super Fudge Chunk");
// "New York Super Fudge Chunk is number 3."
rankFlavor("Peanut Brittle");
// "Peanut Brittle is not among my top 10."
```

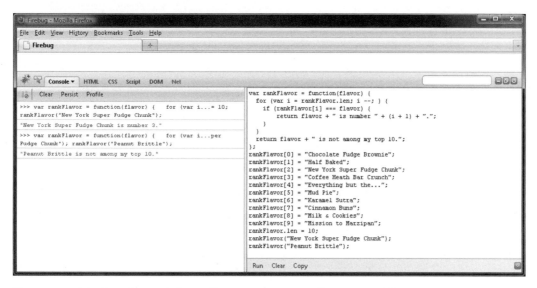

Figure 1–17. The function rankFlavor() *now contains ten elements in addition to a snippet of code.*

Summary

In this chapter, we explored four value types to represent data with. For text like "Chocolate Fudge Brownie", JavaScript has a string value type. Numbers provide a way to do math, while booleans say yes and no.

The object value type provides a way to save related values to the same place in memory, sort of like a folder on your computer. Those may be named with an identifier or string. The array subtype offers a way to numerically order related values, while the function subtype contains snippets of frequently run code.

Although objects, arrays, or functions appear very different, they all may contain members named with a string or identifier or elements named with a non-negative integer. So, they're cut from the same cloth.

CHAPTER 2

Type Conversion

Iron Man, Superman, Batman, Spider-Man, X-Men, and countless other superheroes have many traits in common. Most have a distinctive costume, unwavering morals, underlying motif, secret identity, supervillains to fight, and, of course, extraordinary powers. Those powers may or may not be innate, though. For example, Clark Kent doesn't need his Superman costume to fly, but Tony Stark would drop like a stone without his Iron Man armor.

JavaScript values of object type or array and function subtypes are like Superman or Spider-Man. They innately have extraordinary powers, referred to as *members* or *methods*. On the other hand, values of the string, number, or boolean type are like Iron Man or Batman in that they need to put on their costume, referred to as a *wrapper*, to have extraordinary powers.

So, just as seeing the bat signal appear in the night sky over Gotham City tells Bruce Wayne to put on the bat suit in order to become Batman, seeing the . operator appear to their right tells a string, number, or boolean to put on a wrapper in order to become an object.

Conversely, just as Batman returns to being Bruce Wayne after defeating the Joker, Penguin, or Catwoman, a wrapper object returns to being a string, number, or boolean after invoking a method. To convert a string, number, or boolean to a wrapper object, JavaScript invokes String(), Number(), or Boolean(). Those are referred to as *constructor functions*. To reverse the conversion, that is, to convert a wrapper object back to a string, number, or boolean, JavaScript invokes valueOf() on the wrapper.

Insofar as JavaScript converts string, number, and boolean values to and from wrapper objects behind the scenes, we just need to explore their features. Moreover, string wrappers are useful, but those for numbers and booleans are not. So, we won't waste time on those.

String Members

Open firebug.html in Firefox, and then press F12 to enable Firebug. If you're just joining us, flip back to the preface for details on how to do this. In Chapter 1, you learned how to glue one string to another with the + operator. concat() does the same thing. So in Firebug, let's glue "man" to "Bat" by way of the + operator and concat() method, verifying our work with Figure 2–1:

```
"Bat" + "man";
// "Batman"
"Bat".concat("man");
// "Batman"
```

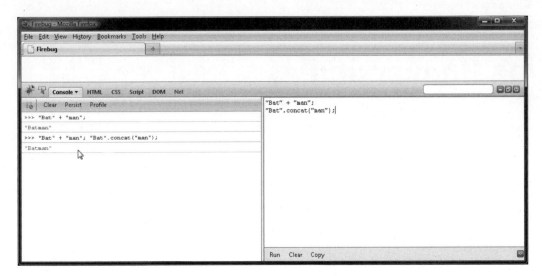

Figure 2–1. concat() works like the + operator.

If you want to append more than one string, separate them with commas. JavaScript will then sequentially append the parameters to the initial string. Try it in Firebug by entering and running the following sample:

```
"Spider".concat("-", "Man");
// "Spider-Man"
```

One thing to note regarding every String method we explore in this chapter is that they return a new, modified string but do not modify the original string. More formally, we would say strings are immutable. To illustrate the point, let's invoke concat() on a variable containing a string like so, verifying our work with Figure 2–2:

```
var name = "Super";
name.concat("man");
// "Superman"
name;
// "Super"
```

Figure 2–2. *String methods do not modify the initial string.*

As you can see, JavaScript used the string in name as the basis for the modification we wanted done. The concat() method returned "Superman", but name still contains "Super".

With this in mind, you will likely want to save the return value of a String method to another variable. Otherwise, it's as if the modification never happened. Let's do so, verifying our work with Figure 2–3:

```
var pre = "Bat";
var post = pre.concat("man");
pre;
// "Bat"
post;
// "Batman";
```

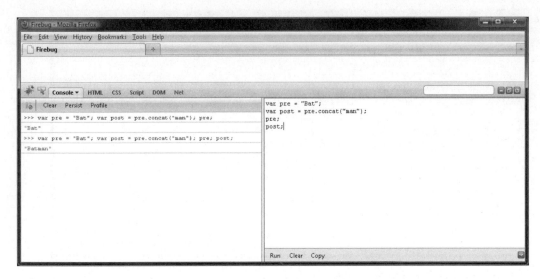

Figure 2–3. Typically you will want to save the return value. Otherwise, it's lost.

If you do not need the original string, you can simply overwrite it with the return value like so. Note that this does not modify the original string. Rather, it writes a new string to the variable:

```
var pre = "Bat";
pre = pre.concat("man");
pre;
// "Batman"
```

Oddly enough, it's quite common not to save the return value of a string method. Say you want to do a case-insensitive comparison of one string to another. Perhaps you're unsure whether a visitor will search for "Superman", "superman", or "SuperMan". To do so, you would call toLowerCase() on a string, comparing the return value, a lowercase literal, to another lowercase literal like so, verifying your work with Figure 2–4:

```
var hero = "Superman";
hero.toLowerCase() === "superman";
// true
```

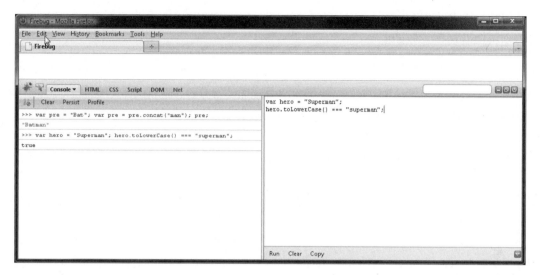

Figure 2–4. But it's also common not to save the return value.

Understanding the three ways to use the return value of any `String` method is as vital as knowing what it does. Here's a recap:

- You can save the return value to a new variable.

- You can replace the string in the original variable with the return value.

- You can immediately use the return value as an operand for an operator such as `===`.

Note that the first two ways apply to object members, array elements, and function parameters, too.
In addition to `concat()`, string wrappers provide the following members. Note that we'll explore only the vital ones. Note too that, except for `String.fromCharCode()`, we'll need to replace identifier `String` with a string literal or string expression, typically just the name of a variable, member, element, or parameter containing a string. However, any expression returning a string will do.

```
String.charAt()
String.charCodeAt()
String.concat()
String.fromCharCode()
String.indexOf()
String.lastIndexOf()
String.length
String.localeCompare()
String.match()
String.replace()
String.search()
String.slice()
String.split()
String.substring()
String.substr()
String.toLocaleLowerCase()
```

```
String.toLocaleUpperCase()
String.toLowerCase()
String.toUpperCase()
```

■ **Note** We use `String.fromCharCode()` as it is because it is a static method. This means JavaScript does not use the `String()` constructor method to create a string when we call this method.

Determining the Number of Characters

For the string `"Batman"`, Firefox would create a wrapper like the following object literal. Recall from Chapter 1 that an object may have elements just like an array. So, this object contains six elements numbered 0 to 5.

```
{"0": "B", "1": "a", "2": "t", "3": "m", "4": "a", "5": "n"}
```

With this in mind, we can query characters in `"Batman"` numerically with the [ ] operator. Try doing so in Firebug, verifying your work with Figure 2–5:

```
"Batman"[3];
// "m"
"Batman"[0];
// "B"
```

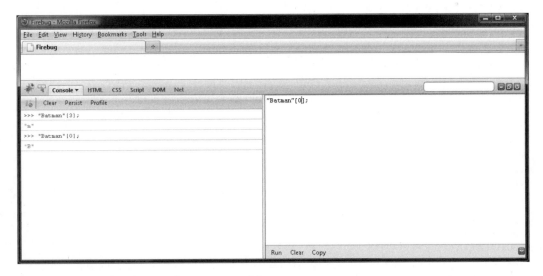

Figure 2–5. Querying elements in a wrapper object

String wrappers have a `length` member equal to the number of elements. That is to say, `length` is equal to the number of characters in the string. Try querying `length` for the Incredibles and a few of their supervillains.

```
"Mr. Incredible, Elastigirl, Violet, Dash, Jack-Jack".length;
// 51
"Underminer, Syndrome, Bomb Voyage".length;
// 33
```

Just as you can query the final element in an array by subtracting 1 from its length member, you can query the final character, which is to say the final element, in a string the very same way. Similarly, subtracting 2 from length returns the second-from-last character, subtracting 3 returns the third-from-last character, and so on:

```
var parrFamily = "Mr. Incredible, Elastigirl, Violet, Dash, Jack-Jack";
parrFamily[parrFamily.length - 1];
// "k"
parrFamily[parrFamily.length - 15];
// "D"
```

Querying elements in a wrapper object with the [ ] operator is a Firefox proprietary feature that is helpful in understanding the way strings are represented with wrapper objects. However, ECMAScript does not require JavaScript interpreters to support it. So, Internet Explorer and other browsers don't. Therefore, it's best to query characters the standard way—by passing the element's index, in other words, its number, to charAt(). Though not as convenient, doing so works cross-browser. Try the following sample in Firebug, verifying your work with Figure 2–6:

```
var parrFamily = "Mr. Incredible, Elastigirl, Violet, Dash, Jack-Jack";
parrFamily.charAt(7);
// "r"
parrFamily.charAt(parrFamily.length - 1);
// "k"
```

Figure 2–6. Querying elements the standard way is less convenient but works cross-browser.

Decoding or Encoding Characters

For nonkeyboard characters, it's typically simpler to work with the Unicode encoding than the character. For example, Dr. Otto Günther Octavius is the secret identity of one of Spider-Man's archenemies, Doctor Octopus. Rather than try to type the ü in Günther, pass its Unicode encoding (252) to `String.fromCharCode()` like so in Firebug, verifying your work with Figure 2–7:

```
var id = "Dr. Otto G" + String.fromCharCode(252) + "nther Octavius";
id;
// "Dr. Otto Günther Octavius"
```

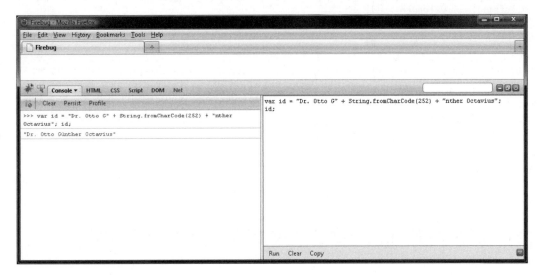

Figure 2–7. `String.fromCharCode()` provides a way to insert nonkeyboard characters.

Conversely, it's simpler to encode the ü and work with 252, say in a comparison, than to try to type the ü. To do so, pass the index to `charCodeAt()`, which returns the Unicode encoding rather than the character, as its partner in crime, `charAt()`, would. Although the following two comparisons are equivalent, I'm guessing you were only able to key in the first in Firebug. Figure 2–8 displays both, however.

```
var id = "Dr. Otto G" + String.fromCharCode(252) + "nther Octavius";
id.charCodeAt(10) === 252;
// true
id.charAt(10) === "ü";
// true
```

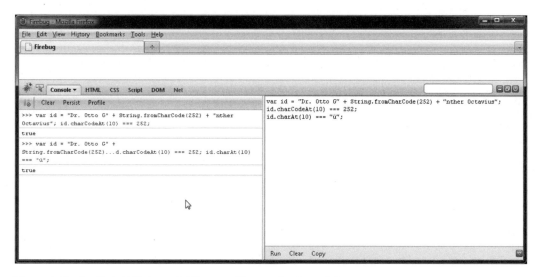

Figure 2–8. charCodeAt() is useful for encoding nonkeyboard characters.

Converting Case

In addition to decoding and encoding characters with String.fromCharCode() and charCodeAt(), you can convert their case to lowercase or uppercase with toLowerCase() or toUpperCase(). For example, fight scenes in Batman comic books would have onomatopoeic words such as *pow*, *bam*, and *zonk* superimposed in uppercase. So in Firebug, let's add some pop to some lowercase onomatopoeic words with the help of toUpperCase():

```
"Pow! Bam! Zonk!".toUpperCase();
// "POW! BAM! ZONK!"
```

Conversely, if the Penguin were to quietly spray a paralytic gas on Batman and Robin with his umbrella, we might want to tone down "PSST...ZZZZ" with toLowerCase(), verifying both samples with Figure 2–9. Note that toLowerCase() or toUpperCase() only manipulate letters. So, nothing weird like the "!" changing to a "1" will happen.

```
"PSST...ZZZZ".toLowerCase();
// "psst...zzzz"
```

Figure 2–9. Converting to uppercase or lowercase

Turkish has dotted and dotless versions of *i*:

- İ i

- I ı

The lowercase version of *I* is *ı*, not *i*. Conversely, the uppercase version of *i* is *İ*, not *I*. So for Turkish, `toLowerCase()` and `toLowerCase()` would mess up the *i* pairings. For Turkish and other alphabets with dotted and dotless *i* versions such as Azerbaijani, Kazakh, Tatar, and Crimean Tatar, JavaScript provides a second pair of methods, `toLocaleLowerCase()` and `toLocaleUpperCase()`, which get the *i* conversions right:

```
"I".toLowerCase();
// "i"
"i".toUpperCase()
// "I"
"I".toLocaleLowerCase();
// "ı"
"i".toLocaleUpperCase()
// "İ"
```

■ **Note** `toLocaleLowerCase()` and `toLocaleUpperCase()` convert case based on your OS settings. You'd have to change those settings to Turkish for the previous sample to work. Or just take my word for it!

Locating a Substring

Sometimes you will want to search a string for a smaller string, referred to as a *substring*. For example, "man" is a substring of "Batman" and "Catwoman". One way to do so is with indexOf(), which works with two parameters:

- The substring to search for

- An optional index for where to begin the search

If the substring is found, indexOf() returns the index of the first matched character. Otherwise, it returns -1 to convey failure. So in Firebug, let's determine where the substring "Ghost" begins in a literal containing some of Iron Man's archenemies:

```
"Iron Monger, Titanium Man, Madame Masque, Ghost, Mandarin".indexOf("Ghost");
// 42
```

Try doing so indirectly through a variable containing the literal. Pass in "Mandarin" and then "Green Goblin", who is Spider-Man's responsibility. So, as Figure 2–10 displays, JavaScript confirms this by returning -1:

```
var villains = "Iron Monger, Titanium Man, Madame Masque, Ghost, Mandarin";
villains.indexOf("Mandarin");
// 49
villains.indexOf("Green Goblin");
-1
```

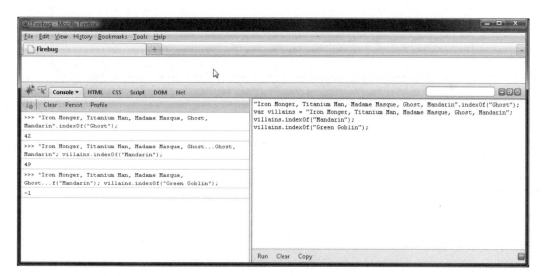

Figure 2–10. *indexOf() returns -1 to convey failure.*

Note that you may call indexOf() on any expression evaluating to string. Those include literals and variables as well as return values for operators or functions, which we'll cover in Chapters 3 and 6, respectively.

indexOf() optionally takes a second parameter telling JavaScript where to begin looking for a substring. Insofar as indexOf() returns the location of the first match, the second parameter provides a way to locate a recurring substring, such as "Man" in our list of Iron Man supervillains. So, we could locate the first and second occurrences of "Man" like so in Firebug. Note that JavaScript evaluates `villains.indexOf("Man") + 1`, which returns 23, prior to passing the parameter to `indexOf()`. Verify your work with Figure 2–11:

```
var villains = "Iron Monger, Titanium Man, Madame Masque, Ghost, Mandarin";
villains.indexOf("Man");
// 22
villains.indexOf("Man", villains.indexOf("Man") + 1);
// 49
```

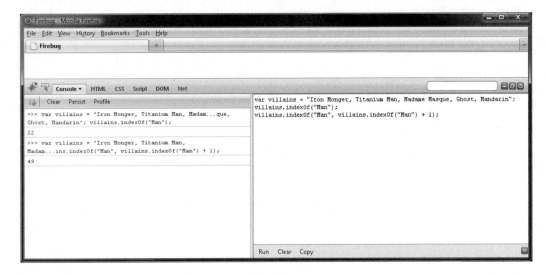

Figure 2–11. *Locating the second occurence of "Man"*

indexOf() has a partner in crime named lastIndexOf() that searches upstream, from the end of a string to the beginning. Insofar as the second occurrence of "Man" is also the last, we could therefore rewrite the previous sample like so:

```
var villains = "Iron Monger, Titanium Man, Madame Masque, Ghost, Mandarin";
villains.lastIndexOf("Man");
// 49
```

Clipping a Substring

Sometimes you may want to cut a slice from a string. To do so, pass two parameters to slice():

- The index of the *first* character in the slice

- The index of the *first* character *after* the slice

So, to slice n characters beginning at index i, pass i for the first parameter and i + n for the second parameter. Just remember that character indexes begin at 0.

```
"Superman, Batman, Spider-Man, Iron Man".slice(18, 24);
// "Spider"
```

Note that, if you omit the second parameter, JavaScript cuts a slice from the index in the first parameter all the way the end of the string. That is, it sets the second index to length. So, the following two samples do the same thing:

```
var heroes = "Superman, Batman, Spider-Man, Iron Man";
heroes.slice(30);
// "Iron Man"
heroes.slice(30, heroes.length);
// "Iron Man"
```

Note too that, if either parameter is negative, JavaScript adds length to them. Verify your work with Figure 2–12:

```
heroes.slice(10, -22);
// "Batman"
```

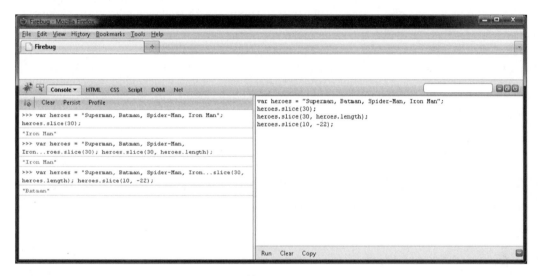

Figure 2–12. *Clipping a substring with* slice()

Replacing a Substring

If you want to replace part of a string, invoke its replace() method, which works with two parameters:

- The string to remove

- The string to insert

However, the first parameter may be a string or RegExp object (we'll explore RegExp objects in Chapter 5), and the second parameter can be a string or a function that returns a string.

■ **Note** Don't worry about the RegExp examples in this chapter; they're fairly simple and are included to keep some common tasks in one place. This means you'll learn the best ways to replace substrings here, rather than having to wait until Chapter 5 to learn all the techniques.

To begin with, we'll make both parameters strings. So, double-clear Firebug as detailed in the preface, and let's use replace() to turn Batman into Superman like so:

```
"Batman".replace("Bat", "Super");
// "Superman"
```

One thing to note when passing a string rather than a RegExp object for the first parameter is that replace() swaps only the first occurrence. To illustrate the point, run the following sample in Firebug:

```
"Batman and Batgirl".replace("Bat", "Super");
// "Superman and Batgirl"
```

To replace two or more occurrences of a search string like "Bat" with a replacement string like "Super", the first parameter must be a RegExp object marked with a g flag, which tells JavaScript to find all matches rather than just the first match. So, just as a primer for Chapter 5, if we make the first parameter in the previous sample a very simple RegExp literal, /Bat/g, we get the desired duo. Verify this and the previous two samples with Figure 2–13:

```
"Batman and Batgirl".replace(/Bat/g, "Super");
// "Superman and Supergirl"
```

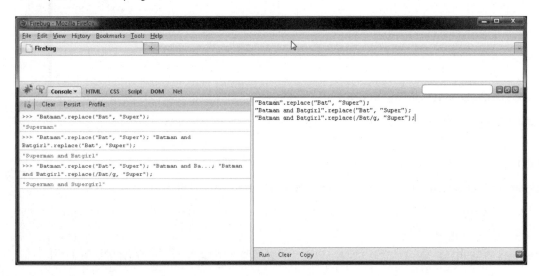

Figure 2–13. Replacing a substring with replace()

Now let's create a title-casing function named titleCase() to pass as the second parameter so that we can replace each hero's name with its title-case version. JavaScript will pass titleCase() the matched text, which we can refer to as m within the function block. There we'll chain invocations of slice() and toUpperCase() in order to convert the first letter in m to uppercase. Then we'll glue that to a slice containing every character in m but the first and return that as the replacement string.

```
var titleCase = function(m) {
  return m.slice(0,1).toUpperCase() + m.slice(1);
};
```

If we then pass a RegExp literal that matches words, /\b\w+\b/g, for the first parameter, JavaScript will pass each word in the string we call replace() to titleCase(). Let's try this on "batman, spider-man, iron man", verifying our work with Figure 2–14. Note that JavaScript invokes titleCase() five times, once for each of the following matches: "batman", "spider", "man", "iron", and "man".

```
var titleCase = function(m) {
  return m.slice(0,1).toUpperCase() + m.slice(1);
};
"batman, spider-man, iron man".replace(/\b\w+\b/g, titleCase);
// "Batman, Spider-Man, Iron Man"
```

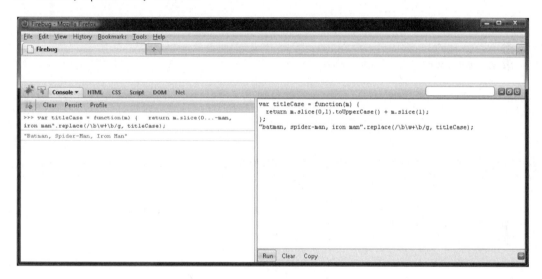

Figure 2–14. The second parameter to replace() may be a function.

Splitting a String into an Array of Smaller Strings

If you want to divide a string into smaller strings, pass the split() method a divider. It will then split the string into smaller strings, referred to as *substrings*, based on where the divider occurs. Those substrings do not include the divider and are returned in an array by split(). Double-clear Firebug, and let's divvy up a list of Spider-Man's archenemies relative to a comma followed by a space. We'll pass ", " to split() like so, verifying our work with Figure 2–15:

```
var villains = "Green Goblin, Doctor Octopus, Venom, Hobgoblin, Sandman";
villains.split(", ");
// ["Green Goblin", "Doctor Octopus", "Venom", "Hobgoblin", "Sandman"]
```

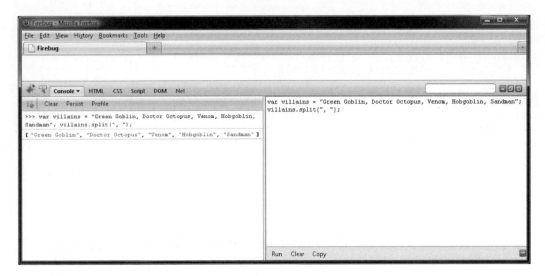

Figure 2–15. *Splitting a string into smaller strings with* `split()`

Say the final villain is prefaced by `", and "` rather than `", "`. That is to say, we want to divvy up a string based on two dividers, `", "` or `", and "`. This can't be done by passing a string divider. Rather, we'd need to pass in a RegExp literal to match both dividers:

`/, (?:and )?/g`

Don't worry, this won't look like gobbledygook by the end of Chapter 5 (note how you can identify the dividers in the expression, and we're using /g again). Try the following sample in Firebug, verifying your work with Figure 2–16:

```
var villains = "Green Goblin, Doctor Octopus, Venom, Hobgoblin, and Sandman";
villains.split(/, (?:and )?/g);
// ["Green Goblin", "Doctor Octopus", "Venom", "Hobgoblin", "Sandman"]
```

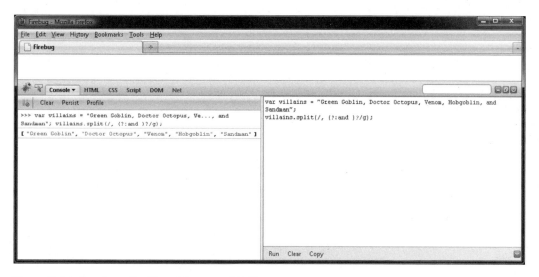

Figure 2–16. Passing a RegExp object to split()

Do you remember from Chapter 1 how you would query the array returned by split()?

Uh-huh. By passing an index to the [ ] operator. So, to return the fourth element, "Hobgoblin", we'd pass [ ] the index 3 since JavaScript numbers elements beginning with 0:

```
var villains = "Green Goblin, Doctor Octopus, Venom, Hobgoblin, and Sandman";
villains.split(/, (?:and )?/g)[3];
// "Hobgoblin"
```

That worked well. But what happened to the array? It's not in villains, as Figure 2–17 displays:

```
var villains = "Green Goblin, Doctor Octopus, Venom, Hobgoblin, and Sandman";
villains.split(/, (?:and )?/g)[3];
// "Hobgoblin"
villains;
// "Green Goblin, Doctor Octopus, Venom, Hobgoblin, and Sandman"
```

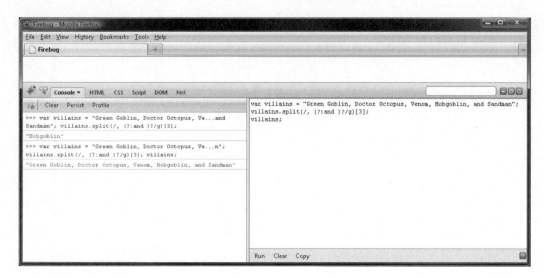

Figure 2–17. Where'd the array of substrings go?

As noted earlier in the chapter, split(), like any other string method, does not modify the string value it's called upon. Rather, split() returns a new value. We'd need to save the array to a new variable or overwrite villains. Let's do the latter, verifying our work with Figure 2–18:

```
var villains = "Green Goblin, Doctor Octopus, Venom, Hobgoblin, and Sandman";
villains = villains.split(/, (?:and )?/g);
villains[1];
// "Doctor Octopus"
```

Figure 2–18. Overwriting the string in villains with the array returned by split()

Searching with Regular Expressions

Whereas indexOf() returns the index of the first match of a string, search() returns the index of the first match of a RegExp object. So, the following samples are equivalent:

```
var villains = "Green Goblin, Doctor Octopus, Venom, Hobgoblin, and Sandman";
villains.indexOf("Goblin");
// 6
villains.search(/Goblin/);
// 6
```

In the event that you want all matches rather than just the first one, pass match() the RegExp instead. JavaScript will then return an array of matching substrings. Let's find any occurrence of goblin regardless of case in Firebug, verifying our work with Figure 2–19:

```
var villains = "Green Goblin, Doctor Octopus, Venom, Hobgoblin, and Sandman";
villains.match(/[Gg]oblin/g);
// ["Goblin", "goblin"]
```

We'll revisit search() and match() in Chapter 5, where you will learn to write more interesting RegExp patterns.

Figure 2–19. *Passing a RegExp object to match()*

Explicitly Creating Wrappers

In addition to the members provided by the String(), Number(), or Boolean() constructor functions, wrapper objects receive the following members from Object() too. The only one we'll explore now is valueOf(); the others are covered in Chapter 5.

```
constructor
hasOwnProperty()
isPrototypeOf()
```

```
propertyIsEnumerable()
toLocaleString()
toString()
valueOf()
```

valueOf() returns the string, number, or boolean associated with a wrapper object. In other words, JavaScript invokes valueOf() on a wrapper to revert it to a string, number, or boolean. So, in Firebug, we can explicitly do what JavaScript does implicitly by creating a wrapper with new and String(), Number(), or Boolean(); querying a member or invoking a method; and then invoking valueOf(). Verify your work with Figure 2–20.

```
var pre = new String("Hob");
var post = pre.concat("goblin");
pre = pre.valueOf();
pre;
// "Hob"
post;
// "Hobgoblin"
```

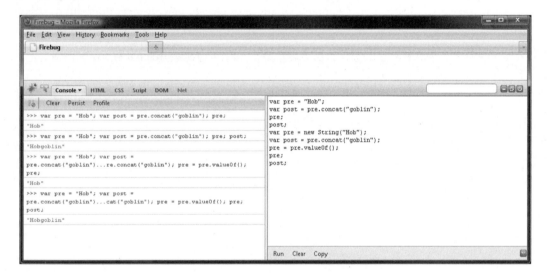

Figure 2–20. *Explicitly converting a string to and from a wrapper object*

JavaScript does not immediately revert an explicitly created wrapper to a string, number, or boolean. They provide a way to create a wrapper that persists past a single line of code.

Converting a Value to Another Type

Elastigirl, Mr. Incredible's wife Helen Parr, can reshape any part of her body to be as large as 30 meters or as small as 1 millimeter. For example, in the 2004 Pixar animated film *The Incredibles*, Elastigirl repeatedly saved the day by reshaping her body into a parachute, rubber raft, and so on. Like Elastigirl, JavaScript values are shape changers, too. They can save the day by changing to another value type, say from a number to a string. Here's how.

Invoking String(), Number(), or Boolean() with the new operator creates a wrapper object. On the other hand, omitting new converts the parameter to a string, number, or boolean. Converting a value to a different type is another thing JavaScript does behind the scenes. So, just as JavaScript quietly converts a string to a wrapper, which is to say to the object type, it also quietly converts a string to the number or boolean type.

You're wondering why would JavaScript ever need to do that for you, aren't you? For one thing, the operators we'll explore typically require their operands to be of a certain type. So, in the event you give them a value of the wrong type to work with, JavaScript saves your bacon by converting it to the correct type. For another, controlling flow with conditional statements, which we'll explore in Chapter 4, relies on JavaScript converting values to the boolean type. In turn, this means that every value you could possibly create has a boolean equivalent. Those that convert to true are referred to as *truthy values*, while those that convert to false are referred to as *falsy values*. There are only six falsy values, which are listed here, so all other values convert to true:

```
undefined
null
false
""
0
NaN
```

But don't take my word for it. Double-clear Firebug, and then pass each of those in turn to Boolean(), verifying your work with Figure 2–21:

```
Boolean(undefined);
// false
Boolean(null);
// false
Boolean(false);
// false
Boolean("");
// false
Boolean(0);
// false
Boolean(NaN);
// false
```

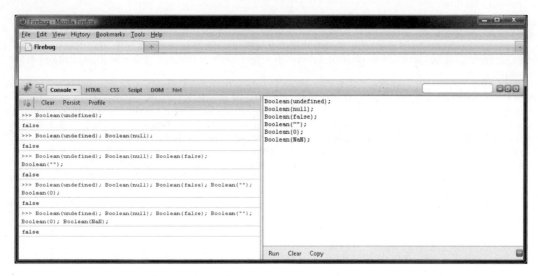

Figure 2–21. Converting values to the boolean type

■ **Note** Converting undefined, the value for a missing method or member, to false is the basis for feature testing, which we'll do quite a bit of in the final few chapters.

Every other value converts to true. So, any string except for "", any number except for 0 and NaN, and any object converts to true:

```
Boolean("Mr. Incredible");
// true
Boolean(["Green Goblin", "Doctor Octopus", "Venom", "Hobgoblin", "Sandman"]);
// true
Boolean(String.fromCharCode);
// true
```

Converting a Value to a Number

Now let's try converting some values to a number by passing them to Number(). Double-clear Firebug, and then try converting nothing, undefined or null, to a number:

```
Number(undefined);
// NaN
Number(null);
// 0
```

Whereas both undefined and null convert to the same boolean (false), they convert to different numbers: undefined to NaN, and null to 0. Note that NaN ("not a number") is a special number literal JavaScript returns for math errors, such as division by 0, or for conversions to the number type that fail.

Note too that, if either operand to a math operator like * or - is NaN, the return value will be NaN, too. Therefore, as Figure 2–22 displays, you can do math with null but not with undefined.

```
var nothing, zilch = null;
nothing * 4;
// NaN
zilch * 4;
// 0
```

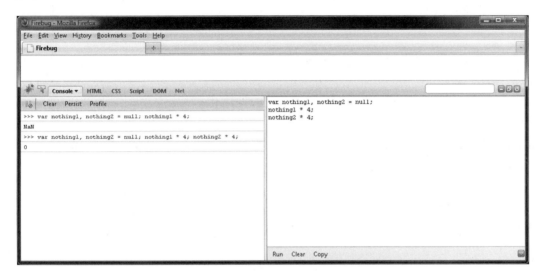

Figure 2–22. JavaScript can do math with null but not with undefined.

Converting strings to numbers is fairly straightforward. Number-like strings such as "4" or "3.33" convert to an equivalent number (4 and 3.33). The "" empty string converts to 0. Everything else converts to NaN. Let's try converting a few strings to a number in Firebug, verifying our work with Figure 2–23:

```
Number("4");
// 4
Number("");
// 0
Number("Mr. Incredible");
// NaN
```

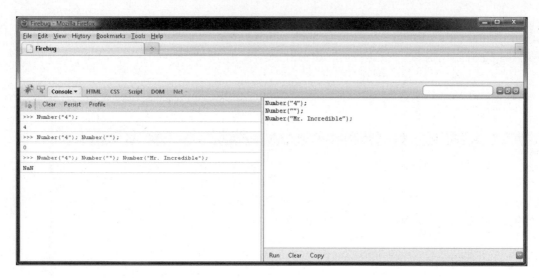

Figure 2–23. Most strings convert to NaN.

One common bugaboo is trying to do math with a CSS value; JavaScript represents all of those as strings. So, if you try to move an element 3 pixels to the left by subtracting 3 from a left value of, say, 30px, you're really doing the following calculation. Note that manipulating CSS is covered in Chapter 8.

```
"30px" - 3;
// NaN
```

Converting booleans to numbers is very simple. true converts to 1, and false converts to 0. Try doing so in Firebug:

```
Number(true);
// 1
Number(false);
// 0
```

Rarely will an object, array, or function convert to a number other than NaN. Trying to do math with an object, array, or function value will generally return NaN to convey failure. Try converting one of each in Firebug, verifying your work with Figure 2–24:

```
Number(["Green Goblin", "Doctor Octopus", "Sandman"]);
// NaN
Number({hero: "Batman", archenemy: "Joker"});
// NaN
Number(String.fromCharCode);
// NaN
```

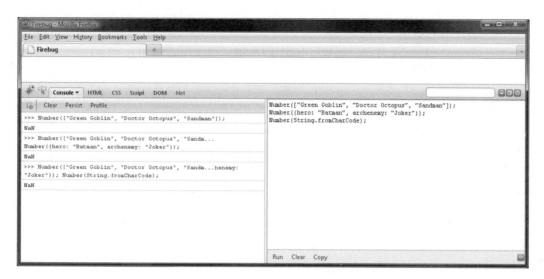

Figure 2–24. Most object, array, and function values convert to NaN.

Table 2–1 displays at a glance the number conversions we explored.

Table 2–1. Samples Displaying Spectrum of Conversions to Number Type

Initial Value	Number()
undefined	NaN
null	0
""	0
"30px"	NaN
"4"	4
"3.33"	3.33
true	1
false	0
["Green Goblin", "Doctor Octopus", "Sandman"]	NaN
{hero:"Batman", archenemy: "Joker"}	NaN
String.fromCharCode	NaN

Converting a Value to a String

In Chapter 1, you learned that the [ ] operator converts a number to a string. So, the following queries both return the member named "3":

```
"Mezmerella"[2];
// "z"
"Mezmerella"["2"];
// "z"
```

Though JavaScript frequently converts numbers to strings behind the scenes, occasionally it will have to convert values of other types to strings. Doing so for undefined, null, or booleans is unsurprising:

```
String(undefined);
// "undefined"
String(null);
// "null"
String(true);
// "true"
String(false);
// "false"
```

On the other hand, converting values of the object type or array and function subtypes to strings in not straightforward or common. To do so, JavaScript calls the value's toString() method. The following array to string conversions are equivalent:

```
String(["Green Goblin", "Doctor Octopus", "Sandman"]);
// "Green Goblin,Doctor Octopus,Sandman"
["Green Goblin", "Doctor Octopus", "Sandman"].toString();
// "Green Goblin,Doctor Octopus,Sandman"
```

So too are the following object to string conversions, as Figure 2–25 displays. Note that the lowercase object indicates the value type, and the uppercase Object indicates the class, which is to say the identifier for the Object() constructor. Figure 2–25 displays the results:

```
({"Bob Parr": "Mr. Incredible", "Helen Parr": "Elastigirl"}).toString();
// "[object Object]"
String({"Bob Parr": "Mr. Incredible", "Helen Parr": "Elastigirl"});
// "[object Object]"
```

Don't devote too many brain cells to converting objects, arrays, or functions to strings. It's not important to know.

Figure 2–25. *Converting an array and object to a string*

Methods for Converting a Number to a String

Mr. Incredible's 10-year-old son, Dashiell "Dash" Robert Parr, is a speedster like the Flash. He can probably run at the speed of light: 299,792,458 meters per second. JavaScript numbers may not contain commas, so the number literal for that would be 299792458. That's pretty ugly.

Not to worry. Number wrappers provide the following three methods to convert a bloated number like 299792458 to a succinct string.

```
Number.toExponential()
Number.toFixed()
Number.toPrecision()
```

Double-clear Firebug, and let's call each of those in turn on 299792458. First, toExponential() converts a number to an exponential string. Optionally, you can indicate the number of decimal places by passing a number between 0 and 20. Try passing 2 and omitting the parameter, verifying your work with Figure 2–26:

```
(299792458).toExponential(2);
// "3.00e+8"
(299792458).toExponential();
// "2.99792458e+8"
```

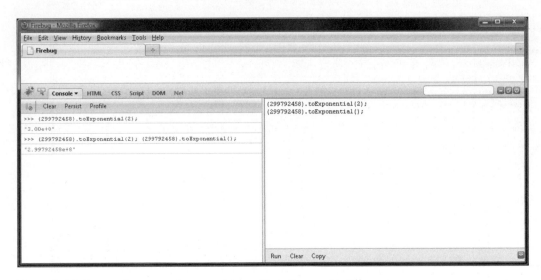

Figure 2–26. Converting a number to a string with toExponential()

The next method, toFixed(), converts a number to a decimal string. Optionally, you can indicate the number of decimal places by passing a number between 0 and 20. Let's divide 299792458 by 1000 to determine kilometers per second. Then convert that to a string with three or no decimal places, verifying your work with Figure 2–27. Note that omitting the parameter is the same as passing 0.

```
(299792458 / 1000).toFixed(3);
// "299792.458"
(299792458 / 1000).toFixed();
//"299792"
```

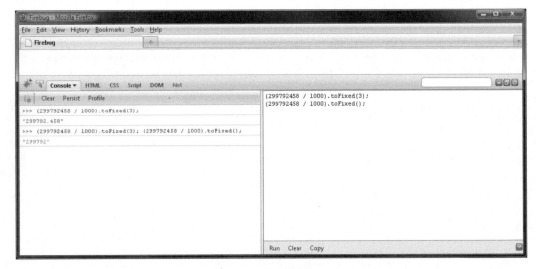

Figure 2–27. Converting a number to a string with toFixed()

If you are indecisive and want JavaScript to choose between exponential and decimal format, call `toPrecision()` on the number. The optional parameter differs this time: it's a number between 1 and 21 indicating the number of significant digits. If the parameter is less than the number of digits in the integer part of the number, JavaScript chooses exponential format. If not, JavaScript chooses decimal format. Finally, if you omit the parameter, JavaScript invokes `Number.toString()`. Try the following samples to clarify how `toPrecision()` works, verifying your work with Figure 2–28. Note that the final two samples are equivalent.

```
(299792458).toPrecision(2);
// "3.0e+8"
(299792458).toPrecision(12);
// "299792458.000"
(299792458).toPrecision();
// "299792458"
(299792458).toString();
// "299792458"
```

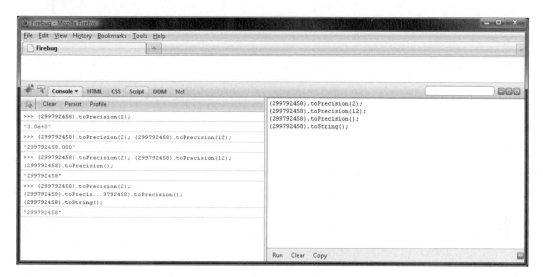

Figure 2–28. Converting a number to a string with `toPrecision()`

Note that `toExponential()`, `toFixed()`, and `toPrecision()` round trailing digits 0–4 down and 5–9 up just like you would.

Putting Off Learning RegExp Syntax

Even though I will cover RegExp objects more fully in Chapter 5, if you are new to both JavaScript and programming, I suggest simply passing string parameters to the four methods that work with RegExp objects. `replace()` and `split()` work with either a string or a RegExp parameter. So, a string will do as is. `match()` and `search()` work only with a RegExp parameter, but JavaScript implicitly converts a string parameter to a RegExp object. So, just as a string is converted to a wrapper object by passing it to `new` and `String()`, it can be converted to a RegExp object by passing it to `new` and `RegExp()`. Insofar as JavaScript does the latter just as quietly as the former, this means that a beginner can put off learning RegExp syntax until after learning JavaScript syntax. I recommend you do.

To illustrate this beginner-friendly JavaScript string to RegExp conversion feature, double-clear Firebug, and then enter and run the following sample. As Figure 2–29 displays, passing a string to match() and search() works just dandy:

```
var incredibles = "Mr. Incredible, Elastigirl, Violet, Dash, Jack-Jack";
incredibles.match("Jack");
// ["Jack"]
incredibles.search("Jack");
// 42
```

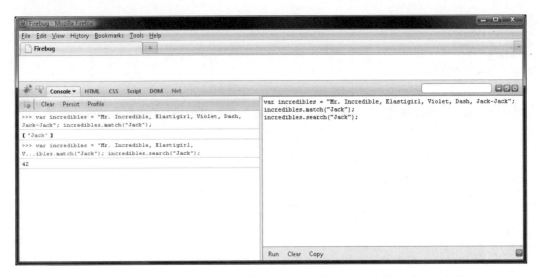

Figure 2–29. JavaScript quietly converts "Jack" to /Jack/ for both match() and search().

JavaScript quietly passed "Jack" to RegExp(), which like String() is referred to as a *constructor function*. So to explicitly do what JavaScript implicitly did, let's enter and run the following in Firebug. As Figure 2–30 displays, the return values are the same:

```
var incredibles = "Mr. Incredible, Elastigirl, Violet, Dash, Jack-Jack";
incredibles.match(new RegExp("Jack"));
// ["Jack"]
incredibles.search(new RegExp("Jack"));
// 42
```

Figure 2–30. Passing a RegExp for a literal string to match() *and* search()

Note, however, that, when JavaScript converts a string to a RegExp object, the g, i, and m flags, which we'll explore in Chapter 5, are not set. There's no way for JavaScript to save the day if we intended to pass /jack/ig but instead passed "jack" to match(), as Figure 2–31 displays:

```
var incredibles = "Mr. Incredible, Elastigirl, Violet, Dash, Jack-Jack";
incredibles.match(/jack/ig);
// ["Jack", "Jack"]
incredibles.match("jack");
// null
```

Note that match() conveys failure, which is to say no array of matching strings, by returning null. Remember from Chapter 1 that null conveys no value on the heap, in other words, no object, array, or function. That is why match() returned null instead of undefined.

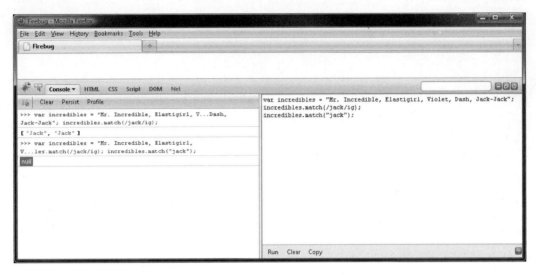

Figure 2–31. JavaScript does not set the i, g, or m flag when converting a string to a RegExp object.

Summary

In this chapter, you learned that JavaScript converts a string to a wrapper object whenever the string is the left operand to the . or [ ] operator, quietly passing the string to the String() constructor and then just as quietly reverting the wrapper to a string by invoking its valueOf() method. String wrappers manipulate characters as if they were read-only elements. In other words, string values are immutable, and wrapper methods return a new value without changing the original. So, typically you will want to save the return value or immediately pass it to one of the operators we'll explore in Chapter 3.

Most JavaScript operators are particular about the value type of their operands. Knowing this, JavaScript will save the day by converting an operand of the wrong type to the correct one. Though JavaScript does so behind the scenes, we explored how to do so by passing values to String(), Number(), Boolean(), and Object(). If invoked without the new operator, those constructors convert their argument to a string, number, boolean, or object. So, a string can be converted to a wrapper by passing it to Object() without new or to String() with new:

```
Object("Spider-Man");
new String("Spider-Man");
```

So, when JavaScript creates a wrapper for a string, it's really converting the value from the string type to the object type. The same thing goes for number or boolean wrappers, too. Therefore, value type conversion is vital for manipulating values with wrapper methods or with operators. You'll learn more about the latter in Chapter 3. Take a breather, and I'll see you there!

CHAPTER 3

■ ■ ■

Operators

Having data is no use if you can't do anything with it, so step forward operators. Operators do just what their name suggests; they operate on things. In the case of JavaScript, those things are the values stored in variables and any other value used in your script. For example, we'd use a division operator to divide one value by another value to return a result. There are some very straightforward operators in JavaScript and some not-so-straightforward ones; we'll cover all the useful ones and mention the others in passing, even though you will never use them.

To work with operators, you must first understand operator precedence, which is how JavaScript decides which operator to apply first if there is more than one in an expression, and operator associativity, which is the direction JavaScript reads through an expression when applying operators. We'll look at precedence and associativity as a general theory at the start of the chapter and then see how JavaScript operators really work. In the course of the chapter, you'll learn how to use operators effectively so that your expressions really zing.

Introducing Operator Precedence and Associativity

I've been running more than 100 miles per week for 14 years. To take in enough daily carbohydrates, I've become not so much a foodie as a doughie. Monday to Friday I run in the evening after work. So by the time I begin making dinner, it's pretty late. To save some time, I typically go with soda leavening rather than yeast.

One of my favorite late-night soda breads is leavened with soda, cream of tartar, and Organic Valley pourable vanilla yogurt, which is drinkable like kefir but tastes like yogurt:

- 2 cups Bob's Red Mill organic whole wheat pastry flour
- 1/3 cup blanched almonds, freshly ground into fine flour
- 1 tsp. Saigon cinnamon
- 2 tsp. minced lemon zest
- 1/4 tsp. sea salt
- 1 tsp. soda
- 1 tsp. cream of tartar
- 1 cup Organic Valley pourable vanilla yogurt
- 1 egg
- 1 1/4 cups fresh wild blueberries

Remember from Chapter 1 that an expression is like a recipe whereby operators combine ingredients referred to as operands to create a value. So, with that analogy in mind, we might write an expression for the dough like so:

```
var dough = pastryFlour + almonds + saigonCinnamon + lemon + seaSalt + soda + tartar +
pourableVanillaYogurt + egg + wildBlueberries;
```

Insofar as that tells JavaScript blindly combine ingredients left to right, not only would the soda leavening fail, but the wild blueberries and lemon would get mulched by the mixer. We'd wind up with a very tart purple stone rather than a yummy loaf. I think I'd just go to bed hungry.

Rather than sequentially mulch everything, we want JavaScript to asynchronously take eight steps:

1. Grind almonds into a very fine flour.

2. Zest lemon.

3. Sift flour, almonds, saigonCinnamon, lemon, and seaSalt.

4. Whisk egg, pourableVanillaYogurt, and tartar.

5. Whisk in soda to touch off alkaline and acid reaction.

6. Mix now bubbling liquid with dry ingredients.

7. Fold in wildBlueberries by hand.

8. Knead dough to form gluten strands.

Okeydokey. But can JavaScript precisely follow a recipe? That is to say, how can it evaluate an expression asynchronously?

Yup, you bet your fern.

Operators have a couple of traits that determine the order of operation. Precedence is a value between 1 and 15 indicating an operator's priority. 1 is very low priority, and 15 is very high priority. So if an expression sequentially contains operators with a priority of 2, 14, 9, and 3, JavaScript does the 14 operation first, followed by the 9, then the 3, and finally the 2.

The other trait, associativity, tells JavaScript what to do when consecutive operators have the same priority. Just two options here. R associativity means do the one on the right first. Conversely, L associativity means do the one on the left first. So if an expression sequentially contains operators with priorities of 15, 15, 3, and 3 and L, L, R, and R associativity, JavaScript does the first 15, then the second 15, then the second 3, then the first 3.

With this in mind, let's create some fictitious operators for JavaScript to cook with:

- G for grind—14 precedence, R associativity

- Z for zest—14 precedence, R associativity

- S for sift—11 precedence, L associativity

- W for whisk—10 precedence, R associativity

- F for fold—3 precedence, L associativity

- K for knead—3 precedence, R associativity

So, we can now express dough to JavaScript with the following expression:

```
var dough = K flour S G almonds S saigonCinnamon S Z lemon S seaSalt W soda W tartar W
pourableVanillaYogurt W egg F wildBlueberries;
```

Let's unpick this in steps:

1. All right, both G and Z have 14 priority. So, does JavaScript evaluate G almonds or Z lemon first? If two operators have equal priority but are not adjacent, JavaScript works left to right. Therefore, the almonds are ground, and then the lemon is zested.

2. Sifting is next up because of S having 11 priority. But there are four S operations in a row, so JavaScript turns to associativity, which is L for sifting, to determine the order of operation. Therefore, JavaScript groups them as follows, evaluating them from left to right:

```
(((flour S almond) S saigonCinnamon) S lemon) S seaSalt
```

3. Insofar as W has 10 priority compared to 3 from K and F, JavaScript does the whisking next. There are four W operations in a row. Associativity, which is R for W, tells JavaScript to do those from right to left. Therefore, JavaScript groups the W operations as follows. Note that W having R associativity does not mean JavaScript whisks the right operand with the left operand.

```
siftedIngredients W (soda W (tartar W (pourableVanillaYogurt W egg)))
```

4. Now we have a K followed by an F, both of which have 3 priority. However, K has R associativity and F has L. Does JavaScript do the K or F first? Yup, the F folding. R followed by R or L means do the one on the right first. Conversely, L followed by L or R means do the one on the left first. So, JavaScript folds in wildBlueberries.

5. Now we just have to K knead the dough for a minute or two to form bubble trapping gluten strands, shape the loaf, and slash a shallow *X* across the top, and we're done.

6. Not quite. = is an operator, too. But it has a very low priority of 2. Only the , operator, which we'll explore a little later, has 1 priority. So, JavaScript does the G, Z, S, W, F, and K operations before assigning the loaf to the variable dough with the = operator.

The = operator having low priority and R associativity enables you to assign an expression to two or more variables. So if we wanted to make three loafs of wild blueberry swope rather than one, we would do so by chaining = operators:

```
var loaf1, loaf2, loaf3;
loaf1 = loaf2 = loaf3 = K flour S almond S saigonCinnamon S lemon S seaSalt W soda W tartar W
pourableVanillaYogurt W egg F wildBlueberries;
```

JavaScript would do the higher priority G, Z, S, W, F, and K operations first. Insofar as = has R associativity, JavaScript would first assign wild blueberry swope to loaf3, then to loaf2, and finally to loaf1.

This section has given you an idea how operator precedence works in principle, so let's look at the actual JavaScript operators, their precedence, and how to use them.

Using JavaScript Operators

As we explore JavaScript operators in this chapter, you might want to refer to the handy Table 3–1, which lists precedence and associativity values. Though you're probably thinking you'll never remember precedence and associativity for all those operators, it's actually very straightforward:

- Unary operators have R associativity and 14 precedence, except for new, which has 15 precedence.

- Binary assignment operators (=, *=, /=, %=, +=, -=) have R associativity and 2 precedence. All other binary operators have L associativity and varying precedence.

- The ?: ternary operator has R associativity and 3 precedence.

Remembering value types for operands will take time. But a year from now, if not by the end of this book, those will be as simple to remember as associativity and precedence.

Table 3–1. Precedence and Associativity for Essential JavaScript Operators

Operator	Precedence	Associativity	Operator	Precedence	Associativity
.	15	L	<=	10	L
[]	15	L	instanceof	10	L
()	15	L	in	10	L
new	15	R	==	9	L
++	14	R	!=	9	L
--	14	R	===	9	L
!	14	R	!==	9	L
delete	14	R	&&	5	L
typeof	14	R	||	4	L
void	14	R	?:	3	R
*	13	L	=	2	R
/	13	L	*=	2	R
%	13	L	/=	2	R
+	12	L	%=	2	R
-	12	L	+=	2	R
>	10	L	-=	2	R
>=	10	L	,	1	L
<	10	L			

> ▓ **Note** JavaScript has a group of operators called bitwise operators. Bitwise operators are generally very fast in other programming languages, but they are very slow in JavaScript. So, no one does bit manipulation with JavaScript. Nor will we, so I won't cover them in this book.

Combining Math and Assignment Operations

Open `firebug.html` in Firefox, and then press F12 to enable Firebug. If you're just joining us, flip back to the preface for details on how to do this. In Chapter 1, we explored the + (addition), - (subtraction), * (multiplication), and / (division) operators, noting that + adds numbers but glues strings. Moreover, we explored how to save a value to a variable with the = (assignment) operator.

In the event that the left operand to +, -, *, or / is a variable, member, element, or parameter, you may replace the = operator and +, -, *, or / operator with a +=, -=, *=, or /= shortcut operator. Those do the math and assignment operations in one fell swoop. In Firebug, let's create the following dough object so that we have some values to explore +=, -=, *=, and /= with.

```
var dough = {
  pastryFlour: [1 + 3/4, "cup"],
  almondFlour: [1/3, "cup"],
  saigonCinnamon: [1, "tsp"],
  mincedLemonZest: [2, "tsp"],
  seaSalt: [1/4, "tsp"],
  soda: [1, "tsp"],
  tartar: [1, "tsp"],
  pourableVanillaYogurt: [1, "cup"],
  egg: [1],
  wildBlueberries: [1 + 1/4, "cup"]
};
```

Say I want to triple the recipe. To do so, we could pass each element and 3 to the *= operator like so in Firebug. Then query the new values of a couple of elements, verifying your work with Figure 3–1:

```
var dough = {
  pastryFlour: [1 + 3/4, "cup"],
  almondFlour: [1/3, "cup"],
  saigonCinnamon: [1, "tsp"],
  mincedLemonZest: [2, "tsp"],
  seaSalt: [1/4, "tsp"],
  soda: [1, "tsp"],
  tartar: [1, "tsp"],
  pourableVanillaYogurt: [1, "cup"],
  egg: [1],
  wildBlueberries: [1 + 1/4, "cup"]
};
dough.pastryFlour[0] *= 3;
dough.almondFlour[0] *= 3;
dough.saigonCinnamon[0] *= 3;
dough.mincedLemonZest[0] *= 3;
dough.seaSalt[0] *= 3;
dough.soda[0] *= 3;
dough.tartar[0] *= 3;
```

61

```
dough.pourableVanillaYogurt[0] *= 3;
dough.egg[0] *= 3;
dough.wildBlueberries[0] *= 3;
dough.pastryFlour[0];
// 5.25
dough.pourableVanillaYogurt[0];
// 3
```

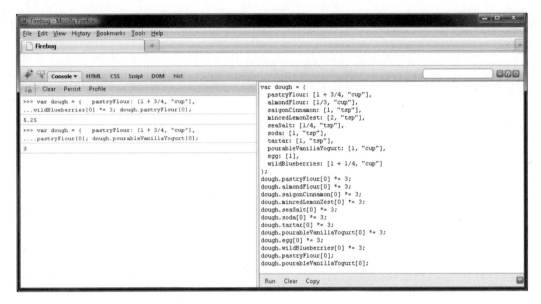

***Figure 3–1.** Doubling elements with *=*

The following is what we would have had to type in if we didn't have *=, so *= saved us from having to separately key in = and * as Figure 3–2 displays.

```
var dough = {
  pastryFlour: [1 + 3/4, "cup"],
  almondFlour: [1/3, "cup"],
  saigonCinnamon: [1, "tsp"],
  mincedLemonZest: [2, "tsp"],
  seaSalt: [1/4, "tsp"],
  soda: [1, "tsp"],
  tartar: [1, "tsp"],
  pourableVanillaYogurt: [1, "cup"],
  egg: [1],
  wildBlueberries: [1 + 1/4, "cup"]
};
dough.pastryFlour[0] = dough.pastryFlour[0] * 3;
dough.almondFlour[0] = dough.almondFlour[0] * 3;
dough.saigonCinnamon[0] = dough.saigonCinnamon[0] * 3;
dough.mincedLemonZest[0] = dough.mincedLemonZest[0] * 3;
dough.seaSalt[0] = dough.seaSalt[0] * 3;
dough.soda[0] = dough.soda[0] * 3;
```

```
dough.tartar[0] = dough.tartar[0] * 3;
dough.pourableVanillaYogurt[0] = dough.pourableVanillaYogurt[0] * 3;
dough.wildBlueberries[0] = dough.wildBlueberries[0] * 3;
dough.pastryFlour[0];
// 5.25
dough.pourableVanillaYogurt[0];
// 3
```

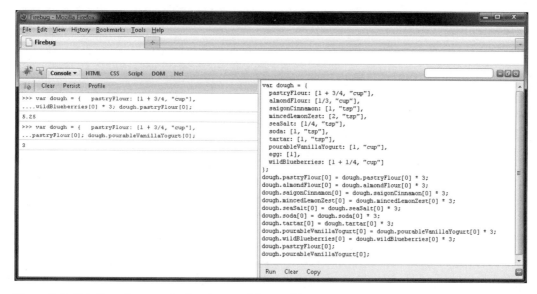

*Figure 3–2. Tripling elements the hard way with = and ***

■ **Note** The `for in` loop, which we'll cover in Chapter 4, would further eliminate drudgery.

Like the * multiplication operator, *= converts its operands to numbers if necessary. So if we inadvertently defined some elements with strings, JavaScript would convert those to numbers so that the multiplication part of *= will work. Insofar as *= does assignment too, values are permanently converted from strings to numbers

Like *=, -= and /= convert their operands to numbers, too. However, += favors gluing strings over adding numbers just as + does. So if one operand is a string and the other is a number, boolean, object, null, or undefined, += converts the nonstring to a string. Therefore, += will do addition only if one operand is a number and the other is not a string.

To illustrate, try doubling pourableVanillaYogurt with += rather than *=. As Figure 3–3 displays, += converts its left operand 1 to 1 and then glues it to its right operand to create the string 11.

```
var dough = {
  pastryFlour: [1 + 3/4, "cup"],
  almondFlour: [1/3, "cup"],
  saigonCinnamon: [1, "tsp"],
```

```
    mincedLemonZest: [2, "tsp"],
    seaSalt: [1/4, "tsp"],
    soda: [1, "tsp"],
    tartar: [1, "tsp"],
    pourableVanillaYogurt: [1, "cup"],
    egg: [1],
    wildBlueberries: [1 + 1/4, "cup"]
};
dough.pourableVanillaYogurt[0] += "1";
dough.pourableVanillaYogurt[0];
// "11"
```

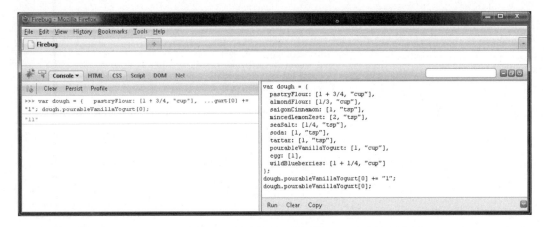

Figure 3–3. *+= only does concatenation if its right operand is not a number.*

Remember that every JavaScript value can be converted to a boolean or string, but not to a number. Not one you can do math with anyway. Most non-numbers convert to the "not a number" literal NaN. Moreover, the return value of any math operation containing a NaN operand will always be NaN.

Insofar as JavaScript returns NaN whenever a value cannot be converted to a number, +=, -=, *=, and /= may overwrite a variable, member, element, or parameter with NaN. To illustrate the point, try the following sample, verifying your work with Figure 3–4. Insofar as we forgot to refine our query with the [ ] operator, JavaScript multiplies the array [1 + 1/4, "cup"] by 3. Therefore, [1 + 1/4, "cup"] is converted to the number NaN and multiplied by 3. So, the array in dough.wildBlueberries is overwritten with the return value of NaN * 3, which of course is NaN.

```
var dough = {
    pastryFlour: [1 + 3/4, "cup"],
    almondFlour: [1/3, "cup"],
    saigonCinnamon: [1, "tsp"],
    mincedLemonZest: [2, "tsp"],
    seaSalt: [1/4, "tsp"],
    soda: [1, "tsp"],
    tartar: [1, "tsp"],
    pourableVanillaYogurt: [1, "cup"],
    egg: [1],
    wildBlueberries: [1 + 1/4, "cup"]
};
```

```
dough.wildBlueberries *= 3;
dough.wildBlueberries;
// NaN
```

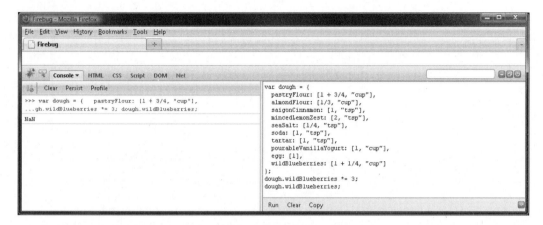

Figure 3–4. Failing to refine our query with [] results in the array being overwritten with NaN.

OK, so what would happen if we try to query the first element in dough.wildBlueberries now that that's NaN, not an array?

Here's a hint: see Chapter 2.

Yup, if you query NaN with the . or [ ] operators, JavaScript creates a number wrapper for NaN. Since that number wrapper does not contain any elements, querying its first element returns undefined, as the following sample and Figure 3–5 illustrate. Note that + converts undefined to "undefined" prior to gluing it to "There are ". Note too that finding and fixing coding typos like this are what debugging primarily entails.

```
var dough = {
  pastryFlour: [1 + 3/4, "cup"],
  almondFlour: [1/3, "cup"],
  saigonCinnamon: [1, "tsp"],
  mincedLemonZest: [2, "tsp"],
  seaSalt: [1/4, "tsp"],
  soda: [1, "tsp"],
  tartar: [1, "tsp"],
  pourableVanillaYogurt: [1, "cup"],
  egg: [1],
  wildBlueberries: [1 + 1/4, "cup"]
};
dough.wildBlueberries *= 3;
"There are " + dough.wildBlueberries[0] + " cups of wild blueberries in the dough.";
// "There are undefined cups of wild blueberries in the dough."
```

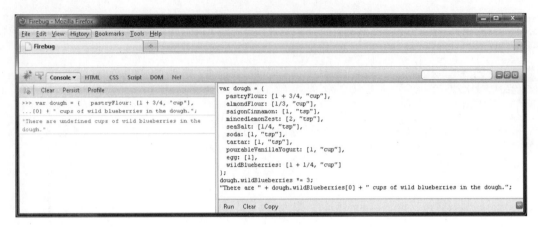

Figure 3–5. JavaScript converts NaN to a wrapper object if you query it with the . or [] operator.

Finally, it's vital to remember that the left operand to +=, -=, *=, or /= must be a variable, member, element, or parameter. Otherwise, JavaScript will slap you upside the head by returning a SyntaxError noting, "invalid assignment left-hand side", which means the left operand must be one of these things.

```
3 -= 1;
// SyntaxError: invalid assignment left-hand side { message="invalid assignment left-hand
side" }
"blue" += "berries";
// SyntaxError: invalid assignment left-hand side { message="invalid assignment left-hand
side" }
```

Incrementing or Decrementing Values

In the event that you are adding or subtracting 1 from a value with += or -=, you may even more succinctly do so with the ++ increment and -- decrement unary operators, which convert it to a number if necessary. Note that although += may do addition or concatenation, ++ always does addition.

So in Firebug, let's double saigonCinnamon with ++ and halve mincedLemonZest with --, verifying our work with Figure 3–6.

```
var dough = {
  pastryFlour: [1 + 3/4, "cup"],
  almondFlour: [1/3, "cup"],
  saigonCinnamon: [1, "tsp"],
  mincedLemonZest: [2, "tsp"],
  seaSalt: [1/4, "tsp"],
  soda: [1, "tsp"],
  tartar: [1, "tsp"],
  pourableVanillaYogurt: [1, "cup"],
  egg: [1],
  wildBlueberries: [1 + 1/4, "cup"]
};
dough.saigonCinnamon[0] ++;
dough.mincedLemonZest[0] --;
```

```
dough.saigonCinnamon[0];
// 2
dough.mincedLemonZest[0];
// 1
```

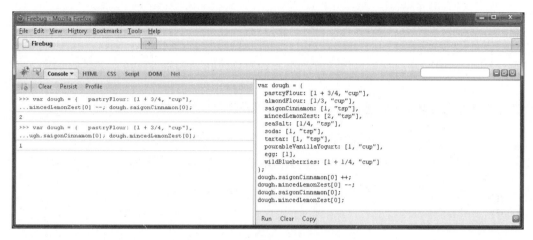

Figure 3–6. *++ is a shortcut for += 1, and -- is a shortcut for -= 1.*

Note that ++ and -- may appear in the prefix or postfix positions, that is to say, to the left or right of their operand. The prefix and postfix positions are irrelevant to the operand's new value: ++ will add 1 to its operand, and -- will subtract 1 from its operand either way. However, the return value of the ++ and -- will differ. In the prefix position, ++ returns the unincremented value, and -- returns the undecremented value. Conversely, in the postfix position, ++ returns the incremented value, and -- returns the decremented value.

To illustrate the point, try the following sample, which has ++ and -- in both the prefix and postfix positions. As Figure 3–7 displays, the return values of the ++ and -- expressions differ in the prefix and postfix positions, but not the new member values. Those are always incremented by ++ or decremented by --. Remember to stop and click Run prior to each comment, as explained in the preface.

```
var dough = {
  pastryFlour: [1 + 3/4, "cup"],
  almondFlour: [1/3, "cup"],
  saigonCinnamon: [1, "tsp"],
  mincedLemonZest: [2, "tsp"],
  seaSalt: [1/4, "tsp"],
  soda: [1, "tsp"],
  tartar: [1, "tsp"],
  pourableVanillaYogurt: [1, "cup"],
  egg: [1],
  wildBlueberries: [1 + 1/4, "cup"]
};
dough.saigonCinnamon[0] ++;
// 1
++ dough.mincedLemonZest[0];
// 3
dough.wildBlueberries[0] --;
```

```
// 1.25
-- dough.pastryFlour[0];
// .75
dough.saigonCinnamon[0];
// 2
dough.mincedLemonZest[0];
// 3
dough.wildBlueberries[0];
// .25
dough.pastryFlour[0];
// .75
```

Figure 3–7. The return value for ++ differs in the prefix and postfix position.

The differing return values of ++ and -- in the prefix and postfix positions provide additional flexibility in limiting the number of roundabouts JavaScript takes of a for, while, or do while loop. Those are covered in Chapter 4.

Testing for Equality

Scones are particularly fast to make—maybe 20 minutes from mixing the dough to putting the scones on the cooling rack. Hazelnut cream scones are among my favorites. I make those with either Organic Valley heavy whipping cream or half & half. Those are deliciously sweet and creamy because of Organic Valley pasturing their cows rather than feeding them corn.

Note that for cream scones the leavening bubbles derive from soda reacting with cream of tartar. That is to say, heavy whipping cream or half & half contain no lactic acid. Note that the ratio of soda tsp. to flour cups is 1:4 for scones compared to 1:2 for bread; we don't want as much lift. Note too that the ratio of soda to tartar is 1:2. Although tartar is tasteless, soda is bitter, so we want to ensure there's soda left in the dough following the leavening reaction.

```
var dough = {
  pastryFlour: [1 + 2/3, "cup"],
  hazelnutFlour: [1/3, "cup"],
  butter: [3, "tbs"],
  sugar: [2, "tbs"],
  seaSalt: [1/4, "tsp"],
  soda: [1/2, "tsp"],
  tartar: [1, "tsp"],
  heavyWhippingCream: [1, "cup"],
  currants: [1/3, "cup"]
};
```

If you're not familiar with making scones, you combine the ingredients in dough like so:

- Sift pastryFlour, hazelnutFlour, sugar, and seaSalt.

- Grate cold butter into flour and work into course meal with pastry blender.

- Sequentially whisk heavyWhippingCream, orangeJuice, mincedLemonZest, tartar, and soda.

- Make a well in center of flour, pour in wet ingredients and currants, and quickly blend with rubber spatula to form soft, slightly moist dough.

- Turn dough onto a well-floured work surface and roll into round 9 inches in diameter (1/2-inch thick).

- Slice into 8 wedges with sharp, floured knife. Cut away and discard center with 3–inch biscuit cutter.

- Bake slightly separated wedges on parchment lined sheet for 12 minutes at 425°F.

- Cool on wire rack for ten minutes.

Note that rolling dough for scones or other pastries can be difficult. So if you're a budding doughie, I recommend buying a marble pastry board. Insofar as marble stays cooler than room temperature, it's easier to roll dough on.

Anyway, say I'd like to compare my guess at how much of an ingredient to add to the dough to what the recipe calls for. I could do so by way of the === identity operator. === returns true if its operands evaluate to identical values and false if not. That boolean verdict derives from the following protocol:

- If the values are of different types, return false.

- If both values are of the undefined type, return true.

- If both values are of the null type, return true.

- If both values are of the number type and one or both are NaN, return false. Otherwise, return true if the numbers are the same and false if not.

- If both values are of the string type and have the same sequence and number of characters, return true. Otherwise, return false.

- If both values are of the boolean type, return true if both are false or both are true. Otherwise, return false.

- If both memory addresses refer to the same location, return true. Otherwise, return false.

Did that final step go over your head? Don't worry, we'll explore comparing memory addresses, which along with pointers are more generally referred to as references, in Chapter 5. For now just know that undefined, null, numbers, strings, and booleans are compared by value while objects, arrays, and functions are compared by memory address, which is to say by reference (which all implies that the two sets are stored in different ways, more of which in Chapter 5).

Note that === does not do datatype conversion, but its predecessor, the == equality operator, does. Insofar as == can tell you whether only one expression is not entirely unlike another, savvy JavaScript programmers frown upon its use. So since you're a clean slate, I won't teach you bad habits here.

Enough with the theory of ===; in Firebug, try the following sample, verifying your work with Figure 3–8:

```
var dough = {
  pastryFlour: [1 + 2/3, "cup"],
  hazelnutFlour: [1/3, "cup"],
  butter: [3, "tbs"],
  sugar: [2, "tbs"],
  seaSalt: [1/4, "tsp"],
  soda: [1/2, "tsp"],
  tartar: [1, "tsp"],
  heavyWhippingCream: [1, "cup"],
  currants: [1/3, "cup"]
};
dough.heavyWhippingCream[0] === 2/3;
// false
dough.currants[0] === dough.hazelnutFlour[0];
// true
dough.hazelnutFlour[0] * 5 === dough.pastryFlour[0];
// true
dough.soda[0] / dough.tartar[0] === 1;
// false
```

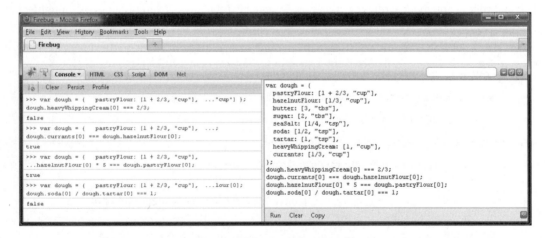

Figure 3–8. Verifying the amount of cream of tartar and soda with ===

Testing for Inequality

Frequently you will want to test for inequality, which is to say for a value you don't want an expression to return. To do so, we might invert the boolean returned by === with the ! logical not operator. ! flips true to false and false to true. However, ! has 14 priority and === 9. To trump the 14 with the 9, we would wrap the === expression in the () grouping operator as the following sample and Figure 3–9 illustrate.

```
var dough = {
  pastryFlour: [1 + 2/3, "cup"],
  hazelnutFlour: [1/3, "cup"],
  butter: [3, "tbs"],
  sugar: [2, "tbs"],
  seaSalt: [1/4, "tsp"],
  soda: [1/2, "tsp"],
  tartar: [1, "tsp"],
  heavyWhippingCream: [1, "cup"],
  currants: [1/3, "cup"]
};
! (dough.heavyWhippingCream[0] === 2/3);
// true
! (dough.currants[0] === dough.hazelnutFlour[0]);
// false
! (dough.hazelnutFlour[0] * 5 === dough.pastryFlour[0]);
// false
! (dough.soda[0] / dough.tartar[0] === 1);
// true
```

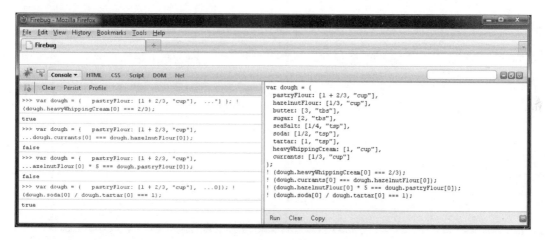

Figure 3–9. Querying JavaScript as to whether two expressions are not equal

As a shortcut for comparing two expressions for equality with === and flipping the verdict with !, JavaScript provides the !== operator. !== first runs through the === protocol and then does a logical not on the verdict. So if === would return true, !== returns false, and if === would false, !== returns true. So !== is quite the contrarian!

The important thing to remember is that both === and !== run through the same protocol; !== just inverts the verdict. It's sort of like a judge sending you to jail when the jury says innocent and letting you go free when the jury says guilty. Wouldn't that be something?

Let's simplify the previous sample with !==, verifying our work with Figure 3–10:

```
var dough = {
  pastryFlour: [1 + 2/3, "cup"],
  hazelnutFlour: [1/3, "cup"],
  butter: [3, "tbs"],
  sugar: [2, "tbs"],
  seaSalt: [1/4, "tsp"],
  soda: [1/2, "tsp"],
  tartar: [1, "tsp"],
  heavyWhippingCream: [1, "cup"],
  currants: [1/3, "cup"]
};
dough.heavyWhippingCream[0] !== 2/3;
// true
dough.currants[0] !== dough.hazelnutFlour[0];
// false
dough.hazelnutFlour[0] * 5 !== dough.pastryFlour[0];
// false
dough.soda[0] / dough.tartar[0] !== 1;
// true
```

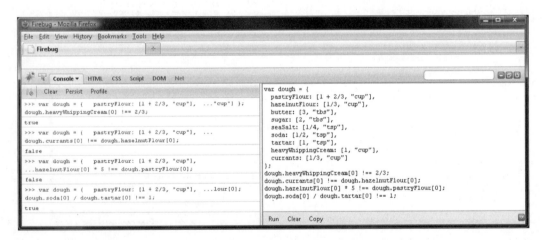

Figure 3–10. !== does a logical not on the verdict of the === protocol.

Comparing Objects, Arrays, and Functions

Thus far we've compared strings and numbers with ===. So, JavaScript never made it to the final step where memory addresses rather than values are compared. Referring to the === protocol, there's no step where JavaScript tediously compares object members, array elements, or function bodies. Not an error on my part. JavaScript never wastes time and memory doing that. Moreover, if you compare an array to a function, === does not return false (or !== true) because of those being different subtypes. Rather, the boolean verdict simply derives from the array and function being in different locations in memory. Remember, JavaScript stores string, number, boolean, undefined, and null values in a different way to object, array, and function values (as we inferred earlier in the chapter).

Now don't be rolling your eyes at me. It's vital to get this point. So, let's compare some of the identical arrays in the following dough object representing the recipe for another of my favorite scones, hazelnut cherry, with === and !== like so in Firebug. As Figure 3–11 displays, === returns false and !== returns true for separate but identical arrays.

```
var dough = {
  pastryFlour: [1 + 2/3, "cup"],
  hazelnutFlour: [1/3, "cup"],
  butter: [3, "tbs"],
  sugar: [2, "tbs"],
  seaSalt: [1/4, "tsp"],
  soda: [1/2, "tsp"],
  tartar: [1, "tsp"],
  heavyWhippingCream: [1, "cup"],
  currants: [1/3, "cup"]
};
dough.pastryFlour === [1 + 2/3, "cup"];
// false
dough.currants !== [1/3, "cup"];
// true
```

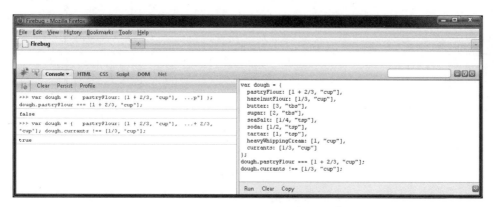

Figure 3–11. Separate but identical arrays are not equal.

Separate but identical values of the object type or array and function subtypes are never equal. Like you and me, those are equal only to themselves, as the following sample and Figure 3–12 display:

```
var dough = {
  pastryFlour: [1 + 2/3, "cup"],
  hazelnutFlour: [1/3, "cup"],
  butter: [3, "tbs"],
  sugar: [2, "tbs"],
  seaSalt: [1/4, "tsp"],
  soda: [1/2, "tsp"],
```

```
  tartar: [1, "tsp"],
  heavyWhippingCream: [1, "cup"],
  currants: [1/3, "cup"]
};
dough === {
  pastryFlour: [1 + 2/3, "cup"],
  hazelnutFlour: [1/3, "cup"],
  butter: [3, "tbs"],
  sugar: [2, "tbs"],
  seaSalt: [1/4, "tsp"],
  soda: [1/2, "tsp"],
  tartar: [1, "tsp"],
  heavyWhippingCream: [1, "cup"],
  currants: [1/3, "cup"]
};
// false
dough === dough;
// true
dough.pastryFlour === [1 + 2/3, "cup"];
// false
dough.pastryFlour === dough.pastryFlour;
// true
```

Figure 3–12. An object, array, or function is only equal to itself.

Furthermore, separate but otherwise identical object, array, or function literals are never equal inasmuch as JavaScript saves those to different locations in memory. To illustrate the point, try the following sample in Firebug:

```
[1 + 2/3, "cup"] === [1 + 2/3, "cup"];
// false
```

We'll more fully explore comparing by value or reference in Chapter 5. It's time to move on to determining the relative order of numbers and strings with the > greater and < less operators.

Determining Whether One Number or String Is Greater Than Another

If you were to strain most of the watery whey from a 1 quart tub of whole milk yogurt, which is 4 percent cream, you would have 1 2/3 cups of delicious full cream Greek yogurt, yiaourti, which is 10 percent cream. Mmmh. Moreover, if you were to strain all of the watery whey, you would have 1 1/3 cups of yogurt cheese, a healthier cream cheese. To do so, simply put a sieve lined with eight layers of cheesecloth overtop a bowl in the fridge, dump in the yogurt, and let the whey drain for 6 hours to make yiaourti or 12 hours to make yogurt cheese. However, Greek yogurt and yogurt cheese makers are inexpensive; I bought mine for $21 from www.kingarthurflour.com, but Target has one for $16.

Insofar as yogurt cheese retains the lactic acid from the yogurt, you can leaven dough with it in place of sour cream. One of my favorite apple cakes does so. Plus the icing is made with whipped yogurt cheese rather than cream cheese. The recipe can be represented by nesting dough and icing objects within the following cake object. Note that you would do the following:

- Strain 2 2/3 cups of watery whey from 4 cups of Stonyfield cream-top yogurt to create 1 1/3 cups yogurt cheese.

- Shred 1 2/3 cups of tart Granny Smith apples.

- Sift Red Mill organic whole wheat pastry flour with the nutmeg and cinnamon.

- Whisk 2 eggs, with 2/3 cup yogurt cheese and 1/3 cup pure maple syrup.

- Dissolve the tartar and soda in the liquid.

- Immediately mix liquid with sifted dry ingredients.

- Fold in the shredded Granny Smith and chopped pecans.

- Bake for 40 minutes at 350ºF.

- To make icing, whisk until creamy the remaining 2/3 cup yogurt cheese with 1 1/3 tbs (4 tsp) pure maple syrup and 2 tsp. ground pecans.

- Wait for cake to cool before topping with icing.

```
var cake = {
  dough: {
    organicPastryFlour: [1 + 1/2, "cup"],
    freshlyGroundNutmeg: [1/4, "tsp"],
    saigonCinnamon: [1/2, "tsp"],
    soda: [1, "tsp"],
    tartar: [1, "tsp"],
    egg: [2],
    yogurtCheese: [2/3, "cup"],
    pureMapleSyrup: [1/3, "cup"],
    shreddedGrannySmith: [1 + 2/3, "cup"],
    choppedPecans: [1/2, "cup"]
  },
  icing: {
    yogurtCheese: [2/3, "cup"],
```

```
      pureMapleSyrup: [1 + 1/3, "tbs"],
      groundPecans: [2, "tsp"]
   }
};
```

What if we want to know whether there's more pastry flour or shredded Granny Smiths in the dough? Neither === nor !== would be of any help. Instead, we'd compare those ingredients with the > greater than operator, which like === and !== returns a boolean verdict—true if its first operand is greater than its second operand, and false if not. Try comparing some members with the > operator, verifying your work with Figure 3–13:

```
var cake = {
  dough: {
    organicPastryFlour: [1 + 1/2, "cup"],
    freshlyGroundNutmeg: [1/4, "tsp"],
    saigonCinnamon: [1/2, "tsp"],
    soda: [1, "tsp"],
    tartar: [1, "tsp"],
    egg: [2],
    yogurtCheese: [2/3, "cup"],
    pureMapleSyrup: [1/3, "cup"],
    shreddedGrannySmith: [1 + 2/3, "cup"],
    choppedPecans: [1/2, "cup"]
  },
  icing: {
    yogurtCheese: [2/3, "cup"],
    pureMapleSyrup: [1 + 1/3, "tbs"],
    groundPecans: [2, "tsp"]
  }
};
cake.dough.organicPastryFlour[0] > cake.dough.shreddedGrannySmith[0];
// false
cake.dough.choppedPecans[0] > cake.dough.pureMapleSyrup[0];
// true
cake.dough.freshlyGroundNutmeg[0] > cake.dough.saigonCinnamon[0];
// false
cake.icing.yogurtCheese[0] > cake.dough.yogurtCheese[0];
// false
```

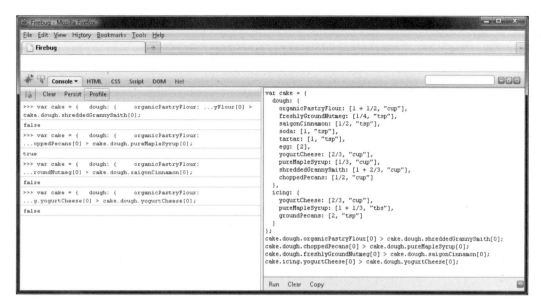

Figure 3–13. Determining whether one number is greater than another with the > operator

In addition to comparing numbers, > is sometimes used to compare strings. However, it does so numerically by the Unicode encoding for each character. Uppercase letters are greater than lowercase characters. Therefore, you want to invoke `toLowerCase()` on both operands to get an alphabetical comparison as Listing 3–1 displays. Note that we explored `toLowerCase()` and other string methods in Chapter 2.

Listing 3–1. Comparing Strings Alphabetically with the > Operator

```
"apple" > "Granny Smith";
// false
"apple".toLowerCase() > "Granny Smith".toLowerCase();
// true
```

Determining Whether One Number or String Is Less Than Another

Now what if we want to do the inverse? In other words, we want to determine whether there's less pure maple syrup than ground pecans in the dough.

Hmm.

Want to take a guess?

Yup, turn the > around and you have the < less than operator, which tells you whether its first operand is less than its second operand. Let's muck around with < in Firebug, verifying our work with Figure 3–14.

```
var cake = {
  dough: {
    organicPastryFlour: [1 + 1/2, "cup"],
    freshlyGroundNutmeg: [1/4, "tsp"],
```

```
    saigonCinnamon: [1/2, "tsp"],
    soda: [1, "tsp"],
    tartar: [1, "tsp"],
    egg: [2],
    yogurtCheese: [2/3, "cup"],
    pureMapleSyrup: [1/3, "cup"],
    shreddedGrannySmith: [1 + 2/3, "cup"],
    choppedPecans: [1/2, "cup"]
  },
  icing: {
    yogurtCheese: [2/3, "cup"],
    pureMapleSyrup: [1 + 1/3, "tbs"],
    groundPecans: [2, "tsp"]
  }
};
cake.dough.organicPastryFlour[0] < cake.dough.shreddedGrannySmith[0];
// true
cake.dough.choppedPecans[0] < cake.dough.pureMapleSyrup[0];
// false
cake.dough.freshlyGroundNutmeg[0] < cake.dough.saigonCinnamon[0];
// true
cake.icing.yogurtCheese[0] < cake.dough.yogurtCheese[0];
// false
```

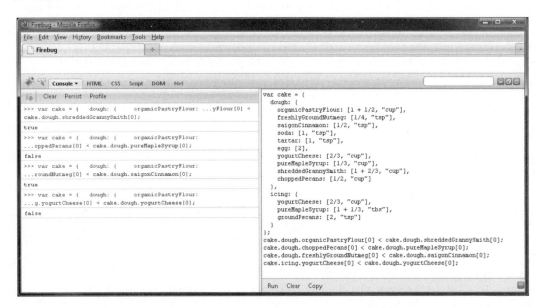

Figure 3–14. Determining whether one number is less than another with the > operator

Greater Than or Equal to, Less Than or Equal to

OK, in both the > and < samples, comparing the yogurt cheese in the dough and icing returned `false` since those are equal—2/3 cup. So if we wanted to know whether one member is greater than or equal to (or less than or equal to) another member, > and < wouldn't be of any help.

Or so it would seem: Saying "not less than" is the same as saying "greater than or equal to," and saying "not greater than" is the same as saying "less than or equal to." So, we'll just flip the boolean verdict of < with ! to do a "greater than or equal to" operation. Conversely, flipping the verdict of > with ! will do a "less than or equal to" operation. So, let's have at it in Firebug, verifying our work with Figure 3–15. Note that > and < have 10 priority, so we need to trump the ! operator's 14 priority by wrapping the > or < expression in parentheses:

```
var cake = {
  dough: {
    organicPastryFlour: [1 + 1/2, "cup"],
    freshlyGroundNutmeg: [1/4, "tsp"],
    saigonCinnamon: [1/2, "tsp"],
    soda: [1, "tsp"],
    tartar: [1, "tsp"],
    egg: [2],
    yogurtCheese: [2/3, "cup"],
    pureMapleSyrup: [1/3, "cup"],
    shreddedGrannySmith: [1 + 2/3, "cup"],
    choppedPecans: [1/2, "cup"]
  },
  icing: {
    yogurtCheese: [2/3, "cup"],
    pureMapleSyrup: [1 + 1/3, "tbs"],
    groundPecans: [2, "tsp"]
  }
};
! (cake.icing.yogurtCheese[0] > cake.dough.yogurtCheese[0]);
// true
! (cake.icing.yogurtCheese[0] < cake.dough.yogurtCheese[0]);
// true
```

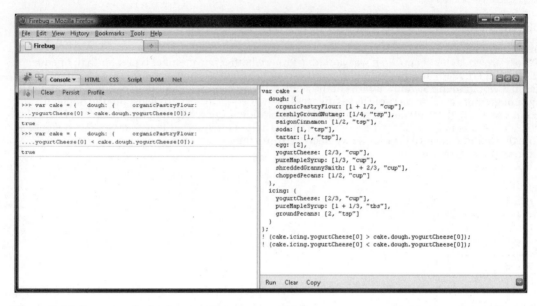

Figure 3–15. *Inverting the boolean verdict of > or < with !*

Just as JavaScript provides !== as a shortcut to flipping the boolean verdict of === with !, it provides >= as a shortcut to flipping the boolean verdict of < with !, and <= as a shortcut to flipping the boolean verdict of > with !. Just remember that neither >= nor <= tests for equality with the === operator. Rather, >= does a "not less than" operation while <= does a "not greater than" operation. Try comparing some ingredients with >= and <=, verifying your work Figure 3–16:

```
var cake = {
  dough: {
    organicPastryFlour: [1 + 1/2, "cup"],
    freshlyGroundNutmeg: [1/4, "tsp"],
    saigonCinnamon: [1/2, "tsp"],
    soda: [1, "tsp"],
    tartar: [1, "tsp"],
    egg: [2],
    yogurtCheese: [2/3, "cup"],
    pureMapleSyrup: [1/3, "cup"],
    shreddedGrannySmith: [1 + 2/3, "cup"],
    choppedPecans: [1/2, "cup"]
  },
  icing: {
    yogurtCheese: [2/3, "cup"],
    pureMapleSyrup: [1 + 1/3, "tbs"],
    groundPecans: [2, "tsp"]
  }
};
cake.icing.yogurtCheese[0] <= cake.dough.yogurtCheese[0];
// true
cake.icing.yogurtCheese[0] >= cake.dough.yogurtCheese[0];
// true
```

```
cake.dough.organicPastryFlour[0] <= cake.dough.shreddedGrannySmith[0];
// true
cake.dough.choppedPecans[0] >= cake.dough.pureMapleSyrup[0];
// true
```

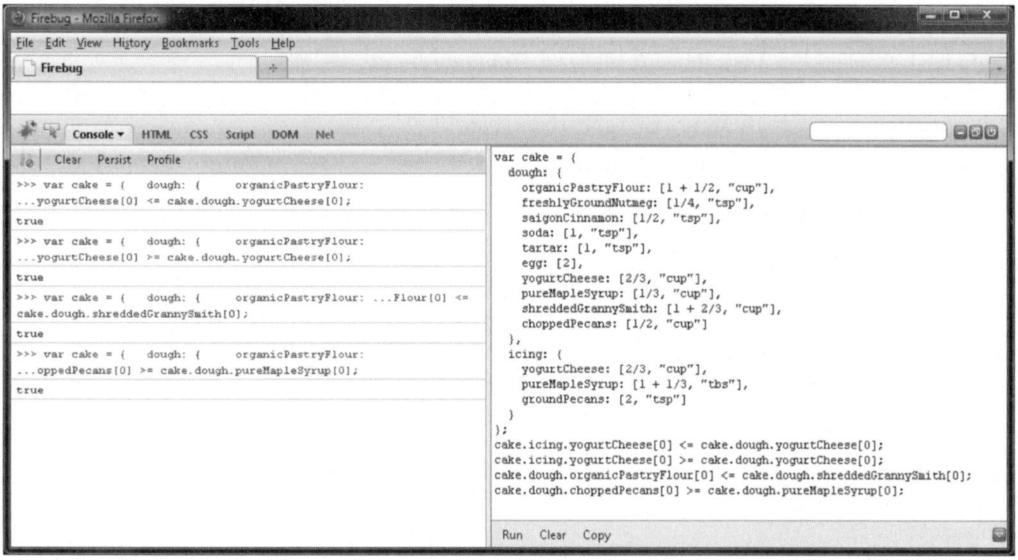

Figure 3–16. Comparing ingredients with >= and <=

Note that >, <, >=, and <= can only compare numbers or strings, so JavaScript converts operands of other value types as follows:

- Convert objects to numbers if possible. Otherwise, convert them to strings.

- If both operands are now strings, compare them by their Unicode encodings.

- Convert any string, boolean, null, or undefined operand to a number, that is, true to 1, false to 0, null to 0, and undefined to NaN, and strings to a number or NaN. Both operands will now be numbers, so compare them mathematically unless one or both are NaN, in which case return false no matter what.

So if one or both operands are of the number, boolean, null, or undefined value type, then >, <, >=, and <= will always compare operands mathematically. That is to say, string comparison is done only when both operands are strings or objects that cannot be converted to numbers.

Creating More Complex Comparisons

Brown Cow, my favorite organic cream-top yogurt, comes in a maple flavor that is just yogurt sweetened with pure maple syrup. Comparing labels of maple and plain Brown Cow to pure maple syrup, I calculated that there's 1 tbsp. pure maple syrup per cup of maple Brown Cow. So if I'm making boysenberry muffins and don't have maple Brown Cow in the fridge, I'll sweeten 1 1/2 cups plain Brown Cow or Stonyfield cream-top with 1 /12 tbs pure maple syrup. Note that boysenberries were created by horticulturist Charles Boysen in 1923 from several varieties of blackberries, raspberries, and loganberries. Note too that Brown Cow is a Stonyfield subsidiary, so their cream-top yogurts taste fairly similar.

The following muffin object represents the recipe for boysenberry muffins. I buy the oat and barley flours from www.kingarthurflour.com. However, you can replace those with the Bob's Red Mill organic whole wheat pastry flour we've been making dough with. To make the muffins, you would do the following:

1. Sift oatFlour, barleyFlour, pastryFlour, sugar, freshlyGroundNutmeg, saigonCinnamon, and seaSalt.

2. Sequentially whisk mapleBrownCow, tartar, and soda.

3. Immediately mix in sifted dry ingredients.

4. Fold in boysenberries and choppedPecans.

5. Fill muffin cups 2/3 full.

6. Bake for 20 minutes at 375°F. However, this will vary depending on the size of the muffin cups.

7. Cool on wire rack for 10 minutes.

```
var muffin = {
  oatFlour: [1/3, "cup"],
  barleyFlour: [1/3, "cup"],
  pastryFlour: [1 + 1/3, "cup"],
  freshlyGroundNutmeg: [1/4, "tsp"],
  saigonCinnamon: [1/2, "tsp"],
  seaSalt: [1/4, "tsp"],
  soda: [1, "tsp"],
  tartar: [1, "tsp"],
  mapleBrownCow: [1 + 1/2, "cup"],
  boysenberries: [2, "cup"],
  choppedPecans: [1/3, "cup"]
};
```

OK, say we'd like to do a more complex comparison. Say verify that one of two comparisons are valid. Or that both of them are. Maybe even that two of five comparisons are valid. Could we do so?

Yup. In addition to being able to say "not" with the ! logical not operator, we can say "or" with the || logical or operator and "and" with the && logical and operator. Both || and && return one of their two operands relative to the boolean their first operand evaluates or converts to. If the first operand evaluates to or converts to true:

• || returns its first operand.

• && returns its second operand.

On the other hand, if the first operand evaluates to or converts to false:

• || returns its second operand.

• && returns its first operand.

Note that && and || only convert their first operand to a boolean in order to determine which operand to return. In other words, if || or && choose to return their first operand, it is the unconverted value that is returned.

The odd way in which || and && choose their return value is the basis for boolean algebra. Scary term, but not to worry. Doing algebra with booleans is simpler than with numbers. Here's how it works.

- The return value for || will convert to true if its first or second operand or both evaluate or convert to true. Otherwise, the return value for || will convert to false.

- The return value for && will convert to true if its first and second operand evaluate or convert to true. Otherwise, the return value for || will convert to false.

That was simple, but why would you want to do boolean algebra? For one thing, the operators we explored for comparing expressions, ===, !==, ==, !=, >, <, >=, and <=, all return a boolean verdict. So, boolean algebra provides a way to express complex comparisons. For another, insofar as objects and functions convert to true and undefined converts to false, boolean algebra is the foundation for DOM feature testing, which we'll explore in gory detail in the final four chapters of this book.

Saying or With ||

Insofar as ===, !==, >, <, >=, and <= return a boolean verdict and || returns one of its operands, you can use || to do boolean algebra on two comparison expressions. If one of two comparisons return true or both of them do, || will return true. That is to say, || will only return false if both comparisons return false. So, we can test if one or both comparisons are valid like so. Note that it's fine to add a new line between a binary operator like || and its second operand. Be sure to click Run prior to each comment. So four times overall. Then verify your work with Figure 3–17.

```
var muffin = {
    oatFlour: [1/3, "cup"],
    barleyFlour: [1/3, "cup"],
    pastryFlour: [1 + 1/3, "cup"],
    freshlyGroundNutmeg: [1/4, "tsp"],
    saigonCinnamon: [1/2, "tsp"],
    seaSalt: [1/4, "tsp"],
    soda: [1, "tsp"],
    tartar: [1, "tsp"],
    mapleBrownCow: [1 + 1/2, "cup"],
    boysenberries: [2, "cup"],
    choppedPecans: [1/3, "cup"]
};
muffin.mapleBrownCow[0] > muffin.boysenberries[0] ||
    muffin.oatFlour[0] === muffin.barleyFlour[0];
// true
muffin.oatFlour[0] === muffin.barleyFlour[0] ||
    muffin.mapleBrownCow[0] > muffin.boysenberries[0];
// true
muffin.boysenberries[0] > muffin.choppedPecans[0] ||
    muffin.pastryFlour[0] > muffin.barleyFlour[0];
// true
muffin.boysenberries[0] < muffin.choppedPecans[0] ||
    muffin.pastryFlour[0] < muffin.barleyFlour[0];
// false
```

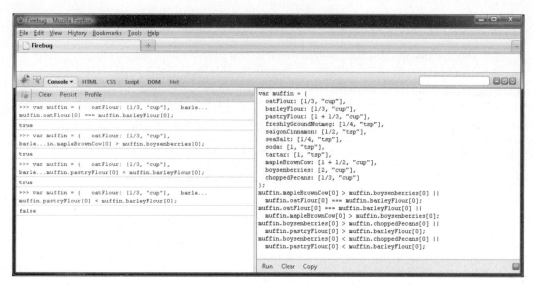

Figure 3–17. || will return true if at least one of two comparisons is valid.

Saying "and" with &&

Though || will return true if one of two comparisons is true, && will return true only if both comparisons
are true. To illustrate, try the following in Firebug, verifying your work with Figure 3–18. Remember to
click Run prior to each comment—so four times overall.

```
var muffin = {
  oatFlour: [1/3, "cup"],
  barleyFlour: [1/3, "cup"],
  pastryFlour: [1 + 1/3, "cup"],
  freshlyGroundNutmeg: [1/4, "tsp"],
  saigonCinnamon: [1/2, "tsp"],
  seaSalt: [1/4, "tsp"],
  soda: [1, "tsp"],
  tartar: [1, "tsp"],
  mapleBrownCow: [1 + 1/2, "cup"],
  boysenberries: [2, "cup"],
  choppedPecans: [1/3, "cup"]
};
muffin.mapleBrownCow[0] > muffin.boysenberries[0] &&
  muffin.oatFlour[0] === muffin.barleyFlour[0];
// false
muffin.oatFlour[0] === muffin.barleyFlour[0] &&
  muffin.mapleBrownCow[0] > muffin.boysenberries[0];
// false
muffin.boysenberries[0] > muffin.choppedPecans[0] &&
  muffin.pastryFlour[0] > muffin.barleyFlour[0];
// true
muffin.boysenberries[0] < muffin.choppedPecans[0] &&
```

```
    muffin.pastryFlour[0] < muffin.barleyFlour[0];
// false
```

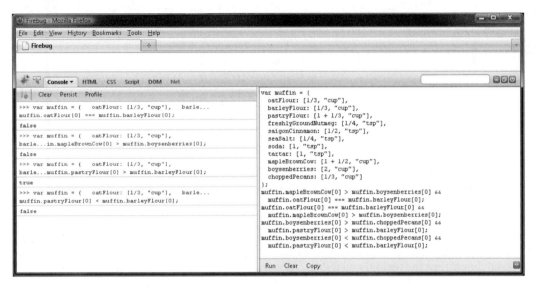

Figure 3–18. && will return true only if both comparisons are valid.

Chaining || Expressions

If you chain two || expressions, you can test whether one of three comparisons is valid. Try it in Firebug, verifying your work with Figure 3–19. Note that || has L associativity and that JavaScript does not evaluate the second operand when the first operand evaluates or converts to true. So in the following sample, since the first comparison is true, JavaScript does not evaluate muffin.oatFlour !== muffin.barleyFlour or muffin.pastryFlour < muffin.barleyFlour.

```
var muffin = {
  oatFlour: [1/3, "cup"],
  barleyFlour: [1/3, "cup"],
  pastryFlour: [1 + 1/3, "cup"],
  freshlyGroundNutmeg: [1/4, "tsp"],
  saigonCinnamon: [1/2, "tsp"],
  seaSalt: [1/4, "tsp"],
  soda: [1, "tsp"],
  tartar: [1, "tsp"],
  mapleBrownCow: [1 + 1/2, "cup"],
  boysenberries: [2, "cup"],
  choppedPecans: [1/3, "cup"]
};
muffin.mapleBrownCow[0] > muffin.boysenberries[0] ||
  muffin.oatFlour[0] !== muffin.barleyFlour[0] ||
  muffin.pastryFlour[0] < muffin.barleyFlour[0];
// true
```

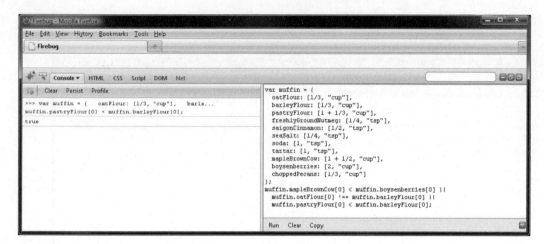

Figure 3–19. Determining whether at least one of three comparisons is true

As you might imagine, you can keep right on going, chaining as many || operations as you like. So in the following sample, we're testing whether at least one of five comparisons is valid. So as Figure 3–20 displays, even though just the second and fourth comparison are valid, which is to say return true, overall the chained || expressions return true:

```
var muffin = {
  oatFlour: [1/3, "cup"],
  barleyFlour: [1/3, "cup"],
  pastryFlour: [1 + 1/3, "cup"],
  freshlyGroundNutmeg: [1/4, "tsp"],
  saigonCinnamon: [1/2, "tsp"],
  seaSalt: [1/4, "tsp"],
  soda: [1, "tsp"],
  tartar: [1, "tsp"],
  mapleBrownCow: [1 + 1/2, "cup"],
  boysenberries: [2, "cup"],
  choppedPecans: [1/3, "cup"]
};
muffin.mapleBrownCow[0] > muffin.boysenberries[0] ||
  muffin.oatFlour[0] !== muffin.barleyFlour[0] ||
  muffin.freshlyGroundNutmeg[0] >= muffin.saigonCinnamon[0] ||
  muffin.choppedPecans[0] <= muffin.mapleBrownCow[0] ||
  muffin.pastryFlour[0] === muffin.barleyFlour[0];
// true
```

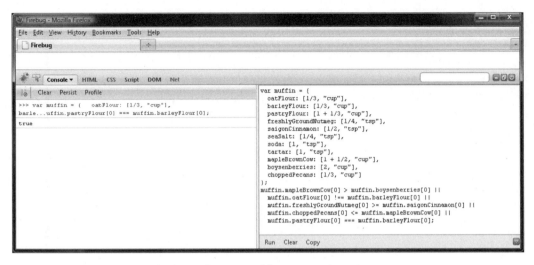

Figure 3–20. *Determining whether at least one of five comparisons is true*

Chaining && Expressions

So || is pretty lenient—just one of two or more chained || has to return true for the whole shebang to return true. && on the other hand, is very strict. Every comparison in a chain of && expressions must be valid for the chain to return true as a whole. So as Figure 3–21 illustrates, even though the first and last two comparisons are true, since the third is false the chain of && expressions return false. So we're asking JavaScript all five comparisons are true, not whether most of them are true.

```
var muffin = {
  oatFlour: [1/3, "cup"],
  barleyFlour: [1/3, "cup"],
  pastryFlour: [1 + 1/3, "cup"],
  freshlyGroundNutmeg: [1/4, "tsp"],
  saigonCinnamon: [1/2, "tsp"],
  seaSalt: [1/4, "tsp"],
  soda: [1, "tsp"],
  tartar: [1, "tsp"],
  mapleBrownCow: [1 + 1/2, "cup"],
  boysenberries: [2, "cup"],
  choppedPecans: [1/3, "cup"]
};
muffin.mapleBrownCow[0] < muffin.boysenberries[0] &&
  muffin.oatFlour[0] === muffin.barleyFlour[0] &&
  muffin.freshlyGroundNutmeg[0] >= muffin.saigonCinnamon[0] &&
  muffin.choppedPecans[0] <= muffin.mapleBrownCow[0] &&
  muffin.pastryFlour[0] > muffin.barleyFlour[0];
// false
```

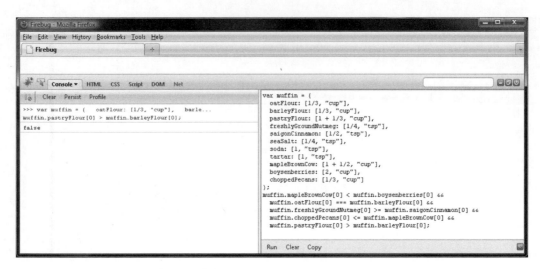

Figure 3–21. *Determining whether all five comparisons are true*

Let's make && happy and change the third comparison "not less than" to "less than." As Figure 3–22 displays, since all five comparisons are true, overall the && chain returns true. Hurray!

```
var muffin = {
  oatFlour: [1/3, "cup"],
  barleyFlour: [1/3, "cup"],
  pastryFlour: [1 + 1/3, "cup"],
  freshlyGroundNutmeg: [1/4, "tsp"],
  saigonCinnamon: [1/2, "tsp"],
  seaSalt: [1/4, "tsp"],
  soda: [1, "tsp"],
  tartar: [1, "tsp"],
  mapleBrownCow: [1 + 1/2, "cup"],
  boysenberries: [2, "cup"],
  choppedPecans: [1/3, "cup"]
};
muffin.mapleBrownCow[0] < muffin.boysenberries[0] &&
  muffin.oatFlour[0] === muffin.barleyFlour[0] &&
  muffin.freshlyGroundNutmeg[0] < muffin.saigonCinnamon[0] &&
  muffin.choppedPecans[0] <= muffin.mapleBrownCow[0] &&
  muffin.pastryFlour[0] > muffin.barleyFlour[0];
// true
```

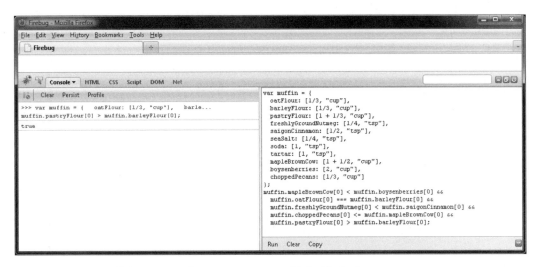

Figure 3–22. Since all five comparisons are true, overall the && chain returns true.

Chaining || and && Expressions

Note that && has a priority of 5 while || has a priority of 4. So in the following sample, JavaScript evaluates the two && expressions prior to the two || expressions. Therefore, as Figure 3–23 illustrates, by the time JavaScript does the || operations, the comparison has been simplified to false || true || muffin.pastryFlour < muffin.barleyFlour. So, it's not necessary for JavaScript to evaluate the final < comparison.

```
var muffin = {
  oatFlour: [1/3, "cup"],
  barleyFlour: [1/3, "cup"],
  pastryFlour: [1 + 1/3, "cup"],
  freshlyGroundNutmeg: [1/4, "tsp"],
  saigonCinnamon: [1/2, "tsp"],
  seaSalt: [1/4, "tsp"],
  soda: [1, "tsp"],
  tartar: [1, "tsp"],
  mapleBrownCow: [1 + 1/2, "cup"],
  boysenberries: [2, "cup"],
  choppedPecans: [1/3, "cup"]
};
muffin.mapleBrownCow[0] < muffin.boysenberries[0] &&
  muffin.oatFlour[0] === muffin.barleyFlour[0] ||
  muffin.freshlyGroundNutmeg[0] < muffin.saigonCinnamon[0] &&
  muffin.choppedPecans[0] <= muffin.mapleBrownCow[0] ||
  muffin.pastryFlour[0] < muffin.barleyFlour[0];
// true
false || true ||  muffin.pastryFlour[0]< muffin.barleyFlour[0];
// true
```

89

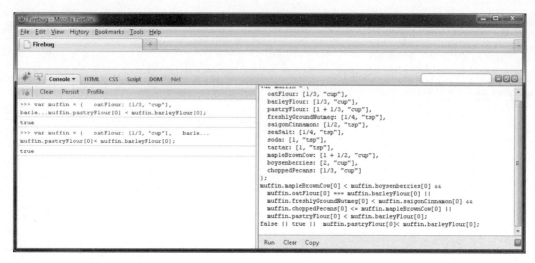

Figure 3–23. Chaining && and || expression to do a complex comparison

To better illustrate the JavaScript's lazy evaluation of || and &&, let's replace the final comparison with an alert() call that would say "Don't panic!" Now click Run in Firebug. Firebug does not open an alert dialog box because JavaScript never bothered to invoke alert().

```
var muffin = {
  oatFlour: [1/3, "cup"],
  barleyFlour: [1/3, "cup"],
  pastryFlour: [1 + 1/3, "cup"],
  freshlyGroundNutmeg: [1/4, "tsp"],
  saigonCinnamon: [1/2, "tsp"],
  seaSalt: [1/4, "tsp"],
  soda: [1, "tsp"],
  tartar: [1, "tsp"],
  mapleBrownCow: [1 + 1/2, "cup"],
  boysenberries: [2, "cup"],
  choppedPecans: [1/3, "cup"]
};
muffin.mapleBrownCow[0] < muffin.boysenberries[0] &&
  muffin.oatFlour[0] === muffin.barleyFlour[0] ||
  muffin.freshlyGroundNutmeg[0] < muffin.saigonCinnamon[0] &&
  muffin.choppedPecans[0] <= muffin.mapleBrownCow[0] ||
  alert("Don't panic!");
// true
```

I think our boysenberry Brown Cow muffins are done, so let's pull them from the oven. Mmmh, share and enjoy.

Conditionally Returning One of Two Values

What if we'd like to conditionally choose a return value rather than just verify it? This is where the ?: conditional operator, JavaScript's only ternary operator, earns its keep. Like || and &&, ?: chooses a return value based on the boolean its first operand evaluates or converts to. If the first operand evaluates to or converts to true:

- || returns its first operand.

- && returns its second operand.

- ?: returns its second operand.

On the other hand, if the first operand evaluates to or converts to false:

- || returns its second operand.

- && returns its first operand.

- ?: returns its third operand.

Though all three operators can be used to conditionally return a value, the ?: conditional operator's separation of the boolean condition from the possible return values make it the preferred way of doing so. Here's a quick example:

```
var first = 30;
var second = 20;
var result = first > second ? "first is larger" : "first is smaller";
result;
//"first is larger"
```

Here the first operand evaluates to true, so ?: returns its second operand. As you can see, the return value is not used as any part of the conditional test.

If I'm making cranberry bread with buttermilk, I'd add 1/2 cup buttermilk as in the following dough object. Note that the leavening bubbles are created by soda reacting with citric acid in the orange juice, lactic acid in the buttermilk, and tartaric acid in the cream of tartar. Note too that for this recipe I like to go with Bob's Red Mill organic hard white whole wheat flour. Though it contains as much fiber-rich bran and vitamin-rich germ as hard red, hard white wheat does have the bitter red tannins. Therefore, hard white whole wheat flour has a milder, sweeter flavor than hard red, making it ideal for sweet soda breads.

```
var dough = {
  hardWhiteWholeWheatFlour: [2, "cup"],
  sugar: [1/3, "cup"],
  madagascarVanilla: [1, "tsp"],
  orangeZest: [1, "tbs"],
  soda: [1, "tsp"],
  tartar: [1, "tsp"],
  orangeJuice: [1/2, "cup"],
  buttermilk: [1/2, "cup"],
  egg: [1],
  cranberries: [2/3, "cup"]
};
```

If I don't have buttermilk and do have kefir, I'd add 9/16 cup kefir. Note that there are 16 tbsp. per cup, so 9/16 cup kefir means 1/2 cup plus 1 tbsp.

```
var dough = {
  hardWhiteWholeWheatFlour: [2, "cup"],
  sugar: [1/3, "cup"],
  madagascarVanilla: [1, "tsp"],
  orangeZest: [1, "tbs"],
  soda: [1, "tsp"],
```

```
    tartar: [1, "tsp"],
    orangeJuice: [1/2, "cup"],
    kefir: [9/16, "cup"],
    egg: [1],
    cranberries: [2/3, "cup"]
};
```

But if I don't have buttermilk or kefir but do have yogurt, I'd add 10/16 cup yogurt, which is 1/2 cup plus 2 tbs:

```
var dough = {
    hardWhiteWholeWheatFlour: [2, "cup"],
    sugar: [1/3, "cup"],
    madagascarVanilla: [1, "tsp"],
    orangeZest: [1, "tbs"],
    soda: [1, "tsp"],
    tartar: [1, "tsp"],
    orangeJuice: [1/2, "cup"],
    yogurt: [10/16, "cup"],
    egg: [1],
    cranberries: [2/3, "cup"]
};
```

With this in mind, let's conditionally set the amount of a culturedMilk[0] element to 1/2, 9/16, or 10/16 depending on whether there's enough buttermilk, kefir, or yogurt in the fridge. To do so, we'll chain two ?: expressions, one as the return value of the other. As Figure 3–24 displays, since there was not enough buttermilk but enough kefir in the fridge, JavaScript set the amount to 9/16, which evaluates to 0.5625 decimal. In other words, the first ?: returns its second operand because the conditional expression is true; if the conditional had been false, it would have returned the second ?: expression, which in turn would have been evaluated:

```
var fridge = {
    buttermilk: [1/3, "cup"],
    kefir: [1 + 1/2, "cup"],
    yogurt: [4, "cup"],
};
var dough = {
    hardWhiteWholeWheatFlour: [2, "cup"],
    sugar: [1/3, "cup"],
    madagascarVanilla: [1, "tsp"],
    orangeZest: [1, "tbs"],
    soda: [1, "tsp"],
    tartar: [1, "tsp"],
    orangeJuice: [1/2, "cup"],
    culturedMilk: [1/2, "cup"],
    egg: [1],
    cranberries: [2/3, "cup"]
};
dough.culturedMilk[0] = fridge.buttermilk[0] < 1/2 && fridge.kefir[0] >= 9/16 ? 9/16 :
    fridge.yogurt[0] >= 10/16 ? 10/16 :
    alert("No cranberry bread for you!");
dough.culturedMilk;
// [0.5625, "cup"]
```

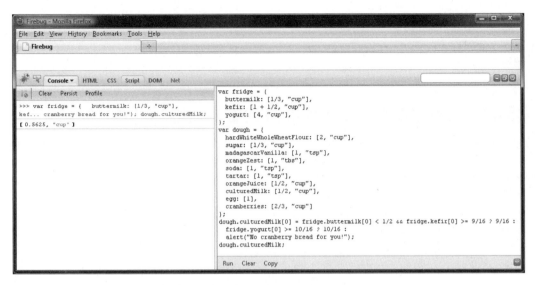

Figure 3–24. Conditionally choosing the amount of cultured milk with the ?: operator

Making Two Expressions Count as One

Now what if we'd like to also update the amount of buttermilk, kefir, or yogurt in the fridge? Insofar as we can put only one expression following the ? and : tokens of the ?: operator, it would appear we're out of luck.

Not so. JavaScript provides the , comma operator for circumstances like this. , works with two operands and simply evaluates both of its operands and returns the value of the second operand. So if we make our updating of the fridge the first operand to , and the value we want to assign to dough.culturedMilk[0] the second operand, that'll work just dandy. Try it in Firebug, verifying your work with Figure 3–25:

```javascript
var fridge = {
  buttermilk: [1/3, "cup"],
  kefir: [1 + 1/2, "cup"],
  yogurt: [4, "cup"],
};
var dough = {
  hardWhiteWholeWheatFlour: [2, "cup"],
  sugar: [1/3, "cup"],
  madagascarVanilla: [1, "tsp"],
  orangeZest: [1, "tbs"],
  soda: [1, "tsp"],
  tartar: [1, "tsp"],
  orangeJuice: [1/2, "cup"],
  culturedMilk: [1/2, "cup"],
  egg: [1],
  cranberries: [2/3, "cup"]
};
dough.culturedMilk[0] = fridge.buttermilk[0] >= 1/2 ? (fridge.buttermilk[0] -= 1/2, 1/2) :
  fridge.kefir[0] >= 9/16 ? (fridge.kefir[0] -= 9/16, 9/16) :
```

93

```
    fridge.yogurt[0] >= 10/16 ? (fridge.yogurt[0] -= 10/16, 10/16) :
    alert("No cranberry bread for you!");
dough.culturedMilk;
// [0.5625, "cup"]
fridge.kefir;
// [0.9375, "cup"]
```

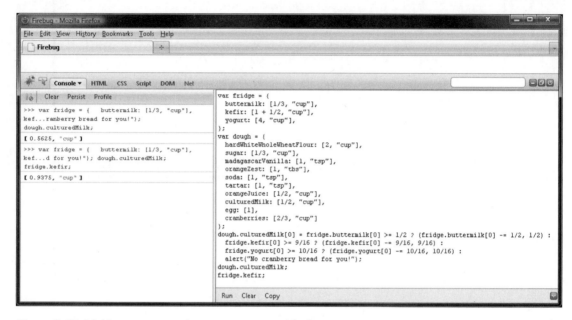

Figure 3–25. *Making two expressions count as one with the* **,** *operator*

Deleting a Member, Element, or Variable

If we don't have buttermilk, kefir, or yogurt, we can still make cranberry bread by doubling the orange juice. How do we tell JavaScript to delete dough.culturedMilk and then double dough.orangeJuice?

To delete the culturedMilk member from dough we'd pass it to the delete operator, which works with an any variable, member, element, or parameter. To double the OJ, we'd pass 2 to the *= operator, which we covered earlier. We can do both in one statement by separating them with the , comma operator.

To verify the demise of culturedMilk, we can pass it to the typeof operator, which returns the value type of its operand as a string. So for a missing member like culturedMilk, typeof would return "undefined". Or we could verify its demise with in, an operator that returns true if an object contains a member named with a particular string. Otherwise, in returns false. Note that typeof has a couple of quirks. For null, typeof returns "object" not "null", and for a function typeof returns "function" not "object". Yep, pretty stupid. But try it, verifying your work with Figure 3–26.

```
var dough = {
  hardWhiteWholeWheatFlour: [2, "cup"],
  sugar: [1/3, "cup"],
```

```
    madagascarVanilla: [1, "tsp"],
    orangeZest: [1, "tbs"],
    soda: [1, "tsp"],
    tartar: [1, "tsp"],
    orangeJuice: [1/2, "cup"],
    culturedMilk: [1/2, "cup"],
    egg: [1],
    cranberries: [2/3, "cup"]
};
delete dough.culturedMilk, dough.orangeJuice[0] *= 2, dough.orangeJuice;
// [1, "cup"]
typeof dough.culturedMilk;
// "undefined"
"culturedMilk" in dough;
// false
"orangeJuice" in dough;
// true
```

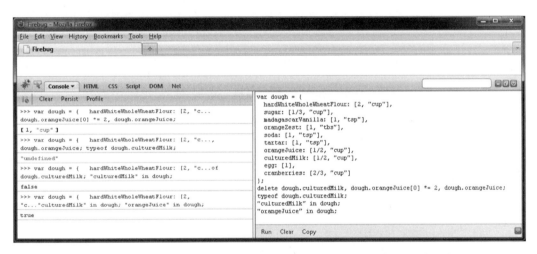

Figure 3–26. Deleting a member with delete and verifying its demise with typeof and in

Summary

In addition to querying objects or arrays, invoking functions, doing math, gluing strings, and assigning values, operators provide a way to verify return values for expressions. Good thing—other than literals, JavaScript expressions tend to evaluate to different values depending on what a visitor does or the browser they're doing it with. So there are many operators to help verify return values with. Those will prove invaluable in Chapter 4, where we'll explore controlling flow, and in the DOM chapters, where we'll test for features before trying to use them.

CHAPTER 4

■■■

Controlling Flow

Running a forest trail in May, I startled a doe and her newborn fawn. The doe made a raspy snort to warn the fawn of danger. Not knowing what to do, the fawn wobbled over to me and plopped down between my legs. Trembling with fear, it looked up at me and bleated faintly, imploring me to keep it safe. The doe stood 20 yards off, quivering with agitation. Obviously, it had wanted the fawn to run away from the predator, not to it.

JavaScript is like the newborn fawn in that it does not know which way you want it to run. So by default, it will simply run forward—that is to say, from the first line in your script to the last. However, there are four ways to manipulate this mindless, sequential flow.

First, you can send JavaScript down different paths with `if` and `switch` statements. They are referred to as *conditional statements* because the paths run conditionally relative to the boolean value of an expression. `true` gives JavaScript the green light to take a path, while `false` tells JavaScript either to do nothing or to take a fall-through path. Second, you can tell JavaScript to take several roundabouts of a loop path with one of the four *looping statements*: `while`, `do while`, `for`, `for`, or `in`. Like `if` and `switch`, loops run conditionally relative to a boolean expression: `true` tells JavaScript to take another roundabout, while `false` tells JavaScript not to. Third, you can disrupt flow with a *disruptive statement* such as `break`, `continue`, or `return`. These statements prevent JavaScript from continuing on its way. Fourth, you can temporarily jump elsewhere in a script by way of *function invocation*. By this, I mean JavaScript goes off and runs the function and then comes back to the spot from which you invoked it.

■ **Note** Chapter 6 more fully covers functions.

Neither disruptive statements nor function invocations are dynamic. That is to say, neither provides a way for JavaScript to make a decision relative to circumstances. So, with them, a fawn would have to run away from squirrels as well as from wolves. On the other hand, conditional and looping statements are dynamic, so they do provide a way for JavaScript to think before it leaps.

So alrighty then, how does JavaScript think? I alluded to this earlier, but the answer is simple: boolean expressions. Truthy expressions, those that return `true` or can be converted to `true`, are a green light, while falsy expressions, those that return `undefined`, `null`, `""`, `0`, `NaN`, or `false`, are a red light. So, not surprisingly, every conditional or looping statement contains a boolean expression, which enables JavaScript to make a decision.

What else do conditional or looping statements contain? They contain paths in the form of child statements or blocks, which are statements wrapped in curly braces. For this reason, conditional and looping statements are referred to as *compound statements*. So, if you want JavaScript to think, you write a compound statement.

The thing is, formal JavaScript syntax limits a compound statement to one child statement. For example, an `if` conditional statement, which we will explore in a moment, can have only one child statement following its boolean expression. In the following if statement, `run(miles);` is the one child statement permitted by JavaScript:

```
if (timeToRun === true) run(miles);
```

Oftentimes this will not do, and JavaScript knows this. If you bundle several child statements in a pair of curly braces, JavaScript will look the other way and view the bundle, referred to as a *block*, as one child statement. So if I want JavaScript to run three child statements whenever it's time to run, which is to say `timeToRun` contains `true`, then I can bundle those statements in a block. JavaScript will be happy as a clam, and I get to run in shoes rather than barefoot:

```
if (timeToRun === true) {
  lace(shoes);
  run(miles);
  shower();
}
```

Note that the block of child statements is not followed by a semicolon. However, the child statements within the block are.

Writing an if Condition

Oftentimes, you will want JavaScript to run a path if circumstances permit but otherwise do nothing and move on. `if` conditional statements will be your bread and butter for this type of decision. To write one of these statements, simply type the keyword `if`, followed by an expression in parentheses, and then a path in the form of a child statement or block. In the event that the expression does not return a boolean, JavaScript will convert the value to a boolean by passing it to `Boolean()`, which we explored in Chapter 2. So if the expression returns any value other than `undefined`, `null`, `""`, `0`, `NaN`, or `false`, JavaScript has a green light to run the path.

Therefore, a JavaScript interpreter views an `if` condition like so:

```
if (Boolean(expression)) path
```

But you write it like this:

```
if (expression) path
```

Open firebug.html in Firefox and then press F12 to enable Firebug. If you're just joining us, flip back to the Preface for details on how to do this.

For any fast running I do, I tend to wear the Nike Mayfly, which weighs just four ounces. By comparison, most running shoes weigh three or four times as much. However, the downside to the Mayfly's minimalist design is that its cushioning goes dead after just 100 kilometers.

Let's create a `mayfly` object containing two methods that may query a secret variable named `tally`, which will contain a tally of kilometers run in a pair of Mayfly shoes. `mayfly.addToTally()` adds its parameter (named `km`) to `tally` only if `km` is safe for addition—that is to say, if `km` is of the number datatype but not the special numbers `NaN` or `Infinity`. The other method, `mayfly.kmLeftToLive()`, will return a message indicating how many kilometers of cushioning the Mayfly has left only if `tally` is less than `100`.

So in Firebug, enter the following code, and click Run. Doing so creates a closure so that `tally` may be queried only by `addToTally()` and `kmLeftToLive()`. Closures are covered in Chapter 6, so just nod knowingly for now. Anyway, just focus on the two `if` conditions.

```
var mayfly = function () {
  var tally = 0;
  return {
```

```
    addToTally: function (km) {
      if (typeof km === "number" && isFinite(km)) {
        return tally += km;
      }
    },
    kmLeftToLive: function () {
      if (tally < 100) {
        return "Mayfly has " + (100 - tally) + " kilometers left to live.";
      }
    }
  }
}();
```

Now that we have initialized `mayfly()` and the secret variable `tally`, click Clear in the bottom-right corner of Firebug. Doing so not only leaves `mayfly()` in memory so that we can invoke it but also prevents us from overwriting it the next several times we click Run.

Now let's add 10 kilometers to `tally`. To do so, pass 10 to `mayfly.addToTally()` by entering the following code and clicking Run:

```
mayfly.addToTally(10);
// 10
```

We can add 10 to `tally` because we've passed in a number that passes the test in the first `if` statement.

Click Run three more times to log a few more 10K races. So now, as Figure 4–1 illustrates, our secret variable `tally` contains 40.

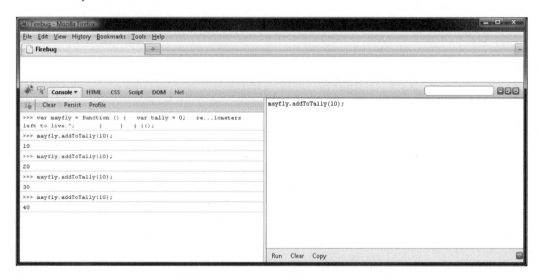

Figure 4–1. Invoking mayfly.addToTally four times with the parameter 10

Click Clear in both Firebug panels and then try calling the other method, `mayfly.kmLeftToLive()`. This one doesn't take any parameters. So, just enter the following code, and click Run in order to find out how many kilometers are left on our pair of Mayfly shoes. We see some output because the `tally` variable is less than 100, and therefore the condition in the second `if` is true.

```
mayfly.kmLeftToLive();
// "Mayfly has 60 kilometers left to live."
```

Appending an else Clause

Now what if you want JavaScript to go down one path when an expression is truthy but another path when it is falsy? Simply append an else clause to your if condition. To do so, simply type the else keyword and then a path in the form of a child statement or block. JavaScript will run the if path when the boolean expression is true and else path when it is false. So, one or the other path will run, but never both.

Currently, both mayfly.addToTally() and mayfly.kmLeftToLive() return undefined whenever JavaScript does not run their if paths. Let's change that by adding else clauses to both methods. To do so, click Clear in Firebug, enter the following, and click Run:

```
var mayfly = function () {
  var tally = 0;
  return {
    addToTally: function (km) {
      if (typeof km === "number" && isFinite(km)) {
        return tally += km;
      } else {
        return "Invalid parameter!";
      }
    },
    kmLeftToLive: function () {
      if (tally < 100) {
        return "Mayfly has " + (100 - tally) + " kilometers left to live.";
      } else {
        return "Mayfly is dead!";
      }
    }
  }
}();
```

Now click Clear, and enter the following:

```
mayfly.addToTally("ten");
// "Invalid parameter!"
```

Here, typeof km returns "string", so the === operator returns false, and in turn the && operator returns false. Therefore, JavaScript goes down the else path, and mayfly.addToTally() returns "Invalid parameter!" rather than adding km to tally, which remains at 0. Let's verify this by clicking Clear and then invoking mayfly.kmLeftToLive() like so:

```
mayfly.kmLeftToLive();
// "Mayfly has 100 kilometers left to live."
```

Great, so our Mayfly still has a full tank. Now let's make sure the else clause for mayfly.kmLeftToLive() works by clicking Clear and then running the following:

```
mayfly.addToTally(110);
mayfly.kmLeftToLive();
// "Mayfly is dead!"
```

So tally < 100 returns false, and JavaScript goes down the else path. Therefore, mayfly.kmLeftToLive() returns "Mayfly is dead!" to indicate that it's time to buy a new Mayfly.

By the way, even if you are not a runner, you might want to try the Mayfly sometime. The upper part is bright orange with a black support grid resembling the wing of a fly—you will be hard to miss in a pair of those!

To Wrap or Not to Wrap

As noted earlier, whenever a compound statement contains a single child statement, you do not have to wrap it in curly braces. So, we could have defined mayfly like so, where the bold code shows the single child statements do not have curly braces:

```
var mayfly = function () {
  var tally = 0;
  return {
    addToTally: function (km) {
      if (typeof km === "number" && isFinite(km))
        return tally += km;
      else
        return "Invalid parameter!";
    },
    kmLeftToLive: function () {
      if (tally < 100)
        return "Mayfly has " + (100 - tally) + " kilometers left to live.";
      else
        return "Mayfly is dead!";
    }
  }
}();
```

Furthermore, we could have omitted the line breaks, too:

```
var mayfly = function () {
  var tally = 0;
  return {
    addToTally: function (km) {
      if (typeof km === "number" && isFinite(km)) return tally += km;
      else return "Invalid parameter!";
    },
    kmLeftToLive: function () {
      if (tally < 100) return "Mayfly has " + (100 - tally) + " kilometers left to live.";
      else return "Mayfly is dead!";
    }
  }
}();
```

The else if idiom, which we will cover next, takes advantage of this single-line, no-bracket JavaScript feature. Moreover, you will encounter both styles in scripts written by others, myself included. However, as a beginner, you may want to wrap single child statements in curly braces inasmuch as this eliminates the need for you to remember that two or more child statements need to be wrapped in curly braces and that an else clause goes with the nearest if condition.

On the other hand, if you wrap all child statements in curly braces, you may find yourself wasting time debugging scripts that have, say, 143 opening braces but only 138 closing braces. Or you may find that peppering your scripts with optional braces makes them less readable.

Regardless of whether you wrap single child statements in curly braces, the important thing to note is that both styles are right. JavaScript does not care which style you go with. Moreover, even programmers who wrap everything in curly braces omit them to use the `else if` idiom. (However, this is probably because they think `else if` is a statement, not an idiom. So, they do not even know they are violating their mantra!)

Coding Several Paths with the else if Idiom

I tend to have a smoothie for dessert most nights. Sometimes if it is late, that is all I will have. I don't worry too much about calories. My favorite full-throttle smoothie contains Brown Cow cream-top yogurt, grass-fed cream and milk, Saigon cinnamon, and wild blueberries. If you like yogurt, treat yourself to Brown Cow cream-top sometime. Trust me, you will never forget your first Brown Cow!

OK, that came out wrong. Anyway, for the Brown Cow and grass-fed cream and milk, I have to go to Whole Foods. But there is just one of those so far in Pittsburgh, and, to get there, I have to drive through murder alley. Most nights when I open the fridge there is no Brown Cow, and I have to choose some other yogurt or kefir for my smoothie. In descending order of preference, those are Stonyfield cream-top, Fage cultured cream, and Lifeway Greek-style kefir.

Alrighty then, let's create an object named `fridge` with boolean members indicating what my cultured milk options are. Life is good tonight because I do have Brown Cow in there:

```
var fridge = {
  brownCow: true,
  stonyfield: false,
  fage: true,
  lifeway: false
};
var smoothie;
```

Now we want JavaScript to choose my favorite available yogurt or kefir by testing the following four expressions in order from top to bottom:

```
fridge.brownCow
fridge.stonyfield
fridge.fage
fridge.lifeway
```

But an `if` condition can test only one expression. So, do we write four of those in a row? It's sort of a clunky solution, but let's do it in Firebug. Note that, for this to work, we have to test the four expressions from bottom to top so that the best available yogurt goes into my smoothie:

```
var fridge = {
  brownCow: true,
  stonyfield: false,
  fage: true,
  lifeway: false
};
var smoothie;
if (fridge.lifeway) {
  smoothie = "Lifeway Greek-style kefir";
}
if (fridge.fage) {
```

```
  smoothie = "Fage cultured cream";
}
if (fridge.stonyfield) {
  smoothie = "Stonyfield cream-top yogurt";
}
if (fridge.brownCow) {
  smoothie = "Brown Cow cream-top yogurt";
}
smoothie += ", grass-fed cream and milk, Saigon cinnamon, and wild blueberries."
// "Brown Cow cream-top yogurt, grass-fed cream and milk, Saigon cinnamon,
// and wild blueberries."
```

Although this kludge works, it makes us look like bumpkins to JavaScript-savvy programmers because we test for every variation, even if we've previously found a match. There is a better way, right?

Yup, you betcha. First, reorder the if conditions in descending order of preference. Second, nest if conditions two through four in an else clause for if conditions one through three. We've now got some opt-outs if an if condition is true; in other words, we don't go on and test for every variation after an if condition is found to be true.

```
var fridge = {
  brownCow: true,
  stonyfield: false,
  fage: true,
  lifeway: false
};
var smoothie;
if (fridge.brownCow) {
  smoothie = "Brown Cow cream-top yogurt";
} else {
  if (fridge.stonyfield) {
    smoothie = "Stonyfield cream-top yogurt";
  } else {
    if (fridge.fage) {
      smoothie = "Fage cultured cream";
    } else {
      if (fridge.lifeway) {
        smoothie = "Lifeway Greek-style kefir";
      }
    }
  }
}
smoothie += ", grass-fed cream and milk, Saigon cinnamon, and wild blueberries."
// "Brown Cow cream-top yogurt, grass-fed cream and milk, Saigon cinnamon,
// and wild blueberries."
```

This is more elegant, but we can do even better by using the else if idiom. So, click Clear in both Firebug panels, and enter and run the following:

```
var fridge = {
  brownCow: true,
  stonyfield: false,
  fage: true,
  lifeway: false
};
var smoothie;
```

```
if (fridge.brownCow) {
  smoothie = "Brown Cow cream-top yogurt";
} else if (fridge.stonyfield) {
  smoothie = "Stonyfield cream-top yogurt";
} else if (fridge.fage) {
  smoothie = "Fage cultured cream";
} else if (fridge.lifeway) {
  smoothie = "Lifeway Greek-style kefir";
}
smoothie += ", grass-fed cream and milk, Saigon cinnamon, and wild blueberries."
// "Brown Cow cream-top yogurt, grass-fed cream and milk, Saigon cinnamon,
// and wild blueberries."
```

Verify your work with Figure 4–2.

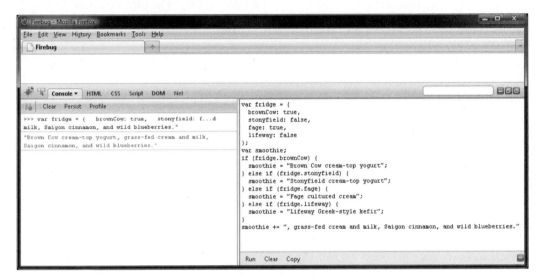

Figure 4–2. Simplifying things with the else if idiom

That's much simpler to code and read, don't you think? Now what is going on here? In a nutshell, since all the else clauses contain a single child statement, the curly braces are optional, so we omitted them along with the line breaks. Doing so means the else and if keywords come together, which is why the idiom is referred to as else if.

But there is one problem: if none of the boolean expression returns true, there's no fall-through path for JavaScript to take. Can we fix that? Oh, you betcha. Simply append an else clause to the final nested if condition. But this time, go with the optional curly braces. Let's make Dannon (Danone in the United Kingdom) the default and then set all fridge members to false so that we can test the fall-through path, as in Figure 4–3:

```
var fridge = {
  brownCow: false,
  stonyfield: false,
  fage: false,
  lifeway: false
};
```

```
var smoothie;
if (fridge.brownCow) {
  smoothie = "Brown Cow cream-top yogurt";
} else if (fridge.stonyfield) {
  smoothie = "Stonyfield cream-top yogurt";
} else if (fridge.fage) {
  smoothie = "Fage cultured cream";
} else if (fridge.lifeway) {
  smoothie = "Lifeway Greek-style kefir";
} else {
  smoothie = "Dannon yogurt";
}
smoothie += ", grass-fed cream and milk, Saigon cinnamon, and wild blueberries."
// "Dannon yogurt, grass-fed cream and milk, Saigon cinnamon, and wild blueberries."
```

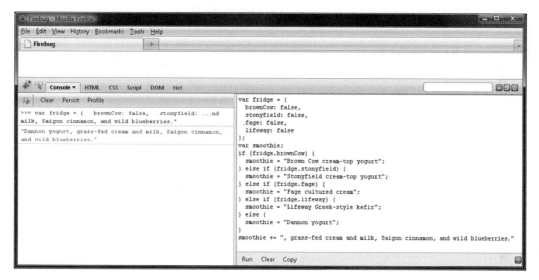

Figure 4–3. Testing the default else path

So there it is. JavaScript has five paths to choose from. Before moving on, note that, since all five paths are single child statements, we may omit curly braces throughout:

```
var fridge = {
  brownCow: false,
  stonyfield: false,
  fage: false,
  lifeway: false
};
var smoothie;
if (fridge.brownCow)
  smoothie = "Brown Cow cream-top yogurt";
else if (fridge.stonyfield)
  smoothie = "Stonyfield cream-top yogurt";
else if (fridge.fage)
```

```
  smoothie = "Fage cultured cream";
else if (fridge.lifeway)
  smoothie = "Lifeway Greek-style kefir";
else
  smoothie = "Dannon yogurt";
smoothie += ", grass-fed cream and milk, Saigon cinnamon, and wild blueberries."
// "Dannon yogurt, grass-fed cream and milk, Saigon cinnamon, and wild blueberries."
```

Controlling Flow with Conditional Expressions

In the event that your if and else clauses contain single expression statements, you may more elegantly control flow with a conditional expression using the ?: operator, which we covered in Chapter 3. Moreover, you may nest conditional expressions to emulate the else if idiom, too.

■ **Note** Even though you can create an expression statement by simply pinning a semicolon tail to any expression, you generally do so only for assignment, invocation, increment, or decrement expressions.

Click Clear in both Firebug panels, and rewrite our else if sample using nested conditional expressions like so:

```
var fridge = {
  brownCow: true,
  stonyfield: false,
  fage: true,
  lifeway: false
};
var smoothie = fridge.brownCow ? "Brown Cow cream-top yogurt" :
(fridge.stonyfield ? "Stonyfield cream-top yogurt" :
(fridge.fage ? "Fage cultured cream" :
(fridge.lifeway ? "Lifeway Greek-style kefir" : "Dannon yogurt")));
smoothie += ", grass-fed cream and milk, Saigon cinnamon, and wild blueberries."
// "Brown Cow cream-top yogurt, grass-fed cream and milk, Saigon cinnamon,
// and wild blueberries."
```

Verify your work with Figure 4–4.

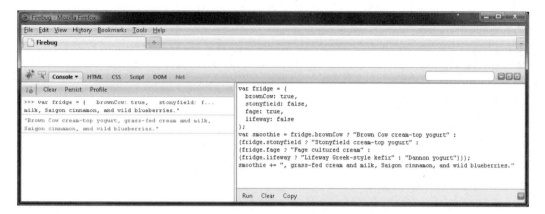

Figure 4–4. Replacing an if else statement with a ?: expression

For reasons of readability, I recommend not nesting more than one ?: expression. So, what we did earlier is not recommended. However, you will encounter such skullduggery in scripts written by others, and being familiar with the technique will prove helpful.

Taking One of Several Paths with a Switch

Now for a less common way to write a multiway branch, let's look at the switch statement. Typically, switch statements are used if all paths depend on the value of the same expression and if that expression returns a string or number.

From a bird's-eye view, if and switch statements look similar:

```
if (expression) {block}
switch (expression) {block}
```

Beyond that, if and switch are markedly different. For one thing, the if block contains just one path, while the switch block contains many paths. Those are marked by one or more case expressions. JavaScript decides which path to take by comparing the switch expression to the case expressions with the === operator. So, no datatype conversion takes place as would occur with the == operator.

For another, case expressions mark only where JavaScript begins running statements in the switch block. You have to manually mark the end of each path with a break or return disruptive statement. Doing so prevents JavaScript from running all paths downstream of the matching case expression.

Finally, whereas an else clause contains the fall-through path for an if statement, a default case clause contains the fall-through for a switch. However, just like else, the default path is optional.

So, refresh Firefox to clear everything we coded thus far from memory. Then click Clear in Firebug to give you a clean slate, and let's try a switch. For your favorite sports team, say you want JavaScript to return the name of a player based on a jersey number. Since all paths depend on the same expression, which returns a number, switch is more efficient than else if. For the Pittsburgh Steelers, a switch for jersey numbers would look like this. Feel free to go with your favorite team rather than mine.

```
var jersey = 34, name = "";
switch (jersey) {
  case 7:
    name = "Roethlisberger";
```

```
        break;
    case 10:
      name = "Holmes";
      break;
    case 17:
      name = "Wallace";
      break;
    case 34:
      name = "Mendenhall";
      break;
    case 43:
      name = "Polamalu";
      break;
    case 83:
      name = "Miller";
      break;
    case 86:
      name = "Ward";
      break;
    case 92:
      name = "Harrison";
      break;
    case 94:
      name = "Timmons";
      break;
    case 96:
      name = "Hood";
      break;
    default:
      name = "not worn by any Steeler";
      break;
}
"Number " + jersey + " is " + name + ".";
// "Number 34 is Mendenhall."
```

Verify your work with Figure 4–5.

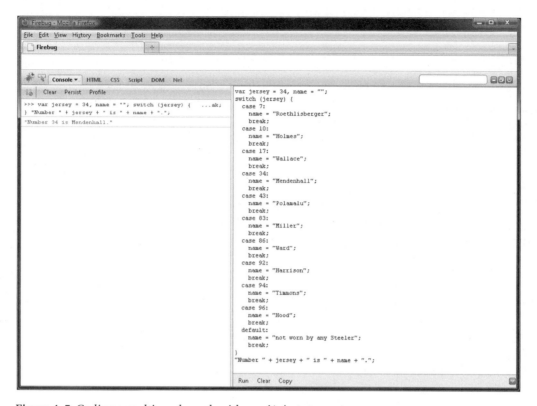

Figure 4–5. Coding a multiway branch with a `switch` statement

Here, JavaScript had to evaluate the first four case clauses in order to identify 34 as Mendenhall. Now change `jersey` to a number no case expression matches in order to make sure the `default` path works:

```
var jersey = 1, name = "";
switch (jersey) {
  case 7:
    name = "Roethlisberger";
    break;
  case 10:
    name = "Holmes";
    break;
  case 17:
    name = "Wallace";
    break;
  case 34:
    name = "Mendenhall";
    break;
  case 43:
    name = "Polamalu";
```

```
    break;
  case 83:
    name = "Miller";
    break;
  case 86:
    name = "Ward";
    break;
  case 92:
    name = "Harrison";
    break;
  case 94:
    name = "Timmons";
    break;
  case 96:
    name = "Hood";
    break;
  default:
    name = "not worn by any Steeler";
    break;
}
"Number " + jersey + " is " + name + ".";
// "Number 1 is not worn by any Steeler."
```

Since there is no case clause for 1, JavaScript ran the default path. Note that, although the default case typically goes last, that is not something JavaScript requires. So let's put it first instead:

```
var jersey = 1, name = "";
switch (jersey) {
  default:
    name = "not worn by any Steeler";
    break;
  case 7:
    name = "Roethlisberger";
    break;
  case 10:
    name = "Holmes";
    break;
  case 17:
    name = "Wallace";
    break;
  case 34:
    name = "Mendenhall";
    break;
  case 43:
    name = "Polamalu";
    break;
  case 83:
    name = "Miller";
    break;
  case 86:
    name = "Ward";
    break;
  case 92:
    name = "Harrison";
```

```
    break;
  case 94:
    name = "Timmons";
    break;
  case 96:
    name = "Hood";
    break;
}
"Number " + jersey + " is " + name + ".";
// "Number 1 is not worn by any Steeler."
```

It works just as well there. Now, as I noted earlier, case clauses can have more than one case expression. This provides a way for you to run a path for more than one string or number. For example, numbers 92 and 97 on the Steelers are both named Harrison, so let's kill two birds with one stone like this:

```
var jersey = 92, name = "";
switch (jersey) {
  case 7:
    name = "Roethlisberger";
    break;
  case 10:
    name = "Holmes";
    break;
  case 17:
    name = "Wallace";
    break;
  case 34:
    name = "Mendenhall";
    break;
  case 43:
    name = "Polamalu";
    break;
  case 83:
    name = "Miller";
    break;
  case 86:
    name = "Ward";
    break;
  case 92:
  case 97:
    name = "Harrison";
    break;
  case 94:
    name = "Timmons";
    break;
  case 96:
    name = "Hood";
    break;
  default:
    name = "not worn by any Steeler";
    break;
}
"Number " + jersey + " is " + name + ".";
```

```
// "Number 92 is Harrison."
```

Verify your work with Figure 4–6.

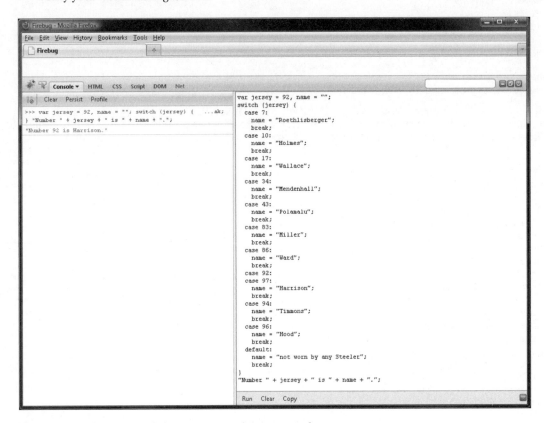

Figure 4–6. Falling through from one case clause to another

JavaScript fell through from the case clause for 92 to the one for 97. Now let's be ornery, omit some break statements, and see what happens:

```
var jersey = 7, name = "";
switch (jersey) {
  case 7:
    name = "Roethlisberger";
  case 10:
    name = "Holmes";
  case 17:
    name = "Wallace";
  case 34:
    name = "Mendenhall";
  case 43:
    name = "Polamalu";
  case 83:
```

```
      name = "Miller";
      break;
    case 86:
      name = "Ward";
      break;
    case 92:
    case 97:
      name = "Harrison";
      break;
    case 94:
      name = "Timmons";
      break;
    case 96:
      name = "Hood";
      break;
    default:
      name = "not worn by any Steeler";
      break;
}
"Number " + jersey + " is " + name + ".";
// "Number 7 is Miller."
```

Here, JavaScript begins running the `switch` block with the statement `name = "Roethlisberger";` and stops when it encounters the break statement after the statement `name = "Miller";`, so for a jersey number of 7, JavaScript incorrectly returns `"Miller"`. Put another way, JavaScript just ran a path like the one for the following ridiculous `if` condition, which overwrites name six times in a row!

```
if (jersey === 7) {
  name = "Roethlisberger";
  name = "Holmes";
  name = "Wallace";
  name = "Mendenhall";
  name = "Polamalu";
  name = "Miller";
}
```

Now put the break statements back in, change jersey to 96, and delete the break after the case clause for 96. Click Run to see what happens:

```
var jersey = 96, name = "";
switch (jersey) {
  case 7:
    name = "Roethlisberger";
    break;
  case 10:
    name = "Holmes";
    break;
  case 17:
    name = "Wallace";
    break;
  case 34:
    name = "Mendenhall";
    break;
  case 43:
    name = "Polamalu";
```

```
      break;
    case 83:
      name = "Miller";
      break;
    case 86:
      name = "Ward";
      break;
    case 92:
    case 97:
      name = "Harrison";
      break;
    case 94:
      name = "Timmons";
      break;
    case 96:
      name = "Hood";
    default:
      name = "not worn by any Steeler";
      break;
}
"Number " + jersey + " is " + name + ".";
// "Number 96 is not worn by any Steeler."
```

As you can see, JavaScript will continue running statements, even those in the default clause, until it either encounters a disruptive statement or encounters the closing curly brace. By neglecting to put a break statement after the case clause for 96, we effectively had JavaScript run the following if condition:

```
if (jersey === 96) {
  name = "Hood";
  name = "not worn by any Steeler";
}
```

Note that had we put the default case at the top of the switch, JavaScript would not have fallen through from the case clause for 96 to the default.

As previously noted, if a switch appears within a function, then you can end paths with a return disruptive statement instead of a break. Oftentimes, the return statement not only marks the end of the path but also is the path itself. So, let's go ahead and put our switch in a function so that we can use return statements:

```
var jersey = 7, name = "";
function identifyPlayer() {
  switch (jersey) {
    case 7:
      return "Roethlisberger";
    case 10:
      return "Holmes";
    case 17:
      return "Wallace";
    case 34:
      return "Mendenhall";
    case 43:
      return "Polamalu";
    case 83:
      return "Miller";
    case 86:
```

```
      return "Ward";
    case 92:
      return "Harrison";
    case 94:
      return "Timmons";
    case 96:
      return "Hood";
    default:
      return "not worn by any Steeler";
  }
}
"Number " + jersey + " is " + identifyPlayer() + ".";
// "Number 7 is Roethlisberger."
```

Verify your work with Figure 4–7.

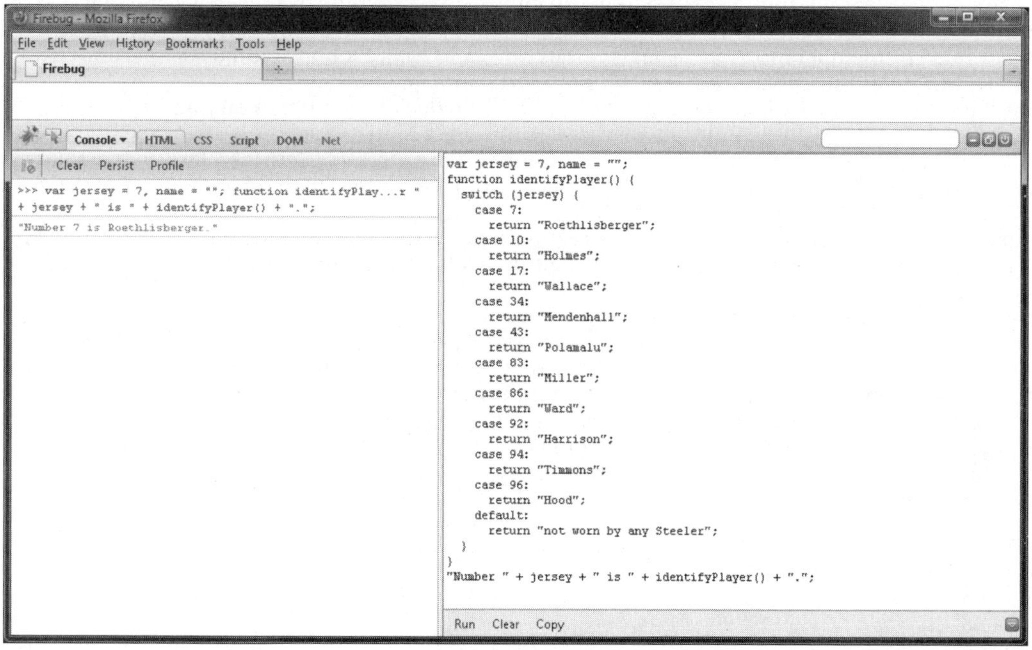

Figure 4–7. Within a function, you can replace break statements with return statements.

One final note on switch statements: case expressions, which go between the case keyword and the colon, typically are string or number literals. However, any expression will do. Just make sure those do not do anything other than return a value for the === operator to test for identity versus the value of the switch expression. I say this because JavaScript does not evaluate case expressions downstream of the one that matches the switch expression. So, you never know how many of your case expressions will run. For example, if your fourth case expression invokes a function that returns a number for === to work with but also changes three variables elsewhere in your script and your second case expression matches the switch expression, then JavaScript never has a chance to change those three variables. This unpredictability is why writing case expressions with secondary effects is frowned upon. Don't do it.

Writing a while Loop

To eliminate the drudgery of coding a slew of identical conditional statements one after another, JavaScript provides you with four looping statements. Remember from earlier that those are while, do while, for, and for in. We will explore each of those in turn, beginning with the simple while loop.

while loops are like an if condition that runs over and over until its expression returns false. Not surprisingly, from a syntax point of view, while and if statements appear similar:

```
if (expression) path
while (expression) path
```

Just as JavaScript converts the value of an if condition's expression to a boolean if necessary, it does so for a while loop's expression, too. So to JavaScript, the game plan looks like this:

```
while (Boolean(expression)) path
```

The first time JavaScript runs a while statement, if the expression returns true or a value that converts to true, then the path runs. On the other hand, if the expression returns false or a value that converts to false (remember those are undefined, null, "", 0, or NaN), then the path does not run. That is to say, on its first iteration, a while loop is no different from an if condition.

Now if the path ran on the first iteration, JavaScript has to decide whether to take another roundabout of the path. To do so, it simply reevaluates the while loop's expression. In the event that the expression again returns a truthy value, the path runs. But if the expression returns a falsy value, the path does not run, so JavaScript moves past the while loop and continues with the remainder of your script.

Iterations of the while loop continue until its expression returns a falsy value. With this in mind, you want to ensure that eventually the expression does return a falsy value. Otherwise, the loop will never stop iterating. Such a mistake is aptly referred to as an *infinite loop*. Those freeze the browser until its long-running script limit, typically between 5 and 10 seconds, is reached.

Essentially, we want to write an if condition but somewhere in the path make sure that expression will eventually return a falsy value. Typically, this is done by incrementing a loop variable, traditionally named i, j, or k, which you in turn compare to the number of roundabouts you want JavaScript to take. So, click Clear in both Firebug panels, and let's enter and run a simple while loop.

I don't know about you, but a cup of tea brightens my mood. So, if I am feeling a little glum and want to rummage through the looseleaf teas in the pantry looking for Borpatra, my favorite Assam tea, I could do so with the following while loop. So, enter and run the following:

```
var looseLeafTea = [
  "Ghillidary",
  "Kenilworth",
  "Milima",
  "Keemun",
  "Boisahabi",
  "Manohari",
  "Borpatra",
  "Lukwah",
  "Khongea"
];
var mood = "glum";
var i = 0;
while (i < looseLeafTea.length) {
  if (looseLeafTea[i] === "Borpatra") {
    mood = "cheery";
    break;
```

```
  }
  i ++;
}
"I feel " + mood + "!";
// "I feel cheery!"
```

Verify your work with Figure 4–8.

Figure 4–8. *Iterating over an array with a* while *loop*

Here we have a `looseLeafTea` array with nine elements. Prior to running the `while` loop, we initialize a loop variable named `i` to 0, the index of the first element in `looseLeafTea`. For the `while` loop's boolean expression, we test whether `i` is less than `looseLeafTea.length`, which is 9. At the very end of the `while` path, we add 1 to `i` with the `++` operator. In this way, the loop will run at most nine times, one iteration per element in `looseLeafTea`.

During a particular roundabout of the `while` path, we can query the next element in `looseLeafTea` with `i` and the `[]` operator. So, for example, during the fourth iteration `i` would be 3 (remember it started at 0), and so `looseLeafTea[i]` would be `"Keemun"`. This behavior is typical of a loop. That is to say, on each roundabout you have JavaScript run the same set of commands on a different variable, member, or element. So, loops provide a way to do things in a batch. It's kind of like baking oatmeal cookies!

Now, unless we tell JavaScript otherwise, it will take all nine roundabouts of the `while` path. There's no harm in that, but it is inefficient. In the event that an element contains `"Borpatra"`, then there's no need to loop through the remainder of `looseLeafTea`. To tell JavaScript that enough is enough, we add break statement to the `while` loop. Doing so tells JavaScript to move past the `while` statement and continue with the next statement in the script, which in our case glues `mood` to a couple of other strings.

So, our `while` loop eliminated the drudgery of having to write separate `if` conditions for the nine elements in `looseLeafTea` like so:

```
var looseLeafTea = [
  "Ghillidary",
  "Kenilworth",
  "Milima",
```

```
    "Keemun",
    "Boisahabi",
    "Manohari",
    "Borpatra",
    "Lukwah",
    "Khongea"
];
var mood = "glum";
if (looseLeafTea[0] === "Borpatra") {
  mood = "cheery";
}
if (looseLeafTea[1] === "Borpatra") {
  mood = "cheery";
}
if (looseLeafTea[2] === "Borpatra") {
  mood = "cheery";
}
if (looseLeafTea[3] === "Borpatra") {
  mood = "cheery";
}
if (looseLeafTea[4] === "Borpatra") {
  mood = "cheery";
}
if (looseLeafTea[5] === "Borpatra") {
  mood = "cheery";
}
if (looseLeafTea[6] === "Borpatra") {
  mood = "cheery";
}
if (looseLeafTea[7] === "Borpatra") {
  mood = "cheery";
}
if (looseLeafTea[8] === "Borpatra") {
  mood = "cheery";
}
"I feel " + mood + "!";
// "I feel cheery!"
```

Bet you're glad now that JavaScript provides looping statements so that you don't have to write all those if conditions! Note that, in addition to saving programmers time, loops let JavaScript work smart. In our while loop, JavaScript knew it was not necessary to query the final three elements, since it had already found "Borpatra".

Aborting an Iteration but Not the Loop

A break statement tells JavaScript to totally abort a loop. But what if you just want to abort an iteration but not the loop? Is there anything less draconian than break? It turns out there is. continue statements simply terminate an iteration. JavaScript then reevaluates the boolean expression to see whether it takes another roundabout.

Typically, continue is used to abort an iteration when a variable contains an undesirable value such as undefined or "". Let's corrupt looseLeafTea by adding "" prior to "Kenilworth" and undefined prior to "Keemun" (by inserting two commas in a row). Then add an else if clause that runs whenever an element in looseLeafTea contains a falsy value. In there we will do two things. First, we will delete the falsy element from looseLeafTea by way of the predefined splice()method, which we will cover in more detail in Chapter 5, that just removes the element from the array and then brings the subsequent elements forward to fill the gap. Second, we will insert a continue statement to abort the iteration. This statement will halt the current iteration of the loop and jump back to the start of the while loop with a new iteration. Note that this means we will skip the i ++ line of code, so the counter will not be incremented. This is exactly what we want to happen because, when we removed the falsy element, JavaScript brought all the remaining elements forward to fill the gap, so there is a new element now occupying the position of the old falsy element. For that reason, we want to loop over the same index in the array twice to make sure we cover all the elements. Finally, let's increment i within an else clause just to make things read better.

So, modify the previous sample like so, and click Run in Firebug:

```
var looseLeafTea = [
  "Ghillidary",
  "",
  "Kenilworth",
  "Milima",
  ,
  "Keemun",
  "Boisahabi",
  "Manohari",
  "Borpatra",
  "Lukwah",
  "Khongea"
];
var mood = "glum";
var i = 0;
while (i < looseLeafTea.length) {
  if (looseLeafTea[i] === "Borpatra") {
    mood = "cheery";
    break;
  } else if (! looseLeafTea[i]) {
    looseLeafTea.splice(i, 1);
    continue;
  } else {
    i ++;
  }
}
"I feel " + mood + "!";
// "I feel cheery!"
```

Before moving on, let's check to make sure JavaScript did weed out the "" and undefined values from looseLeafTea. So, click Clear, and then query looseLeafTea like so, verifying your work with Figure 4–9:

```
looseLeafTea;
// ["Ghillidary", "Kenilworth", "Milima", "Keemun", "Boisahabi", "Manohari",
// "Borpatra", "Lukwah", "Khongea"]
```

So there it is. JavaScript deleted the "" and undefined elements just like we wanted.

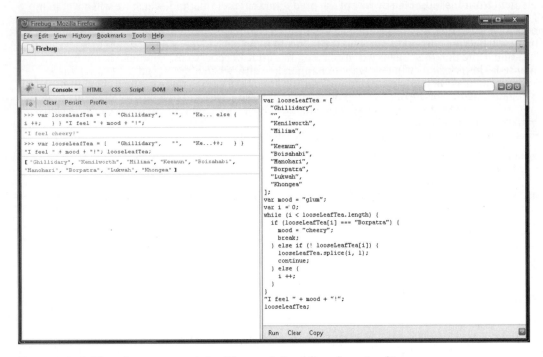

Figure 4–9. Culling elements containing "" or undefined from looseLeafTea

Replacing Break with Return in a Function

Now just as you can abort a switch with return rather than break whenever the switch appears in a function, you can abort a loop (while, do while, for, for in) with return rather than break whenever the loop appears in a function. So, click Clear in both Firebug panels, and let's rewrite our while loop inside a function, replacing break with return:

```
var looseLeafTea = [
  "Ghillidary",
  "Kenilworth",
  "Milima",
  "Keemun",
  "Boisahabi",
  "Manohari",
  "Borpatra",
  "Lukwah",
  "Khongea"
];
function findTea(tea) {
  var i = 0;
  while (i < looseLeafTea.length) {
    if (looseLeafTea[i] === tea) {
      return "cheery";
```

```
  } else if (! looseLeafTea[i]) {
    looseLeafTea.splice(i, 1);
    continue;
  } else {
    i ++;
  }
  }
  return "glum";
}
"I feel " + findTea("Kenilworth") + "!";
// "I feel cheery!"
```

As Figure 4–10 illustrates, invoking our function findTea() evaluates to "cheery" or "glum" depending upon whether JavaScript can find the value of the tea parameter in looseLeafTea.

Figure 4–10. Inside a function, you can abort a while loop with a return statement.

■ **Note** Chapter 6 covers functions more fully.

Writing a do while loop

while loops provide a way to conditionally run a path zero or more times. That is, if the loop expression equates to false when it is first evaluated, then the path will not run at all. Now what if you want to make sure the path runs at least one time? For this circumstance, you would write a do while loop. The syntax for do while is as follows:

```
do path while (expression);
```

As you might guess by now, path can be either a single child statement or a block, and the value of expression is converted to a boolean if necessary by passing it to Boolean(). Though it is easy to overlook, the semicolon following the expression in parentheses is required. With those things in mind, click Clear in both Firebug panels, and let's try a do while loop.

More often than not, when it comes time to follow a recipe, there is a spice that if unavailable would put the kaibosh on my plans. Say I want to make lemon scones; the limiting ingredient would be, oddly enough, lemon peel. Being a foodie, it is safe to assume I have at least one spice. Therefore, it makes sense to rummage through the spice shelf with a do while loop like so, because we want to check at least one spice:

```
var spices = [
  "cinnamon",
  "ginger",
  "nutmeg",
  "cloves",
  "sesame seed",
  "pepper",
  "rosemary",
  "tarragon",
  "basil",
  "mace",
  "poppy seed",
  "lemon peel",
  "vanilla",
  "oregano",
  "allspice",
  "thyme"
];
var putTheKaiboshOn = true;
var i = 0;
do {
  if (spices[i] === "lemon peel") {
    putTheKaiboshOn = false;
    break;
  }
  i ++;
} while (i < spices.length);
(putTheKaiboshOn) ? "No can do!" : "Go right ahead!";
// "Go right ahead!"
```

Verify your work with Figure 4–11.

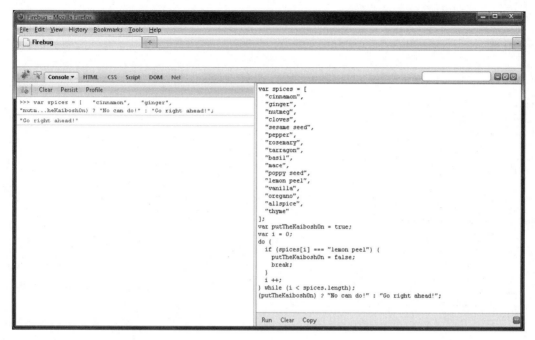

Figure 4–11. Rummaging through the spices array with a do while loop

Here, === will compare "cinnamon" to "lemon peel" no matter what, since JavaScript always takes at least one roundabout of a do while loop. Thereafter, JavaScript will do another iteration only if i < spices.length returns true. Since spices.length evaluates to 15, JavaScript will run the do while path 15 times unless we tell it otherwise with a break statement, which we do in the event we find "lemon peel" in spices. Finally, our loop variable i contains the index by which we query elements in spices, so we increment i with the ++ operator at the end of the path. In this way, JavaScript can decide whether there is any point to taking another roundabout.

In the event that JavaScript finds "lemon peel" while rummaging through spices, it assigns false to putTheKaiboshOn. This variable in turn enables JavaScript to decide whether our recipe is doable. If putTheKaiboshOn is false, JavaScript prints "Go right ahead!". Otherwise, it prints "No can do!". Test that your code works both ways by running the sample with and without "lemon peel" in the spices array.

Before moving on, let's rework our do while loop as a while loop. Doing so illustrates that JavaScript unconditionally takes the first roundabout of a do while loop and then conditionally takes any subsequent ones. Therefore, to emulate such behavior with a while loop, you would have to key in the path twice like so:

```
path
while (expression) path
```

With this in mind, click Clear in both Firebug panels, and let's try to pull this off:

```
var spices = [
  "cinnamon",
  "ginger",
```

```
    "nutmeg",
    "cloves",
    "sesame seed",
    "pepper",
    "rosemary",
    "tarragon",
    "basil",
    "mace",
    "poppy seed",
    "lemon peel",
    "vanilla",
    "oregano",
    "allspice",
    "thyme"
];
var putTheKaiboshOn = true;
var i = 0;
if (spices[i] === "lemon peel") {
  putTheKaiboshOn = false;
} else {
  i ++;
  while (i < spices.length) {
    if (spices[i] === "lemon peel") {
      putTheKaiboshOn = false;
      break;
    }
    i ++;
  }
}
(putTheKaiboshOn) ? "No can do!" : "Go right ahead!";
// "Go right ahead!"
```

As Figure 4–12 illustrates, the while equivalent to our do while loop is much more verbose. Therefore, for circumstances where you want JavaScript to go down a path one or more times, it is much more elegant to control flow with do while rather than while. Many beginners shy away from do while. Don't be one of them!

Figure 4–12. Replacing a do while loop with a while loop takes some doing!

Writing a for Loop

Observant readers will notice that in both our while and do while samples, we initialized a loop variable prior to the loop and then incremented it at the very end of the loop's path. It's a bit of a pain to have to remember to initialize and increment a loop variable, don't you think? JavaScript thinks so, too. Consequently, there is a third kind of looping statement, for, which puts the initialization to the left of the boolean expression and the increment to the right. Note that semicolons separate the initialization, boolean, and increment expressions.

Click Clear in both Firebug panels, and let's try a for loop.

Norah Jones is one of my favorite recording artists. I was listening to a prerelease of her new album, *The Fall*, today. I am thinking that "Back to Manhattan" will be a hit. It is with me anyway. However, since the album is new, I have a hard time remembering the track number for "Back to Manhattan."

Let's create an array named theFall containing a chronological list of tracks on *The Fall* and then have JavaScript iterate through those with a for loop looking for "Back to Manhattan", which we will save to a variable named song. JavaScript will then add 1 to the index of the matching element and store the result in j, which represents the track number. We do so since array elements are numbered with integers beginning with 0, while album tracks obviously are numbered with integers beginning with 1.

Enter and run the following for loop, then verify your work with Figure 4–13:

```
var theFall = [
  "Chasing Pirates",
  "Even Though",
  "Light as a Feather",
  "Young Blood",
  "I Wouldn't Need You",
  "Waiting",
  "It's Gonna Be",
  "You've Ruined Me",
  "Back to Manhattan",
  "Stuck",
  "December",
  "Tell Yer Mama",
  "Man of the Hour"
];
var song = "Back to Manhattan";
for (var i = 0, j = 0; i < theFall.length; i ++) {
  if (theFall[i] === song) {
    j = i + 1;
    break;
  }
}
song + (j > 0 ? " is track " + j : " is not") + " on The Fall.";
// "Back to Manhattan is track 9 on The Fall."
```

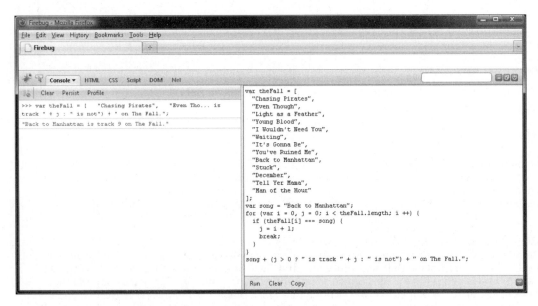

Figure 4–13. Iterating over theFall with a for loop

Here, JavaScript initializes i and j to 0 prior to evaluating the boolean expression i < theFall.length. Following any roundabout of the for loop, JavaScript increments i with the ++ operator. Then it reevaluates the boolean expression to see whether it should run the path again. Note that the initialization expressions are not reevaluated. That is to say, JavaScript runs those just the first time. Note too that we use the comma operator to separate the two initialization expressions. Recall from Chapter 3 that doing so makes i = 0 and j = 0 count as one expression rather than two. So, the comma operator does for expressions what curly braces do for statements—it makes two or more count as one.

■ **Tip** In the event that you have previously declared the loop variables, i and j in our sample, the var keyword is optional.

Enumerating Members with a for in Loop

The fourth and final looping statement, for in, provides a way to enumerate the members of an object. JavaScript ensures the boolean expression, which uses the in operator from Chapter 3, returns true by assigning the name of a different member to the left operand of in prior to an iteration. There's no need to initialize and increment a loop variable in order to prevent an infinite loop; JavaScript already knows to do one iteration per member.

```
for (member in object) path
```

There are three things to note. First, regardless of whether the member was named with an identifier or string, JavaScript returns its name as a string. Second, the left operand to in may be a variable, member, or element. That is to say, it can be anything you can assign a string to. Third, the right operand to in may be any expression for an object—typically, an identifier or function invocation. With those things in mind, click Clear in both Firebug panels, and let's work through a sample for in loop.

I like to wear a shoe tailored to the pace and distance of a run. So, I have a number of running shoes in the cellar. There are eight Nikes down there at the moment. Let's create an object named shoes containing the weight in ounces of each shoe I could run in this evening:

```
var shoes = {
  "LunaRacer": 6.6,
  "Air Max": 13,
  "LunarGlide": 10.2,
  "Zoom Streak XC": 7,
  "Free": 8.6,
  "Mayfly": 4,
  "Zoom Vomero": 11.6,
  "LunarElite": 9.7
}
```

Generally, the more a shoe weighs, the more cushioning it provides. Therefore, if I am running far afield, I wear a pair of shoes weighing more than 10 ounces. Let's enumerate the members in shoes, saving the name of any shoe weighing more than 10 ounces to an array named myOptions. In this way, I will know what my options are.

Note that during each roundabout of the for in loop, JavaScript assigns the name of a member in shoes to shoe. So, shoes[shoe] will return the weight of a shoe. In the event that this weight is greater than or equal to 10, we add the name of the shoe to myOptions by way of the push() method, which I will cover in Chapter 5.

Try entering and running the following for in loop in Firebug, then verify your work with Figure 4–14:

```
var shoes = {
```

```
    "LunaRacer": 6.6,
    "Air Max": 13,
    "LunarGlide": 10.2,
    "Zoom Streak XC": 7,
    "Free": 8.6,
    "Mayfly": 4,
    "Zoom Vomero": 11.6,
    "LunarElite": 9.7
}
var myOptions = [];
for (var shoe in shoes) {
  if (shoes[shoe] >= 10) {
    myOptions.push(shoe);
  }
}
myOptions;
// ["Air Max", "LunarGlide", "Zoom Vomero"]
```

Figure 4–14. Enumerating members with a for in loop

Our for in loop eliminated the drudgery of having to write the following eight if conditions:

```
if (shoes["LunaRacer"] >= 10) {
  myOptions.push("LunaRacer");
}
if (shoes["Air Max"] >= 10) {
  myOptions.push("Air Max");
}
if (shoes["LunarGlide"] >= 10) {
  myOptions.push("LunarGlide");
}
if (shoes["Zoom Streak XC"] >= 10) {
  myOptions.push("Zoom Streak XC");
}
```

```
if (shoes["Free"] >= 10) {
  myOptions.push("Free");
}
if (shoes["Mayfly"] >= 10) {
  myOptions.push("Mayfly");
}
if (shoes["Zoom Vomero"] >= 10) {
  myOptions.push("Zoom Vomero");
}
if (shoes["LunarElite"] >= 10) {
  myOptions.push("LunarElite");
}
```

Snappier Conditionals

Now that we have explored conditionals and loops, let's work through some techniques to make them run snappier—not just a little but two to seven times snappier, if not more. Insofar as the bulk of any JavaScript behavior is comprised of conditionals and loops, doing so will in turn make your behaviors feel that much more responsive to visitors. Yup, I like the sound of that, too!

Let's begin with a few ways to code speedier switch and if else conditionals. One simple thing you can do is favor switch over if else whenever coding five or more paths for JavaScript to conditionally take. Past four, incrementally adding conditions to a switch decrements speed much less than doing so for an if else.

OK, that was painless. And so is the second way to code snappier conditionals—just order their paths from the one JavaScript is most likely to take to the one JavaScript is least likely to take. Doing so minimizes the number of boolean expressions JavaScript has to evaluate.

Now for the third way to code snappier conditionals: don't code them in the first place. No, that's not a typo. In the event that you have written an if else or switch for variations of a string or number and every path does the same thing (just with a different value of that string or number), replacing the if else or switch with an array or object member query will result in an extraordinary speed gain, to put it mildly.

There are a couple of reasons why doing so is preferable to conditional statements. For one thing, JavaScript does not have to drill down through conditions, just one [ ] operation. For another, whereas adding conditions to a switch or if else decrements evaluation speed, adding members to an object or elements to an array does not decrement query speed.

Ideally, you are sold on replacing conditionals with an object or array query whenever possible. Now let's give the technique a try. Double-clear Firebug, and then enter the following function, which contains a switch mapping jersey numbers to player names for Opening Day, 2010 as my Pittsburgh Pirates try to avert their eighteenth losing season in a row. Insofar as 17 of 25 Pirates were not in the dugout last April, namePirate() will come in handy!

```
function namePirate(jersey) {
  var name;
  switch(jersey) {
    case 77:
      name = "D.J. Carrasco";
      break;
    case 53:
      name = "Brendan Donnelly";
      break;
    case 29:
      name = "Octavio Dotel";
```

```
    break;
case 57:
  name = "Zach Duke";
  break;
case 48:
  name = "Javier Lopez";
  break;
case 28:
  name = "Paul Maholm";
  break;
case 34:
  name = "Daniel McCutchen";
  break;
case 47:
  name = "Evan Meek";
  break;
case 37:
  name = "Charlie Morton";
  break;
case 49:
  name = "Ross Ohlendorf";
  break;
case 62:
  name = "Hayden Penn";
  break;
case 43:
  name = "Jack Taschner";
  break;
case 41:
  name = "Ryan Doumit";
  break;
case 35:
  name = "Jason Jaramillo";
  break;
case 13:
  name = "Ronny Cedeno";
  break;
case 6:
  name = "Jeff Clement";
  break;
case 2:
  name = "Bobby Crosby";
  break;
case 3:
  name = "Akinori Iwamura";
  break;
case 15:
  name = "Andy LaRoche";
  break;
case 19:
  name = "Ryan Church";
  break;
case 46:
  name = "Garrett Jones";
```

```
      break;
    case 22:
      name = "Andrew McCutchen";
      break;
    case 85:
      name = "Lastings Milledge";
      break;
    case 58:
      name = "John Raynor";
      break;
    case 24:
      name = "Delwyn Young";
      break;
    default:
      name = "not worn by any Pirate";
  }
  return jersey + " is " + name + ".";
}
```

We're only two games into the season, but the big fella wearing 46 has already hit three home runs. One of those even landed in the Allegheny River, which flows past PNC Park where the Pirates play. So, let's pass 46 to namePirate() and find out who that thumper is. Verify your work with Figure 4–15.

```
function namePirate(jersey) {
  var name;
  switch(jersey) {
    case 77:
      name = "D.J. Carrasco";
      break;
    case 53:
      name = "Brendan Donnelly";
      break;
    case 29:
      name = "Octavio Dotel";
      break;
    case 57:
      name = "Zach Duke";
      break;
    case 48:
      name = "Javier Lopez";
      break;
    case 28:
      name = "Paul Maholm";
      break;
    case 34:
      name = "Daniel McCutchen";
      break;
    case 47:
      name = "Evan Meek";
      break;
    case 37:
      name = "Charlie Morton";
      break;
    case 49:
```

```
      name = "Ross Ohlendorf";
      break;
    case 62:
      name = "Hayden Penn";
      break;
    case 43:
      name = "Jack Taschner";
      break;
    case 41:
      name = "Ryan Doumit";
      break;
    case 35:
      name = "Jason Jaramillo";
      break;
    case 13:
      name = "Ronny Cedeno";
      break;
    case 6:
      name = "Jeff Clement";
      break;
    case 2:
      name = "Bobby Crosby";
      break;
    case 3:
      name = "Akinori Iwamura";
      break;
    case 15:
      name = "Andy LaRoche";
      break;
    case 19:
      name = "Ryan Church";
      break;
    case 46:
      name = "Garrett Jones";
      break;
    case 22:
      name = "Andrew McCutchen";
      break;
    case 85:
      name = "Lastings Milledge";
      break;
    case 58:
      name = "John Raynor";
      break;
    case 24:
      name = "Delwyn Young";
      break;
    default:
      name = "not worn by any Pirate";
  }
  return jersey + " is " + name + ".";
}
namePirate(46);
// "46 is Garrett Jones."
```

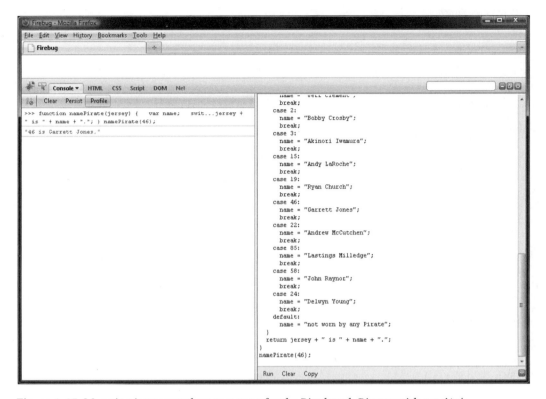

Figure 4–15. Mapping jersey numbers to names for the Pittsburgh Pirates with a `switch`

Now then, I ordered the `switch` like a scorecard (pitchers, catchers, infielders, outfielders) and then by surname. JavaScript had to evaluate 21 `case` clauses to determine who wears 46. But if we were to replace the `switch` with an object member query, we would in turn replace those 21 `===` operations with 1 `[ ]` operation. Yup, that sounds like a good idea to me, too.

So, double-clear Firebug, and then enter the following object literal. Note that, although we are adding members in the same order as in the `switch`, which is to say by position and then by surname, remember that ECMAScript does not define an order for object members. So, neither D. J. Carrasco nor any other Pirate is the first member in `pirates`. Note too that, since the jersey numbers are integers, we could have done this with an array. However, that would be a bear to type. Insofar as an object may have elements just like an array, a feature I will explore in Chapter 5, there is no point in doing all the extra typing to create an array lookup.

```
var pirates = {
  "77": "D.J. Carrasco",
  "53": "Brendan Donnelly",
  "29": "Octavio Dotel",
  "57": "Zach Duke",
  "48": "Javier Lopez",
  "28": "Paul Maholm",
  "34": "Daniel McCutchen",
  "47": "Evan Meek",
```

```
    "37": "Charlie Morton",
    "49": "Ross Ohlendorf",
    "62": "Hayden Penn",
    "43": "Jack Taschner",
    "41": "Ryan Doumit",
    "35": "Jason Jaramillo",
    "13": "Ronny Cedeno",
    "6": "Jeff Clement",
    "2": "Bobby Crosby",
    "3": "Akinori Iwamura",
    "15": "Andy LaRoche",
    "19": "Ryan Church",
    "46": "Garrett Jones",
    "22": "Andrew McCutchen",
    "85": "Lastings Milledge",
    "58": "John Raynor",
    "24": "Delwyn Young"
};
```

Now let's code a much simpler version of namePirate(). There's just one line of code in the body now:

```
var pirates = {
    "77": "D.J. Carrasco",
    "53": "Brendan Donnelly",
    "29": "Octavio Dotel",
    "57": "Zach Duke",
    "48": "Javier Lopez",
    "28": "Paul Maholm",
    "34": "Daniel McCutchen",
    "47": "Evan Meek",
    "37": "Charlie Morton",
    "49": "Ross Ohlendorf",
    "62": "Hayden Penn",
    "43": "Jack Taschner",
    "41": "Ryan Doumit",
    "35": "Jason Jaramillo",
    "13": "Ronny Cedeno",
    "6": "Jeff Clement",
    "2": "Bobby Crosby",
    "3": "Akinori Iwamura",
    "15": "Andy LaRoche",
    "19": "Ryan Church",
    "46": "Garrett Jones",
    "22": "Andrew McCutchen",
    "85": "Lastings Milledge",
    "58": "John Raynor",
    "24": "Delwyn Young"
};
function namePirate(jersey) {
    return jersey + " is " + (pirates[jersey] ? pirates[jersey] : "not worn by a Pirate") + ".";
}
```

Alright, let's test this thing and see if it works. Hmm. Someone wearing 3 is playing second base now that Freddy Sanchez has been traded to the Giants for prospects. Let's find out who's on second (no, not first base) by passing 3 to namePirate(). Remember from Chapter 3 that [ ] converts its operand to a string; therefore, you can pass either 3 or "3" to namePirate(). Inasmuch as numbers take fewer keystrokes, let's pass 3. Then verify your work with Figure 4–16.

```
var pirates = {
  "77": "D.J. Carrasco",
  "53": "Brendan Donnelly",
  "29": "Octavio Dotel",
  "57": "Zach Duke",
  "48": "Javier Lopez",
  "28": "Paul Maholm",
  "34": "Daniel McCutchen",
  "47": "Evan Meek",
  "37": "Charlie Morton",
  "49": "Ross Ohlendorf",
  "62": "Hayden Penn",
  "43": "Jack Taschner",
  "41": "Ryan Doumit",
  "35": "Jason Jaramillo",
  "13": "Ronny Cedeno",
  "6": "Jeff Clement",
  "2": "Bobby Crosby",
  "3": "Akinori Iwamura",
  "15": "Andy LaRoche",
  "19": "Ryan Church",
  "46": "Garrett Jones",
  "22": "Andrew McCutchen",
  "85": "Lastings Milledge",
  "58": "John Raynor",
  "24": "Delwyn Young"
};
function namePirate(jersey) {
  return jersey + " is " + (pirates[jersey] ? pirates[jersey] : "not worn by a Pirate") + ".";
}
namePirate(3);
// "3 is Akinori Iwamura."
```

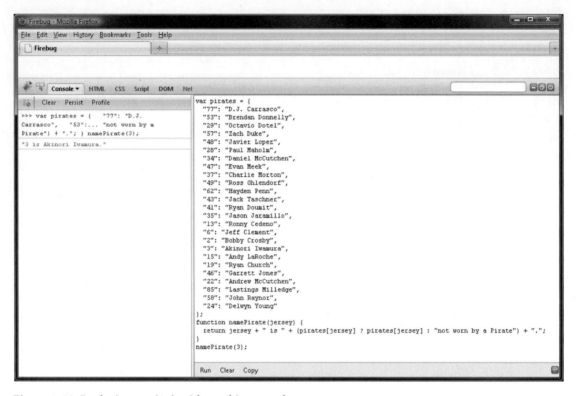

Figure 4–16. Replacing a switch *with an object member query*

Now that you know three ways to make conditionals run snappy, let's explore some ways to do so for loops.

Snappier Loops

So, which of the four loops is fastest?

No, not for.

Not while either.

Definitely not for in. That one runs like a tortoise.

So then, it has to be do while, right? Sorry, no.

Alright, so that was a trick question. for in loops are the slowest. Sometimes they're seven times slower than the others. But while, for, and do while loops run neck and neck. So, of those three, code the one that you prefer for a particular job.

On the other hand, try to replace for in loops with one of the other three whenever you can. That might seem to be a tall order, though. After all, for in is the only loop that can enumerate members in an object, right?

Yes and no: for in loops are the only one that can enumerate unknown object members, in other words, members you do not know the name of. However, you can enumerate members that you know the name of with one of the other three loops. Just put those names in an array and iterate through them.

Taking this tack can speed up your code sevenfold. Yup, that's a lot! So, double-clear Firebug, and I'll show you how.

First, let's create an object to loop through. Hmm. OK, I thought of one: there are a couple of games remaining in the NHL regular season, and several players are vying for the Rocket Richard trophy, which is awarded annually to the top goal scorer. Right now, Sidney Crosby for my Pittsburgh Penguins has the most at 49. Let's create an object containing the top 20 goal scorers entering the final weekend of play:

```
var topTwenty = {
    "Crosby": 49,
    "Ovechkin": 48,
    "Stamkos": 48,
    "Marleau": 43,
    "Gaborik": 41,
    "Kovalchuk": 40,
    "Heatley": 39,
    "Semin": 39,
    "Parise": 37,
    "Burrows": 35,
    "Kopitar": 34,
    "Ryan": 34,
    "Carter": 33,
    "Nash": 33,
    "Iginla": 32,
    "Penner": 32,
    "Backstrom": 31,
    "Hornqvist": 30,
    "Jokinen": 30,
    "Kane": 30
};
```

Now with two games to go, most of those players have no chance whatsoever of passing Crosby and winning the Rocket Richard. So, not only would enumerating every topTwenty member with a for in loop be slow, it would also be irrational. Not wanting to appear ridiculous, let's create an array named rocketRichard containing just the names of the four players that have a chance of finishing first in goals. While we're at it, let's create a note string for later:

```
var topTwenty = {
    "Crosby": 49,
    "Ovechkin": 48,
    "Stamkos": 48,
    "Marleau": 43,
    "Gaborik": 41,
    "Kovalchuk": 40,
    "Heatley": 39,
    "Semin": 39,
    "Parise": 37,
    "Burrows": 35,
    "Kopitar": 34,
    "Ryan": 34,
    "Carter": 33,
    "Nash": 33,
    "Iginla": 32,
    "Penner": 32,
    "Backstrom": 31,
    "Hornqvist": 30,
```

```
  "Jokinen": 30,
  "Kane": 30
};
var rocketRichard = ["Ovechkin", "Crosby", "Marleau", "Stamkos"], note = "";
```

Now let's order the names in rocketRichard by goals and then by name. To do so, we will use the sort() method that every array, including rocketRichard, defines so that you can order its elements. We will cover sort() and other Array methods in the next chapter. So for now, just type carefully!

```
var topTwenty = {
  "Crosby": 49,
  "Ovechkin": 48,
  "Stamkos": 48,
  "Marleau": 43,
  "Gaborik": 41,
  "Kovalchuk": 40,
  "Heatley": 39,
  "Semin": 39,
  "Parise": 37,
  "Burrows": 35,
  "Kopitar": 34,
  "Ryan": 34,
  "Carter": 33,
  "Nash": 33,
  "Iginla": 32,
  "Penner": 32,
  "Backstrom": 31,
  "Hornqvist": 30,
  "Jokinen": 30,
  "Kane": 30
};
var rocketRichard = ["Ovechkin", "Crosby", "Marleau", "Stamkos"], note = "";
rocketRichard.sort(function(p1, p2) {
  var d = topTwenty[p2] - topTwenty[p1];
  if (d !== 0) {
    return d;
  } else {
    return (p1 < p2) ? -1 : 1;
  }
});
```

Now we can code either a for, while, or do while loop to indirectly enumerate members in topTwenty by way of the member names in rocketRichard. Let's go with a for loop. This one will build up a string in note that lists the top four goal scorers. Following the for loop, let's clip off the ", " from the end of note with String.slice(), a method we covered in Chapter 2. Then click Run, and verify your work with Figure 4–17.

```
var topTwenty = {
  "Crosby": 49,
  "Ovechkin": 48,
  "Stamkos": 48,
  "Marleau": 43,
  "Gaborik": 41,
  "Kovalchuk": 40,
```

```
    "Heatley": 39,
    "Semin": 39,
    "Parise": 37,
    "Burrows": 35,
    "Kopitar": 34,
    "Ryan": 34,
    "Carter": 33,
    "Nash": 33,
    "Iginla": 32,
    "Penner": 32,
    "Backstrom": 31,
    "Hornqvist": 30,
    "Jokinen": 30,
    "Kane": 30
};
var rocketRichard = ["Ovechkin", "Crosby", "Marleau", "Stamkos"], note = "";
rocketRichard.sort(function(p1, p2) {
  var d = topTwenty[p2] - topTwenty[p1];
  if (d !== 0) {
    return d;
  } else {
    return (p1 < p2) ? -1 : 1;
  }
});
for (var i = 0; i < rocketRichard.length; i ++) {
  note = note + rocketRichard[i] + ": " + topTwenty[rocketRichard[i]] + ", ";
}
note.slice(0, -2);
// "Crosby: 49, Ovechkin: 48, Stamkos: 48, Marleau: 43"
```

By the way, the previous sample illustrates a hidden perk in enumerating object members with a helper array. Doing so enables you to set the order members are enumerated.

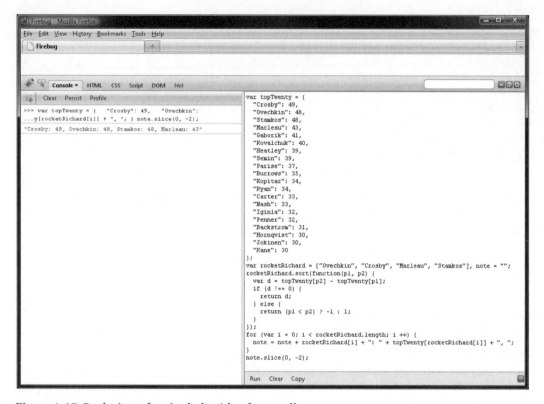

Figure 4–17. *Replacing a for in sloth with a for gazelle*

Now that you know how to replace a for in sloth with a for, while, or do while gazelle, let's explore a couple of ways to make those three snappier. Let's begin with our for loop from the previous sample.

First, JavaScript can query local variables within a function or global variables outside of a function faster than object members such as length—like two times as fast in Explorer 7 and 8. So, rather than query length over and over in the boolean expression, i < rocketRichard.length, let's do so one time in the initialization expression, replacing i = 0 with i = rocketRichard.length. Second, it's faster to iterate over an array in reverse because doing so provides a way to combine the boolean expression with the increment or decrement expression. Therefore, omit the latter, and decrement the loop variable i in the boolean expression. In turn, since we are now iterating over the array in reverse, we need to tweak the function literal we pass to sort() so that rocketRichard is ordered from fewest to most goals and then from Z to A. Make the following changes, click Run, and then verify your work with Figure 4–18:

```
var topTwenty = {
  "Crosby": 49,
  "Ovechkin": 48,
  "Stamkos": 48,
  "Marleau": 43,
  "Gaborik": 41,
  "Kovalchuk": 40,
  "Heatley": 39,
```

```
    "Semin": 39,
    "Parise": 37,
    "Burrows": 35,
    "Kopitar": 34,
    "Ryan": 34,
    "Carter": 33,
    "Nash": 33,
    "Iginla": 32,
    "Penner": 32,
    "Backstrom": 31,
    "Hornqvist": 30,
    "Jokinen": 30,
    "Kane": 30
}
var rocketRichard = ["Ovechkin", "Crosby", "Marleau", "Stamkos"], note = "";
rocketRichard.sort(function(p1, p2) {
  var d = topTwenty[p1] - topTwenty[p2];
  if (d !== 0) {
    return d;
  } else {
    return (p2 < p1) ? -1 : 1;
  }
});
for (var i = rocketRichard.length; i --; ) {
  note = note + rocketRichard[i] + ": " + topTwenty[rocketRichard[i]] + ", ";
}
note.slice(0, -2);
// "Crosby: 49, Ovechkin: 48, Stamkos: 48, Marleau: 43"
```

Note that in i --, the -- operator is in the post-decrement position. Why does that matter? It matters for a couple of reasons. For one thing, if you wrote -- i instead of i --, JavaScript would never query the fourth element in rocketRichard. For another, if rocketRichard were empty, which is to say its length was 0, then our for loop would never stop iterating. So, be sure that -- is in the post-decrement position!

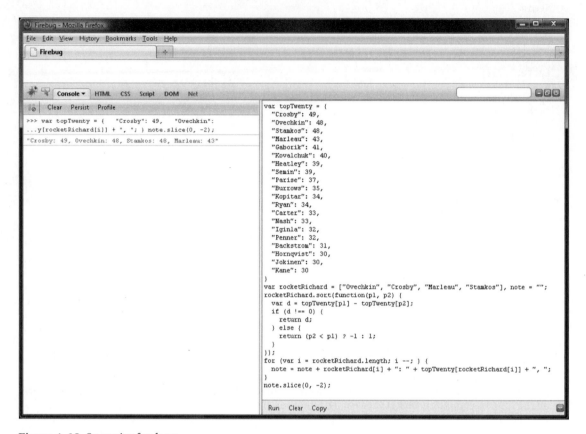

Figure 4–18. Snappier for loop

Alright, now let's try rewriting our snappy for loop as an equally snappy while loop. Just move the initialization of i to rocketRichard.length to a separate statement prior to the while loop, and decrement i in the boolean expression. Make those two quick edits like so, and click Run:

```
var topTwenty = {
  "Crosby": 49,
  "Ovechkin": 48,
  "Stamkos": 48,
  "Marleau": 43,
  "Gaborik": 41,
  "Kovalchuk": 40,
  "Heatley": 39,
  "Semin": 39,
  "Parise": 37,
  "Burrows": 35,
  "Kopitar": 34,
  "Ryan": 34,
  "Carter": 33,
```

```
    "Nash": 33,
    "Iginla": 32,
    "Penner": 32,
    "Backstrom": 31,
    "Hornqvist": 30,
    "Jokinen": 30,
    "Kane": 30
}
var rocketRichard = ["Ovechkin", "Crosby", "Marleau", "Stamkos"], note = "";
rocketRichard.sort(function(p1, p2) {
    var d = topTwenty[p1] - topTwenty[p2];
    if (d !== 0) {
        return d;
    } else {
        return (p2 < p1) ? -1 : 1;
    }
});
var i = rocketRichard.length;
while (i --) {
    note = note + rocketRichard[i] + ": " + topTwenty[rocketRichard[i]] + ", ";
}
note.slice(0, -2);
// "Crosby: 49, Ovechkin: 48, Stamkos: 48, Marleau: 43"
```

Finally, let's rewrite our snappy while loop as a snappy do while. That makes sense since we want to run the loop at least one time. OK, four times. With that in mind, be sure to initialize i to one less than rocketRichard.length. Otherwise, note will contain "undefined: undefined, Crosby: 49, Ovechkin: 48, Stamkos: 48, Marleau: 43" since there is no element with an index of 4 in rocketRichard. Edit the while loop from the previous sample like so, and then click Run:

```
var topTwenty = {
    "Crosby": 49,
    "Ovechkin": 48,
    "Stamkos": 48,
    "Marleau": 43,
    "Gaborik": 41,
    "Kovalchuk": 40,
    "Heatley": 39,
    "Semin": 39,
    "Parise": 37,
    "Burrows": 35,
    "Kopitar": 34,
    "Ryan": 34,
    "Carter": 33,
    "Nash": 33,
    "Iginla": 32,
    "Penner": 32,
    "Backstrom": 31,
    "Hornqvist": 30,
    "Jokinen": 30,
    "Kane": 30
}
var rocketRichard = ["Ovechkin", "Crosby", "Marleau", "Stamkos"], note = "";
rocketRichard.sort(function(p1, p2) {
```

```
    var d = topTwenty[p1] - topTwenty[p2];
    if (d !== 0) {
      return d;
    } else {
      return (p2 < p1) ? -1 : 1;
    }
});
var i = rocketRichard.length - 1;
do {
  note = note + rocketRichard[i] + ": " + topTwenty[rocketRichard[i]] + ", ";
} while (i --);
note.slice(0, -2);
// "Crosby: 49, Ovechkin: 48, Stamkos: 48, Marleau: 43"
```

So, there it is. We're done exploring conditionals and loops. By the way, Sidney Crosby and Steven Stamkos finished in a tie for most goals in the NHL with 51 apiece. They'll share the Rocket Richard trophy. Note to NHL: I'd suggest fewest empty net goals being the tie-breaker for the Rocket Richard in the future. Crosby had just one empty net goal this year, while Stamkos had five, including number 51!

Summary

In this chapter, you learned how to control flow with if and switch conditional statements and with while, do while, for, and for in looping statements. You also learned to make decisions, as JavaScript does, with boolean expressions. true is a green light to do something, and false is a red light not to.

In the next chapter, we will delve more deeply into objects and arrays, folder-like datatypes for organizing data. Take a well-deserved break, and I'll see you there!

CHAPTER 5

Member Inheritance

In this chapter, I'll cover a feature of JavaScript called *inheritance*, which is a very useful and powerful tool to acquire. It allows us to write much more ordered and efficient code, because it is a great way to organize your code into useful little lumps. I will cover the following four ways to approach inheritance, each of which has its own place in your programs:

- Classical
- Prototypal
- Deep copy
- Mixin

As you may have guessed from the chapter title, this chapter covers only member inheritance; Chapter 6 covers how to use inheritance with object functions.

To get to grips with inheritance, you first have to get to know objects a little bit better, so I will start by covering object constructors to see how objects are defined and created. You've already seen a few constructors in previous chapters (anything preceded by the new keyword is a constructor), but in this chapter, you will see how to define constructors for yourself.

Creating Objects with a Constructor

Ben & Jerry's Wild Maine Blueberry rests peacefully in a small graveyard on a grassy knoll encircled by a white picket fence in Waterbury, Vermont. The epitaph on its humble tombstone reads as follows:

> *Wild Maine Blueberry*
> *Wild Maine Blueberry*
> *From the land of the puffin,*
> *Now when we crave you,*
> *We turn to the muffin.*
> *1990–92*

Blueberries are my favorite fruit—my mom nicknamed me Blueberry as a child for that reason and because it rhymes with Terry—so I took it pretty hard when Wild Maine Blueberry died. I may have even stopped talking for a while.

But time heals all wounds. Or in this case, an ice cream maker did. So, now I churn my own Wild Maine Blueberry from the following recipe. Note that I puree one of the two cups of wild Maine blueberries, the pulp for which is removed with the vanilla pod and seeds by straining the French-style custard through a fine mesh sieve.

- 1 cup, Organic Valley heavy whipping cream

- 1 cup, Organic Valley half & half

- 5/8 cup, sugar

- 6 egg yolks

- 2 cups, wild Maine blueberries

- 1 Madagascar Bourbon vanilla bean

- 2 tsp. fresh lemon juice

Open `firebug.html` in Firefox, and then press F12 to enable Firebug. If you're just joining us, flip back to the preface for details on how do this. So anyway, we can represent this recipe with the following `wildMaineBlueberry` object:

```
var wildMaineBlueberry = {
  heavyCream: [1, "cup", "Organic Valley"],
  halfHalf: [1, "cup", "Organic Valley"],
  sugar: [5/8, "cup"],
  yolks: [6],
  blueberries: [2, "cup", "fresh wild Maine blueberries"],
  vanilla: [1, "bean", "Madagascar Bourbon"],
  freshLemonJuice: [2, "tsp"]
};
```

However, other than a few short months, fresh wild Maine blueberries are tough to find. So for most of the year, I'd have to set `wildMaineBlueberry.blueberries` to either `[2, "cup", "Dole frozen wild blueberries"]` or `[2, "cup", "Wyman frozen wild blueberries"]`. Moreover, Madagascar Bourbon is my favorite type of vanilla bean. But if I'm out of those, I'll steep a Tahitian or Mexican one instead. The former is milder than Madagascar Bourbon while the latter is more intense.

So, what do you do? Modify `wildMaineBlueberry.blueberries` and `wildMaineBlueberry.vanilla` by hand whenever my preferred ingredients are not to be had? Well, we could, but that's so greenhorn. There's a better way: create a constructor to churn custom quarts of Wild Maine Blueberry for us. Here's how:

Constructors are functions invoked with the `new` operator. Unlike typical functions, constructors are named in upper camel case to indicate that `new` is required. Omitting `new` for a constructor adds members to the global `window` object, which would not be good.

So, anyway, when you invoke a constructor with `new`, JavaScript creates a private variable named `this`, which contains an empty object for you to add members to. Whereas functions implicitly return `undefined`, constructors implicitly return `this`. So you don't have to create a private `this` variable in the body of the constructor or explicitly write a return statement. JavaScript does that for you.

That's really nice. But even better, `this` inherits any members you add to the constructor's `prototype` object. With all of this in mind, we can create a constructor named `WildMaineBlueberry()`. Carved in stone members will go in `WildMaineBlueberry.prototype`, while the values we pass in parameters cleverly named `blueberries` and `vanilla` will be assigned to the `blueberries` and `vanilla` members of `this`. In other words, we set the `prototype` to contain all the ingredients that never change and use the constructor to customize the ingredients that do change, which are then combined with the unchanging set.

In the following constructor, you can see how we use `?:` to set the default values of `blueberries` and `vanilla`, should we not supply a `blueberries` parameter or a `vanilla` parameter (in other words, the value of the `blueberries` parameter is returned by `?:` if it is set; otherwise, the default string is returned):

```
var WildMaineBlueberry = function(blueberries, vanilla) {
  this.blueberries = [2, "cup", blueberries ? blueberries : "fresh wild Maine blueberries"];
```

```
  this.vanilla = [1, "bean", vanilla ? vanilla : "Madagascar Bourbon"];
};
WildMaineBlueberry.prototype = {
  heavyCream: [1, "cup", "Organic Valley"],
  halfHalf: [1, "cup", "Organic Valley"],
  sugar: [5/8, "cup"],
  yolks: [6],
  freshLemonJuice: [2, "tsp"]
};
```

Now let's have `WildMaineBlueberry()` churn us a quart of Ben & Jerry's Wild Maine Blueberry with the preferable default values for blueberries and vanilla. Then pass that to Firebug's `console.dir()` method, which as Figure 5–1 displays, prints an object's own and inherited members. Note that **own members** are those we add to this, so blueberries and vanilla:

```
var WildMaineBlueberry = function(blueberries, vanilla) {
  this.blueberries = [2, "cup", blueberries ? blueberries : "fresh wild Maine blueberries"];
  this.vanilla = [1, "bean", vanilla ? vanilla : "Madagascar Bourbon"];
};
WildMaineBlueberry.prototype = {
  heavyCream: [1, "cup", "Organic Valley"],
  halfHalf: [1, "cup", "Organic Valley"],
  sugar: [5/8, "cup"],
  yolks: [6],
  freshLemonJuice: [2, "tsp"]
};
var wildMaineBlueberry = new WildMaineBlueberry();
console.dir(wildMaineBlueberry);
```

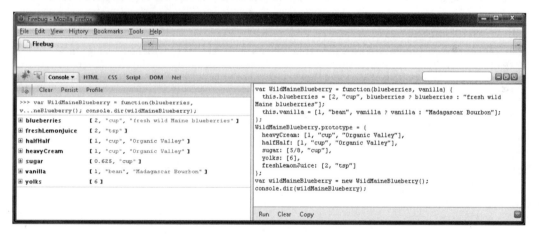

Figure 5–1. Firebug's `console.dir()` method prints an object's own and inherited members.

Now this time, let's churn a less preferable but still yummy quart with Dole frozen wild blueberries and a Tahitian bean, verifying our work with Figure 5–2:

```
var WildMaineBlueberry = function(blueberries, vanilla) {
  this.blueberries = [2, "cup", blueberries ? blueberries : "fresh wild Maine blueberries"];
  this.vanilla = [1, "bean", vanilla ? vanilla : "Madagascar Bourbon"];
```

```
};
WildMaineBlueberry.prototype = {
  heavyCream: [1, "cup", "Organic Valley"],
  halfHalf: [1, "cup", "Organic Valley"],
  sugar: [5/8, "cup"],
  yolks: [6],
  freshLemonJuice: [2, "tsp"]
};
var wildMaineBlueberry = new WildMaineBlueberry("Dole frozen wild blueberries", "Tahitian");
console.dir(wildMaineBlueberry);
```

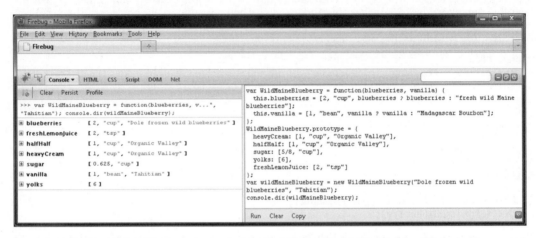

Figure 5–2. Churning a quart with Dole frozen wild blueberries and a Tahitian bean

Finally, let's be ding-dongs and forget to invoke WildMaineBlueberry() with new. As Figure 5–3 displays, WildMaineBlueberry() returns undefined, and there are now global variables named blueberries and vanilla. Great googly moogly!

```
var WildMaineBlueberry = function(blueberries, vanilla) {
  this.blueberries = [2, "cup", blueberries ? blueberries : "fresh wild Maine blueberries"];
  this.vanilla = [1, "bean", vanilla ? vanilla : "Madagascar Bourbon"];
};
WildMaineBlueberry.prototype = {
  heavyCream: [1, "cup", "Organic Valley"],
  halfHalf: [1, "cup", "Organic Valley"],
  sugar: [5/8, "cup"],
  yolks: [6],
  freshLemonJuice: [2, "tsp"]
};
var wildMaineBlueberry = WildMaineBlueberry();
typeof wildMaineBlueberry;
// "undefined"
blueberries;
// [2, "cup", "fresh wild Maine blueberries"]
vanilla;
// [1, "bean", "Madagascar Bourbon"]
```

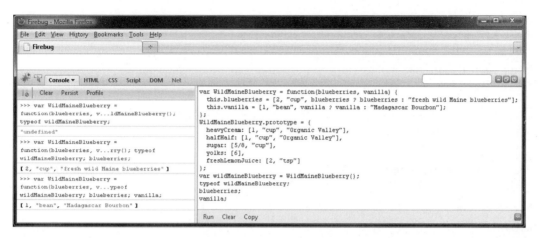

Figure 5–3. Don't forget to invoke constructors like WildMaineBlueberry() *with new, or you'll be creating or overwriting global variables.*

Now that you know how to create custom objects using a constructor, it's time to talk about inheritance. This will show you how to take advantage of constructors.

Classical Inheritance

Like Wild Maine Blueberry, many ice cream flavors begin with a vanilla base, which other ingredients are then added to. This is something we'd often like to do in JavaScript; in other words, if we have some object that has some desirable members, we can take that object and add other members to it to create another kind of object. The new object is based on the old one and has all the members of the old one, in addition to all the new ones we have added. This means we can place useful common members in one object and then base other, more specialized, objects on it, as well as make more specialized versions of useful objects in our code. The feature in JavaScript to do this is called *inheritance*, because the new object inherits the members of the old object.

Back to the ice cream to see inheritance in action: the very best vanilla ice cream is made by steeping a vanilla bean rather than adding vanilla extract. There are three types of vanilla beans. Madagascar Bourbon is the most common. I prefer those to the more floral Tahitian or intense Mexican beans.

So, let's create a VanillaBean() constructor that optionally takes a vanilla parameter, which would contain the bean type as a string. By way of the ?: operator, we'll default vanilla to "Madagascar Bourbon":

```
var VanillaBean = function(vanilla) {
  this.vanilla = [1, "bean", vanilla ? vanilla : "Madagascar Bourbon"];
}
```

Oftentimes I'll steep a stick of Saigon cinnamon with the vanilla bean. That works especially well for fruit flavors like peach or if you're serving the ice cream with pie. So, let's add an optional boolean parameter named cinnamon. By way of the && operator, VanillaBean() will add a cinnamon stick only if cinnamon is true. Note that insofar as && has higher precedence than =, we need to wrap the = expression in parentheses.

```
var VanillaBean = function(vanilla, cinnamon) {
```

149

```
  this.vanilla = [1, "bean", vanilla ? vanilla : "Madagascar Bourbon"];
  cinnamon && (this.cinnamon = [1, "stick", "Saigon"]);
};
```

Having defined VanillaBean(), we can now put add carved in stone members to VanillaBean.prototype:

```
var VanillaBean = function(vanilla, cinnamon) {
  this.vanilla = [1, "bean", vanilla ? vanilla : "Madagascar Bourbon"];
  cinnamon && (this.cinnamon = [1, "stick", "Saigon"]);
};
VanillaBean.prototype = {
  heavyCream: [1, "cup", "Organic Valley"],
  halfHalf: [2, "cup", "Organic Valley"],

  sugar: [5/8, "cup"],

  yolks: [6]
};
```

Having done so, let's create a VanillaBean() instance named vanilla, verifying our work with Figure 5–4. Note that vanilla has its own vanilla and cinnamon members but inherits other members from VanillaBean.prototype.

```
var VanillaBean = function(vanilla, cinnamon) {
  this.vanilla = [1, "bean", vanilla ? vanilla : "Madagascar Bourbon"];
  cinnamon && (this.cinnamon = [1, "stick", "Saigon"]);
};
VanillaBean.prototype = {
  heavyCream: [1, "cup", "Organic Valley"],
  halfHalf: [2, "cup", "Organic Valley"],
  sugar: [5/8, "cup"],
  yolks: [6]
};
var vanilla = new VanillaBean("Tahitian", true);
console.dir(vanilla);
```

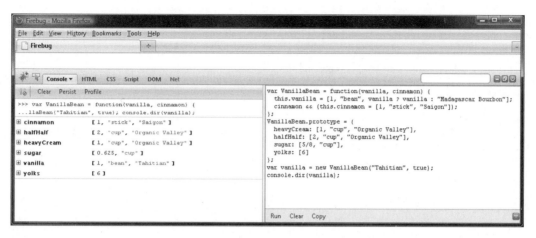

Figure 5–4. vanilla has its own vanilla and cinnamon members but inherits other members from VanillaBean.prototype.

Now let's create a Coffee() constructor that will inherit from VanillaBean(). Unless otherwise specified in an optional coffee parameter, we'll steep coarsely ground Starbucks Espresso with a Madagascar Bourbon vanilla bean.

```
var VanillaBean = function(vanilla, cinnamon) {
  this.vanilla = [1, "bean", vanilla ? vanilla : "Madagascar Bourbon"];
  cinnamon && (this.cinnamon = [1, "stick", "Saigon"]);
};
VanillaBean.prototype = {
  heavyCream: [1, "cup", "Organic Valley"],
  halfHalf: [2, "cup", "Organic Valley"],
  sugar: [5/8, "cup"],
  yolks: [6]
};
var Coffee = function(coffee) {
  this.coffee = coffee || [1/4, "cup, coarsely ground", "Starbucks Espresso"];
};
Coffee.prototype = new VanillaBean();
```

Note that Coffee.prototype contains just one member, vanilla, which contains [1, "bean", "Madagascar Bourbon"], because we didn't supply the optional cinnamon parameter to the Vanilla() constructor. So for Coffee(), the prototype chain would be as follows:

```
VanillaBean.prototype = {
  heavyCream: [1, "cup", "Organic Valley"],
  halfHalf: [2, "cup", "Organic Valley"],
  sugar: [5/8, "cup"],
  yolks: [6]
};
Coffee.prototype = {
  vanilla: [1, "bean", "Madagascar Bourbon"],
};
```

Having done so, let's create a Coffee() instance named coffee, verifying our work with Figure 5–5. Note that coffee has its own coffee member but inherits other members from Coffee.prototype and VanillaBean.prototype.

```
var VanillaBean = function(vanilla, cinnamon) {
  this.vanilla = [1, "bean", vanilla ? vanilla : "Madagascar Bourbon"];
  cinnamon && (this.cinnamon = [1, "stick", "Saigon"]);
};
VanillaBean.prototype = {
  heavyCream: [1, "cup", "Organic Valley"],
  halfHalf: [2, "cup", "Organic Valley"],
  sugar: [5/8, "cup"],
  yolks: [6]
};
var Coffee = function(coffee) {
  this.coffee = coffee || [1/4, "cup, coarsely ground", "Starbucks Espresso"];
};
Coffee.prototype = new VanillaBean();
var coffee = new Coffee();
console.dir(coffee);
```

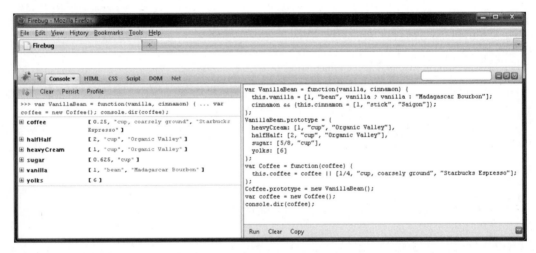

Figure 5–5. coffee has its own coffee member but inherits other members from Coffee.prototype and VanillaBean.prototype.

Now let's create a Chocolate() constructor that also inherits members from VanillaBean(). Optional cocoa and bittersweet parameters will allow us to specify Dutch cocoa and bittersweet chocolate other than Callebaut, though Callebaut will be substituted in different quantities for each parameter if they are missing. We'll then set the prototype, as we did for Coffee(). However, we'll add a yolks member to override the one on VanillaBean.prototype, because chocolate ice cream takes fewer yolks than vanilla:

```
var VanillaBean = function(vanilla, cinnamon) {
  this.vanilla = [1, "bean", vanilla ? vanilla : "Madagascar Bourbon"];
  cinnamon && (this.cinnamon = [1, "stick", "Saigon"]);
};
```

```
VanillaBean.prototype = {
  heavyCream: [1, "cup", "Organic Valley"],
  halfHalf: [2, "cup", "Organic Valley"],
  sugar: [5/8, "cup"],
  yolks: [6]
};
var Coffee = function(coffee) {
  this.coffee = coffee || [1/4, "cup, coarsely ground", "Starbucks Espresso"];
};
Coffee.prototype = new VanillaBean();

var Chocolate = function(cocoa, bittersweet) {

  this.cocoa = cocoa || [3/16, "cup", "Callebaut"];

  this.bittersweet = bittersweet || [1 + 1/2, "cup", "Callebaut"];
};
Chocolate.prototype = new VanillaBean();
Chocolate.prototype.yolks = [4];
```

Having done so, let's create a Chocolate() instance named chocolate, verifying our work with Figure 5–6. Note that chocolate has its own cocoa and bittersweet members and inherits other members from Chocolate.prototype and VanillaBean.prototype.

```
var VanillaBean = function(vanilla, cinnamon) {
  this.vanilla = [1, "bean", vanilla ? vanilla : "Madagascar Bourbon"];
  cinnamon && (this.cinnamon = [1, "stick", "Saigon"]);
};
VanillaBean.prototype = {
  heavyCream: [1, "cup", "Organic Valley"],
  halfHalf: [2, "cup", "Organic Valley"],
  sugar: [5/8, "cup"],
  yolks: [6]
};
var Coffee = function(coffee) {
  this.coffee = coffee || [1/4, "cup, coarsely ground", "Starbucks Espresso"];
};
Coffee.prototype = new VanillaBean();

var Chocolate = function(cocoa, bittersweet) {
  this.cocoa = cocoa || [3/16, "cup", "Callebaut"];
  this.bittersweet = bittersweet || [1 + 1/2, "cup", "Callebaut"];
};
Chocolate.prototype = new VanillaBean();
Chocolate.prototype.yolks = [4];
var chocolate = new Chocolate([1/4, "cup", "Bensdorp"]);
console.dir(chocolate);
```

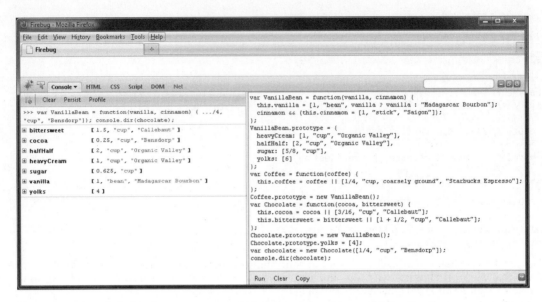

Figure 5–6. *chocolate has its own cocoa and bittersweet members and inherits other members from*
`Chocolate.prototype` *and* `VanillaBean.prototype`.

Though it's not in my top 10, Ben & Jerry's Mint Chocolate Chunk is pretty good, so let's define a
`MintChocolateChunk()` constructor and chain `MintChocolateChunk.prototype` to `Chocolate.prototype` by
invoking `Chocolate()` with the new operator. Note that you would steep the mint leaves with the vanilla
pod and seeds, later removing both by straining through a fine mesh sieve. Note too that you would add
the Callebaut bittersweet chunks at the very end of the churning phase.

```
var VanillaBean = function(vanilla, cinnamon) {
  this.vanilla = [1, "bean", vanilla ? vanilla : "Madagascar Bourbon"];
  cinnamon && (this.cinnamon = [1, "stick", "Saigon"]);
};
VanillaBean.prototype = {
  heavyCream: [1, "cup", "Organic Valley"],
  halfHalf: [2, "cup", "Organic Valley"],
  sugar: [5/8, "cup"],
  yolks: [6]
};
var Coffee = function(coffee) {
  this.coffee = coffee || [1/4, "cup, coarsely ground", "Starbucks Espresso"];
};
Coffee.prototype = new VanillaBean();
var Chocolate = function(cocoa, bittersweet) {
  this.cocoa = cocoa || [3/16, "cup", "Callebaut"];
  this.bittersweet = bittersweet || [1 + 1/2, "cup", "Callebaut"];
};
Chocolate.prototype = new VanillaBean();
Chocolate.prototype.yolks = [4];
```

```
var MintChocolateChunk = function(mint) {
  this.mint = mint || [1, "cup", "fresh mint leaves"];
};
MintChocolateChunk.prototype = new Chocolate();
```

Now let's add a vanilla member to override `Chocolate.prototype.vanilla`. Insofar as we're chipping the Callebaut bittersweet chocolate, we need only 1 cup, rather than 1 1/2 cups. So, let's modify the first element in the `MintChocolateChunk.prototype.bittersweet` array. Finally, we don't want the cocoa, so pass that member to the `delete` operator, which we covered in Chapter 3.

```
var VanillaBean = function(vanilla, cinnamon) {
  this.vanilla = [1, "bean", vanilla ? vanilla : "Madagascar Bourbon"];
  cinnamon && (this.cinnamon = [1, "stick", "Saigon"]);
};
VanillaBean.prototype = {
  heavyCream: [1, "cup", "Organic Valley"],
  halfHalf: [2, "cup", "Organic Valley"],
  sugar: [5/8, "cup"],
  yolks: [6]
};
var Coffee = function(coffee) {
  this.coffee = coffee || [1/4, "cup, coarsely ground", "Starbucks Espresso"];
};
Coffee.prototype = new VanillaBean();
var Chocolate = function(cocoa, bittersweet) {
  this.cocoa = cocoa || [3/16, "cup", "Callebaut"];
  this.bittersweet = bittersweet || [1 + 1/2, "cup", "Callebaut"];
};
Chocolate.prototype = new VanillaBean();
Chocolate.prototype.yolks = [4];

var MintChocolateChunk = function(mint) {
  this.mint = mint || [1, "cup", "fresh mint leaves"];
};
MintChocolateChunk.prototype = new Chocolate();
MintChocolateChunk.prototype.vanilla = [1/3, "bean", "Madagascar Bourbon"];
MintChocolateChunk.prototype.bittersweet[0] = 1;
delete MintChocolateChunk.prototype.cocoa;
```

Having done so, let's create a `MintChocolateChunk()` instance named `mintChocolateChunk`, verifying our work with Figure 5–7. Note that `mintChocolateChunk` has its own mint member and inherits other members from `MintChocolateChunk.prototype`, `Chocolate.prototype`, and `VanillaBean.prototype`.

```
var VanillaBean = function(vanilla, cinnamon) {
  this.vanilla = [1, "bean", vanilla ? vanilla : "Madagascar Bourbon"];
  cinnamon && (this.cinnamon = [1, "stick", "Saigon"]);
};
VanillaBean.prototype = {
  heavyCream: [1, "cup", "Organic Valley"],
  halfHalf: [2, "cup", "Organic Valley"],
  sugar: [5/8, "cup"],
  yolks: [6]
};
var Coffee = function(coffee) {
```

```
    this.coffee = coffee || [1/4, "cup, coarsely ground", "Starbucks Espresso"];
};
Coffee.prototype = new VanillaBean();
var Chocolate = function(cocoa, bittersweet) {
    this.cocoa = cocoa || [3/16, "cup", "Callebaut"];
    this.bittersweet = bittersweet || [1 + 1/2, "cup", "Callebaut"];
};
Chocolate.prototype = new VanillaBean();
Chocolate.prototype.yolks = [4];

var MintChocolateChunk = function(mint) {
    this.mint = mint || [1, "cup", "fresh mint leaves"];
};
MintChocolateChunk.prototype = new Chocolate();
MintChocolateChunk.prototype.vanilla = [1/3, "bean", "Madagascar Bourbon"];
MintChocolateChunk.prototype.bittersweet[0] = 1;
delete MintChocolateChunk.prototype.cocoa;
var mintChocolateChunk = new MintChocolateChunk();
console.dir(mintChocolateChunk);
```

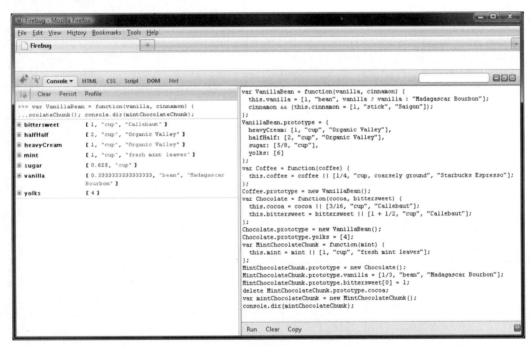

Figure 5–7. mintChocolateChunk *has its own mint member and inherits other members from*
MintChocolateChunk.prototype, Chocolate.prototype, *and* VanillaBean.prototype.

Determining Which Type or Types an Object Is an Instance Of

The prototype chain, such as those we saw earlier, determines which type or types an object such as mintChocolateChunk is an instance of, that is, what constructor or constructors an object inherits members from. To figure this out, you would use the aptly named instanceof operator, which we didn't cover in Chapter 3. Note that instanceof, like typeof, is in lowercase, not camel case.

Let's query JavaScript in regard to what types mintChocolateChunk is an instance of with instanceof. Note that the second operand to instanceof is the identifier for the constructor, so don't append the () operator. Note too that like every object, mintChocolateChunk is an instance of the Object() constructor, from which it inherits methods like valueOf() and toString(). So as Figure 5–8 displays, mintChocolateChunk is an instance of four types, which is to say it inherits members from four constructors.

```
var VanillaBean = function(vanilla, cinnamon) {
  this.vanilla = [1, "bean", vanilla ? vanilla : "Madagascar Bourbon"];
  cinnamon && (this.cinnamon = [1, "stick", "Saigon"]);
};
VanillaBean.prototype = {
  heavyCream: [1, "cup", "Organic Valley"],
  halfHalf: [2, "cup", "Organic Valley"],
  sugar: [5/8, "cup"],
  yolks: [6]
};
var Coffee = function(coffee) {
  this.coffee = coffee || [1/4, "cup, coarsely ground", "Starbucks Espresso"];
};
Coffee.prototype = new VanillaBean();
var Chocolate = function(cocoa, bittersweet) {
  this.cocoa = cocoa || [3/16, "cup", "Callebaut"];
  this.bittersweet = bittersweet || [1 + 1/2, "cup", "Callebaut"];
};
Chocolate.prototype = new VanillaBean();
Chocolate.prototype.yolks = [4];
var MintChocolateChunk = function(mint) {
  this.mint = mint || [1, "cup", "fresh mint leaves"];
};
MintChocolateChunk.prototype = new Chocolate();
MintChocolateChunk.prototype.vanilla = [1/3, "bean", "Madagascar Bourbon"];
MintChocolateChunk.prototype.bittersweet[0] = 1;
delete MintChocolateChunk.prototype.cocoa;
var mintChocolateChunk = new MintChocolateChunk();


mintChocolateChunk instanceof MintChocolateChunk;

// true
mintChocolateChunk instanceof Chocolate;
// true
mintChocolateChunk instanceof Coffee;
// false
mintChocolateChunk instanceof VanillaBean;
// true
mintChocolateChunk instanceof Object;
// true
```

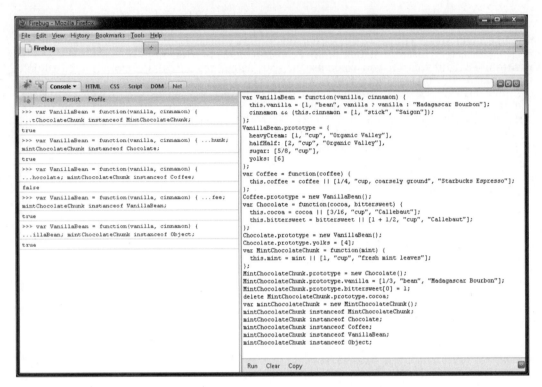

Figure 5–8. *mintChocolateChunk is an instance of four types, which is to say it inherits members from four constructors.*

Inherited Members Are Shared Not Copied

It's important to note inherited members are shared among instances. So if you recall from Chapter 3, the === will return true for a member that two instances share, even a member that is an object, array, or function. To illustrate the point, let's chain && comparisons in order to confirm that instances of VanillaBean, Coffee, Chocolate, and MintChocolateChunk share the heavyCream array, [1, "cup", "Organic Valley"], verifying our work with Figure 5–9:

```
var VanillaBean = function(vanilla, cinnamon) {
  this.vanilla = [1, "bean", vanilla ? vanilla : "Madagascar Bourbon"];
  cinnamon && (this.cinnamon = [1, "stick", "Saigon"]);
};
VanillaBean.prototype = {
  heavyCream: [1, "cup", "Organic Valley"],
  halfHalf: [2, "cup", "Organic Valley"],
  sugar: [5/8, "cup"],
  yolks: [6]
};
var Coffee = function(coffee) {
  this.coffee = coffee || [1/4, "cup, coarsely ground", "Starbucks Espresso"];
```

```
};
Coffee.prototype = new VanillaBean();
var Chocolate = function(cocoa, bittersweet) {
  this.cocoa = cocoa || [3/16, "cup", "Callebaut"];
  this.bittersweet = bittersweet || [1 + 1/2, "cup", "Callebaut"];
};
Chocolate.prototype = new VanillaBean();
Chocolate.prototype.yolks = [4];
var MintChocolateChunk = function(mint) {
  this.mint = mint || [1, "cup", "fresh mint leaves"];
};
MintChocolateChunk.prototype = new Chocolate();
MintChocolateChunk.prototype.vanilla = [1/3, "bean", "Madagascar Bourbon"];
MintChocolateChunk.prototype.bittersweet[0] = 1;
delete MintChocolateChunk.prototype.cocoa;

var vanilla = new VanillaBean("Tahitian", true);

var coffee = new Coffee();
var chocolate = new Chocolate([1/4, "cup", "Bensdorp"]);
var mintChocolateChunk = new MintChocolateChunk();

vanilla.heavyCream === coffee.heavyCream &&
  vanilla.heavyCream === chocolate.heavyCream &&
  vanilla.heavyCream === mintChocolateChunk.heavyCream &&
  mintChocolateChunk.heavyCream === coffee.heavyCream &&
  coffee.heavyCream === chocolate.heavyCream &&
  mintChocolateChunk.heavyCream === chocolate.heavyCream;
// true
```

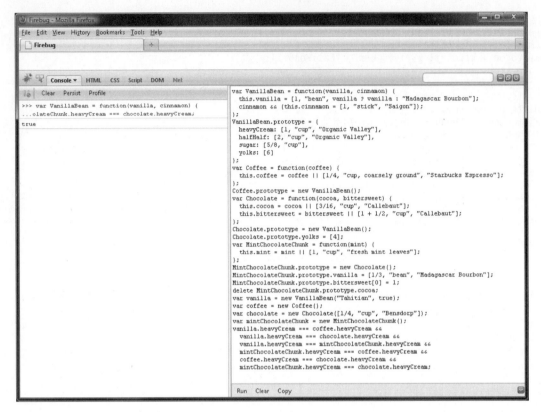

Figure 5–9. Any instance of VanillaBean, Coffee, Chocolate, or MintChocolateChunk shares the heavyCream array, [1, "cup", "Organic Valley"].

What are the implications of sharing inherited members? Changing an inherited member immediately changes all instances, both old and new, that inherit it. If you're thinking this would make it easier to look after your code when something has to change, I owe you a Smiley Cookie!

Modifying New and Past Instances of a Type

Now then, if we modify, add, or delete a member in MintChocolateChunk.prototype, Chocolate.prototype, Coffee.prototype, or VanillaBean.prototype, the change will be evident in any instance, both new and old, that inherits the member. So for example, if we change MintChocolateChunk.prototype.bittersweet[2] from "Callebaut" to "Lindt" after creating mintChocolateChunk, its bittersweet member reflects the change as Figure 5–10 displays:

```
var VanillaBean = function(vanilla, cinnamon) {
  this.vanilla = [1, "bean", vanilla ? vanilla : "Madagascar Bourbon"];
  cinnamon && (this.cinnamon = [1, "stick", "Saigon"]);
};
VanillaBean.prototype = {
  heavyCream: [1, "cup", "Organic Valley"],
```

```
  halfHalf: [2, "cup", "Organic Valley"],
  sugar: [5/8, "cup"],
  yolks: [6]
};
var Coffee = function(coffee) {
  this.coffee = coffee || [1/4, "cup, coarsely ground", "Starbucks Espresso"];
};
Coffee.prototype = new VanillaBean();
var Chocolate = function(cocoa, bittersweet) {
  this.cocoa = cocoa || [3/16, "cup", "Callebaut"];
  this.bittersweet = bittersweet || [1 + 1/2, "cup", "Callebaut"];
};
Chocolate.prototype = new VanillaBean();
Chocolate.prototype.yolks = [4];
var MintChocolateChunk = function(mint) {
  this.mint = mint || [1, "cup", "fresh mint leaves"];
};
MintChocolateChunk.prototype = new Chocolate();
MintChocolateChunk.prototype.vanilla = [1/3, "bean", "Madagascar Bourbon"];
MintChocolateChunk.prototype.bittersweet[0] = 1;
delete MintChocolateChunk.prototype.cocoa;
var mintChocolateChunk = new MintChocolateChunk();
console.dir(mintChocolateChunk);
```

MintChocolateChunk.prototype.bittersweet[2] = "Lindt";
console.dir(mintChocolateChunk);

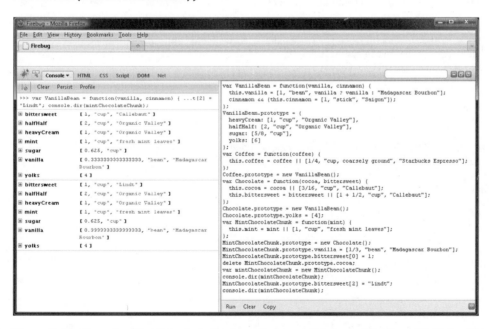

Figure 5–10. Changing MintChocolateChunk.prototype.bittersweet[2] from "Callebaut" to "Lindt" after creating mintChocolateChunk still changes its bittersweet member.

Now let's add four chopped Heath Bars to VanillaBean.prototype in order to change vanilla to Ben & Jerry's Vanilla Heath Bar Crunch and coffee to Ben & Jerry' Coffee Heath Bar Crunch. However, as Figure 5–11 displays, by doing so we also wind up with Chocolate Heath Bar Crunch and Mint Chocolate Chip Heath Bar Crunch, because everything that inherits from VanillaBean gets the heathBars member!

```javascript
var VanillaBean = function(vanilla, cinnamon) {
  this.vanilla = [1, "bean", vanilla ? vanilla : "Madagascar Bourbon"];
  cinnamon && (this.cinnamon = [1, "stick", "Saigon"]);
};
VanillaBean.prototype = {
  heavyCream: [1, "cup", "Organic Valley"],
  halfHalf: [2, "cup", "Organic Valley"],
  sugar: [5/8, "cup"],
  yolks: [6]
};
var Coffee = function(coffee) {
  this.coffee = coffee || [1/4, "cup, coarsely ground", "Starbucks Espresso"];
};
Coffee.prototype = new VanillaBean();
var Chocolate = function(cocoa, bittersweet) {
  this.cocoa = cocoa || [3/16, "cup", "Callebaut"];
  this.bittersweet = bittersweet || [1 + 1/2, "cup", "Callebaut"];
};
Chocolate.prototype = new VanillaBean();
Chocolate.prototype.yolks = [4];
var MintChocolateChunk = function(mint) {
  this.mint = mint || [1, "cup", "fresh mint leaves"];
};
MintChocolateChunk.prototype = new Chocolate();
MintChocolateChunk.prototype.vanilla = [1/3, "bean", "Madagascar Bourbon"];
MintChocolateChunk.prototype.bittersweet[0] = 1;
delete MintChocolateChunk.prototype.cocoa;
var vanilla = new VanillaBean();
var coffee = new Coffee();
var chocolate = new Chocolate();
var mintChocolateChunk = new MintChocolateChunk();

VanillaBean.prototype.heathBars = [4, "Heath Bars, chopped in chunks"];
console.dir(vanilla);
console.dir(coffee);
console.dir(chocolate);
console.dir(mintChocolateChunk);
```

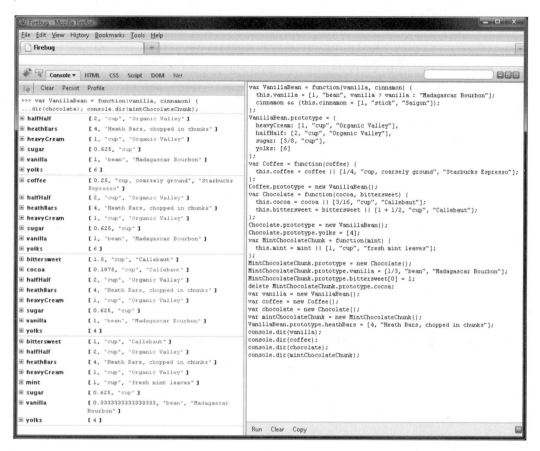

Figure 5–11. Adding four Heath Bars *to* VanillaBean.prototype *has unintended effects, which are that the three other objects also include* Heath Bars.

Sharing a Prototype but Forgoing the Chain

One drawback of chaining prototypes is that own members turn into inherited members. For example, linking MintChocolateChunk.prototype to Chocolate.prototype by invoking Chocolate() put cocoa and bittersweet members on MintChocolateChunk.prototype, so we had to delete MintChocolateChunk.prototype.cocoa and modify MintChocolateChunk.prototype.bittersweet[0].

One way around this bugaboo would be to have two constructors share a prototype object, thereby dispensing with the chain link. Let's look at an example: to make blueberry, strawberry, mango, or raspberry ice cream, I'll typically puree one of the two cups of fresh fruit. Then cut the half & half from 2 cups to 1 and the yolks from 6 to 3. With this in mind, we can have constructors for blueberry and strawberry ice cream share a parent prototype object, as shown next.

Note that fraises des bois are smaller, sweeter, and more flavorful than traditional strawberries. Create an instance of Blueberry() and Strawberry(), verifying your work with Figure 5–12.

```
var Berry = function() {}
Berry.prototype = {
  heavyCream: [1, "cup", "Organic Valley"],
  halfHalf: [1, "cup", "Organic Valley"],
  sugar: [5/8, "cup"],
  yolks: [3],
  vanilla: [1, "bean", "Madagascar Bourbon"]
};

var Blueberry = function(blueberry, lemon) {
  this.blueberry = [2, "cup", blueberry ? blueberry : "Maine wild blueberries"];
  this.freshLemonJuice = [2, "tsp", lemon ? lemon : "Meyer"];
};
Blueberry.prototype = Berry.prototype;

var Strawberry = function(strawberry) {
  this.strawberry = [2, "cup", strawberry ? strawberry : "fraises des bois"];
};
Strawberry.prototype = Berry.prototype;
var blueberry = new Blueberry();
var strawberry = new Strawberry();
console.dir(blueberry);
console.dir(strawberry);
```

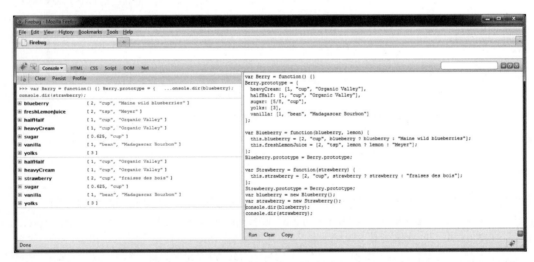

Figure 5–12. *There's no prototype chain link between* Strawberry.prototype *and* Blueberry.prototype.

So, forgoing the prototype chain link prevented our having to delete
Strawberry.prototype.blueberry and Strawberry.prototype.freshLemonJuice members as in the
following sample and Figure 5–13, where the strawberry recipe is based on the blueberry recipe:

```
var Blueberry = function(blueberry, lemon) {
  this.blueberry = [2, "cup", blueberry ? blueberry : "Maine wild blueberries"];
  this.freshLemonJuice = [2, "tsp", lemon ? lemon : "Meyer"];
```

```
};
Blueberry.prototype = {
  heavyCream: [1, "cup", "Organic Valley"],
  halfHalf: [1, "cup", "Organic Valley"],
  sugar: [5/8, "cup"],
  yolks: [3],
  vanilla: [1, "bean", "Madagascar Bourbon"]
};
var Strawberry = function(strawberry) {
  this.strawberry = [2, "cup", strawberry ? strawberry : "fraises des bois"];
};
Strawberry.prototype = new Blueberry();
delete Strawberry.prototype.blueberry;
delete Strawberry.prototype.freshLemonJuice;
var blueberry = new Blueberry();
var strawberry = new Strawberry();
console.dir(blueberry);
console.dir(strawberry);
```

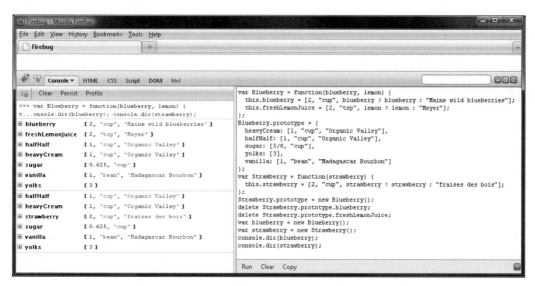

Figure 5–13. Having to delete unwanted Strawberry.prototype.blueberry and
Strawberry.prototype.freshLemonJuice members

That's the good news. Now for the bad. Since Blueberry.prototype and Strawberry.prototype are the same object, there's no way to add, delete, or modify inherited members for Strawberry() without identically changing inherited embers for Blueberry(), and vice versa. To illustrate the point, try the following sample, verifying your work with Figure 5–14:

```
var Berry = function() {}
Berry.prototype = {
  heavyCream: [1, "cup", "Organic Valley"],
  halfHalf: [1, "cup", "Organic Valley"],
  sugar: [5/8, "cup"],
```

```
  yolks: [3],
  vanilla: [1, "bean", "Madagascar Bourbon"]
};

var Blueberry = function(blueberry, lemon) {
  this.blueberry = [2, "cup", blueberry ? blueberry : "Maine wild blueberries"];
  this.freshLemonJuice = [2, "tsp", lemon ? lemon : "Meyer"];
};
Blueberry.prototype = Berry.prototype;

var Strawberry = function(strawberry) {
  this.strawberry = [2, "cup", strawberry ? strawberry : "fraises des bois"];
};
Strawberry.prototype = Berry.prototype;
var blueberry = new Blueberry();
var strawberry = new Strawberry();
Blueberry.prototype.cinnamon = [1, "stick", "Saigon"];
console.dir(blueberry);
console.dir(strawberry);
```

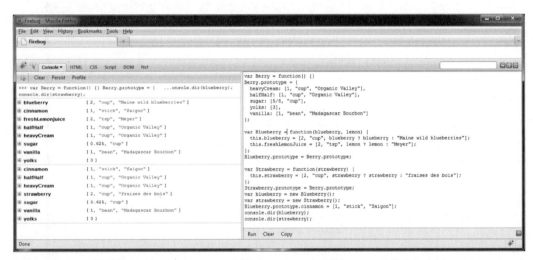

Figure 5–14. Adding a cinnamon member to Blueberry.prototype is no different from adding it to Strawberry.prototype or Berry.prototype since they're the same object.

Adding an Empty Chain Link

Both of the previous patterns have a downside. Chaining prototypes turns own members into inherited members, adding those to the child constructor's prototype. Forgoing the prototype chain solves that problem but then effectively prevents us from adding, deleting, or modifying prototype members.

Hmm. Would there be a way for a child constructor to inherit members from a parent constructor's prototype yet have its own, blank prototype to add inherited members to?

Yup, but you'll need to be ten toes in for a few moments to get it. First we'll create a helper function named extend that takes two parameters:

- child will be the constructor we want to have a blank prototype.

- parent will be a constructor we want the child to inherit members from.

```
var extend = function (child, parent) {
};
```

Now we'll create a constructor named Proxy() with an empty code block. In this way, when we invoke Proxy() with new, it will return an empty object.

```
var extend = function (child, parent) {
  var Proxy = function () {};
};
```

Now just as we did for Strawberry.prototype and Blueberry.prototype, we'll have Proxy.prototype refer to parent.prototype. That is to say, there's no prototype chain between Proxy.prototype and parent.prototype. Rather, they're just two names for the same object.

```
var extend = function (child, parent) {
  var Proxy = function () {};
  Proxy.prototype = parent.prototype;
};
```

Now just as we linked MintChocolateChunk.prototype to Chocolate.prototype with the assignment expression MintChocolateChunk.prototype = new Chocolate(), we'll link child.prototype to parent.prototype with the assignment expression child.prototype = new Proxy(). Note that in terms of creating a link from child.prototype to parent.prototype, the expressions new parent() and new Proxy() would be equivalent because parent.prototype and Proxy.prototype refer to the same object. However, since Proxy() has an empty body, it returns an empty object linked to parent.prototype. It's that empty object that is assigned to child.prototype.

```
var extend = function (child, parent) {
  var Proxy = function () {};
  Proxy.prototype = parent.prototype;
  child.prototype = new Proxy();
};
```

Now it's inefficient to create Proxy() every time we invoke extend(), so by way of a self-invoking function, we'll save Proxy() to a closure. Just nod knowingly for now; we'll cover self-invoking functions and closures in Chapter 6.

```
var extend = (function () {
  var Proxy = function () {};
  return function (child, parent) {
    Proxy.prototype = parent.prototype;
    child.prototype = new Proxy();
  }
}());
```

Chaining prototypes or using extend() overwrites the default prototype and its constructor member, which simply refers to the function that constructed the object, so let's add a constructor member to child.prototype:

```
var extend = (function () {
  var Proxy = function () {};
  return function (child, parent) {
    Proxy.prototype = parent.prototype;
```

```
    child.prototype = new Proxy();
    child.prototype.constructor = child;
  }
}());
```

The downside of doing so is that while the default constructor member would not be enumerated in a for in loop, the one you add by hand would be enumerated. For this reason, you may want to forgo adding a constructor member, but I have added it here so you can say you've seen one in action. Note that JavaScript does not need the constructor member for the prototype chain, instanceof operator, or any feature to work.

A common practice is to add a static member to child (not to child.prototype) referring to parent.prototype. Doing so provides a way to query a type's parent (known as its *superclass*). That's not something you'll do as a beginner. Still, you'll see it around, so let's add one named donor:

```
var extend = (function () {
  var Proxy = function () {};
  return function (child, parent) {
    Proxy.prototype = parent.prototype;
    child.prototype = new Proxy();
    child.prototype.constructor = child;
    child.donor = parent.prototype;
  }
}());
```

Now that we have extend() written, let's use it to create a blank prototype for a CherryGarcia() constructor that is chained to Strawberry.prototype. In this way, instances of CherryGarcia will inherit members from Strawberry.prototype but not the strawberry member created in the body of Strawberry(). Cherries are sweeter than strawberries, so let's override Strawberry.prototype.sugar by adding a sugar member to CherryGarcia.prototype.

Now for the moment of truth. Create instances of Strawberry() and CherryGarcia(), passing them to Firebug's console.dir() method. Then verify your work with Figure 5–15.

Cherry Garcia. Mmmh.

```
var extend = (function () {
  var Proxy = function () {};
  return function (child, parent) {
    Proxy.prototype = parent.prototype;
    child.prototype = new Proxy();
    child.prototype.constructor = child;
    child.donor = parent.prototype;
  }
}());
var Strawberry = function(strawberry) {
  this.strawberry = [2, "cup", strawberry ? strawberry : "fraises des bois"];
};
Strawberry.prototype = {
  heavyCream: [1, "cup", "Organic Valley"],
  halfHalf: [1, "cup", "Organic Valley"],
  sugar: [5/8, "cup"],
  yolks: [3],

  vanilla: [1, "bean", "Madagascar Bourbon"]

};
var CherryGarcia = function(cherry, bittersweet) {
```

```
    this.cherries = [2, "cup, pitted and halved", cherry ? cherry : "Bing"];
    this.bittersweet = [1, "cup, coarsely chopped", bittersweet ? bittersweet : "Callebaut"];
};

extend(CherryGarcia, Strawberry);

CherryGarcia.prototype.sugar = [9/16, "cup"];
var strawberry = new Strawberry();
var cherryGarcia = new CherryGarcia();
console.dir(strawberry);
console.dir(cherryGarcia);
```

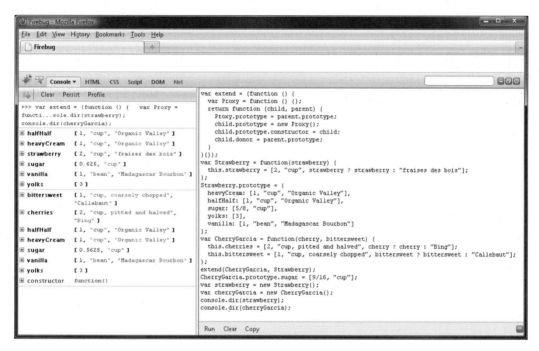

Figure 5–15. cherryGarcia inherits members only from Strawberry.prototype.

Stealing a Constructor

With extend(), we can chain the prototype of one constructor to the prototype of another. But what if we want to fully duplicate a constructor? In other words, say we want to inherit members from its prototype and borrow all its other members that aren't in the prototype. We'd do the former with extend() and the latter invoking the parent constructor's apply() method from within the child constructor, passing this and an array of parameters.

For example, if we wanted to make CherryGarcia() be a Cherry() clone that adds Callebaut bittersweet chunks, we'd chain CherryGarcia.prototype to Cherry.prototype with extend(). Then invoke Cherry.apply() from within CherryGarcia(), passing this and the cherry parameter as in the following sample and Figure 5–16:

```
var extend = (function () {
  var Proxy = function () {};
  return function (child, parent) {
    Proxy.prototype = parent.prototype;
    child.prototype = new Proxy();
    child.prototype.constructor = child;
    child.donor = parent.prototype;
  }
}());
var Cherry = function(cherry) {
  this.cherries = [2, "cup, pitted and halved", cherry ? cherry : "Bing"];
};
Cherry.prototype = {
  heavyCream: [1, "cup", "Organic Valley"],
  halfHalf: [1, "cup", "Organic Valley"],
  sugar: [9/16, "cup"],
  yolks: [3],

  vanilla: [1, "bean", "Madagascar Bourbon"]

};
var CherryGarcia = function(cherry, bittersweet) {
  Cherry.apply(this, [cherry]);
  this.bittersweet = [1, "cup, coarsely chopped", bittersweet ? bittersweet : "Callebaut"];
};
extend(CherryGarcia, Cherry);

var cherry = new Cherry();

var cherryGarcia = new CherryGarcia();
console.dir(cherry);
console.dir(cherryGarcia);
```

Figure 5–16. CherryGarcia( ) is a Cherry( ) clone that adds Callebaut bittersweet chunks.

Prototypal Inheritance

Oftentimes you will want to create one object that is pretty similar to another. The techniques we saw previously can do this, but there was a fair amount of work involved when writing all the constructors and chaining their prototypes if there are lots of similarities between the objects. For circumstances like this, we'll forgo the previous classical inheritance and turn to prototypal inheritance instead, which clones from prototypes, rather than using inheritance such as that we saw earlier. Though ECMAScript 5 defines an Object.create() function for prototypal inheritance, no browsers yet implement it. So, we'll write our own prototypal inheritance function named clone() while we wait for Firefox, Safari, Opera and eventually Internet Explorer to implement Object.create().

■ **Note** The beta versions of the next major releases for Internet Explorer, Firefox, Chrome, and Safari all support Object.create(), so it might not be so long before it's in general use.

clone() works with one parameter named donor, which contains the object you want to clone. Similar to extend(), we'll create an empty constructor function named Proxy(). Unlike extend(), we'll set Proxy.prototype to donor rather than to donor.prototype and return an empty object, which will inherit both own and inherited members from donor. We'll then add whatever additional members we need to the empty object.

```
var clone = function (donor) {
  var Proxy = function () {};
  Proxy.prototype = donor;
  return new Proxy();
};
```

171

So, say we have a quart of banana ice cream and want to make a quart of Ben & Jerry's Chunky Monkey based on the contents of the banana ice cream. We'd do so with the help of clone() as in the following sample and Figure 5–17:

```
var clone = function (donor) {
  var Proxy = function () {};
  Proxy.prototype = donor;
  return new Proxy();
};
var banana = {

  heavyCream: [1, "cup", "Organic Valley"],

  halfHalf: [1, "cup", "Organic Valley"],
  sugar: [9/16, "cup"],
  yolks: [3],
  banana: [1 + 1/2, "cup, puréed"],
  coconutMilk: [1/4, "cup"],
  lemon: [2, "tsp", "freshly juiced Meyer lemon"],
  vanilla: [1, "bean", "Madagascar Bourbon"]
};
var chunkyMonkey = clone(banana);
chunkyMonkey.walnuts = [3/4, "cup, coarsely chopped"];
chunkyMonkey.bittersweet = [1, "cup, coarsely chopped", "Callebaut"];
console.dir(banana);
console.dir(chunkyMonkey);
```

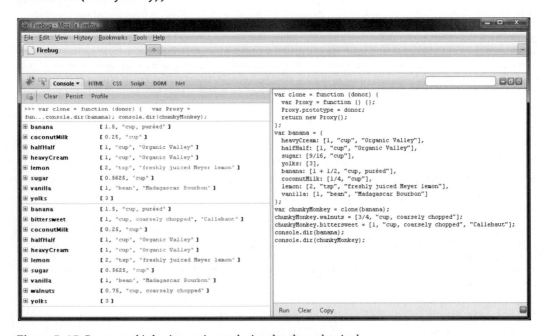

Figure 5–17. Prototypal inheritance is much simpler than classical.

Now then, `Object.create()` will take an optional second parameter when it eventually arrives, which is an object containing members to add to the clone. So, let's define a second function named `emulate()` that does the same thing while we wait for better days:

```
var emulate = function (donor, more) {
  var Proxy = function () {}, child, m;
  Proxy.prototype = donor;
  child = new Proxy();
  for (var m in more) {
    child[m] = more[m];
  }
  return child;
};
```

Now say we've made a quart of chocolate ice cream and want to make a quart of Ben & Jerry's New York Super Fudge Chunk. We can do so by passing the chocolate quart plus the additional ingredients to `emulate()`. Try it, verifying your work with Figure 5–18:

```
var emulate = function (donor, more) {
  var Proxy = function () {}, child, m;
  Proxy.prototype = donor;
  child = new Proxy();
  for (var m in more) {
    child[m] = more[m];
  }
  return child;
};
var chocolate = {
  heavyCream: [1, "cup", "Organic Valley"],

  halfHalf: [2, "cup", "Organic Valley"],

  sugar: [5/8, "cup"],
  yolks: [6],
  cocoa: [3/8, "cup", "Callebaut, Dutch process"],
  vanilla: [1, "bean", "Madagascar Bourbon"]
};
var newYorkSuperFudgeChunk = emulate(chocolate, {
  pecans: [1/4, "cup, coarsely chopped"],

  walnuts: [1/4, "cup, coarsely chopped"],

  almonds: [1/4, "cup, coarsely chopped"],
  whiteChocolate: [1/3, "cup, coarsely chopped", "Callebaut"],
  bittersweetChocolate: [1/3, "cup, coarsely chopped", "Callebaut"]
});
console.dir(chocolate);
console.dir(newYorkSuperFudgeChunk);
```

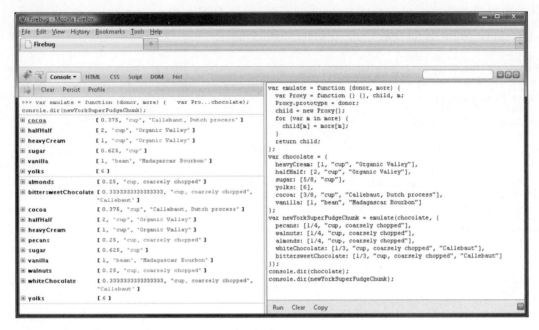

Figure 5–18. Adding members in prototypal inheritance

Cloning Members

Another way to clone an object is to do a deep copy of its members. Unlike `emulate()` shown earlier, which does a shallow copy of members (that is, members of the object type are copied by reference), a deep copy recursively clones those. Let's write a helper function named `cloneMembers()` that will clone an object by doing a deep copy of its members, deferring the explanation of recursion until Chapter 6.

```
var cloneMembers = function (donor, donee) {
  donee = donee || {};
  for (var m in donor) {
    if (typeof donor[m] === "object" && donor[m] !== null) {
      donee[m] = typeof donor[m].pop === "function" ? [] : {};
      cloneMembers(donor[m], donee[m]);
    } else {
      donee[m] = donor[m];
    }
  }
  return donee;
};
```

Now if we want to make a quart of Ben & Jerry's Coffee Heath Bar Crunch from Vanilla Heath Bar Crunch, we'd clone the latter by doing a deep copy of its members. Then add a `coffee` member, verifying our work with Figure 5–19. Note that `coffeeHeathBarCrunch` does not inherit members from `vanillaHeathBarCrunch` via the prototype chain. Rather, `coffeeHeathBarCrunch` has deep copies of `vanillaHeathBarCrunch` members. So, no prototype chain this time.

```
var cloneMembers = function (donor, donee) {
  donee = donee || {};
  for (var m in donor) {
    if (typeof donor[m] === "object" && donor[m] !== null) {
      donee[m] = typeof donor[m].pop === "function" ? [] : {};
      cloneMembers(donor[m], donee[m]);
    } else {
      donee[m] = donor[m];
    }
  }
  return donee;
};
var vanillaHeathBarCrunch = {
  heavyCream: [1, "cup", "Organic Valley"],
  halfHalf: [2, "cup", "Organic Valley"],
  sugar: [5/8, "cup"],
  yolks: [6],
  heathBars: [4, "bars, coarsely chopped"],
  vanilla: [1, "bean", "Madagascar Bourbon"]
};
var coffeeHeathBarCrunch = cloneMembers(vanillaHeathBarCrunch);
coffeeHeathBarCrunch.coffee = [1/4, "cup, coarsely ground", "Starbucks Espresso"];
console.dir(vanillaHeathBarCrunch);

console.dir(coffeeHeathBarCrunch);
```

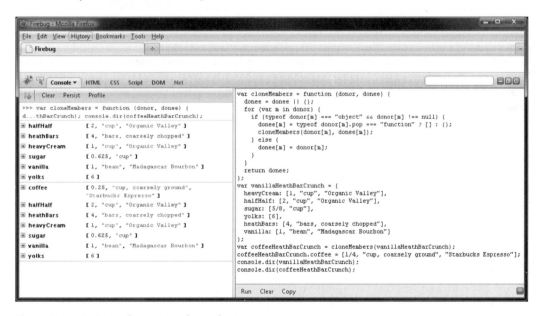

Figure 5–19. Doing a deep copy of members

Mixins

Finally, we can create an object by doing a deep copy of the members of two or more objects. Doing so is called a *mixin*. So, we'll write a merge() function that takes an array of mixins named mixins and optionally a donee to clone members to. Note that merge() will have cloneMembers() do the deep copy.

```
var cloneMembers = function (donor, donee) {
  donee = donee || {};
  for (var m in donor) {
    if (typeof donor[m] === "object" && donor[m] !== null) {
      donee[m] = typeof donor[m].pop === "function" ? [] : {};
      cloneMembers(donor[m], donee[m]);
    } else {
      donee[m] = donor[m];
    }
  }
  return donee;
};

var merge = function (mixins, donee) {
  var i, j, donee = donee || {};
  for (i = 0, j = mixins.length; i < j; i ++) {

    cloneMembers(mixins[i], donee);

  }
  return donee;
};
```

Now let's create some mixins. Throughout this chapter, we've used a French sweet cream base; other kinds of ice cream bases include Philadelphia, which contains no yolks, and Italian gelato, which has a higher yolk to cream ratio than French and therefore delivers a denser ice cream. In addition to those bases, we'll create some mixins for flavors.

```
var cloneMembers = function (donor, donee) {
  donee = donee || {};
  for (var m in donor) {
    if (typeof donor[m] === "object" && donor[m] !== null) {
      donee[m] = typeof donor[m].pop === "function" ? [] : {};
      cloneMembers(donor[m], donee[m]);
    } else {
      donee[m] = donor[m];
    }
  }
  return donee;
};
var merge = function (mixins, donee) {
  var i, j, donee = donee || {};
  for (i = 0, j = mixins.length; i < j; i ++) {
    cloneMembers(mixins[i], donee);
  }
  return donee;
};
```

```
var french = {
  heavyCream: [1, "cup", "Organic Valley"],
  halfHalf: [2, "cup", "Organic Valley"],
  sugar: [5/8, "cup"],
  yolks: [6]
};
var philly = {

  heavyCream: [2, "cup", "Organic Valley"],

  halfHalf: [1, "cup", "Organic Valley"],
  sugar: [5/8, "cup"]
};
var gelato = {
  halfHalf: [3, "cup", "Organic Valley"],
  sugar: [5/8, "cup"],
  yolks: [6]
};
var vanilla = {
  vanilla: [1, "bean", "Madagascar Bourbon"]
};
var heathBar = {
  heathBars: [4, "bars, coarsely chopped"]
};
var coffee = {
  coffee: [1/4, "cup, coarsely ground", "Starbucks Espresso"]
};
```

Having done so, we'll create Italian-style Coffee Heath Bar Crunch, Philadelphia-style Coffee, and French-style Vanilla Heath Bar Crunch, verifying our work with Figure 5–20:

```
var cloneMembers = function (donor, donee) {
  donee = donee || {};
  for (var m in donor) {
    if (typeof donor[m] === "object" && donor[m] !== null) {
      donee[m] = typeof donor[m].pop === "function" ? [] : {};
      cloneMembers(donor[m], donee[m]);
    } else {
      donee[m] = donor[m];
    }
  }
  return donee;
};
var merge = function (mixins, donee) {
  var i, j, donee = donee || {};
  for (i = 0, j = mixins.length; i < j; i ++) {
    cloneMembers(mixins[i], donee);
  }
  return donee;
};
var french = {
  heavyCream: [1, "cup", "Organic Valley"],
  halfHalf: [2, "cup", "Organic Valley"],
```

```
    sugar: [5/8, "cup"],
    yolks: [6]
};
var philly = {
  heavyCream: [2, "cup", "Organic Valley"],
  halfHalf: [1, "cup", "Organic Valley"],
  sugar: [5/8, "cup"]
};
var gelato = {
  halfHalf: [3, "cup", "Organic Valley"],
  sugar: [5/8, "cup"],
  yolks: [6]
};
var vanilla = {
  vanilla: [1, "bean", "Madagascar Bourbon"]
};
var heathBar = {
  heathBars: [4, "bars, coarsely chopped"]
};
var coffee = {
  coffee: [1/4, "cup, coarsely ground", "Starbucks Espresso"]
};

var coffeeHeathBarCrunch = merge([gelato, vanilla, coffee, heathBar]);
console.dir(coffeeHeathBarCrunch);
var coffee = merge([philly, vanilla, coffee]);
console.dir(coffee);
var vanillaHeathBarCrunch = merge([french, vanilla, heathBar]);
console.dir(vanillaHeathBarCrunch);
```

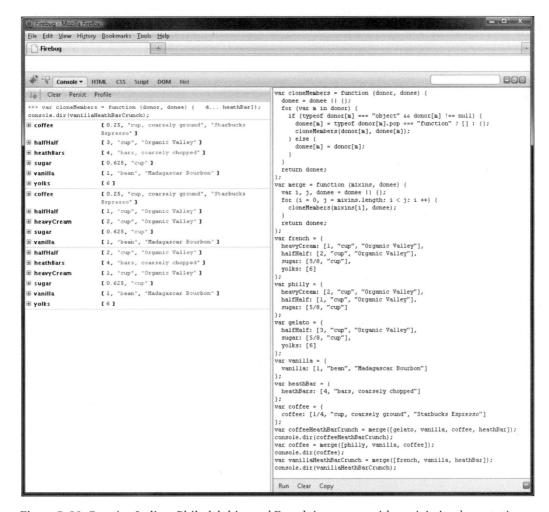

Figure 5–20. Creating Italian, Philadelphia, and French ice creams with a mixin implementation

Summary

In this chapter, we explored inheriting members by way of classical, prototypal, deep copy, and mixin implementations. However, more often than not, it's methods, which is to say functions, that are inherited. We'll cover that and other function essentials in Chapter 6.

Have a well-deserved scoop or two of your favorite ice cream, and I'll see you there.

CHAPTER 6

■ ■ ■

Functions and Arrays

In the previous chapter, you learned about inheritance and saw how to pass members onto child objects using classical, prototypal, deep copy, and mixin inheritance. As I noted at the end of that chapter, it's actually functions that are more often passed on to child objects. This is because common processes, as provided by a function, are frequently more useful than common data, as provided by members. In this chapter, I'll cover why you would want to use functions and how to take advantage of function inheritance. There are a lot of cool tricks to learn in this area and we'll take advantage of a lot of them in later chapters, as you'll see from the copious forward references. In other words, this is quite an important chapter.

In addition to the function subtype, arrays are a second subtype of the `object` value type. Arrays are special primarily due to the predefined methods they inherit from `Array.prototype`. We'll explore those methods in this chapter.

Why Use Functions?

Ben & Jerry's, Häagen-Dazs, and other French-style ice creams are made by creating a satiny custard from cream, milk, and egg yolks. Compared to Philadelphia-style ice cream, which is made by simply churning cream and milk, French-style ice cream can be tricky for a beginner to make. So, it's best to start with vanilla before gilding the lily. Err, gilding the orchid—vanilla flavoring derives from the fruit of the vanilla orchid.

Anyway, the most delicious vanilla ice cream is made by steeping the pod and seeds from a vanilla bean rather than by stirring in vanilla extract, which is less flavorful. Vanilla beans differ in taste depending on where the vanilla orchids are grown. Madagascar Bourbon are my favorite. Compared to those, Tahitian are milder in flavor, and Mexican are bolder.

If you are an ice-cream beginner, take your lumps with the following recipe for French vanilla before gilding the orchid with chocolate, fruit, and so on:

```
1 cup, Organic Valley heavy whipping cream
2 cups, Organic Valley half & half
5/8 cup, sugar
6 egg yolks
1 Madagascar Bourbon vanilla bean
```

- Separate the egg yolks into mixing bowl.

- Slit the vanilla bean length-wise with a paring knife.

- Scrape the tiny, pasty seeds into a saucepan. Then add the empty pod halves—most of the vanilla flavor derives from the pod.

- Add 2 cups half & half, 1/2 cup heavy whipping cream, and 5/8 cup sugar to saucepan containing the vanilla seeds and pod halves.

- Add the remaining 1/2 cup heavy whipping cream to the 6 egg yolks and whisk vigorously until smooth.

- Stirring frequently with wooden spoon, put the saucepan over medium heat for 4 minutes or just until the liquid begins to ripple but do not boil.

- Temper the egg yolks by gradually adding 1/4 of the hot liquid from the saucepan while whisking continuously. Tempering prevents the yolks from curdling, which would ruin the custard.

- Pour the tempered yolk mixture into the saucepan while whisking constantly.

- Stirring constantly with wooden spoon, put the saucepan over medium heat for 4 minutes or until custard thickens at roughly 170 F—do not boil.

- Pressing with the wooden spoon, strain the custard through a fine mesh sieve into a bowl to remove the vanilla pod, seeds, and any custard lumps.

- Stirring occasionally, cool the custard by placing the bowl into a larger bowl halfway filled with ice water.

- Remove the custard from ice bath and chill in refrigerator for at least a few hours if not overnight as well-chilled custard freezes into ice cream more effectively.

- Finally, churn chilled custard in ice-cream maker and then freeze for a few hours or until firm.

Once you've mastered French vanilla, it's easy to embellish it, as many flavors derive from it. For example, to make coffee ice cream, just steep 1/4 cup coarsely ground espresso beans with the vanilla pod and seeds. Then strain away the espresso grinds along with the vanilla pod and seeds and any custard lumps with a fine mesh sieve. Or to make chocolate, whisk 3/8 cup Dutch process cocoa—I recommend Callebaut—into the yolks and cream prior to tempering.

The French-style ice-cream recipes for vanilla, coffee, and chocolate displayed here are similar:

```
1 cup, Organic Valley heavy whipping cream
2 cups, Organic Valley half & half
5/8 cup, sugar
6 egg yolks
1 Madagascar Bourbon vanilla bean

1 cup, Organic Valley heavy whipping cream
2 cups, Organic Valley half & half
5/8 cup, sugar
6 egg yolks
1/4 cup, Starbucks Espresso beans, freshly and coarsely ground
1 Madagascar Bourbon vanilla bean

1 cup, Organic Valley heavy whipping cream
2 cups, Organic Valley half & half
5/8 cup, sugar
6 egg yolks
3/8 cup, Callebaut cocoa
1 Madagascar Bourbon vanilla bean
```

In JavaScript, if you find yourself writing a certain sequence of statements over and over that differ just slightly as the steps in our recipes for vanilla, coffee, and chocolate ice cream do, then you would want to create a function for those statements. Then define parameters for the differences. The constructor and helper functions in Chapter 5 such as CherryGarcia() and extend() are good examples of this.

You already know when to create a function. Therefore, in this chapter, we'll explore two vital features of JavaScript functions that make them distinctive. First, functions are values that may be expressed with literal notation. In geeky terms, this means JavaScript has first-class functions. Second, JavaScript has function scope, which makes functions vital for variable lookup.

Open firebug.html in Firefox, and then press F12 to enable Firebug—if you're just joining us, flip back to the preface for details on how to do this—and let's begin exploring functions as values.

■ **Note** If you save a function to an object, the function is referred to as a method.

Functions Are Values

First-class functions may be expressed with literals. Typically, those are unnamed or anonymous. You invoke a function through the variable, member, or element you saved it to. For example, in Chapter 5, we saved an unnamed function expression to a variable named WildMaineBlueberry and invoked the anonymous function by way of the variable's name, WildMaineBlueberry:

```
var WildMaineBlueberry = function (blueberries, vanilla) {
  this.blueberries = [2, "cup", blueberries ? blueberries : "fresh wild Maine blueberries"];
  this.vanilla = [1, "bean", vanilla ? vanilla : "Madagascar Bourbon"];
};
WildMaineBlueberry.prototype = {
  heavyCream: [1, "cup", "Organic Valley"],
  halfHalf: [1, "cup", "Organic Valley"],
  sugar: [5/8, "cup"],
  yolks: [6],
  freshLemonJuice: [2, "tsp"]
};
var wildMaineBlueberry = new WildMaineBlueberry();
console.dir(wildMaineBlueberry);
```

Named function values can be created with a *function declaration*. In turn, you can invoke the function by its name. So, rather than save a function expression to a variable named WildMaineBlueberry, we could create a function named WildMaineBlueberry like so:

```
function WildMaineBlueberry (blueberries, vanilla) {
  this.blueberries = [2, "cup", blueberries ? blueberries : "fresh wild Maine blueberries"];
  this.vanilla = [1, "bean", vanilla ? vanilla : "Madagascar Bourbon"];
}
WildMaineBlueberry.prototype = {
  heavyCream: [1, "cup", "Organic Valley"],
  halfHalf: [1, "cup", "Organic Valley"],
  sugar: [5/8, "cup"],
  yolks: [6],
  freshLemonJuice: [2, "tsp"]
};
var wildMaineBlueberry = new WildMaineBlueberry();
console.dir(wildMaineBlueberry);
```

What's the difference? For one thing, functions declarations cannot be assigned to variables, members, or elements. That is to say, you have to declare the function and then assign its name to a variable, member, or element. It's two steps rather than one. Moreover, you cannot pass a function declaration to a function. Rather, you have to pass its name. Again, it's two steps rather than one. Finally, declarations create functions that may be called prior to being defined, though doing so is frowned upon. For those reasons and so that you get used to using functions as values just like objects or booleans, we'll continue using function expressions rather than declarations for the remainder of our journey.

Function Members

Functions are values of the object value type, so they inherit members from `Object.prototype` like `valueOf()` as well as the following ones from `Function.prototype`. Note that `Function.prototype.constructor` and `Function.prototype.toString()` override `Object.prototype.constructor` and `Object.prototype.toString()`.

```
constructor
length
apply()
bind()
call()
toString()
```

`Function.prototype.constructor` just refers to `Function()`, `length` contains the number of named parameters defined for the function, and `toString()` contains the function definition as a string. Query those for `WildMaineBlueberry()`. Note that we'll explore `apply()`, `bind()`, and `call()` in just a bit.

```
function WildMaineBlueberry (blueberries, vanilla) {
  this.blueberries = [2, "cup", blueberries ? blueberries : "fresh wild Maine blueberries"];
  this.vanilla = [1, "bean", vanilla ? vanilla : "Madagascar Bourbon"];
}
WildMaineBlueberry.prototype = {
  heavyCream: [1, "cup", "Organic Valley"],
  halfHalf: [1, "cup", "Organic Valley"],
  sugar: [5/8, "cup"],
  yolks: [6],
  freshLemonJuice: [2, "tsp"]
};
WildMaineBlueberry.constructor;
// Function()
WildMaineBlueberry.length;
// 2
WildMaineBlueberry.toString()
// "function WildMaineBlueberry(blueberries, vanilla) { this.blueberries = [2, "cup",
blueberries ? blueberries : "fresh wild Maine blueberries"]; this.vanilla = [1, "bean",
vanilla ? vanilla : "Madagascar Bourbon"]; }"
```

■ **Tip** It's worth noting that JavaScript initializes an element in the `arguments` object for every named or unnamed parameter. You can use this object to obtain the number of parameters used (`arguments.length`) or get the name of the function that called the current function (`arguments.callee`), which we will cover a bit later in the "Recursion" section. You can also obtain parameters by using their place in the parameter list (for example, `arguments[0]` to obtain the first parameter).

Conditional Advance Loading

One implication of functions being values is that you can conditionally choose one of two or more values for a function as your script loads. This technique, referred to as *conditional advance loading* or *load-time branching*, is one we'll turn to quite a bit in Chapters 9 and 10.

Conditional advance loading can be used to choose a value for a function relative to what ECMAScript or DOM features a browser's JavaScript interpreter implements. This means we set the function's value to use a particular feature if it is available or write that particular feature in the function's value if it is not available. For example, ECMAScript 5 defines the following 12 new methods. Note that those are static methods, which is to say they are saved to `Object`, not to `Object.prototype`.

```
Object.create()
Object.defineProperty()
Object.defineProperties()
Object.getOwnPropertyDescriptor()
Object.keys()
Object.getOwnPropertyNames()
Object.preventExtensions()
Object.isExtensible()
Object.seal()
Object.isSealed()
Object.freeze()
Object.isFrozen()
```

Right now, no browser supports these methods, but the JavaScript interpreters in Explorer 9 and Firefox 4 will do so. However, those methods will greatly improve JavaScript's inheritance features. So, if available, we'd want to work those into the functions we wrote in Chapter 5.

One way to do so is with conditional advance loading. The "conditional" bit means an `if` conditional statement or `?:` conditional expression that checks to see whether a particular feature is available, while the "advance loading" bit means doing the feature detection as the script loads, which is to say in advance.

So jargon in hand, let's rewrite `extend()` from Chapter 5 so that Explorer 9 and Firefox 4 can use the following ECMAScript 5 methods, each of which I will explain as I show you how to implement them:

```
Object.create()
Object.defineProperty()
Object.defineProperties()
```

The first thing we want to do is define methods not quite unlike the ECMAScript 5 ones for current versions of Explorer, Firefox, Safari, and Opera; in other words, we're going to write our own versions of `create()`, `defineProperty()`, and `defineProperties()` for browsers to use if they don't support

ECMAScript5. Let's begin by roughing out an `if` condition for missing members. Do you remember what the value of a missing member is?

Yup, `undefined`.

Thus far, we have this:

```
if (Object.defineProperty === undefined) {
}
if (Object.defineProperties === undefined) {
}
if (Object.create === undefined) {
}
```

Now, within the empty `if` blocks, create the missing members and just assign an empty function literal. Take care not to omit the semicolon following each assignment statement:

```
if (Object.defineProperty === undefined) {
  Object.defineProperty = function () {
  };
}
if (Object.defineProperties === undefined) {
  Object.defineProperties = function () {
  };
}
if (Object.create === undefined) {
  Object.create = function () {
  };
}
```

Writing Object.defineProperty()

With `Object.defineProperty()`, you can assign a value to a member as well as define whether a member is writable, enumerable, or deletable.

■ **Note** Enumerable means that a member is enumerated in a `for in` loop, while writable simply means we can assign a value to the member. So, you can see that an array is enumerable, as are the properties of an object.

Prior to ECMAScript 5, any member you added to an object was writable, enumerable, and deletable. For most members, that's what you want. So, `Object.defineProperty()` is not a replacement for adding members with the `.`, `[]`, and `=` operators. Rather, it is just for doing things such as ensuring that members like `constructor` (for a prototype object) don't appear in a `for in` loop.

To do so, you pass `Object.defineProperty()` three parameters.

- First, an object to add a member to or that contains a member you want to modify.

- Second, the name of a member, as a string, that you want to add or modify.

- Third, a data descriptor or accessor descriptor object. Data descriptors may contain the following four members. Minimally, a data descriptor must contain a value or writable member.

    - value contains the member's value, which defaults to undefined.

    - writable contains a boolean indicating whether the member's value is writable. true means that it is, and false, which is the default, means that it is not. So, false means that you cannot assign a new value to a member with the = operator.

    - configurable contains a boolean indicating whether a member may be deleted and whether its descriptor attributes are writable, with the exception of writable, which is carved in stone. false, the default, means that a member may not be deleted and that its configurable and enumerable attributes may not be changed. true means the inverse.

    - enumerable contains a boolean indicating whether the member would be enumerated in a for in loop. true means that it would be, and false, the default, means that it would not. So, enumerable provides a way to ensure a member such as constructor doesn't appear in a for in loop.

Note that the writable, configurable, and enumerable descriptor attributes default to false. On the other hand, for a member traditionally created or modified with the = operator, writable, configurable, and enumerable default to true. That's your clue to continue using = for most assignment operations. Note that, if you add a member with the =, you may later change its writable, configurable, and enumerable attributes with Object.defineProperty().

■ **Note** I will not cover accessor descriptors in this book. You use them to provide a function that is called whenever a property value is accessed or set.

For browsers that do not implement Object.defineProperty(), we'd simply want to assign the descriptor's value member with the = operator and disregard the writable, configurable, and enumerable members. Note that, if the descriptor just has a writable member, descriptor.value evaluates to undefined.

```
if (Object.defineProperty === undefined) {
  Object.defineProperty = function (obj, name, descriptor) {
    obj[name] = descriptor.value;
  };
}
if (Object.defineProperties === undefined) {
  Object.defineProperties = function () {
  };
}
if (Object.create === undefined) {
  Object.create = function () {
  };
}
```

Writing Object.defineProperties()

Object.defineProperties() is sort of the plural version of Object.defineProperty(). That is to say, it can create or modify more than one member. Unlike Object.defineProperty(), this one takes two parameters.

- The first one is the same as Object.defineProperty()—the object on which to add or modify members.

- The second one is an object containing one or more descriptor objects.

So, for pre-ECMAScript 5 browsers, we'll loop through the descriptors parameter with a for in loop, disregarding descriptor members other than value:

```
if (Object.defineProperty === undefined) {
  Object.defineProperty = function (obj, name, descriptor) {
    obj[name] = descriptor.value;
  };
}
if (Object.defineProperties === undefined) {
  Object.defineProperties = function (obj, descriptors) {
      for (descriptor in descriptors) {
        if (descriptors.hasOwnProperty(descriptor)) {
          obj[descriptor] = descriptors[descriptor].value;
        }
      }
  };
}
if (Object.create === undefined) {
  Object.create = function () {
  };
}
```

Writing Object.create()

Finally, Object.create() works with two parameters (recall we discussed create() in Chapter 5).

- The first one is the object to inherit members from.

- The optional second one is an object containing descriptors of its own members to add to the child object.

For pre-ECMAScript 5 browsers, we'll write a function similar to clone() in Chapter 5. In the event that the optional descriptors parameter is defined, we'll pass those to Object.defineProperties():

```
if (Object.defineProperty === undefined) {
  Object.defineProperty = function (obj, name, descriptor) {
    obj[name] = descriptor.value;
  };
}
if (Object.defineProperties === undefined) {
  Object.defineProperties = function (obj, descriptors) {
      for (descriptor in descriptors) {
        if (descriptors.hasOwnProperty(descriptor)) {
```

```
      obj[descriptor] = descriptors[descriptor].value;
      }
    }
  };
}
if (Object.create === undefined) {
  Object.create = function (parent, descriptors) {
    var Proxy = function () {},
      child;
    Proxy.prototype = parent;
    child = new Proxy();
    if (descriptors !== undefined) {
      Object.defineProperties(child, descriptors);
    }
    return child;
  };
}
```

Using the new Functions

Now let's invoke toString() on Object.defineProperty, Object.defineProperties, and Object.create and then pass the string to Firebug's console.log() method. If you're running Firefox 3, JavaScript will print our pre-ECMAScript 5 functions in the left panel of Firebug, as in Figure 6–1. On the other hand, if you're running Firefox 4, JavaScript will print the native ECMAScript 5. Note that native functions are written in a compiled language like C++, so rather than print compiled gobbledygook for the body of a native function, JavaScript simply prints [native code]:

```
if (Object.defineProperty === undefined) {
  Object.defineProperty = function (obj, name, descriptor) {
    obj[name] = descriptor.value;
  };
}
if (Object.defineProperties === undefined) {
  Object.defineProperties = function (obj, descriptors) {
      for (descriptor in descriptors) {
        if (descriptors.hasOwnProperty(descriptor)) {
          obj[descriptor] = descriptors[descriptor].value;
        }
      }
  };
}
if (Object.create === undefined) {
  Object.create = function (parent, descriptors) {
    var Proxy = function () {},
      child;
    Proxy.prototype = parent;
    child = new Proxy();
    if (descriptors !== undefined) {
      Object.defineProperties(child, descriptors);
    }
    return child;
  };
```

```
}
console.log(Object.defineProperty.toString());
console.log(Object.defineProperties.toString());
console.log(Object.create.toString());
```

***Figure 6–1.** Firefox 3 opts for our pre-ECMAScript 5 functions.*

Now with those conditional advance loaders written, we can rework extend() from Chapter 5 so that the constructor members we add to the child and parent prototype objects are not enumerated in a for in loop. That is to say, our constructor members will behave like the native ones that get overwritten during prototype chaining or prototype replacement. Moreover, we'll set writable to true and configurable to false so that the constructor member can be changed but not deleted. Finally, we'll make the child constructor's superclass member writable and configurable but not enumerable. In this way, we retain the option to have the child not inherit from a parent.

```
if (Object.defineProperty === undefined) {
  Object.defineProperty = function (obj, name, descriptor) {
    obj[name] = descriptor.value;
  };
}
if (Object.defineProperties === undefined) {
  Object.defineProperties = function (obj, descriptors) {
      for (descriptor in descriptors) {
        if (descriptors.hasOwnProperty(descriptor)) {
          obj[descriptor] = descriptors[descriptor].value;
        }
      }
```

```
    };
}
if (Object.create === undefined) {
  Object.create = function (parent, descriptors) {
    var Proxy = function () {},
      child;
    Proxy.prototype = parent;
    child = new Proxy();
    if (descriptors !== undefined) {
      Object.defineProperties(child, descriptors);
    }
    return child;
  };
}
var extend = function (child, parent, descriptors) {
  child.prototype = Object.create(parent.prototype, descriptors);
  Object.defineProperty(child.prototype, "constructor", {
    value: child,
    writable: true,
    enumerable: false,
    configurable: false
  });
  if (! parent.prototype.hasOwnProperty("constructor")) {
    Object.defineProperty(parent.prototype, "constructor", {
      value: parent,
      writable: true,
      enumerable: false,
      configurable: false
    });
  }
  Object.defineProperty(child, "superclass", {
    value: parent.prototype,
    writable: true,
    enumerable: false,
    configurable: true
  });
};
```

Insofar as writable, enumerable, and configurable default to false, we can more succinctly write extend() like so. Just be sure to remove the comma following the final descriptor member. After all, descriptors are just object literals, so those must abide by object literal notation.

```
if (Object.defineProperty === undefined) {
  Object.defineProperty = function (obj, name, descriptor) {
    obj[name] = descriptor.value;
  };
}
if (Object.defineProperties === undefined) {
  Object.defineProperties = function (obj, descriptors) {
    for (descriptor in descriptors) {
      if (descriptors.hasOwnProperty(descriptor)) {
        obj[descriptor] = descriptors[descriptor].value;
      }
```

```
      }
    };
  }
  if (Object.create === undefined) {
    Object.create = function (parent, descriptors) {
      var Proxy = function () {},
        child;
      Proxy.prototype = parent;
      child = new Proxy();
      if (descriptors !== undefined) {
        Object.defineProperties(child, descriptors);
      }
      return child;
    };
  }
  var extend = function (child, parent, descriptors) {
    child.prototype = Object.create(parent.prototype, descriptors);
    Object.defineProperty(child.prototype, "constructor", {
      value: child,
      writable: true
    });
    if (! parent.prototype.hasOwnProperty("constructor")) {
      Object.defineProperty(parent.prototype, "constructor", {
        value: parent,
        writable: true
      });
    }
    Object.defineProperty(child, "superclass", {
      value: parent.prototype,
      writable: true,
      configurable: true
    });
  };
```

Now let's rework the extend() sample from Chapter 5 in which we had CherryGarcia() inherit from Strawberry. In ECMAScript 5 compliant browsers like Explorer 9 and Firefox 4, Strawberry.prototype.constructor and CherryGarcia.prototype.constructor will not be enumerated in a for in loop or deleted by the delete operator. Moreover, CherryGarcia.superclass will not be enumerated in a for in loop but would be deleted by the delete operator. On the other hand, in pre-ECMAScript 5 browsers extend() would create constructor and superclass members by simple assignment with the = operator. So, Firebug's console.dir() method, which prints an object's enumerable members, would print the constructor member for strawberry and cherryGarcia if you're running Firefox 3 as in Figure 6–2, but not if you're running Firefox 4.

```
if (Object.defineProperty === undefined) {
  Object.defineProperty = function (obj, name, descriptor) {
    obj[name] = descriptor.value;
  };
}
if (Object.defineProperties === undefined) {
  Object.defineProperties = function (obj, descriptors) {
    for (descriptor in descriptors) {
      if (descriptors.hasOwnProperty(descriptor)) {
        obj[descriptor] = descriptors[descriptor].value;
```

```
      }
    }
  };
}
if (Object.create === undefined) {
  Object.create = function (parent, descriptors) {
    var Proxy = function () {},
      child;
    Proxy.prototype = parent;
    child = new Proxy();
    if (descriptors !== undefined) {
      Object.defineProperties(child, descriptors);
    }
    return child;
  };
}
var extend = function (child, parent, descriptors) {
  child.prototype = Object.create(parent.prototype, descriptors);
  Object.defineProperty(child.prototype, "constructor", {
    value: child,
    writable: true
  });
  if (! parent.prototype.hasOwnProperty("constructor")) {
    Object.defineProperty(parent.prototype, "constructor", {
      value: parent,
      writable: true
    });
  }
  Object.defineProperty(child, "superclass", {
    value: parent.prototype,
    writable: true,
    configurable: true
  });
};

var Strawberry = function(strawberry) {
  this.strawberry = [2, "cup", strawberry ? strawberry : "fraises des bois"];
};
Strawberry.prototype = {
  heavyCream: [1, "cup", "Organic Valley"],
  halfHalf: [1, "cup", "Organic Valley"],
  sugar: [5/8, "cup"],
  yolks: [3],
  vanilla: [1, "bean", "Madagascar Bourbon"]
};
var CherryGarcia = function(cherry, bittersweet) {
  this.cherries = [2, "cup, pitted and halved", cherry ? cherry : "Bing"];
  this.bittersweet = [1, "cup, coarsely chopped", bittersweet ? bittersweet : "Callebaut"];
};
extend(CherryGarcia, Strawberry, {
    sugar: {
      value: [9/16, "cup"],
```

```
        writable: true,
        enumerable: true,
        configurable: true
    }});
var strawberry = new Strawberry();
var cherryGarcia = new CherryGarcia();
console.dir(strawberry);
console.dir(cherryGarcia);
```

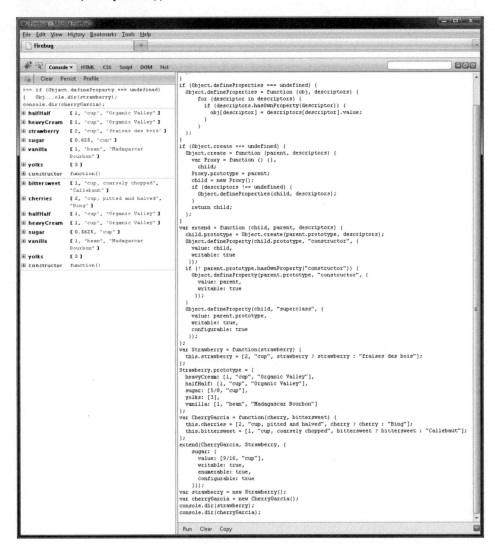

Figure 6–2. strawberry *and* cherryGarcia *will have enumerable constructor members in pre-ECMAScript 5 browsers.*

Lazy Loading

Another implication of functions being values is that you can conditionally change a function value while it's running. This technique, referred to as *lazy loading* or *lazy definition*, is one we'll turn to often in Chapters 9 and 10.

Because native functions such as `Object.create()` are compiled into gobbledygook, they run much faster than your plain-text functions. So, it's best to opt for a native function to do some work if one is available. Conditional advance loading is one way to ensure that JavaScript opts for fast-running gobbledygook. Lazy loading—that is, having a function redefine itself the first time it's called—is another way.

Lazy loaders are appropriate for functions that may not be needed or that are not needed right away. *Lazy* refers to not redefining a function unless or until you have to. On the other hand, conditional advance loading is appropriate for functions you definitely need, especially those that are needed right away.

In Chapter 5, we wrote the following `clone()` function to implement prototypal inheritance:

```
var clone = function (donor) {
  var Proxy = function () {};
  Proxy.prototype = donor;
  return new Proxy();
};
```

If you omit its optional second parameter, `Object.create()` does the same thing as `clone()` but much faster. Insofar as descriptors are too unwieldy to add members that are writable, enumerable, and configurable, which is to say like those added with the = operator, more often than not you'll be omitting the second parameter. With this in mind, let's rework `clone()` into a lazy loader that opts for `Object.create()` in Explorer 9, Firefox 4, and other ECMAScript 5-savvy browsers.

Begin by putting our definition of `clone` in the `else` clause of an `if` condition that determines whether `Object.create` is defined. However, omit the var keyword because we want to overwrite the containing `clone()` function, not create a nested `clone()` function.

```
var clone = function (donor) {
  if (Object.create !== undefined) {
  } else {
    clone = function (donor) {
      var Proxy = function () {};
      Proxy.prototype = donor;
      return new Proxy();
    };
  }
};
```

Now, within the `if` clause, simply return the empty object created by passing donor to `Object.create()`:

```
var clone = function (donor) {
  if (Object.create !== undefined) {
    clone = function (donor) {
      return Object.create(donor);
    };
  } else {
    clone = function (donor) {
      var Proxy = function () {};
      Proxy.prototype = donor;
```

```
      return new Proxy();
    };
  }
};
```

Unfortunately, right now clone() would simply redefine itself the first time we call it. That is, it would return undefined rather than an empty object that inherits members from donor.

Hmmm.

What to do?

I know. Following the if else statement, we'll pass donor from the old clone() to the new clone():

```
var clone = function (donor) {
  if (Object.create !== undefined) {
    clone = function (donor) {
      return Object.create(donor);
    };
  } else {
    clone = function (donor) {
      var Proxy = function () {};
      Proxy.prototype = donor;
      return new Proxy();
    };
  }
  clone(donor);
};
```

But that will still return undefined the first time we call clone() inasmuch as a function that does not explicitly return a value with a return statement will implicitly return undefined. With this in mind, how would we fix our lazy loader?

Yup, have the old clone() explicitly return the value of passing its donor parameter to the new clone(). Note that if you are redefining a function that does not explicitly return a value, such as the thwart() or burst() functions we'll write in Chapter 9, then you can omit the return keyword.

```
var clone = function (donor) {
  if (Object.create !== undefined) {
    clone = function (donor) {
      return Object.create(donor);
    };
  } else {
    clone = function (donor) {
      var Proxy = function () {};
      Proxy.prototype = donor;
      return new Proxy();
    };
  }
  return clone(donor);
};
```

Now let's create some Ben & Jerry's Chunky Monkey with our lazy loading clone() just as we did in Chapter 5, before verifying our work with Figure 6–3. If you're running Firefox 4, then chunkyMonkey is churned by Object.create(). But if you're running Firefox 3, then chunkyMonkey is churned by Proxy(). It's delicious either way, but you'll have a scoop sooner if Object.create() is doing the churning.

```
var clone = function (donor) {
  if (Object.create !== undefined) {
    clone = function (donor) {
```

```
      return Object.create(donor);
    };
  } else {
    clone = function (donor) {
      var Proxy = function () {};
      Proxy.prototype = donor;
      return new Proxy();
    };
  }
  return clone(donor);
};

var banana = {
  heavyCream: [1, "cup", "Organic Valley"],
  halfHalf: [1, "cup", "Organic Valley"],
  sugar: [9/16, "cup"],
  yolks: [3],
  banana: [1 + 1/2, "cup, puréed"],
  coconutMilk: [1/4, "cup"],
  lemon: [2, "tsp", "freshly juiced Meyer lemon"],
  vanilla: [1, "bean", "Madagascar Bourbon"]
};
var chunkyMonkey = clone(banana);
chunkyMonkey.walnuts = [3/4, "cup, coarsely chopped"];
chunkyMonkey.bittersweet = [1, "cup, coarsely grated", "Callebaut"];
console.dir(banana);
console.dir(chunkyMonkey);
```

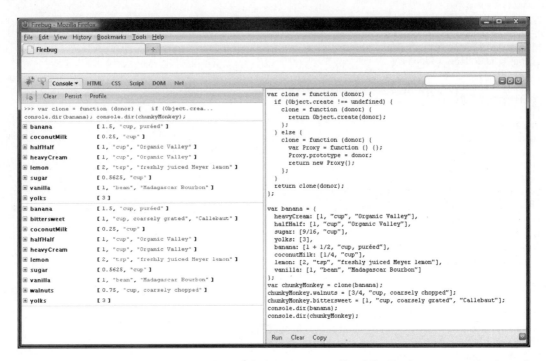

Figure 6–3. Firefox 4 creates chunkyMonkey with `Object.create()`, *while Firefox 3 creates chunkyMonkey with* `Proxy()`.

Recursion

Whereas function literal expressions create function values, function invocation expressions create values of any type, typically by manipulating one or more values referred to as parameters or arguments. Insofar as a function value can self-invoke, a function can do work on parameters and then pass those back to itself. Doing so, referred to as **recursion**, provides a way to do a lot of mind numbing work in small steps. Recursive functions are invaluable for traversing the DOM, something we'll explore in Chapter 7. But we've already written a recursive function in Chapter 5. There we churned a quart of Ben & Jerry's Coffee Heath Bar Crunch from Vanilla Heath Bar Crunch by simply cloning members with a recursive function named cloneMembers() like so:

```
var cloneMembers = function cloneMembers (donor, donee) {
  donee = donee || {};
  for (var m in donor) {
    if (donor.hasOwnProperty(m)) {
      if (typeof donor[m] === "object" && donor[m] !== null) {
        donee[m] = typeof donor[m].pop === "function" ? [] : {};
        cloneMembers(donor[m], donee[m]);
      } else {
        donee[m] = donor[m];
      }
    }
```

```
    }
    return donee;
};
var vanillaHeathBarCrunch = {
    heavyCream: [1, "cup", "Organic Valley"],
    halfHalf: [2, "cup", "Organic Valley"],
    sugar: [5/8, "cup"],
    yolks: [6],
    heathBars: [4, "bars, coarsely chopped"],
    vanilla: [1, "bean", "Madagascar Bourbon"]
};
var coffeeHeathBarCrunch = cloneMembers(vanillaHeathBarCrunch);
coffeeHeathBarCrunch.coffee = [1/4, "cup, coarsely ground", "Starbucks Espresso"];
```

Note how we test whether an object is an array by checking if it has a pop() method. We'll cover arrays and their methods later in this chapter, but for now remember that arrays have a pop() method of type function.

If we rewrote cloneMembers() as a nonrecursive function, which is to say deleted cloneMembers(donor[m], donee[m]);, then we'd have to invoke cloneMembers() eight times rather than one time. So, recursion spares us from having to key in the following, which as Figure 6–4 displays still works fine.

```
var cloneMembers = function cloneMembers (donor, donee) {
    donee = donee || {};
    for (var m in donor) {
        if (donor.hasOwnProperty(m)) {
            if (typeof donor[m] === "object" && donor[m] !== null) {
                donee[m] = typeof donor[m].pop === "function" ? [] : {};
            } else {
                donee[m] = donor[m];
            }
        }
    }
    return donee;
};
var vanillaHeathBarCrunch = {
    heavyCream: [1, "cup", "Organic Valley"],
    halfHalf: [2, "cup", "Organic Valley"],
    sugar: [5/8, "cup"],
    yolks: [6],
    heathBars: [4, "bars, coarsely chopped"],
    vanilla: [1, "bean", "Madagascar Bourbon"]
};
var coffeeHeathBarCrunch = cloneMembers(vanillaHeathBarCrunch);

coffeeHeathBarCrunch.heavyCream = cloneMembers(vanillaHeathBarCrunch.heavyCream,
    coffeeHeathBarCrunch.heavyCream);
coffeeHeathBarCrunch.halfHalf = cloneMembers(vanillaHeathBarCrunch.halfHalf,
    coffeeHeathBarCrunch.halfHalf);
coffeeHeathBarCrunch.sugar = cloneMembers(vanillaHeathBarCrunch.sugar,
    coffeeHeathBarCrunch.sugar);
coffeeHeathBarCrunch.yolks = cloneMembers(vanillaHeathBarCrunch.yolks,
    coffeeHeathBarCrunch.yolks);
coffeeHeathBarCrunch.heathBars = cloneMembers(vanillaHeathBarCrunch.heathBars,
```

```
      coffeeHeathBarCrunch.heathBars);
coffeeHeathBarCrunch.vanilla = cloneMembers(vanillaHeathBarCrunch.vanilla,
   coffeeHeathBarCrunch.vanilla);
coffeeHeathBarCrunch.heavyCream = cloneMembers(vanillaHeathBarCrunch.heavyCream,
   coffeeHeathBarCrunch.heavyCream);
coffeeHeathBarCrunch.coffee = [1/4, "cup, coarsely ground", "Starbucks Espresso"];
console.dir(vanillaHeathBarCrunch);
console.dir(coffeeHeathBarCrunch);
```

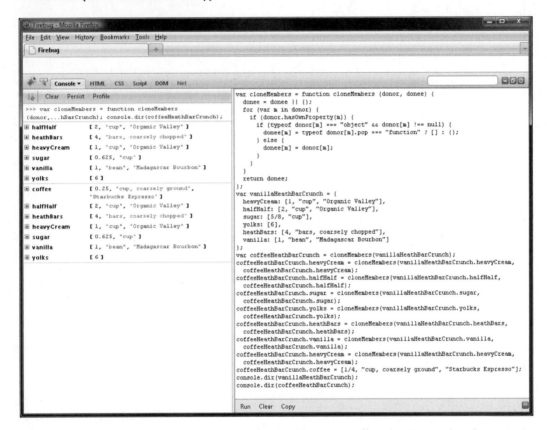

Figure 6–4. Recursion prevents our having to invoke cloneMembers() eight times rather than one time.

Don't know about you, but I'd rather work smart than hard. So, recursion is a keeper. Note that in Chapter 7 we'll write a recursive function named traverseTree() to traverse the DOM tree. Doing so possibly prevents our having to invoke traverseTree() hundreds of times by hand.

Another way to implement recursion is by way of arguments.callee, which refers to the running function. We'll use this approach a bit more later in the book:

```
var cloneMembers = function cloneMembers (donor, donee) {
  donee = donee || {};
  for (var m in donor) {
    if (donor.hasOwnProperty(m)) {
```

```
      if (typeof donor[m] === "object" && donor[m] !== null) {
        donee[m] = typeof donor[m].pop === "function" ? [] : {};
        arguments.callee(donor[m], donee[m]);
      } else {
        donee[m] = donor[m];
      }
    }
  }
  return donee;
};
var vanillaHeathBarCrunch = {
  heavyCream: [1, "cup", "Organic Valley"],
  halfHalf: [2, "cup", "Organic Valley"],
  sugar: [5/8, "cup"],
  yolks: [6],
  heathBars: [4, "bars, coarsely chopped"],
  vanilla: [1, "bean", "Madagascar Bourbon"]
};
var coffeeHeathBarCrunch = cloneMembers(vanillaHeathBarCrunch);
coffeeHeathBarCrunch.coffee = [1/4, "cup, coarsely ground", "Starbucks Espresso"];
```

Borrowing Methods with apply() or call()

Insofar as functions are values of the object value type, they inherit members from `Object.prototype` and `Function.prototype` by way of a prototype chain in the same way as our `cherryGarcia` object inherits members from `Object.prototype`, `Strawberry.prototype`, and `CherryGarcia`. Two methods inherited from `Function.prototype`, `apply()` and `call()`, provide a way to borrow function values. These functions mean that you can define a function in one object and use it in another as if it were inherited, without having to inherit the whole object. In both cases, you pass the object that is inheriting the function as the first parameter (which becomes `this` in the inherited function), followed by either of these:

- The arguments to the function as a series of values separated by commas, in the case of `call()`

- The arguments to the function as an array, in the case of `apply()`

ECMAScript 5 defines an `Array.isArray()` method to verify whether or not a value is an array. This is a much-needed addition to JavaScript inasmuch as `typeof` returns `"object"` for an object, array, or `null`, and the `instanceof` operator does not work with frames in some Explorer versions. Let's see how `call()` and `apply()` can help.

Overriding toString()

So, for Explorer 9, Firefox 4, and other ECMAScript 5-savvy browsers, we want to verify arrayness with `Array.isArray()` rather than testing for an array method like `pop()` or `slice()` as we did in `cloneMembers()`. After all, there's no reason why an object or function could not have a method named `pop()` or `slice()`.

To do so, we'd want to write a conditional advance loader for `Array.isArray()`. So, just like we did for `Object.create()`. The tricky part is writing something not quite unlike `Array.isArray()` for Explorer 8, Firefox, 3, and other ECMAScript 5 dummies. To do so, we're going to work with the `toString()` function to extract information about the object in question.

If you invoke toString() on an object that does not override Object.prototype.toString() with its own toString() method, it will return "[object Object]". For example, even though we churned wildMaineBlueberry with the WildMaineBlueberry() constructor in Chapter 5, as Figure 6–5 displays, invoking wildMaineBlueberry.toString() returns "[object Object]" inasmuch as we did not override Object.prototype.toString():

```
var WildMaineBlueberry = function(blueberries, vanilla) {
  this.blueberries = [2, "cup", blueberries ? blueberries : "fresh wild Maine blueberries"];
  this.vanilla = [1, "bean", vanilla ? vanilla : "Madagascar Bourbon"];
};
WildMaineBlueberry.prototype = {
  heavyCream: [1, "cup", "Organic Valley"],
  halfHalf: [1, "cup", "Organic Valley"],
  sugar: [5/8, "cup"],
  yolks: [6],
  freshLemonJuice: [2, "tsp"]
};
var wildMaineBlueberry = new WildMaineBlueberry("Dole frozen wild blueberries", "Tahitian");
wildMaineBlueberry.toString();
// "[object Object]"
```

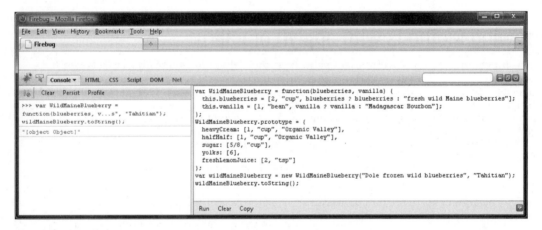

Figure 6–5. Invoking toString() on an object that does not override Object.prototype.toString() with its own toString() method, it will return "[object Object]".

However, if we add a toString() method to WildMaineBlueberry.prototype, that will override Object.prototype.toString() as the following sample and Figure 6–6 display:

```
var WildMaineBlueberry = function(blueberries, vanilla) {
  this.blueberries = [2, "cup", blueberries ? blueberries : "fresh wild Maine blueberries"];
  this.vanilla = [1, "bean", vanilla ? vanilla : "Madagascar Bourbon"];
};
WildMaineBlueberry.prototype = {
  heavyCream: [1, "cup", "Organic Valley"],
  halfHalf: [1, "cup", "Organic Valley"],
  sugar: [5/8, "cup"],
  yolks: [6],
```

```
  freshLemonJuice: [2, "tsp"],
  toString: function () { return "[object WildMaineBlueberry]";}
};
var wildMaineBlueberry = new WildMaineBlueberry("Dole frozen wild blueberries", "Tahitian");
wildMaineBlueberry.toString();
// "[object WildMaineBlueberry]"
```

Figure 6–6. WildMaineBlueberry.prototype.toString() overrides Object.prototype.toString().

Native JavaScript constructors defined by ECMAScript or DOM always override
`Object.prototype.toString()`. For example, if we call `toString()` on the array in
`wildMaineBlueberry.heavyCream`, JavaScript glues the elements together with commas instead of
returning `"[object Array]"`, which is what `Object.prototype.toString()` returns for an array when it is
not overridden. Similarly, if we call `toString()` on the constructor function `WildMaineBlueberry`,
JavaScript return its definition as a string. Try doing both, verifying your work with Figure 6–7.

```
var WildMaineBlueberry = function(blueberries, vanilla) {
  this.blueberries = [2, "cup", blueberries ? blueberries : "fresh wild Maine blueberries"];
  this.vanilla = [1, "bean", vanilla ? vanilla : "Madagascar Bourbon"];
};
WildMaineBlueberry.prototype = {
  heavyCream: [1, "cup", "Organic Valley"],
  halfHalf: [1, "cup", "Organic Valley"],
  sugar: [5/8, "cup"],
  yolks: [6],
  freshLemonJuice: [2, "tsp"],
  toString: function () { return "[object WildMaineBlueberry]";}
};
var wildMaineBlueberry = new WildMaineBlueberry("Dole frozen wild blueberries", "Tahitian");
wildMaineBlueberry.heavyCream.toString();
// "1,cup,Organic Valley"
WildMaineBlueberry.toString();
// "function (blueberries, vanilla) { this.blueberries = [2, "cup", blueberries ? blueberries
: "fresh wild Maine blueberries"]; this.vanilla = [1, "bean", vanilla ? vanilla : "Madagascar
Bourbon"]; }"
```

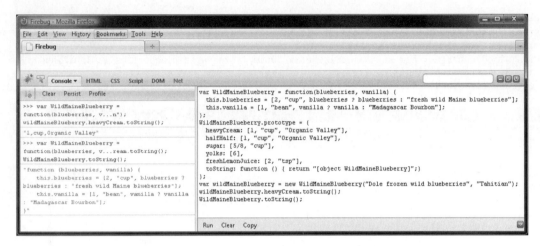

Figure 6–7. Native JavaScript constructors defined by ECMAScript or DOM always override
`Object.prototype.toString()`.

Testing for an Array

To test for arrayness like `Array.isArray()` in ECMAScript 5 dummies like Explorer 8, we need to circumvent any `toString()` method overriding `Object.prototype.toString()` to avoid the gluey string that JavaScript shows us when we call `toString()` on an array. Having done so, we would then return true if `Object.prototype.toString()` returns `"[object Array]"` and false if not.

ECMAScript defines a couple of methods for function values, `apply()` and `call()`, that provide a way to borrow a method like `Object.prototype.toString()` and use it as if it were inherited (so we have access to it over the head of any overridden methods).

The first parameter to `apply()` or `call()` is an object to bind to `this` for the method you are borrowing. If you wanted to invoke `Object.prototype.toString()` on `[1, "cup", "Organic Valley"]`, which is to say circumvent `Array.prototype.toString()`, you'd pass `[1, "cup", "Organic Valley"]` as the first parameter to `apply()` or `call()`. Try both methods, verifying your work with Figure 6–8. Note that, to save some typing, you can just replace `Object.prototype` with an empty object literal wrapped in parentheses.

```
var WildMaineBlueberry = function(blueberries, vanilla) {
  this.blueberries = [2, "cup", blueberries ? blueberries : "fresh wild Maine blueberries"];
  this.vanilla = [1, "bean", vanilla ? vanilla : "Madagascar Bourbon"];
};
WildMaineBlueberry.prototype = {
  heavyCream: [1, "cup", "Organic Valley"],
  halfHalf: [1, "cup", "Organic Valley"],
  sugar: [5/8, "cup"],
  yolks: [6],
  freshLemonJuice: [2, "tsp"],
  toString: function () { return "[object WildMaineBlueberry]";}
};
var wildMaineBlueberry = new WildMaineBlueberry("Dole frozen wild blueberries", "Tahitian");

Object.prototype.toString.apply(wildMaineBlueberry.halfHalf);
```

```
// "[object Array]"
Object.prototype.toString.call(wildMaineBlueberry.freshLemonJuice);
// "[object Array]"
({}).toString.apply(wildMaineBlueberry.blueberries);
// "[object Array]"
({}).toString.call(wildMaineBlueberry.vanilla);
// "[object Array]"
```

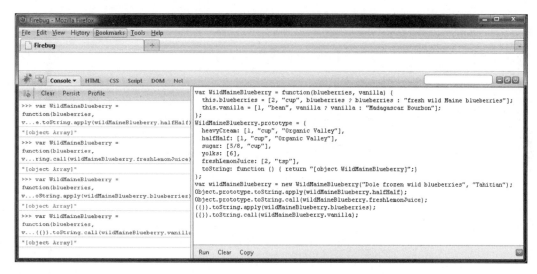

Figure 6–8. *Circumventing* `Array.prototype.toString()` *to verify arrayness*

OK, with `apply()` and `call()` now in our noggins, we can now write a conditional advance loader as shown next. Note that it's only necessary to wrap an empty object literal in parentheses when it begins a line of code (to prevent confusion as to whether it's an object or a block), so we can omit those here. Verify a couple of values for arrayness with `Array.isArray()`, comparing your work to Figure 6–9. If you're running Firefox 4, JavaScript will use the native ECMAScript 5 function, but, if you're running Firefox 3, it will use our knock-off.

```
if (Array.isArray === undefined) {
  Array.isArray = function(v) {
    return {}.toString.apply(v) === "[object Array]";
  };
}
var WildMaineBlueberry = function(blueberries, vanilla) {
  this.blueberries = [2, "cup", blueberries ? blueberries : "fresh wild Maine blueberries"];
  this.vanilla = [1, "bean", vanilla ? vanilla : "Madagascar Bourbon"];
};
WildMaineBlueberry.prototype = {
  heavyCream: [1, "cup", "Organic Valley"],
  halfHalf: [1, "cup", "Organic Valley"],
  sugar: [5/8, "cup"],
  yolks: [6],
  freshLemonJuice: [2, "tsp"],
```

```
    toString: function () { return "[object WildMaineBlueberry]";}
};
var wildMaineBlueberry = new WildMaineBlueberry("Dole frozen wild blueberries", "Tahitian");
```

```
Array.isArray(wildMaineBlueberry.halfHalf);
// true
Array.isArray(wildMaineBlueberry.halfHalf[2]);
// false
```

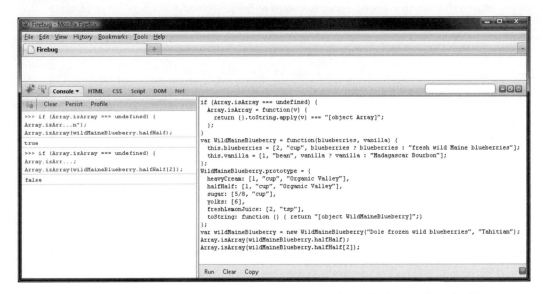

Figure 6–9. Verifying arrayness with the native `Array.isArray()` *method or our knock-off*

Rewriting cloneMembers()

Now that we have a better way to verify arrayness than simply groking whether a method like pop() or slice() is defined, let's rework cloneMembers() accordingly. Then try churning a quart of Coffee Heath Bar Crunch by cloning and augmenting a quart of Vanilla Heath Bar Crunch, verifying your work with Figure 6–10:

```
if (Array.isArray === undefined) {
  Array.isArray = function(v) {
    return {}.toString.apply(v) === "[object Array]";
  };
}
var cloneMembers = function (donor, donee) {
  donee = donee || {};
  for (var m in donor) {
    if (donor.hasOwnProperty(m)) {
      if (typeof donor[m] === "object" && donor[m] !== null) {
        donee[m] = Array.isArray(donor[m]) ? [] : {};
        cloneMembers(donor[m], donee[m]);
      } else {
```

```
        donee[m] = donor[m];
      }
    }
  }
  return donee;
};
var vanillaHeathBarCrunch = {
  heavyCream: [1, "cup", "Organic Valley"],
  halfHalf: [2, "cup", "Organic Valley"],
  sugar: [5/8, "cup"],
  yolks: [6],
  heathBars: [4, "bars, coarsely chopped"],
  vanilla: [1, "bean", "Madagascar Bourbon"]
};
var coffeeHeathBarCrunch = cloneMembers(vanillaHeathBarCrunch);
coffeeHeathBarCrunch.coffee = [1/4, "cup, coarsely ground", "Starbucks Espresso"];
console.dir(vanillaHeathBarCrunch);
console.dir(coffeeHeathBarCrunch);
```

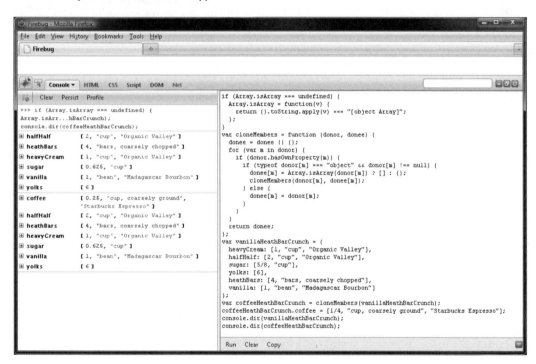

Figure 6–10. Churning a quart of Coffee Heath Bar Crunch with an improved cloneMembers() function

Currying

Because both functions and their parameters are values, we can create a new function value by combining an old function and one or more parameters, so those parameters are preset in the new function. Doing so is referred to as *currying* in honor of its creator, Haskell Curry, who also has the Haskell programming language named after him.

ECMAScript 5 defines one new method for function values, `Function.prototype.bind()`, that is ideal for currying. Though Explorer 9 and Firefox 4 will implement `Function.prototype.bind`, as of this writing Explorer 8, Firefox, 3, and other pre-ECMAScript 5 browsers do not. So, even when the cavalry arrives, we'll still need to emulate `Function.prototype.bind()`.

Let's roll up our sleeves and do so with the help of our conditional advance loaders for `Object.defineProperties()` and `Object.create()`. Those two conditional advance loaders were implemented with an `if` statement. But `if` isn't the only way to write a conditional advance loader—the `||` and `?:` operators work, too. Therefore, let's choose a value for `Function.prototype.bind()` with the `||` this time.

Remember from Chapter 3 that, if the first operand to `||` is falsey, which is to say evaluates to `""`, 0, `NaN`, `false`, `undefined`, or `null`, then the overall `||` expression evaluates to the second operand. So, if querying `Function.prototype.bind` returns `undefined`, as it would for any pre-ECMAScript 5 browser, then our `||` expression will evaluate to the second operand, which will be our emulation of `Function.prototype.bind()`. For now, just make that an empty literal that works with an `obj` parameter:

```
if (Object.defineProperties === undefined) {
  Object.defineProperties = function (obj, descriptors) {
      for (descriptor in descriptors) {
        if (descriptors.hasOwnProperty(descriptor)) {
          obj[descriptor] = descriptors[descriptor].value;
        }
      }
  };
}
if (Object.create === undefined) {
  Object.create = function (parent, descriptors) {
    var Proxy = function () {},
      child;
    Proxy.prototype = parent;
    child = new Proxy();
    if (descriptors !== undefined) {
      Object.defineProperties(child, descriptors);
    }
    return child;
  };
}

Function.prototype.bind = Function.prototype.bind ||
  function (obj) {
  };
```

Now the this keyword will refer to the function that inherits the `bind()` method. We'll save it to a variable named that so we can use that to build the new function. Traditionally, when you want to save this, you do so to a variable named that. But you don't have to. Like Haskell Curry, you could name the variable after yourself if you wanted.

```
if (Object.defineProperties === undefined) {
```

```
    Object.defineProperties = function (obj, descriptors) {
      for (descriptor in descriptors) {
        if (descriptors.hasOwnProperty(descriptor)) {
          obj[descriptor] = descriptors[descriptor].value;
        }
      }
    };
}
if (Object.create === undefined) {
  Object.create = function (parent, descriptors) {
    var Proxy = function () {},
      child;
    Proxy.prototype = parent;
    child = new Proxy();
    if (descriptors !== undefined) {
      Object.defineProperties(child, descriptors);
    }
    return child;
  };
}
Function.prototype.bind = Function.prototype.bind ||
  function (obj) {
    var that = this;
  };
```

By way of the comma operator, define another variable named ossify. Then borrow the slice() method from an empty array literal with the call() method, which slice() inherits from Function.prototype as any other function would. Then we'll invoke slice() in order to save any unnamed arguments passed to bind() as an array. So, ossify does not contain obj, just any additional arguments.

```
if (Object.defineProperties === undefined) {
  Object.defineProperties = function (obj, descriptors) {
    for (descriptor in descriptors) {
      if (descriptors.hasOwnProperty(descriptor)) {
        obj[descriptor] = descriptors[descriptor].value;
      }
    }
  };
}
if (Object.create === undefined) {
  Object.create = function (parent, descriptors) {
    var Proxy = function () {},
      child;
    Proxy.prototype = parent;
    child = new Proxy();
    if (descriptors !== undefined) {
      Object.defineProperties(child, descriptors);
    }
    return child;
  };
}
Function.prototype.bind = Function.prototype.bind ||
  function (obj) {
```

```
      var that = this,
        ossify = [].slice.call(arguments, 1);
    };
```

By way of the comma operator, we'll define a third variable with the var statement. That one will be named fn and will contain the function value created by currying that and ossify.

```
if (Object.defineProperties === undefined) {
  Object.defineProperties = function (obj, descriptors) {
      for (descriptor in descriptors) {
        if (descriptors.hasOwnProperty(descriptor)) {
          obj[descriptor] = descriptors[descriptor].value;
        }
      }
  };
}
if (Object.create === undefined) {
  Object.create = function (parent, descriptors) {
    var Proxy = function () {},
      child;
    Proxy.prototype = parent;
    child = new Proxy();
    if (descriptors !== undefined) {
      Object.defineProperties(child, descriptors);
    }
    return child;
  };
}
Function.prototype.bind = Function.prototype.bind ||
  function (obj) {
    var that = this,
      ossify = [].slice.call(arguments, 1),
      fn = function () {
        return that.apply(this instanceof that ? this : obj,
ossify.concat([].slice.call(arguments, 0)));
      };
  };
```

Now in the event that that contains a constructor function, we need to ensure fn has the same prototype chain. To do so, we'd assign to fn.prototype the return value of passing that.prototype to Object.create(). This ensures that objects created by that and fn inherit the same members. Finally, we want to return the function value in fn, which is a combination of the function value in that and the parameters in ossify.

```
if (Object.defineProperties === undefined) {
  Object.defineProperties = function (obj, descriptors) {
      for (descriptor in descriptors) {
        if (descriptors.hasOwnProperty(descriptor)) {
          obj[descriptor] = descriptors[descriptor].value;
        }
      }
  };
}
if (Object.create === undefined) {
  Object.create = function (parent, descriptors) {
```

```
    var Proxy = function () {},
      child;
    Proxy.prototype = parent;
    child = new Proxy();
    if (descriptors !== undefined) {
      Object.defineProperties(child, descriptors);
    }
    return child;
  };
}
Function.prototype.bind = Function.prototype.bind ||
  function (obj) {
    var that = this,
      ossify = [].slice.call(arguments, 1),
      fn = function () {
        return that.apply(this instanceof that ? this : obj,
ossify.concat([].slice.call(arguments, 0)));
      };
    fn.prototype = Object.create(that.prototype);
    return fn;
  };
```

Now for the moment of truth. Let's try currying a constructor that churns Wild Maine Blueberry ice cream with its blueberries and lemon parameters. Insofar as we're presetting those parameters to their typical winter values—no fresh wild blueberries to be had now—we'll name the new constructor `WinterWildMaineBlueberry`. Then since `WinterWildMaineBlueberry` just takes a vanilla parameter—the blueberries and lemon parameters are preset—we'll just pass `"Tahitian"` to choose a mild vanilla bean, verifying our work with Figure 6–11:

```
if (Object.defineProperties === undefined) {
  Object.defineProperties = function (obj, descriptors) {
      for (descriptor in descriptors) {
        if (descriptors.hasOwnProperty(descriptor)) {
          obj[descriptor] = descriptors[descriptor].value;
        }
      }
  };
}
if (Object.create === undefined) {
  Object.create = function (parent, descriptors) {
    var Proxy = function () {},
      child;
    Proxy.prototype = parent;
    child = new Proxy();
    if (descriptors !== undefined) {
      Object.defineProperties(child, descriptors);
    }
    return child;
  };
}
Function.prototype.bind = Function.prototype.bind ||
  function (obj) {
    var that = this,
      ossify = [].slice.call(arguments, 1),
```

```
        fn = function () {
            return that.apply(this instanceof that ? this : obj,
ossify.concat([].slice.call(arguments, 0)));
        };
        fn.prototype = Object.create(that.prototype);
        return fn;
    };

var WildMaineBlueberry = function(blueberries, lemon, vanilla) {
    this.blueberries = [2, "cup", blueberries ? blueberries : "fresh wild Maine blueberries"];
    this.freshLemonJuice = [2, "tsp", lemon ? lemon : "Meyer"];
    this.vanilla = [1, "bean", vanilla ? vanilla : "Madagascar Bourbon"];
};
WildMaineBlueberry.prototype = {
    heavyCream: [1, "cup", "Organic Valley"],
    halfHalf: [1, "cup", "Organic Valley"],
    sugar: [5/8, "cup"],
    yolks: [6]
};
var WinterWildMaineBlueberry = WildMaineBlueberry.bind(null, "Dole frozen wild blueberries",
"Eureka");
var iceCream = new WinterWildMaineBlueberry("Tahitian");
console.dir(iceCream);
```

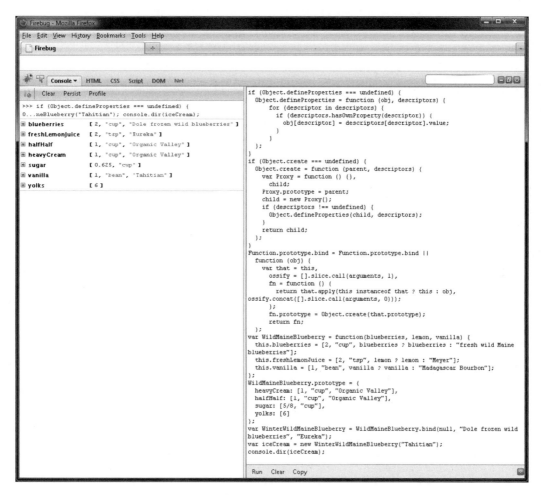

Figure 6–11. WinterWildMaineBlueberry() *is created by combining* WildMaineBlueberry() *and its*
blueberries and lemon parameters.

Chaining Methods

If you save a function to an object, the function is referred to as a method. Moreover, within the body of
the method, this refers to the object you saved the method to. So, when you invoke a function as a
constructor, this refers to the object the constructor returns, but when you invoke a function as a
method, this refers to the object containing the function. Finally, if you invoke a function traditionally
as a global method, then this refers to the global object window. However, ECMAScript 5 changes the
value of this to null from window to prevent your coming to grief if you forget to invoke a constructor
with new.

So anyway, to illustrate the point let's use Object.create() to create an object named iceCream that
inherits methods named _french(), _vanilla(), and _coffee() from another object named churn. Then

if we invoke those methods on iceCream, this will refer to iceCream and populate the members of iceCream. Therefore, as Figure 6–12 displays, iceCream will contain heavyCream, halfHalf, sugar, yolks, vanilla, and coffee members, which we can display by calling _print():

```
if (Object.defineProperties === undefined) {
  Object.defineProperties = function (obj, descriptors) {
      for (descriptor in descriptors) {
        if (descriptors.hasOwnProperty(descriptor)) {
          obj[descriptor] = descriptors[descriptor].value;
        }
      }
  };
}
if (Object.create === undefined) {
  Object.create = function (parent, descriptors) {
    var Proxy = function () {},
      child;
    Proxy.prototype = parent;
    child = new Proxy();
    if (descriptors !== undefined) {
      Object.defineProperties(child, descriptors);
    }
    return child;
  };
}
var churn = {};
churn._french = function (heavyCream, halfHalf, sugar, yolks) {
  this.heavyCream = [1, "cup", heavyCream || "Organic Valley"],
  this.halfHalf = [1, "cup", halfHalf || "Organic Valley"],
  this.sugar = [sugar || 5/8, "cup"],
  this.yolks = [yolks || 6]
};
churn._vanilla = function (vanilla) {
  this.vanilla = [1, "bean", vanilla || "Madagascar Bourbon"];
};
churn._coffee = function (coffee) {
  this.coffee = [1/4, "cup, coarsely ground", coffee || "Starbucks Espresso"];
};
churn._print = function () {
  var copy = {};
  for (var m in this) {
    this.hasOwnProperty(m) && (copy[m] = this[m]);
  }
  console.dir(copy);
};
var iceCream = Object.create(churn);
iceCream._french();
iceCream._vanilla();
iceCream._coffee();
iceCream._print();
```

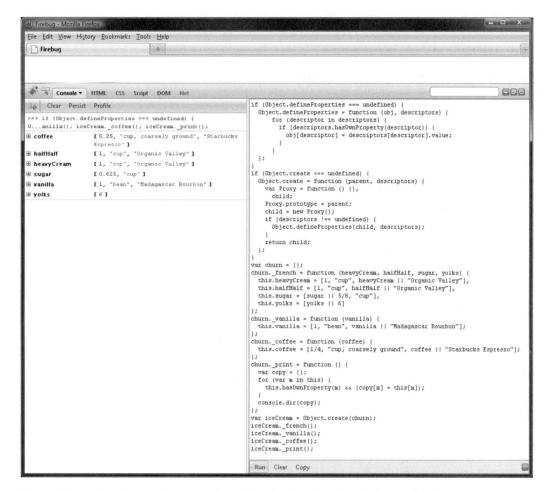

Figure 6–12. *this refers to the containing object for functions invoked as methods.*

That all worked fine, but there is a more elegant way to achieve what we just did, by chaining method calls together.

```
iceCream._french()._vanilla()._coffee()._print();
```

Let's see how to enable this technique.

Right now, our methods return `undefined`, but to chain a method to another one, we have to return `this` instead. As Figure 6–13 displays, doing so works just as well as, but more elegantly than, invoking the methods separately. Note that chaining methods is also referred to as cascades. Note too that chaining is very common in DOM and JavaScript libraries.

```
var clone = typeof Object.create === "function" ?
  Object.create :
  function (donor) {
    var Proxy = function () {};
    Proxy.prototype = donor;
```

```
      return new Proxy();
   };
var churn = {};
churn._vanilla = function (vanilla) {
   this.vanilla = [1, "bean", vanilla || "Madagascar Bourbon"];
   return this;
};
churn._coffee = function (coffee) {
   this.coffee = [1/4, "cup, coarsely ground", coffee || "Starbucks Espresso"];
   return this;
};
churn._french = function (heavyCream, halfHalf, sugar, yolks) {
   this.heavyCream = [1, "cup", heavyCream || "Organic Valley"],
   this.halfHalf = [1, "cup", halfHalf || "Organic Valley"],
   this.sugar = [sugar || 5/8, "cup"],
   this.yolks = [yolks || 6]
   return this;
};
churn._coffee = function (coffee) {
   this.coffee = [1/4, "cup, coarsely ground", coffee || "Starbucks Espresso"];
   return this;
};
churn._print = function () {
   var copy = {};
   for (var m in this) {
      this.hasOwnProperty(m) && (copy[m] = this[m]);
   }
   console.dir(copy);
};
var iceCream = clone(churn);
iceCream._french()._vanilla()._coffee()._print();
```

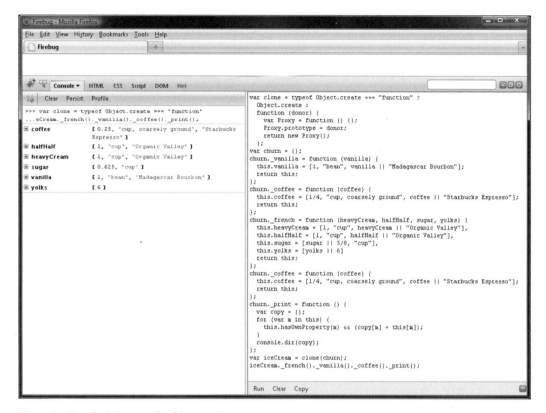

***Figure 6–13.** Chaining method invocations*

Closure and Returning Functions

Vanilla is among the most powerful flavor enhancers, which is to say it enhances our ability to taste chocolate, coffee, fruit, nuts, and other foods. Moreover, vanilla elevates our perception of sweetness. For this reason, most ice-cream flavors are embellishments of vanilla ice cream.

So, while you could make chocolate ice cream from a sweet cream base, adding a vanilla bean boosts the chocolate flavor of the cocoa. To further do so, we could coarsely chop a cup, roughly 4 ounces, of bittersweet chocolate—I'd recommend Callebaut, Ghirardelli, or Lindt—and melt that into the custard.

Note that chocolate is made by crushing cacao beans and pressing them into an unsweetened paste, referred to as chocolate liqueur, which is comprised of cocoa and cocoa butter. So cocoa is made by removing the cocoa butter and grinding the now fat-free cacao paste into a powder. To remove some acidity and enhance the chocolate flavor, cocoa may be Dutched with alkali.

On the other hand, bittersweet chocolate is made by adding additional cocoa butter to pure chocolate liqueur and sweetening it with sugar. Fine bittersweet chocolate by Callebaut, Lindt, Ghirardelli, and others contain 60 to 70 percent pure cacao paste, while inexpensive bittersweet chocolate typically contains just 15 percent cacao, the FDA minimum. So paying an extra dollar or two for four or five times as much cacao is worth it if you love chocolate ice cream.

Let's get to the JavaScript to see what we can do with all this information. First, some background: any variable that you declare within the curly braces wrapping the block of an if, for, while, or other compound statement *is* visible outside the block, as you have seen throughout this book. Put another way, curly braces do not provide a way to create private variables.

In contrast, functions have **function scope**, which means that any variables or functions declared within the curly braces wrapping a function block normally *are not* visible outside of the block. Let's find out why.

Whenever you define a function, JavaScript saves the **scope chain** as part of the new function object; that is to say, the scope chain is the sequence of objects, beginning with the function's own call object and ending with the global window object. This means this part of the scope chain is set in stone before the function ever runs. However, any variables, functions, or arguments contained by the call and global objects comprising that scope chain are live.

Then, when you invoke a function, JavaScript adds any variables defined locally within the function, named parameters, the arguments object, and this to the scope chain. So these variable objects will differ every time you invoke the function. JavaScript looks in this complete set of items in the scope chain when it is looking up the value of a variable. In other words, when you invoke a function that uses a variable, JavaScript can only use the variable if it is declared in the scope chain.

Normally, after an invoked function returns, everything added to the scope chain when you invoked the function is destroyed. However, if you create a **closure**, the objects contained in function scope are not destroyed. Therefore, you may query the named parameters and locally defined variables for that invocation even after it has ended. Let's look at closures now.

Insofar as closure is a wildly popular technique, do yourself a favor and go ten toes in while we explore those now. Say we want to save some default values for bittersweet chocolate, cocoa, and vanilla to a closure our ChocolateChocolate() constructor can query. One way would be to define those as local variables for a self-invoking function and then have its return value be the ChocolateChocolate() constructor.

So, in the following sample, chocolateChocolate is churned with Callebaut cocoa and Madagascar Bourbon vanilla due to closure, as Figure 6–14 displays, along with the function JavaScript assigns to ChocolateChocolate.

```javascript
var ChocolateChocolate = function () {
  var _bittersweet = "Ghirardelli",
    _cocoa = "Callebaut",
    _vanilla = "Madagascar Bourbon";
  return function (bittersweet, cocoa, vanilla) {
    this.bittersweet = [1, "cup", bittersweet || _bittersweet];
    this.cocoa = [3, "tbs", cocoa || _cocoa];
    this.vanilla = [1, "bean", vanilla || _vanilla];
  };
}();
ChocolateChocolate.prototype = {
  heavyCream: [1, "cup", "Organic Valley"],
  halfHalf: [1, "cup", "Organic Valley"],
  sugar: [5/8, "cup"],
  yolks: [6]
};
var chocolateChocolate = new ChocolateChocolate("Lindt");
console.dir(chocolateChocolate);
ChocolateChocolate.toString();
```

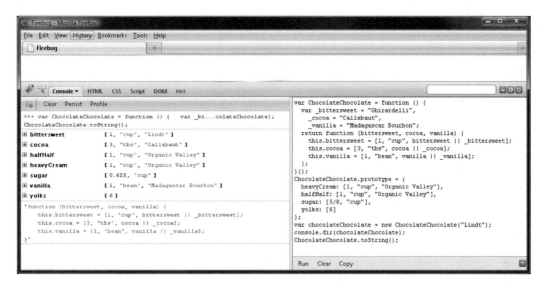

Figure 6–14. *Querying local variables saved to a closure*

Another way to save default values for bittersweet chocolate, cocoa, and vanilla to a closure would be to define _bittersweet, _cocoa, and _vanilla parameters for the self-invoking function that returns the ChocolateChocolate() constructor. Then pass their values to the self-invoking function.

So, as Figure 6–15 displays, saving our default values as named parameters for a closure works just as well as saving those as local variables for the closure. Note that the definition of ChocolateChocolate() is the same as in the previous sample. The reason why we did not have to change the definition of ChocolateChocolate() is that there's no difference between named parameters and local variables on an activation object. That is to say, named parameters become local variables. The only difference between the two is the way you assign a value to them.

```
var ChocolateChocolate = function (_bittersweet, _cocoa, _vanilla) {
  return function (bittersweet, cocoa, vanilla) {
    this.bittersweet = [1, "cup", bittersweet || _bittersweet];
    this.cocoa = [3, "tbs", cocoa || _cocoa];
    this.vanilla = [1, "bean", vanilla || _vanilla];
  };
}("Ghirardelli", "Callebaut", "Madagascar Bourbon");
ChocolateChocolate.prototype = {
  heavyCream: [1, "cup", "Organic Valley"],
  halfHalf: [1, "cup", "Organic Valley"],
  sugar: [5/8, "cup"],
  yolks: [6]
};
var chocolateChocolate = new ChocolateChocolate("Lindt");
console.dir(chocolateChocolate);
ChocolateChocolate.toString();
```

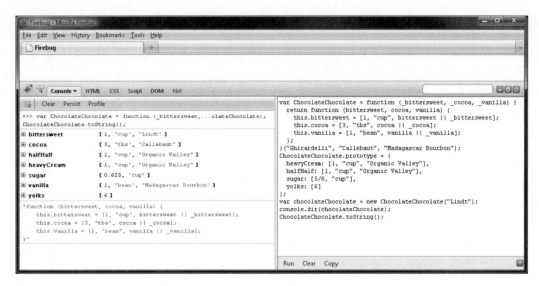

Figure 6–15. Querying named parameters saved to a closure

A third way to save default values for bittersweet chocolate, cocoa, and vanilla to a closure would be to first declare the variable ChocolateChocolate and then assign a function to it from within the self-invoking function. That is to say, export a locally defined function to a global variable as in the following sample and Figure 6–16. Note that, as in the previous two samples, we did not have to change definition for the ChocolateChocolate() constructor. It's just the way we create a closure for it to query that differs. Note too that we wrap the self-invoking function within parentheses. Those are mandatory inasmuch as we want JavaScript to interpret the function as a function expression rather than a function declaration. That is to say, to prevent a syntax error.

```
var ChocolateChocolate = null;
(function (_bittersweet, _cocoa, _vanilla) {
  ChocolateChocolate = function (bittersweet, cocoa, vanilla) {
    this.bittersweet = [1, "cup", bittersweet || _bittersweet];
    this.cocoa = [3, "tbs", cocoa || _cocoa];
    this.vanilla = [1, "bean", vanilla || _vanilla];
  };
}("Ghirardelli", "Callebaut", "Madagascar Bourbon"));
ChocolateChocolate.prototype = {
  heavyCream: [1, "cup", "Organic Valley"],
  halfHalf: [1, "cup", "Organic Valley"],
  sugar: [5/8, "cup"],
  yolks: [6]
};
var chocolateChocolate = new ChocolateChocolate("Lindt");
console.dir(chocolateChocolate);
ChocolateChocolate.toString();
```

***Figure 6–16.** Exporting the constructor function from a self-invoking function expression*

The previous sample could be reworked to use locally defined _bittersweet, _cocoa, and _vanilla variables rather than _bittersweet, _cocoa, and _vanilla named parameters. Try it, verifying your work with Figure 6–17.

```
var ChocolateChocolate = null;
(function () {
  var _bittersweet = "Ghirardelli",
    _cocoa = "Callebaut",
    _vanilla = "Madagascar Bourbon";
  ChocolateChocolate = function (bittersweet, cocoa, vanilla) {
    this.bittersweet = [1, "cup", bittersweet || _bittersweet];
    this.cocoa = [3, "tbs", cocoa || _cocoa];
    this.vanilla = [1, "bean", vanilla || _vanilla];
  };
}());
ChocolateChocolate.prototype = {
  heavyCream: [1, "cup", "Organic Valley"],
  halfHalf: [1, "cup", "Organic Valley"],
  sugar: [5/8, "cup"],
  yolks: [6]
};
var chocolateChocolate = new ChocolateChocolate("Lindt");
console.dir(chocolateChocolate);
ChocolateChocolate.toString();
```

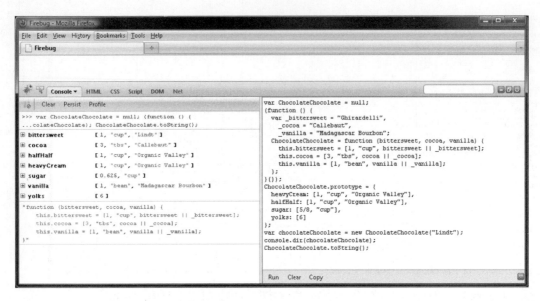

Figure 6–17. Reworking the previous sample to use locally defined _bittersweet, _cocoa, and _vanilla variables rather than _bittersweet, _cocoa, and _vanilla named parameters

Finally, note that, rather than wrapping the self-invocation in parentheses, you will often see the function expression wrapped in parentheses, which are then followed by the () operator as in the following sample. Try it, verifying your work with Figure 6–18:

```javascript
var ChocolateChocolate = null;
(function (_bittersweet, _cocoa, _vanilla) {
  ChocolateChocolate = function (bittersweet, cocoa, vanilla) {
    this.bittersweet = [1, "cup", bittersweet || _bittersweet];
    this.cocoa = [3, "tbs", cocoa || _cocoa];
    this.vanilla = [1, "bean", vanilla || _vanilla];
  };
})("Ghirardelli", "Callebaut", "Madagascar Bourbon");
ChocolateChocolate.prototype = {
  heavyCream: [1, "cup", "Organic Valley"],
  halfHalf: [1, "cup", "Organic Valley"],
  sugar: [5/8, "cup"],
  yolks: [6]
};
var chocolateChocolate = new ChocolateChocolate("Lindt");
console.dir(chocolateChocolate);
ChocolateChocolate.toString();
```

Figure 6–18. Moving the ( ) operator outside the parentheses works fine, too.

Passing a Configuration Object

Often, if you have a number of optional parameters, such as in our closure samples, you will want to pass a configuration object rather than separate parameters. Doing so prevents your having to pass "" or some other falsy value parameters prior to the one you want to explicitly pass as in the following sample:

```
var ChocolateChocolate = function () {
  var _bittersweet = "Ghirardelli",
    _cocoa = "Callebaut",
    _vanilla = "Madagascar Bourbon";
  return function (bittersweet, cocoa, vanilla) {
    this.bittersweet = [1, "cup", bittersweet || _bittersweet];
    this.cocoa = [3, "tbs", cocoa || _cocoa];
    this.vanilla = [1, "bean", vanilla || _vanilla];
  };
}();
ChocolateChocolate.prototype = {
  heavyCream: [1, "cup", "Organic Valley"],
  halfHalf: [1, "cup", "Organic Valley"],
  sugar: [5/8, "cup"],
  yolks: [6]
};
var chocolateChocolate = new ChocolateChocolate("", "", "Tahitian");
console.dir(chocolateChocolate);
```

So here's how we can remedy that bugaboo by defining one parameter named pref. As Figure 6–19 displays, this prevents our having to pass empty strings for bittersweet and cocoa in order to pass "Tahitian" for vanilla.

```
var ChocolateChocolate = function () {
  var _bittersweet = "Ghirardelli",
    _cocoa = "Callebaut",
    _vanilla = "Madagascar Bourbon";
  return function (pref) {
    pref || (pref = {});
    this.bittersweet = [1, "cup", pref.bittersweet || _bittersweet];
    this.cocoa = [3, "tbs", pref.cocoa || _cocoa];
    this.vanilla = [1, "bean", pref.vanilla || _vanilla];
  };
}();
ChocolateChocolate.prototype = {
  heavyCream: [1, "cup", "Organic Valley"],
  halfHalf: [1, "cup", "Organic Valley"],
  sugar: [5/8, "cup"],
  yolks: [6]
};
var chocolateChocolate = new ChocolateChocolate({vanilla: "Tahitian"});
console.dir(chocolateChocolate);
```

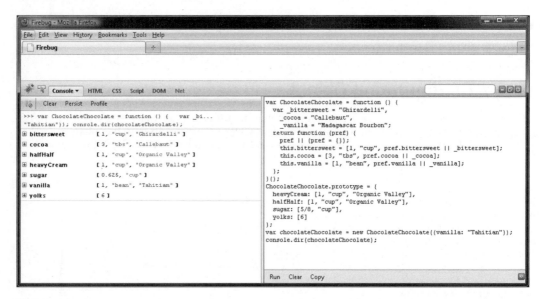

Figure 6–19. Defining a configuration object in place of several defaut parameters

Callback Functions

Insofar as functions are values, you can pass a function as a parameter to another function, which can then invoke it. A function passed and invoked this way is referred to as a **callback function**. Event listener functions, which we'll explore in Chapter 9, are the most common type of callback function. But they're not the only way to implement this pattern.

For example, we could rework our clone function from earlier in the chapter so that we can pass it either an object or a callback constructor function. So let's do so now, and then test it both ways by passing it a constructor named SweetCream as well as by passing it SweetCream.prototype. As Figure 6–20 displays, the end result is the same.

```
var clone = typeof Object.create === "function" ?
  function (donor) {
    return typcof donor !== "function" ?
      Object.create(donor) :
      Object.create(new donor());
  } :
  function (donor) {
    var Proxy = function () {};
    Proxy.prototype = typeof donor !== "function" ?
      donor :
      new donor();
    return new Proxy();
  };

var SweetCream = function () {};
SweetCream.prototype = {
  heavyCream: [1, "cup", "Organic Valley"],
  halfHalf: [1, "cup", "Organic Valley"],
  sugar: [5/8, "cup"],
  yolks: [6]
};
var sweetCream = clone(SweetCream);
console.dir(sweetCream);
var sweetCream2 = clone(SweetCream.prototype);
console.dir(sweetCream2);
```

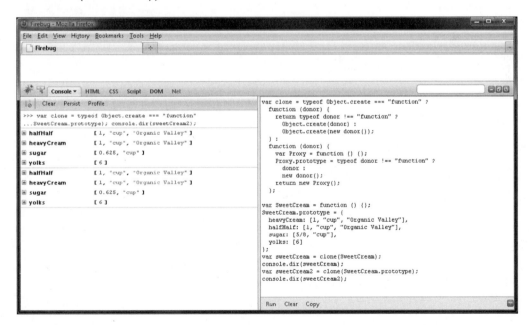

Figure 6–20. Passing a SweetCream() callback function to clone()

Memoization

In the event that you have a function that does memory-intensive or identically repetitive work, you might want to cache its return values to a closure. Doing so is referred to as *memoization*. To illustrate this technique, let's memoize our ChocolateChocolate() constructor. To do so, we'll save a local variable named memo to a closure. Then, every time ChocolateChocolate() is invoked, we'll add a member to memo containing the returned object. Those members will be named with a string created by gluing the parameter values together with underscores. Just for the purposes of running this in Firebug, we'll pass the memo object to console.dir so that we can view its members following each invocation of ChocolateChocolate().

So, as Figure 6–21 displays, invoking ChocolateChocolate() two times in a row with the same parameters, returns the object from memo the second time. To verify that, we can compare the return values with ===. Remember from Chapter 3 that === returns true for two objects only if their heap memory locations are the same. That is to say, to ===, no two quarts of double chocolate ice cream are the same—a quart of double chocolate ice cream can only be equal to itself.

```
var ChocolateChocolate = function () {
  var memo = {};
  return function (bittersweet, cocoa, vanilla) {
    var m = bittersweet + "_" + cocoa + "_" + vanilla;
    if (typeof memo[m] === "object") {
      return memo[m];
    }
    this.bittersweet = [1, "cup", bittersweet || "Callebaut"];
    this.cocoa = [3, "tbs", cocoa || "Callebaut"];
    this.vanilla = [1, "bean", vanilla || "Madagascar Bourbon"];
    memo[m] = this;
    console.dir(memo);
  };
}();
ChocolateChocolate.prototype = {
  heavyCream: [1, "cup", "Organic Valley"],
  halfHalf: [1, "cup", "Organic Valley"],
  sugar: [5/8, "cup"],
  yolks: [6]
};
var chocolateChocolate = new ChocolateChocolate("Lindt");
console.dir(chocolateChocolate);
var chocolateChocolate2 = new ChocolateChocolate("Lindt");
console.dir(chocolateChocolate);
chocolateChocolate === chocolateChocolate2;
```

Figure 6–21. Memoizing `ChocolateChocolate()`

Global Abatement with Modules

Self-invoking function expressions, which we used earlier in the closure samples, can be used to eliminate global variables, referred to as global abatement, by way of modules. Eliminating global variables is often a good idea to avoid name clashes with local variables. In other words, a global variable could easily have the same name as a local variable, which is not a good idea. The script we'll hand-code at the end of this book will leave no global footprint due to the module pattern, which is quite simple.

Just put your script within the body of a self-invoking function expression. As discussed earlier, the () operator may go inside or outside the parentheses wrapping the function expression. So one of the following two patterns will do:

```
(function () {
// paste script here
}());
```

```
(function () {
// paste script here
})();
```

Using the first way, let's paste in our callback sample from earlier in the chapter. As Figure 6–22 and 6–23 display, we can invoke clone() from within the module but not outside of it for the reason that clone() and SweetCream() are not globally defined. So JavaScript returns a reference error in Figure 6–23.

```
(function () {
var clone = typeof Object.create === "function" ?
  function (donor) {
    return typeof donor !== "function" ?
      Object.create(donor) :
      Object.create(new donor());
  } :
  function (donor) {
    var Proxy = function () {};
    Proxy.prototype = typeof donor !== "function" ?
      donor :
      new donor();
    return new Proxy();
  };

var SweetCream = function () {};
SweetCream.prototype = {
  heavyCream: [1, "cup", "Organic Valley"],
  halfHalf: [1, "cup", "Organic Valley"],
  sugar: [5/8, "cup"],
  yolks: [6]
};
console.dir(clone(SweetCream));
}());
```

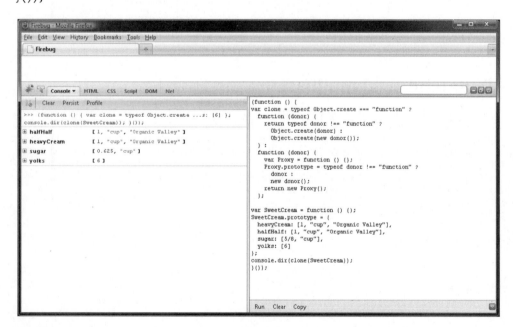

Figure 6–22. Calling clone() within the module works

```javascript
(function () {
var clone = typeof Object.create === "function" ?
  function (donor) {
    return typeof donor !== "function" ?
      Object.create(donor) :
      Object.create(new donor());
  } :
  function (donor) {
    var Proxy = function () {};
    Proxy.prototype = typeof donor !== "function" ?
      donor :
      new donor();
    return new Proxy();
  };

var SweetCream = function () {};
SweetCream.prototype = {
  heavyCream: [1, "cup", "Organic Valley"],
  halfHalf: [1, "cup", "Organic Valley"],
  sugar: [5/8, "cup"],
  yolks: [6]
};
}());
console.dir(clone(SweetCream));
```

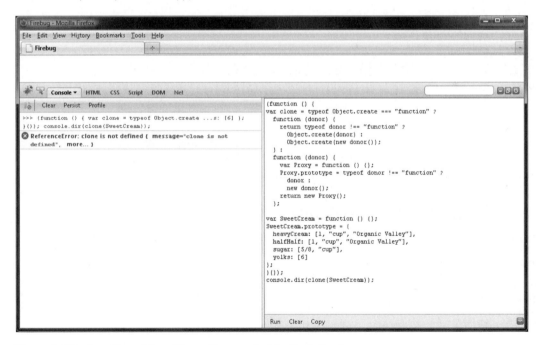

Figure 6–23. clone() and SweetCream() are not globally defined.

Arrays

Not only did Ben & Jerry's churn Wild Maine Blueberry from 1990 to 1992, but my Pittsburgh Pirates made it to the NL championship series during those years, too. But in 1993, Wild Maine Blueberry was laid to rest, and Barry Bonds left for San Francisco, where he would set MLB marks for most MVP awards (7), homeruns in a season (73), and homeruns in a career (762). My Pirates then embarked on a streak of losing seasons, 18 as of this writing, unrivaled in the history of North American pro sports (MLB, NFL, NBA, NHL).

So anyway, let's explore some predefined array methods with an array of arrays representing the Pirates' unenviable streak of futility, which we'll assign to a variable named `pirates`. Note that these predefined methods are saved to `Array.prototype`. So every array inherits those methods by way of the prototype chain in the same way that our ice-cream objects inherited members like `halfHalf` and `yolks` from the prototype chain.

```
var pirates = [[2010, 57, 105],
  [2009, 62, 99],
  [2008, 67, 95],
  [2007, 68, 94],
  [2006, 67, 95],
  [2005, 67, 95],
  [2004, 72, 89],
  [2003, 75, 87],
  [2002, 72, 89],
  [2001, 62, 100],
  [2000, 69, 93],
  [1999, 78, 83],
  [1998, 69, 93],
  [1997, 79, 83],
  [1996, 73, 89],
  [1995, 58, 86],
  [1994, 53, 61],
  [1993, 75, 87]];
```

■ **Note** `pirates` is a valid JSON array. We'll explore JSON, the popular Ajax data exchange format in Chapter 10.

Plucking Elements from an Array

Alright, to pluck the first element in `pirates` we'd invoke its `shift()` method. So, if we pass the return value of `shift()` to `console.dir()`, JavaScript will print the 2010 season for us in Firebug as Figure 6–24 displays.

```
var pirates = [[2010, 57, 105],
  [2009, 62, 99],
  [2008, 67, 95],
  [2007, 68, 94],
  [2006, 67, 95],
  [2005, 67, 95],
  [2004, 72, 89],
  [2003, 75, 87],
```

```
  [2002, 72, 89],
  [2001, 62, 100],
  [2000, 69, 93],
  [1999, 78, 83],
  [1998, 69, 93],
  [1997, 79, 83],
  [1996, 73, 89],
  [1995, 58, 86],
  [1994, 53, 61],
  [1993, 75, 87]];
console.dir(pirates.shift());
```

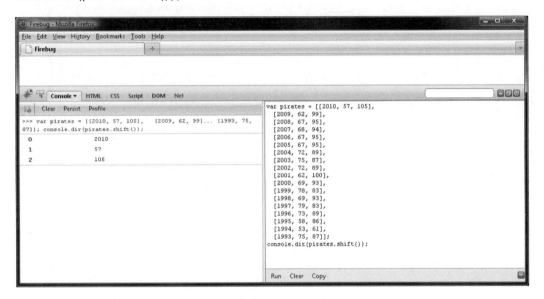

Figure 6–24. shift() removes and returns the first element in an array.

Note that shift() modifies pirates, too, by shifting the contents down one place in the array every time it is invoked. This means that element 0 is removed, element 1 becomes element 0, and so on. So, after invoking shift() three times in a row, pirates has just 15 elements rather than 18 as Figure 6–25 displays.

```
var pirates = [[2010, 57, 105],
  [2009, 62, 99],
  [2008, 67, 95],
  [2007, 68, 94],
  [2006, 67, 95],
  [2005, 67, 95],
  [2004, 72, 89],
  [2003, 75, 87],
  [2002, 72, 89],
  [2001, 62, 100],
  [2000, 69, 93],
  [1999, 78, 83],
```

```
    [1998, 69, 93],
    [1997, 79, 83],
    [1996, 73, 89],
    [1995, 58, 86],
    [1994, 53, 61],
    [1993, 75, 87]];
pirates.shift(),
  pirates.shift(),
  pirates.shift(),
  console.dir(pirates);
```

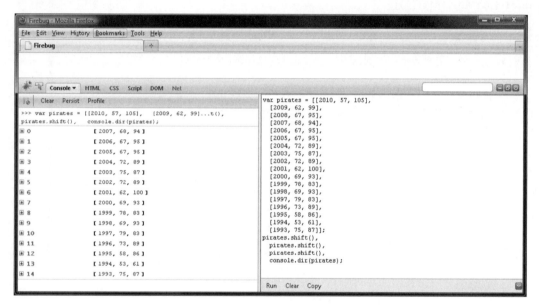

Figure 6–25. *pirates has 15 elements rather than 18 after invoking its shift() method three times.*

Naturally, JavaScript provides a method to pluck the last element from an array, which is named pop(). So, invoking pop() on pirates three times in a row removes and returns the 1993, 1994, and 1995 seasons, as Figure 6–26 displays.

```
var pirates = [[2010, 57, 105],
  [2009, 62, 99],
  [2008, 67, 95],
  [2007, 68, 94],
  [2006, 67, 95],
  [2005, 67, 95],
  [2004, 72, 89],
  [2003, 75, 87],
  [2002, 72, 89],
  [2001, 62, 100],
  [2000, 69, 93],
  [1999, 78, 83],
  [1998, 69, 93],
  [1997, 79, 83],
```

```
  [1996, 73, 89],
  [1995, 58, 86],
  [1994, 53, 61],
  [1993, 75, 87]];
console.dir(pirates.pop()),
  console.dir(pirates.pop()),
  console.dir(pirates.pop());
```

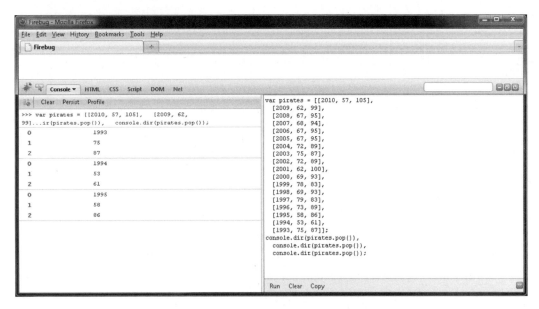

Figure 6–26. pop( ) *removes and returns the last element in an array.*

Note that, like shift(), pop() modifies the array it is invoked upon. So, after invoking pop() three times on pirates, there are just 15 elements left as Figure 6–27 displays:

```
var pirates = [[2010, 57, 105],
  [2009, 62, 99],
  [2008, 67, 95],
  [2007, 68, 94],
  [2006, 67, 95],
  [2005, 67, 95],
  [2004, 72, 89],
  [2003, 75, 87],
  [2002, 72, 89],
  [2001, 62, 100],
  [2000, 69, 93],
  [1999, 78, 83],
  [1998, 69, 93],
  [1997, 79, 83],
  [1996, 73, 89],
  [1995, 58, 86],
  [1994, 53, 61],
  [1993, 75, 87]];
```

```
pirates.pop(),
  pirates.pop(),
  pirates.pop(),
  console.dir(pirates);
```

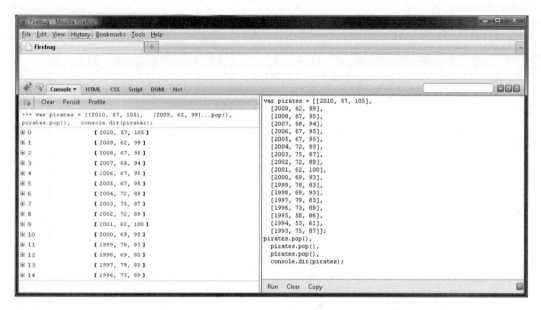

Figure 6–27. pirates has 15 elements rather than 18 after invoking its pop( ) method three times.

Adding Elements to an Array

To do the inverse of shift( ), which is to say add an element to the beginning of an array, call an array's unshift( ) method. The Pirates hired a new manager, Clint Hurdle, for 2011. So I'm hopeful they'll win say 15 more games than in 2010. Let's add that prediction of 72 wins and 90 losses to pirates by invoking its unshift( ) method. Then pass pirates to console.dir( ) and JavaScript will print the modified array in Firebug as Figure 6–28 displays.

```
var pirates = [[2010, 57, 105],
  [2009, 62, 99],
  [2008, 67, 95],
  [2007, 68, 94],
  [2006, 67, 95],
  [2005, 67, 95],
  [2004, 72, 89],
  [2003, 75, 87],
  [2002, 72, 89],
  [2001, 62, 100],
  [2000, 69, 93],
  [1999, 78, 83],
  [1998, 69, 93],
  [1997, 79, 83],
  [1996, 73, 89],
```

```
  [1995, 58, 86],
  [1994, 53, 61],
  [1993, 75, 87]];
pirates.unshift([2011, 72, 90]),
console.dir(pirates);
```

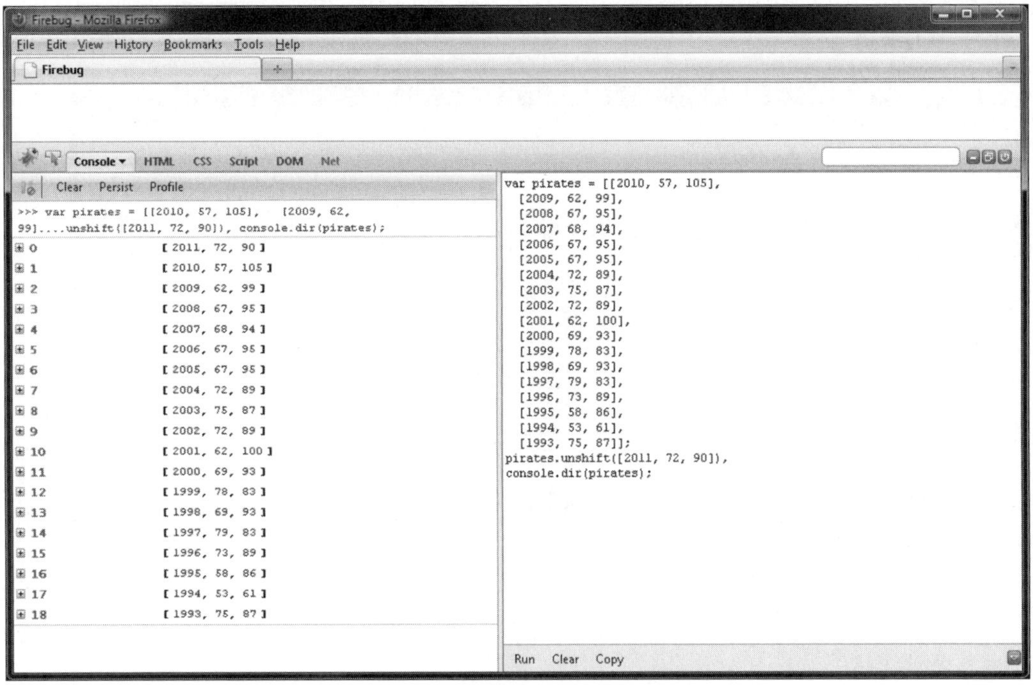

Figure 6–28. *unshift() adds an element to the beginning of an array.*

Similarly, pop() has an inverse, too. But it's not named unpop(), but push(). So let's add the 1992, 1991, and 1990 glory years to pirates by calling push() three times in a row. Then pass pirates to console.dir(), verifying our work with Figure 6–29.

```
var pirates = [[2010, 57, 105],
  [2009, 62, 99],
  [2008, 67, 95],
  [2007, 68, 94],
  [2006, 67, 95],
  [2005, 67, 95],
  [2004, 72, 89],
  [2003, 75, 87],
  [2002, 72, 89],
  [2001, 62, 100],
  [2000, 69, 93],
  [1999, 78, 83],
  [1998, 69, 93],
  [1997, 79, 83],
```

```
    [1996, 73, 89],
    [1995, 58, 86],
    [1994, 53, 61],
    [1993, 75, 87]];
pirates.push([1992, 96, 66]),
  pirates.push([1991, 98, 64]),
  pirates.push([1990, 95, 67]);
console.dir(pirates);
```

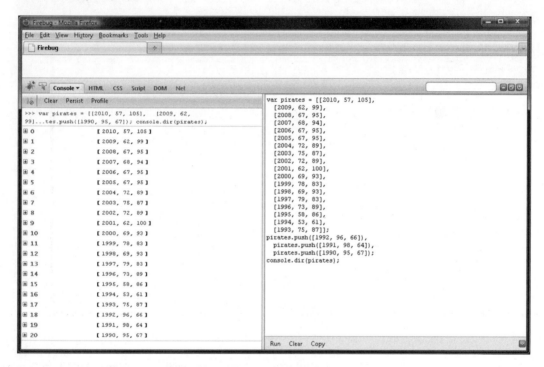

Figure 6–29. push( ) adds an element to the end of an array.

Gluing Two Arrays Together

Alrighty, to glue two arrays together, you would invoke concat( ) on the first array, passing the second array as a parameter. So, if we had the past nine seasons in an array named pirates1 and the nine seasons prior to those in pirates2, we'd create the losing streak array by calling concat( ) on pirates1 while passing in pirates2. Try it and then query the first and last elements in pirates, verifying your work with Figure 6–30.

```
var pirates1 = [[2010, 57, 105],
  [2009, 62, 99],
  [2008, 67, 95],
  [2007, 68, 94],
  [2006, 67, 95],
  [2005, 67, 95],
```

```
    [2004, 72, 89],
    [2003, 75, 87],
    [2002, 72, 89]];
var pirates2 = [[2001, 62, 100],
    [2000, 69, 93],
    [1999, 78, 83],
    [1998, 69, 93],
    [1997, 79, 83],
    [1996, 73, 89],
    [1995, 58, 86],
    [1994, 53, 61],
    [1993, 75, 87]];
var pirates = pirates1.concat(pirates2);
console.dir(pirates[0]);
console.dir(pirates[pirates.length - 1]);
```

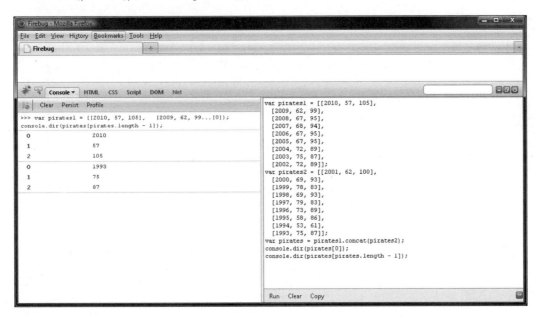

Figure 6–30. Gluing arrays together with concat()

Note that creating pirates by gluing pirates1 to pirates2 does not modify pirates1 or pirates2. That is to say, the last element in pirates1 is still the 2002 season and the first element in pirates2 is still the 2001 season as Figure 6–31 displays. So, unlike methods like pop(), push(), shift(), and unshift(), a concat() does not modify the array it's invoked upon. In geeky terms, we would say that pop() is a mutator method while concat() is an accessor method.

```
var pirates1 = [[2010, 57, 105],
    [2009, 62, 99],
    [2008, 67, 95],
    [2007, 68, 94],
    [2006, 67, 95],
    [2005, 67, 95],
```

```
      [2004, 72, 89],
      [2003, 75, 87],
      [2002, 72, 89]];
var pirates2 = [[2001, 62, 100],
      [2000, 69, 93],
      [1999, 78, 83],
      [1998, 69, 93],
      [1997, 79, 83],
      [1996, 73, 89],
      [1995, 58, 86],
      [1994, 53, 61],
      [1993, 75, 87]];
var pirates = pirates1.concat(pirates2);
console.dir(pirates1[pirates.length - 1]);
console.dir(pirates2[0]);
```

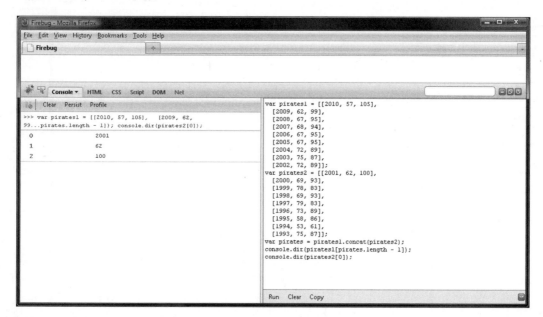

Figure 6–31. concat() does not modify the array its invoked upon nor the one passed to it as an argument.

Reversing the Elements in an Array

Now say we wanted to reverse the order of seasons in `pirates` from 2010–1993 to 1993–2010. To do so, we'd simply call the aptly named method `reverse()` on `pirates`. So, as Figure 6–32 displays, querying the first element in `pirates` before and after calling `reverse()` returns the 2010 and 1993 season, respectively:

```
var pirates = [[2010, 57, 105],
      [2009, 62, 99],
      [2008, 67, 95],
      [2007, 68, 94],
```

```
        [2006, 67, 95],
        [2005, 67, 95],
        [2004, 72, 89],
        [2003, 75, 87],
        [2002, 72, 89],
        [2001, 62, 100],
        [2000, 69, 93],
        [1999, 78, 83],
        [1998, 69, 93],
        [1997, 79, 83],
        [1996, 73, 89],
        [1995, 58, 86],
        [1994, 53, 61],
        [1993, 75, 87]];
console.dir(pirates[0]);
pirates.reverse();
console.dir(pirates[0]);
```

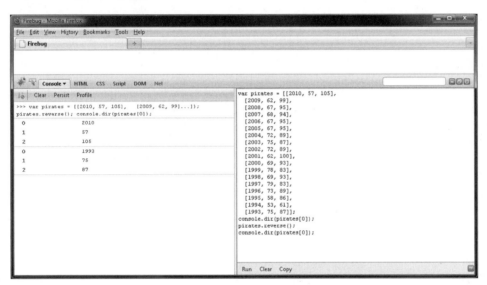

Figure 6–32. Reversing the order of elements in an array by invoking its reverse() method

Sorting the Elements in an Array

Though reversing the order of elements in pirates is interesting, it would be more helpful if we could reorder those by wins or losses. To do so, we'd invoke sort() on pirates and pass a function value to do the reordering work. JavaScript will pass that function two elements from pirates—yup, happens by magic—and the function will then return -1 if the first element ought to come before the second element, 0 if there is a tie, and 1 if the second element ought to come before the first element. Though it's typical for the function to return -1 and 1, any negative or positive integer will do. The only return value set in stone is 0, which conveys a tie.

So alrighty then, let's save a function to a variable named sortByLosses that will sort pirates by losses. Begin by defining parameters named e1 and e2 for JavaScript to pass elements in pirates to sortByLosses() with.

```
var pirates = [[2010, 57, 105],
  [2009, 62, 99],
  [2008, 67, 95],
  [2007, 68, 94],
  [2006, 67, 95],
  [2005, 67, 95],
  [2004, 72, 89],
  [2003, 75, 87],
  [2002, 72, 89],
  [2001, 62, 100],
  [2000, 69, 93],
  [1999, 78, 83],
  [1998, 69, 93],
  [1997, 79, 83],
  [1996, 73, 89],
  [1995, 58, 86],
  [1994, 53, 61],
  [1993, 75, 87]];
var sortByLosses = function (e1, e2) {
};
```

Then write an if condition to handle the case where the Pirates lost the same number of games in e1 and e2. If so, we want to sort the seasons by year, putting the most recent season first. So we'll have sortByLosses() return -1 if the year in e1[0] is more recent than e2[0], and 1 if e1[0] is more recent than e2[0]:

```
var pirates = [[2010, 57, 105],
  [2009, 62, 99],
  [2008, 67, 95],
  [2007, 68, 94],
  [2006, 67, 95],
  [2005, 67, 95],
  [2004, 72, 89],
  [2003, 75, 87],
  [2002, 72, 89],
  [2001, 62, 100],
  [2000, 69, 93],
  [1999, 78, 83],
  [1998, 69, 93],
  [1997, 79, 83],
  [1996, 73, 89],
  [1995, 58, 86],
  [1994, 53, 61],
  [1993, 75, 87]];
var sortByLosses = function (e1, e2) {
  if (e1[2] === e2[2]) {
    return e1[0] > e2[0] ? -1 : 1;
  }
};
```

Now append an `else` clause that has `sortByLosses()` return -1 if the Pirates lost more games in e1 than e2, and 1 if the Pirates lost more games in e2 than e1:

```
var pirates = [[2010, 57, 105],
  [2009, 62, 99],
  [2008, 67, 95],
  [2007, 68, 94],
  [2006, 67, 95],
  [2005, 67, 95],
  [2004, 72, 89],
  [2003, 75, 87],
  [2002, 72, 89],
  [2001, 62, 100],
  [2000, 69, 93],
  [1999, 78, 83],
  [1998, 69, 93],
  [1997, 79, 83],
  [1996, 73, 89],
  [1995, 58, 86],
  [1994, 53, 61],
  [1993, 75, 87]];
var sortByLosses = function (e1, e2) {
  if (e1[2] === e2[2]) {
    return e1[0] > e2[0] ? -1 : 1;
  } else {
    return e1[2] > e2[2] ? -1 : 1;
  }
};
```

OK, time to see if `sortByLosses()` does what we want it to. So invoke `sort()` on `pirates` and pass the `sortByLosses` identifier—don't invoke `sortByLosses` with the () operator or you'll come to grief. `sort()` will then reorder and return `pirates`. So if we invoke `console.dir()` on the return value of `sort()`, JavaScript will print the reordered array in Firebug as Figure 6–33 displays.

```
var pirates = [[2010, 57, 105],
  [2009, 62, 99],
  [2008, 67, 95],
  [2007, 68, 94],
  [2006, 67, 95],
  [2005, 67, 95],
  [2004, 72, 89],
  [2003, 75, 87],
  [2002, 72, 89],
  [2001, 62, 100],
  [2000, 69, 93],
  [1999, 78, 83],
  [1998, 69, 93],
  [1997, 79, 83],
  [1996, 73, 89],
  [1995, 58, 86],
  [1994, 53, 61],
  [1993, 75, 87]];
var sortByLosses = function (e1, e2) {
  if (e1[2] === e2[2]) {
    return e1[0] > e2[0] ? -1 : 1;
```

```
  } else {
    return e1[2] > e2[2] ? -1 : 1;
  }
};
console.dir(pirates.sort(sortByLosses));
```

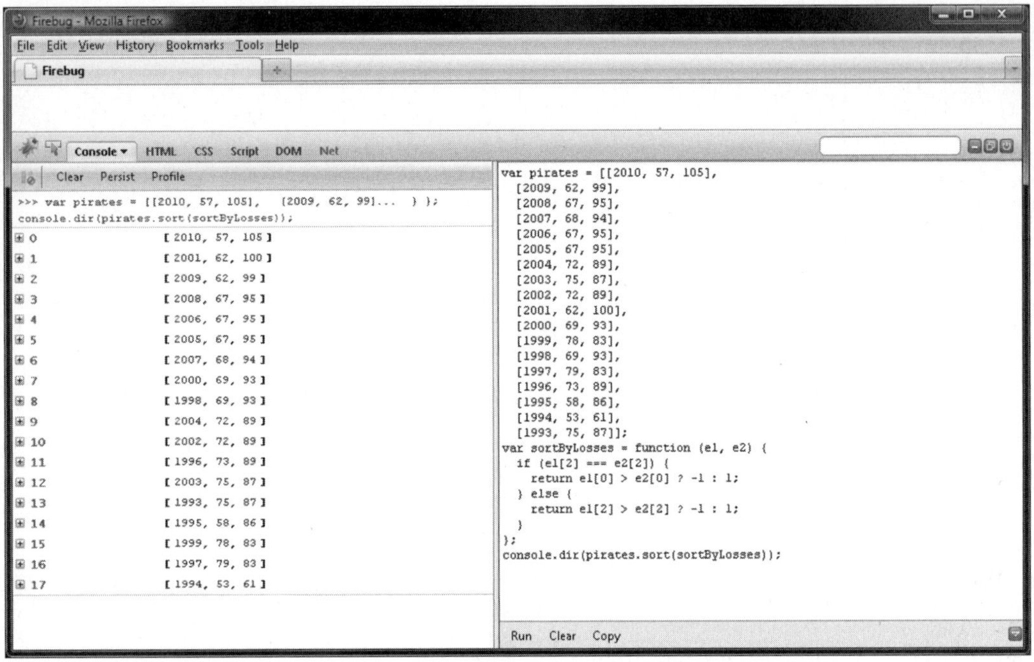

Figure 6–33. Sorting elements in the pirates *array by losses and then by year*

Forgive me for being negative and sorting by losses. In Pittsburgh, between the end of the Penguins season and beginning of the Steelers season, guessing how many games the Pirates will lose and which star players they'll trade away for prospects is pretty much all there is to do sports-wise. So let's be optimistic and sort pirates by wins instead. Doing so is trivial, just rename the function sortByWins and change the indexes in the boolean expression and else clause from 2 to 1 like so.

```
var pirates = [[2010, 57, 105],
  [2009, 62, 99],
  [2008, 67, 95],
  [2007, 68, 94],
  [2006, 67, 95],
  [2005, 67, 95],
  [2004, 72, 89],
  [2003, 75, 87],
  [2002, 72, 89],
  [2001, 62, 100],
  [2000, 69, 93],
  [1999, 78, 83],
  [1998, 69, 93],
```

```
  [1997, 79, 83],
  [1996, 73, 89],
  [1995, 58, 86],
  [1994, 53, 61],
  [1993, 75, 87]];
var sortByWins = function (e1, e2) {
  if (e1[1] === e2[1]) {
    return e1[0] > e2[0] ? -1 : 1;
  } else {
    return e1[1] > e2[1] ? -1 : 1;
  }
};
```

Then invoke `sort()` on `pirates`, but pass the identifier `sortByWins` instead of `sortByLosses`. As before, pass the return value of `sort()` to `console.dir()` and JavaScript will print the reordered `pirates` array in Firebug as in Figure 6–34.

```
var pirates = [[2010, 57, 105],
  [2009, 62, 99],
  [2008, 67, 95],
  [2007, 68, 94],
  [2006, 67, 95],
  [2005, 67, 95],
  [2004, 72, 89],
  [2003, 75, 87],
  [2002, 72, 89],
  [2001, 62, 100],
  [2000, 69, 93],
  [1999, 78, 83],
  [1998, 69, 93],
  [1997, 79, 83],
  [1996, 73, 89],
  [1995, 58, 86],
  [1994, 53, 61],
  [1993, 75, 87]];
var sortByWins = function (e1, e2) {
  if (e1[1] === e2[1]) {
    return e1[0] > e2[0] ? -1 : 1;
  } else {
    return e1[1] > e2[1] ? -1 : 1;
  }
};
console.dir(pirates.sort(sortByWins));
```

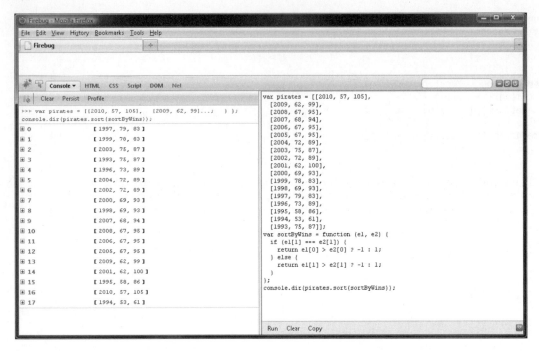

Figure 6–34. Sorting elements in the `pirates` *array by wins and then by year*

Creating a String from an Array

Often, you will want to create a string from an array. To do so, you would invoke the array's `join()` method, which converts the elements in the array to strings and then sequentially glues them together. `join()` takes an optional parameter, which is a separator to glue the elements together with. Note that, if you omit the separator, then JavaScript will use `","` by default.

So say we'd like to create a comma-separated list from `pirates`, with each entry on a single line, we would pass `"/n"` as the separator. JavaScript will then invoke `toString()` on each element in `pirates` and join those strings together with `"/n"`.

■ **Note** This format is called a comma-separated value (CSV) string. It can be imported into spreadsheets or processed by other applications, because it is a standard format.

So, as Figure 6–35 displays, `join()` returns the Pirates' 18 years of futility as a CSV string:

```
var pirates = [[2010, 57, 105],
  [2009, 62, 99],
  [2008, 67, 95],
  [2007, 68, 94],
  [2006, 67, 95],
```

```
        [2005, 67, 95],
        [2004, 72, 89],
        [2003, 75, 87],
        [2002, 72, 89],
        [2001, 62, 100],
        [2000, 69, 93],
        [1999, 78, 83],
        [1998, 69, 93],
        [1997, 79, 83],
        [1996, 73, 89],
        [1995, 58, 86],
        [1994, 53, 61],
        [1993, 75, 87]];
pirates.join("\n");
```

Figure 6–35. Gluing elements together with join()

Taking a Slice of an Array

Sometimes you will want to copy two or more elements from an array. To do so, you would invoke its slice() method, passing two parameters.

- First, the *index* of the first element to copy.

- Second, the *number* of elements to copy.

■ **Note** slice() makes a shallow copy of an array. That is to say, elements containing object, array, and function values are copied by reference, not duplicated.

So, say we'd like to know how the Pirates did during the past five years, we'd invoke slice() on pirates and pass 0 and 5. As Figure 6–36 displays, slice() returns copies of those five seasons, but does not remove them from pirates.

```
var pirates = [[2010, 57, 105],
  [2009, 62, 99],
  [2008, 67, 95],
  [2007, 68, 94],
  [2006, 67, 95],
  [2005, 67, 95],
  [2004, 72, 89],
  [2003, 75, 87],
  [2002, 72, 89],
  [2001, 62, 100],
  [2000, 69, 93],
  [1999, 78, 83],
  [1998, 69, 93],
  [1997, 79, 83],
  [1996, 73, 89],
  [1995, 58, 86],
  [1994, 53, 61],
  [1993, 75, 87]];
console.dir(pirates.slice(0, 5));
pirates.length;
// 18
```

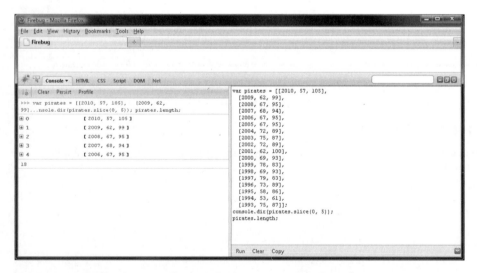

Figure 6–36. Shallow copying elements from an array with slice()

Converting a Read-only Array-like Object to an Array

slice() is commonly borrowed by read-only array-like objects such as arguments in order to copy their elements to a real, read-write array. To very simply illustrate this technique, let's create a function named argumentsToArray() that will copy elements from its arguments object to an array and then return that array. Then if we pass 18 parameters to argumentsToArray(), one for each losing season in the Pirates' streak of futility, those will first get saved to its arguments object. Then we'll have arguments borrow slice(), which will return a real array containing 18 elements, one for each losing season. Therefore, if we save the return value of argumentsToArray() to a variable named pirates, it will contain the very same array we've been mucking around with in this chapter as Figure 6–37 displays.

```
var argumentsToArray = function () {
  return Array.prototype.slice.call(arguments);
};
var pirates = argumentsToArray([2010, 57, 105],
  [2009, 62, 99],
  [2008, 67, 95],
  [2007, 68, 94],
  [2006, 67, 95],
  [2005, 67, 95],
  [2004, 72, 89],
  [2003, 75, 87],
  [2002, 72, 89],
  [2001, 62, 100],
  [2000, 69, 93],
  [1999, 78, 83],
  [1998, 69, 93],
  [1997, 79, 83],
  [1996, 73, 89],
  [1995, 58, 86],
  [1994, 53, 61],
  [1993, 75, 87]);
console.dir(pirates);
```

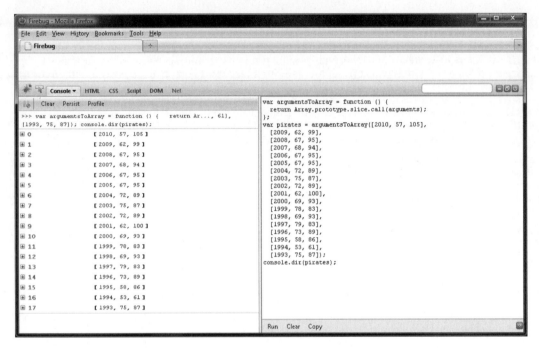

Figure 6–37. Shallow copying members from arguments to an array by borrowing slice()*.*

Or more succinctly, we can borrow slice() from an empty array literal rather than from Array.prototype. As Figure 6–38 displays, this works just as well and saves some keystrokes. Consequently, borrowing slice() this way is very common.

```
var argumentsToArray = function () {
  return [].slice.call(arguments);
}
var pirates = argumentsToArray([2010, 57, 105],
  [2009, 62, 99],
  [2008, 67, 95],
  [2007, 68, 94],
  [2006, 67, 95],
  [2005, 67, 95],
  [2004, 72, 89],
  [2003, 75, 87],
  [2002, 72, 89],
  [2001, 62, 100],
  [2000, 69, 93],
  [1999, 78, 83],
  [1998, 69, 93],
  [1997, 79, 83],
  [1996, 73, 89],
  [1995, 58, 86],
  [1994, 53, 61],
  [1993, 75, 87]);
console.dir(pirates);
```

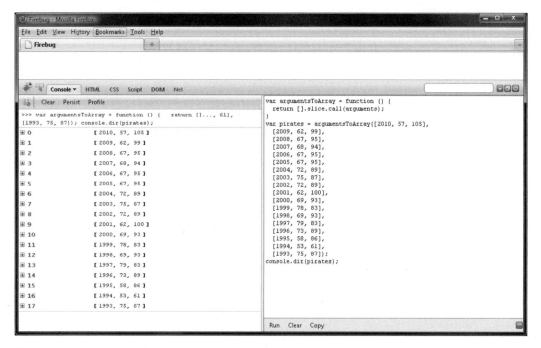

Figure 6–38. A more succinct way of creating an array from the members in arguments

So argumentsToArray() invoked the array method slice() on the arguments object, which is like the arg object below, but read-only. Then, insofar as we did not pass an index to begin the slice at the number of elements to copy, slice() copies every element in arguments and returns those in an array. This works for the reason that any member in an object named with a non-negative integer string is really an element. So while an object like arguments does not inherit any array methods, it can contain elements. So slice() copies the members named "0" through "17", but not the one named "length" or "callee". Pretty cool, don't you think?

```
var arg = {
  "0": [2010, 57, 105],
  "1": [2009, 62, 99],
  "2": [2008, 67, 95],
  "3": [2007, 68, 94],
  "4": [2006, 67, 95],
  "5": [2005, 67, 95],
  "6": [2004, 72, 89],
  "7": [2003, 75, 87],
  "8": [2002, 72, 89],
  "9": [2001, 62, 100],
  "10": [2000, 69, 93],
  "11": [1999, 78, 83],
  "12": [1998, 69, 93],
  "13": [1997, 79, 83],
  "14": [1996, 73, 89],
  "15": [1995, 58, 86],
```

```
    "16": [1994, 53, 61],
    "17": [1993, 75, 87],
    "length": 18,
    "callee": argumentsToArray
};
```

Inserting or Deleting Elements from an Array

Now then, say the elements for the 2000–2002 seasons are invalid inasmuch as the wins and losses are reversed, and 2002 is in there twice. To delete those four invalid elements and insert new ones in their place, we can invoke splice() on pirates.

- The first parameter is the index of the first element to delete, so 8 for the 2002 season.

- The second parameter is the number of elements to delete, which would be 4.

- From there, any additional parameters are elements to splice into the array. Note that it's OK to add more or fewer elements than you deleted; JavaScript will keep the array indexes sequential behind the scenes.

So if we add three elements in place of the four invalid ones, the indexes in pirates remain sequential, ordered 0 to 17 as Figure 6–39 displays.

```
var pirates = [[2010, 57, 105],
  [2009, 62, 99],
  [2008, 67, 95],
  [2007, 68, 94],
  [2006, 67, 95],
  [2005, 67, 95],
  [2004, 72, 89],
  [2003, 75, 87],
  [2002, 89, 72],
  [2002, 89, 72],
  [2001, 100, 62],
  [2000, 93, 69],
  [1999, 78, 83],
  [1998, 69, 93],
  [1997, 79, 83],
  [1996, 73, 89],
  [1995, 58, 86],
  [1994, 53, 61],
  [1993, 75, 87]];
pirates.splice(8, 4, [2002, 72, 89], [2001, 62, 100], [2000, 69, 93]);
console.dir(pirates);
```

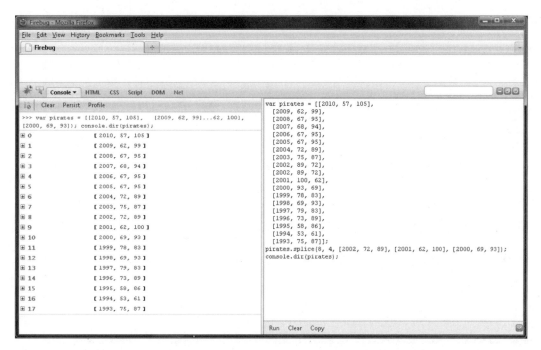

Figure 6–39. Deleting and inserting elements into an array with splice()

Now, say the 2000–2002 seasons are simply missing. We can use splice() to insert those. That is to say, splice() does not require you to delete any elements. So if we pass 0 for the second parameter to splice(), JavaScript will insert the three new elements, and, as before, keep the indexes sequential behind the scenes, as Figure 6–40 displays.

```
var pirates = [[2010, 57, 105],
  [2009, 62, 99],
  [2008, 67, 95],
  [2007, 68, 94],
  [2006, 67, 95],
  [2005, 67, 95],
  [2004, 72, 89],
  [2003, 75, 87],
  [1999, 78, 83],
  [1998, 69, 93],
  [1997, 79, 83],
  [1996, 73, 89],
  [1995, 58, 86],
  [1994, 53, 61],
  [1993, 75, 87]];
pirates.splice(8, 0, [2002, 72, 89], [2001, 62, 100], [2000, 69, 93]);
console.dir(pirates);
```

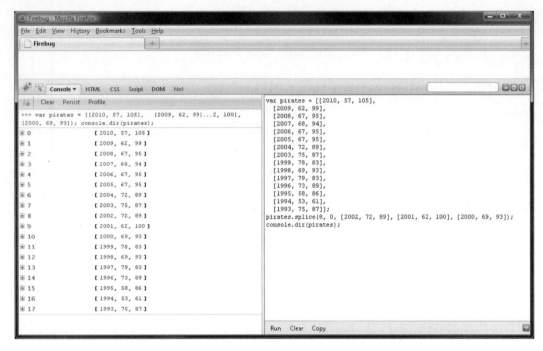

Figure 6–40. *There's no need to delete elements prior to inserting new ones with* splice()*.*

Conversely, splice() can be used just to delete elements. That is to say, we're not required to insert new elements in place of the ones we delete. So say pirates contains elements for the 1990–92 seasons and we want to delete those so that only the seasons comprising the 18-year losing streak remain. To do so, we'd simply pass 18 and 3 to splice(). JavaScript will then clip those three winning seasons from pirates, as Figure 6–41 displays.

```
var pirates = [[2010, 57, 105],
    [2009, 62, 99],
    [2008, 67, 95],
    [2007, 68, 94],
    [2006, 67, 95],
    [2005, 67, 95],
    [2004, 72, 89],
    [2003, 75, 87],
    [2002, 72, 89],
    [2001, 62, 100],
    [2000, 69, 93],
    [1999, 78, 83],
    [1998, 69, 93],
    [1997, 79, 83],
    [1996, 73, 89],
    [1995, 58, 86],
    [1994, 53, 61],
    [1993, 75, 87],
    [1992, 96, 66],
```

```
    [1991, 98, 64],
    [1990, 95, 67]];
pirates.splice(18, 3);
console.dir(pirates);
```

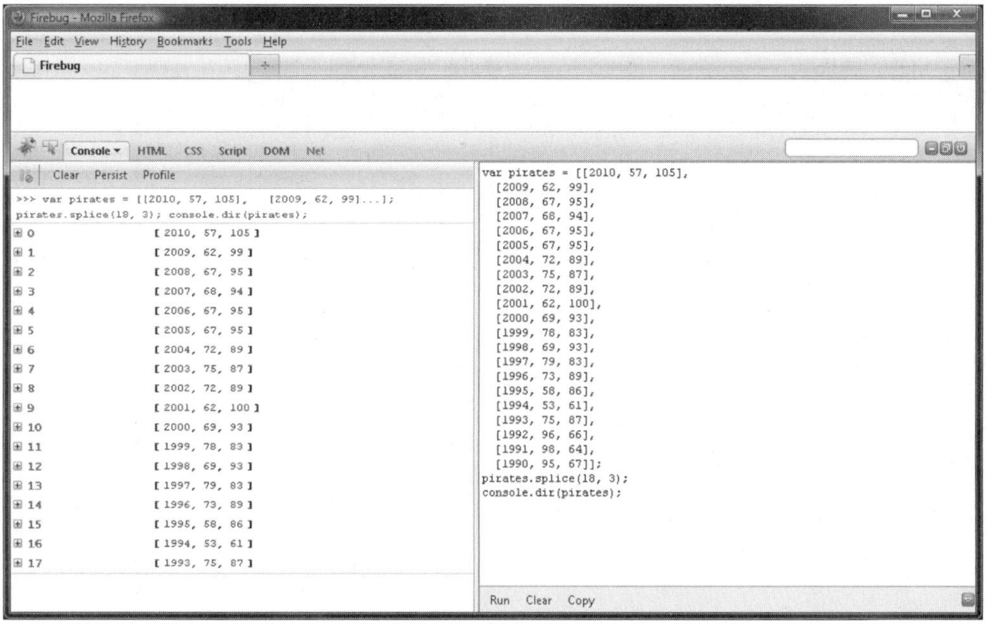

***Figure 6–41.** There's no need to replace deleted elements with new ones when invoking splice().*

Even more succinctly, we could accomplish the same thing by simply passing 18. JavaScript will then delete any elements from that index all the way to the end of the array. So, as Figure 6–42 displays, passing 18 modifies pirates, just as passing 18 and 3 did.

```
var pirates = [[2010, 57, 105],
    [2009, 62, 99],
    [2008, 67, 95],
    [2007, 68, 94],
    [2006, 67, 95],
    [2005, 67, 95],
    [2004, 72, 89],
    [2003, 75, 87],
    [2002, 72, 89],
    [2001, 62, 100],
    [2000, 69, 93],
    [1999, 78, 83],
    [1998, 69, 93],
    [1997, 79, 83],
    [1996, 73, 89],
    [1995, 58, 86],
    [1994, 53, 61],
```

```
            [1993, 75, 87],
            [1992, 96, 66],
            [1991, 98, 64],
            [1990, 95, 67]];
pirates.splice(18);
console.dir(pirates);
```

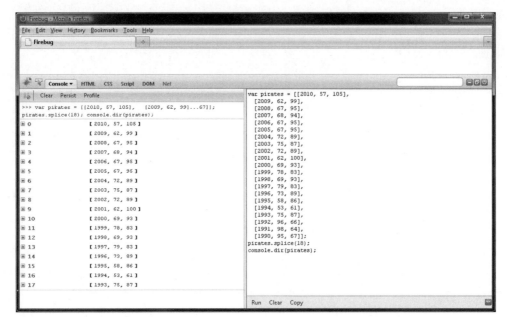

Figure 6–42. If we omit the second parameter, JavaScript deletes elements all the way to the end of the array.

Summary

In this chapter, we explored functions and arrays, which are subtypes of the object value type. JavaScript functions are first-class objects, which is to say they are values that can be expressed with function literal notation. Functions also provide local scope. The diverse array of function techniques we explored in this chapter derive from those two distinctive features.

I expanded on Chapter 5's discussion of inheritance by showing how to pass on functions to child objects. This technique allows you to build scripts for all sorts of purposes, including conditional advance loading, lazy loading, recursion, function borrowing, and currying. All of these cunning tricks have their place in a JavaScript application and make life a lot easier when you have to make a snappy and useful application. You've learned a lot of advanced programming techniques in this chapter, maybe without realizing it, which will stand you in good stead for the chapters to come.

We also explored methods that all arrays inherit by way of the prototype chain from Array.prototype. Some of those like pop() and splice() modify, which is to say mutate, the array they are invoked upon. Others like slice() or join() query an array in order to return a new value, but do not modify the array. Those inherited methods, along with the length member, differentiate the array subtype from the object type.

CHAPTER 7

■ ■ ■

Traversing and Modifying the DOM Tree

One of my favorite books as a child was *Where the Wild Things Are* by Maurice Sendak. If you are not familiar with the story, it goes like this: one night, a little boy named Max, dressed in a wolf costume, misbehaves and is sent to bed without supper. There, a sea, a wild forest, and mysterious creatures spring from his imagination. Max sails to the land of the wild things, who crown him king. But even though the creatures do his bidding, Max grows hungry for love. So, he sails home to find his supper waiting for him, still hot.

In 2009, Spike Jonze directed a film adaptation of *Where the Wild Things Are*. As the book contains just 338 words, Jonze and cowriter Dave Eggers obviously had to add dialogue. For example, prior to the wild rumpus in the book, Jonze and Eggers have Max blurt, "I'll be on my own side. By myself." Then later, as warring factions emerge, they have Max wonder, "How do I make everyone OK?"

Those two quotes came to mind as I wrote this chapter. Though Internet Explorer, Firefox, Safari, and Opera faithfully implement ECMAScript, a standard we explored in the first six chapters, such is not the case with DOM, a standard we will explore in this chapter and the next two. Not entirely anyway. Firefox, Safari, and Opera faithfully implement DOM, too. Internet Explorer, on the other hand, does not—at least not always. For some DOM features, Internet Explorer abides by DOM. For others, it blurts, like little Max, "I'll be on my own side. By myself."

That's the bad news. Now for the good. There's no need for you to wonder like Max, "How do I make everyone OK?" That is to say, how to solve the problem of warring browser factions in regard to DOM. By way of feature testing, we will script DOM in the standard way for Firefox, Safari, or Opera, but in a proprietary way for Internet Explorer. Note too that the three DOM chapters were written in order of increasing Internet Explorer childishness. In other words, we will have to do some cross-browser scripting in this chapter, a little more in Chapter 8, and quite a bit in Chapter 9. But you will be battle hardened by then!

DOM Tree

DOM provides a way for JavaScript to represent the nested tags in HTML or XML markup as a tree of nested objects, referred to as *nodes*. Like any other JavaScript value of the object datatype, a node is a container for related variables and functions. Moreover, node members provide a way for scripters like us to query and manipulate markup, doing things like finding, creating, or deleting content. But just remember that a node is an object. Everything you learned in Chapter 5 works for a node.

Why not just call a node an *object*? Things are already confusing enough with having to remember that arrays and functions are of the object datatype. Now we're adding nodes to the list. Enough already! Now before you get your dander up, bumpkin, there is a reason for saying *node* rather than simply *object*. Not a bad one either. DOM is not just for JavaScript. Many other languages use it too, such as Java, PHP, Perl, and so on. Those languages have their own datatypes. So, saying *node* rather than

255

JavaScript *object* makes DOM language neutral. Internet Explorer, for example, implements DOM with COM objects, while Firefox, Safari, and Opera implement DOM with JavaScript objects. For this reason, DOM objects do not behave like JavaScript objects in Internet Explorer, but do so in Firefox, Safari, and Opera. So, there's your first taste of Internet Explorer's "I'll be on my own side. By myself." mischief.

■ **Note** If you are curious as to what COM objects are, visit the following Wikipedia page: http://en.wikipedia.org/wiki/Component_Object_Model.

DOM is language-neutral, but it is a pretty loose standard, too. Rather than very specifically documenting classes, DOM tells Internet Explorer, Firefox, Safari, and Opera what to do by way of *interfaces*. Interfaces list methods and members that must be implemented together. Just as an interface is an intentionally vague blueprint for an object, the JavaScript interpreter for Firefox implements DOM features differently than the JavaScript interpreter for Internet Explorer or Safari does. Moreover, a node in the DOM tree can implement more than one interface. For example, a `<div>` tag from your markup is represented with an `Element` node in the DOM tree. Those have all the features listed in the `Node`, `Element`, and `HTMLElement` interfaces, among others.

With this in mind, in order to know what members and methods are available for you to manipulate a node with, you have to know which interfaces list those features. Although DOM is comprised of hundreds of interfaces, we will explore just 11 in this chapter. Did I hear a sigh of relief?

Thought so. Anyway, knowing key interface names will also prove invaluable whenever you need to look up features in a DOM reference, printed or online. For those reasons, I preface DOM methods and members with their interface names. For example, the method `createElement()` is listed in the `Document` interface, so I refer to it as `Document.createElement()`. That way, you know it can be invoked only on a `Document` node. Also, you know to look under the `Document` interface in a DOM reference whenever you want more information.

Alrighty then, these are the 11 DOM interfaces we will explore in this chapter:

```
Attr
CharacterData
Document
Element
HTMLCollection
HTMLDocument
HTMLElement
NamedNodeMap
Node
NodeList
Text
```

Is Every Node the Same?

Every node is not the same; there are 12 different kinds of nodes. But as a DOM scripting beginner, and even later in life when you are a guru, you will really only ever work with four. First, every tag in your markup is represented with an `Element` node. Second, tag attributes like `id` or `href` are represented with `Attr` nodes. Next, not surprisingly, text content is represented with `Text` nodes. And finally, the whole enchilada is represented with a `Document` node—in other words, the root to the DOM tree is a `Document` node. Every other kind of node is a descendant of this root node.

This brings to mind one further point. Much DOM jargon is borrowed from traditional family trees. So, this chapter will be sprinkled with terms like *parent*, *child*, *sibling*, *ancestor*, and *descendant*. These terms mean what you think they mean. So, you already are in good shape with the tree jargon.

Interfaces Are Sensibly Named

Now then, as you might guess, every kind of node has the methods and members defined by the Node interface, so every kind of node implements Node. That's simple to remember, and things do not get any harder from here. Element nodes have those defined by the Element interface. Text nodes pick up features from the Text and CharacterData interfaces; Document nodes from the Document interface; Attr nodes from the Attr interface. You get the picture.

For a DOM tree representing a web page (that is, HTML markup rather than XML), nodes pick up some HTML-only features. For example, Element nodes representing HTML tags like <div> receive members from the HTMLElement and HTMLDivElement interfaces. Note that the former defines members common to every element in an HTML node tree, such as id and class.

Querying the DOM Tree

To start this example, download seven.html (shown here) from the chapter downloads at www.apress.com. Then open it with Firefox and press F12 to enable Firebug.

```
<!DOCTYPE html PUBLIC "-//W3C//DTD XHTML 1.0 Strict//EN"
"http://www.w3.org/TR/xhtml1/DTD/xhtml1-strict.dtd">
<html xmlns="http://www.w3.org/1999/xhtml">
<head>
<meta http-equiv="Content-Type" content="text/html; charset=utf-8" />
<title>Firebug</title>
</head>
<body>
<div>
  <h4>Talk to me:</h4>
  <ul>
    <li id="twitter" class="sprite"><a href="http://www.twitter.com">Twitter</a></li>
    <li id="facebook" class="sprite"><a href="http://www.facebook.com">Facebook</a></li>
    <li id="flickr" class="sprite"><a href="http://www.flickr.com">Flickr</a></li>
    <li id="linkedin" class="sprite"><a href="http://www.linkedin.com">LinkedIn</a></li>
  </ul>
</div>
</body>
</html>
```

As noted, the root to the DOM tree representing this simple XHTML file is a Document node. Typically, you query this object by way of the document member of window. In other words, document is an identifier for a global variable. With this in mind, let's query document in Firebug by typing its identifier and clicking Run:

```
document;
// Document dom.html
```

Firebug tells you the node's type and the URL of the markup it represents. Now let's query a few members that document, like any other node in the DOM tree, receives from the Node interface. First, nodeType contains an integer between 1 and 12 that tells you the kind of node you have on your hands:

```
document.nodeType;
// 9
```

Did you get 9? Yup, me too. nodeType will always be 9 for a Document node. And for Element and Text nodes, nodeType will always be 1 and 3, respectively. Write those down for later reference, as in Table 7–1.

Table 7–1. nodeType Literals for Commonly Scripted Nodes

Node	nodeType **Literal**
Element	1
Text	3
Document	9

nodeType commonly appears in the boolean expression for if conditions. Say you want to be sure you have an Element node on your hands, you might write an if condition comparing nodeType to 3. If === returns true, you may query any of the members or invoke any of the methods listed in the Element interface in the if block. So, you do something like this:

```
if (nodeFromTree.nodeType === 3) {
  // do something to Element node
}
```

In addition to testing nodeType with number literals, you can do so with constants, that is to say, in Firefox, Safari, and Opera. As of version 8, Internet Explorer still does not implement nodeType constants. However, you can create those for Internet Explorer. Just code an if condition testing whether window has a Node member. If not, create one like so:

```
if (typeof Node === "undefined") {
  var Node = {ELEMENT_NODE: 1, TEXT_NODE: 3, DOCUMENT_NODE: 9}
}
```

Note that you are just adding the nodeType constants commonly scripted. There are nine more of those. But you won't need them for anything.

Having created the Node object in the event that it is missing, you can now rewrite the nodeType test like so:

```
if (nodeFromTree.nodeType === Node.ELEMENT_NODE) {
  // do something to Element node
}
```

Constants do read better than number literals. But most JavaScript programmers just go with the number literals, viewing laziness as a virtue. Even so, let's add a nodeType constant column, as in Table 7–2.

Table 7–2. nodeType Literals and Constants for Commonly Scripted Nodes

Node	nodeType **Literal**	nodeType **Constant**
Element	1	Node.ELEMENT_NODE
Text	3	Node.TEXT_NODE
Document	9	Node.DOCUMENT_NODE

Now let's query the `nodeName` member. Note that, for a `Document` node, this will always be the string `"#document"`:

```
document.nodeName;
// "#document"
```

For `Element` nodes, `nodeName` will be the name of the markup tag in uppercase letters, such as `"DIV"` for a `<div>` element and `"LI"` for an `<li>` element. It doesn't matter whether your markup contains lowercase or uppercase tags; `nodeName` always contains a string of uppercase letters.

On the other hand, `nodeName` for a `Text` node, like that for a `Document` node, is carved in stone. This will always be the string `"#text"`. Let's add a column for `nodeName`, as in Table 7–3.

Table 7–3. nodeType Literals, nodeType Constants, and nodeName Values for Commonly Scripted Nodes

Node	nodeType **Literal**	nodeType **Constant**	nodeName
Element	1	Node.ELEMENT_NODE	Tag name from markup
Text	3	Node.TEXT_NODE	"#text"
Document	9	Node.DOCUMENT_NODE	"#document"

Finally, in addition to `nodeType` and `nodeName`, every node regardless of type has a `nodeValue` member. So, let's query this member for document in Firebug:

```
document.nodeValue;
// null
```

Did you get `null`? Good. For a `Document` or `Element` node, `nodeValue` will always be `null`. On the other hand, for a `Text` node, `nodeValue` will contain the text content from your markup. So, add a fourth column for `nodeValue` to finish our node decoder table, which appears in Table 7–4.

Table 7–4. Our Final Secret Decoder Table for Commonly Scripted Nodes

Node	nodeType **Literal**	nodeType **Constant**	nodeName	nodeValue
Element	1	Node.ELEMENT_NODE	Tag name from markup	null
Text	3	Node.TEXT_NODE	"#text"	Text from markup
Document	9	Node.DOCUMENT_NODE	"#document" null	null

Now that you can figure out the kind of node you are sitting on in the DOM tree, let's go ahead and start climbing about the nodes representing the markup.

Same Jargon as for a Family Tree

The DOM tree is like a family tree in that terms like *parent*, *child*, and *sibling* apply. So, the node one tier above another is its parent. Conversely, any nodes one tier beneath another are its children. Sibling nodes are those on the same tier.

A Document node will never have a parent or siblings but will always have children. On the other hand, a Text node will always have a parent but will never have children. Like a Text node, an Element node will always have a parent. But unlike a Text node, an Element node, unless it is representing an empty tag such as `<img>` or `<meta>`, will always have children. Both a Text or Element node may have siblings.

With that in mind, if you ascend the DOM, you will eventually dead end at a Document node. Conversely, if you descend the DOM, you will likely dead end at a Text or empty Element node. Moving laterally generally takes you to an Element or Text node.

Traversing the DOM Tree

To traverse the DOM tree, you simply jump to a child, sibling, or parent node by way of one of the following members listed in the Node interface:

```
Node.childNodes
Node.firstChild
Node.lastChild
Node.nextSibling
Node.previousSibling
Node.parentNode
```

Let's begin with the first one in the list, `Node.childNodes`.

Descending with childNodes

Now then, like any of the 12 node types, Document, Element, and Text nodes have a childNodes member containing a NodeList, which is an arraylike object. Remember from earlier in the book that an arraylike object contains elements and a length property but lacks array methods such as slice() or pop(). childNodes is aptly named in that it contains any child nodes, which is to say direct descendants, of a parent node. Note that, for Text nodes, childNodes will always be empty and therefore have a length of 0. Note too that childNodes will never contain null. That is, childNodes will always contain a NodeList object, even if the parent node is childless.

So, how many children does document have?

```
document.childNodes;
// [DocumentType, html]
```

Just two. First, a DocumentType node for:

```
<!DOCTYPE html PUBLIC "-//W3C//DTD XHTML 1.0 Strict//EN"
"http://www.w3.org/TR/xhtml1/DTD/xhtml1-strict.dtd">
```

Second, an Element node representing our `<html>` element. Note that, for document, childNodes may contain only one Element node and one DocumentType node. Note too that document has a member named documentElement that refers to the one Element child node that it is permitted by DOM. For web pages, documentElement will always refer to the <html> Element node. Finally, although Firefox, Safari, and Opera implement DocumentType nodes, Internet Explorer does not. So for Internet Explorer, document.childNodes would contain just one member, the <html> Element node.

To query an element in a NodeList, use the [] operator like so:

```
document.childNodes[1].nodeName;
// "HTML"
```

Another way to query a NodeList element is with NodeList.item():

```
document.childNodes.item(1).nodeType;
// 1
```

But since [] takes fewer keystrokes, no one ever queries a NodeList with item().

document has a few shortcut members referring to <body>, <html>, and window. Those are named body, documentElement, and defaultView, respectively. So try them out in Firebug. Remember that a commented line is your cue to click Run; in the following example, you would do so five times.

```
document.body.nodeName;
// "BODY"
document.documentElement.nodeName;
// "HTML"
var yogurt = "Brown Cow";
document.defaultView.yogurt;
// "Brown Cow"
window.yogurt;
// "Brown Cow"
yogurt = "Stonyfield";
document.defaultView.yogurt;
// "Stonyfield"
```

Verify your work with Figure 7–1.

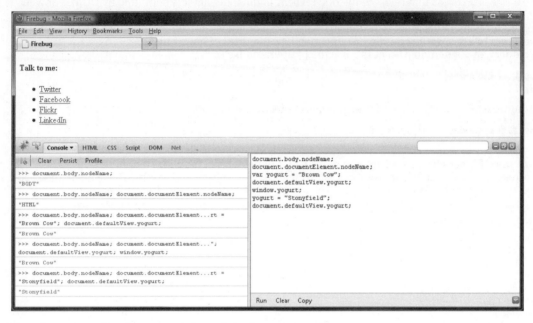

Figure 7–1. Querying shortcut members of the document node

Ascending with parentNode

You can descend the DOM tree with childNodes, but is there a way to do the inverse? Of course. You can ascend with parentNode, a member defined by every type of node. This one is fairly predictable. For a Document node, parentNode is null. For a Text node, parentNode is an Element node. And for an Element node, parentNode is either an Element or a Document node. So, although people have two parents, Text and Element nodes have just one. Kind of like bacteria.

Alright, given that the <html> element contains the <body> element, document.body.parentNode ought to refer to the <html> element. Let's see whether this is so:

```
document.body.parentNode.nodeName;
// "HTML"
```

In turn, document is the parent of the <html> element:

```
document.body.parentNode.parentNode.nodeName;
// "#document"
```

But as I said, document is an orphan, which means its parentNode member contains null:

```
document.parentNode;
// null
```

Muddying the Waters with Whitespace

Now for some bad news. For an `Element` node, `childNodes` may contain `Text` nodes representing the whitespace you formatted your markup with. Browsers create a single `Text` node to represent the whitespace between tags. If you separate two tags with a new line and four spaces, the browser will create a `Text` node with the data member "\n   " to represent the whitespace. Note that browsers only ever create one `Text` node to represent any combination of whitespace between markup tags. So initially, `childNodes` will not have two consecutive whitespace `Text` nodes. However, if you later add or remove nodes by script, `childNodes` may then contain consecutive whitespace `Text` nodes. Later in the chapter, that very thing will happen.

Let's take a look at the markup and figure out where the whitespace `Text` nodes are:

```
<!DOCTYPE html PUBLIC "-//W3C//DTD XHTML 1.0 Strict//EN"
"http://www.w3.org/TR/xhtml1/DTD/xhtml1-strict.dtd">
<html xmlns="http://www.w3.org/1999/xhtml">
<head>
<meta http-equiv="Content-Type" content="text/html; charset=utf-8" />
<title>Firebug</title>
</head>
<body>
<div>
  <h4>Talk to me:</h4>
  <ul>
    <li id="twitter" class="sprite"><a href="http://www.twitter.com">Twitter</a></li>
    <li id="facebook" class="sprite"><a href="http://www.facebook.com">Facebook</a></li>
    <li id="flickr" class="sprite"><a href="http://www.flickr.com">Flickr</a></li>
    <li id="linkedin" class="sprite"><a href="http://www.linkedin.com">LinkedIn</a></li>
  </ul>
</div>
</body>
</html>
```

First, since `childNodes` for a `Document` node may not contain `Text` nodes, JavaScript does not create a `Text` node for the new line between our doctype and html tags:

```
document.childNodes;
// [DocumentType, html]
```

On the other hand, for the `<ul>` tag, which is represented by an `Element` node, `childNodes` contains five whitespace `Text` nodes. To verify this, enter and run the following in Firebug:

```
document.childNodes[1].childNodes[1].childNodes[1].childNodes[3].childNodes;
 // [
// <TextNode textContent="\n ">,
// li#twitter,
// <TextNode textContent="\n ">,
// li#facebook,
// <TextNode textContent="\n ">,
// li#flickr,
// <TextNode textContent="\n ">,
// li#linkedin,
// <TextNode textContent="\n ">
// ]
```

With this in mind, you would query the Flickr `<li>` with the `childNodes` index of 5 rather than 2:

```
document.childNodes[1].childNodes[1].childNodes[1].childNodes[3].childNodes[5];
// <li id="flickr">
```

■ **Note** Internet Explorer does not bother to represent markup formatting with whitespace Text nodes. Don't you wish that Firefox, Safari, and Opera would disregard this most stupid of all DOM requirements, too?

Coding Cascade Style

Oftentimes. you will find yourself chaining together a bunch of . or [ ] refinements while querying the DOM. Rather than write one extraordinarily long line of code, break the statement over several lines by coding cascade style. To do so, follow the . operator with a new line and indentation of two or four spaces. Note that in this book all indents are two spaces. Remember from Chapter 3 that breaking a statement between the operands of a binary operator prevents JavaScript from implicitly terminating lines with semicolons. Therefore, separating the . operator from its right operand by a new line and two spaces is totally safe. So, enter and run the following in Firebug. Do not key in the comments; they are present for information as you read the book only:

```
document.
  childNodes[1]. // <html>
  childNodes[1]. // <body>
  childNodes[1]. // <div>
  childNodes[3]. // <ul>
  childNodes[5]. // <li>
  childNodes[0]. // <a>
  childNodes[0]. // Text node
  data;
// "Flickr"
```

So here you descended seven tiers of the DOM tree in order to query the "Flickr" Text node with a single statement spanning nine lines.

```
document.
  childNodes[1].
  childNodes[1].
  childNodes[1].
  childNodes[3].
  childNodes[5].
  childNodes[0].
  childNodes[0].
  nodeValue;
// "Flickr"
```

As illustrated in Figure 7–2, data and nodeValue both contain the string of text the Text node represents.

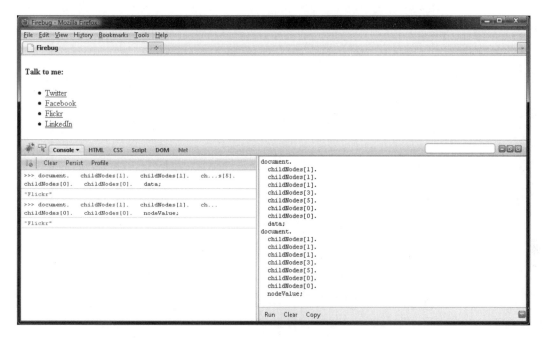

Figure 7–2. nodeValue and data contain the same string of text.

However, data requires fewer keystrokes and so is preferable to nodeValue. But either way will do, since both members contain the same value. To illustrate this in Firebug, let's change the final link from "LinkedIn" to "Linked In" with data and then read the new value with nodeValue.

```
document.
  childNodes[1].
  childNodes[1].
  childNodes[1].
  childNodes[3].
  childNodes[7].
  childNodes[0].
  childNodes[0].
  data = "Linked In";
document.
  childNodes[1].
  childNodes[1].
  childNodes[1].
  childNodes[3].
  childNodes[7].
  childNodes[0].
  childNodes[0].
  nodeValue;
// "Linked In";
```

Verify your work with Figure 7–3.

265

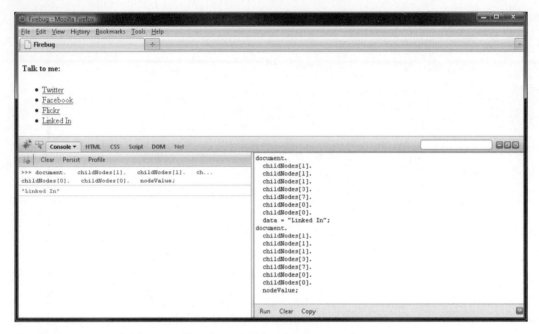

Figure 7–3. *Writing the data member changes the nodeValue member, too.*

Note that this changes the display in Firefox. However, if you press Ctrl+U (Cmd+U) to view the XHTML markup, the link still contains "LinkedIn", as Figure 7–4 displays. So, JavaScript modifies the DOM tree floating around in memory, not the XHTML file on the server.

```
File  Edit  View  Help
<!DOCTYPE html PUBLIC "-//W3C//DTD XHTML 1.0 Strict//EN" "http://www.w3.org/TR/xhtml1/DTD/xhtml1-strict.dtd">
<html xmlns="http://www.w3.org/1999/xhtml">
<head>
<meta http-equiv="Content-Type" content="text/html; charset=utf-8" />
<title>Firebug</title>
</head>
<body>
<div>
  <h4>Talk to me:</h4>
  <ul>
    <li id="twitter" class="sprite"><a href="http://www.twitter.com">Twitter</a></li>
    <li id="facebook" class="sprite"><a href="http://www.facebook.com">Facebook</a></li>
    <li id="flickr" class="sprite"><a href="http://www.flickr.com">Flickr</a></li>
    <li id="linkedin" class="sprite"><a href="http://www.linkedin.com">LinkedIn</a></li>
  </ul>
</div>
</body>
</html>
```

Figure 7–4. *JavaScript modifies the DOM tree, not the markup it represents.*

Finally, let's try ascending cascade style with `parentNode`. Doing so is much simpler than descending with `childNodes` insofar as there are no element indexes, muddied by whitespace Text nodes, for you to worry about. So, in Firebug, click Clear in both panels, and save the `"Flickr"` Text node to a variable named `myText`.

```
var myText = document.
  childNodes[1].
  childNodes[1].
  childNodes[1].
  childNodes[3].
  childNodes[5].
  childNodes[0].
  childNodes[0];
```

Then ascend from `myText` to the `<html>` element by chaining `parentNode` queries.

```
myText.parentNode.
  parentNode.
  parentNode.
  parentNode.
  parentNode.
  parentNode;
// <html xmlns="http://www.w3.org/1999/xhtml">
```

Verify your work with Figure 7–5.

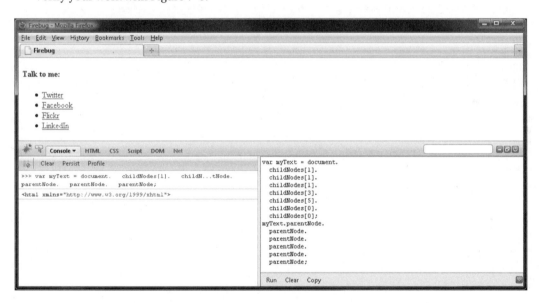

Figure 7–5. Chaining parentNode queries

Note that, while ascending the DOM tree with `parentNode` from a `Text` or `Element` node, you will only ever pass through an `Element` node, and eventually you will dead end at the `Document` node. In Chapter 9, you will learn to lay event listener functions such as traps along this `parentNode` path upward through the

DOM tree. Those event listeners will then be triggered as event objects move along this parentNode trail. We will cover event objects in Chapter 9.

Moving Laterally

So, with childNodes and parentNode, you can move vertically within the DOM tree. But what if you want to move laterally? Two Node members, nextSibling and previousSibling, provide a way to do so. Like human siblings, node siblings have the same parent. So in the markup, the four <li> Element nodes and five formatting Text nodes are all siblings.

Click Clear in both Firebug panels, and try the following nextSibling sample:

```
var myLI = document.
  childNodes[1].
  childNodes[1].
  childNodes[1].
  childNodes[3]. // <ul>
  childNodes[0]. // <TextNode textContent="\n ">
  nextSibling; // <li>
myLI;
// <li id="twitter" class="sprite">
```

So here you went from the first formatting Text node contained by the <ul> to the first <li> Element node. Just as with childNodes and parentNode, you can chain nextSibling queries, too. Try the following cascade, and then verify your work with Figure 7–6.

```
var myLI = document.
  childNodes[1].
  childNodes[1].
  childNodes[1].
  childNodes[3].
  childNodes[1];
myLI.nextSibling.
  nextSibling.
  nextSibling.
  nextSibling.
  nextSibling.
  nextSibling;
// <li id="linkedin" class="sprite">
```

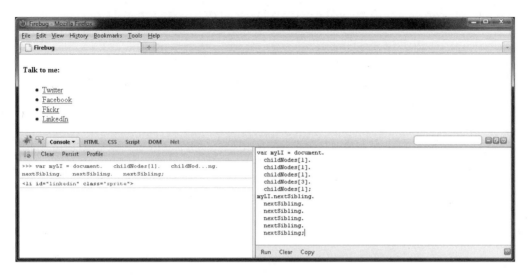

***Figure 7–6.** Moving laterally by chaining nextSibling queries*

Here you went from the first `<li>` to the fourth `<li>`. Not surprisingly, `previousSibling` does the reverse of `nextSibling`. So, let's go from the fourth `<li>` to the first `<li>` with `previousSibling`:

```
var myLI = document.
  childNodes[1].
  childNodes[1].
  childNodes[1].
  childNodes[3].
  childNodes[7];
myLI;
// <li id="linkedin" class="sprite">
myLI.previousSibling.
  previousSibling.
  previousSibling.
  previousSibling.
  previousSibling;
// <li id="twitter" class="sprite">
```

Now then, what would happen if a node does not have a next or previous sibling? I'll give you a hint: DOM nodes are of the object datatype and are therefore saved to the heap just like an ordinary object, array, or function would be. So, how do you represent no data on the heap? Yup, with `null`.

So, there it is. Let's verify this in Firebug by querying `nextSibling` on the final child node of the `<ul>` like so:

```
var myUL = document.
  childNodes[1].
  childNodes[1].
  childNodes[1].
  childNodes[3];
myUL.childNodes[myUL.childNodes.length - 1].nextSibling;
// null
```

Similarly, querying previousSibling on the first child node of the <ul> returns null, too:

```
var myUL = document.
  childNodes[1].
  childNodes[1].
  childNodes[1].
  childNodes[3];
myUL.childNodes[0].previousSibling;
// null
```

Now then, is there a simpler way to query the last child node of the <ul> than keying in childNodes[myUL.childNodes.length - 1]? Oh, you betcha. Just query the aptly named lastChild member:

```
var myUL = document.
  childNodes[1].
  childNodes[1].
  childNodes[1].
  childNodes[3];
myUL.lastChild.previousSibling;
// <li id="linkedin" class="sprite">
```

Conversely, every kind of node has a firstChild member referring to its first child node. So rather than querying childNodes[0], you can save a few keystrokes with firstChild. Note that, in addition to saving keystrokes, lastChild and firstChild read better than their childNodes equivalents.

So, click Clear in both Firebug panels and give firstChild a try, verifying this and the previous sample with Figure 7–7:

```
var myUL = document.
  childNodes[1].
  childNodes[1].
  childNodes[1].
  childNodes[3];
myUL.firstChild.nextSibling;
// <li id="twitter" class="sprite">
```

Figure 7–7. Querying `lastChild` *and* `firstChild` *members*

Converting a NodeList to an Array

Even though `childNodes` contains elements that you query like an array (with an integer index and the [ ] operator), `childNodes` is not an array. Rather, as mentioned earlier, `childNodes` is a `NodeList` object. So, it does not have any array methods like `slice()` or `pop()`. Additionally, `NodeList` objects are live DOM queries. That is, JavaScript has to re-create the `NodeList` any time you query one of its members, including `length`. With those two things in mind, scripters oftentimes convert `NodeList` objects to an array. Doing so not only makes the array methods available but also eliminates the live DOM query sluggishness.

Click Clear in both Firebug panels, and let's convert a `NodeList` object to an array. For this sample, you will work with the `NodeList` returned by the `childNodes` member of the `<ul>` element. Yup, the one with five `Text` nodes and four `<li>` element nodes in it.

```
var myArray = document.
  childNodes[1].
  childNodes[1].
  childNodes[1].
  childNodes[3].
  childNodes;
myArray = Array.prototype.slice.call(myArray, 0);
```

Now loop through `myArray`, deleting formatting `Text` nodes with the array method, `splice()`:

```
var i = 0;
while (i < myArray.length) {
  if (myArray[i].nodeType !== 1) {
    myArray.splice(i, 1);
    continue;
  }
  i ++;
```

```
}
myArray;
// [li#twitter.sprite, li#facebook.sprite, li#flickr.sprite, li#linkedin.sprite]
```

Now `myArray` just contains the four `<li>` Element nodes and therefore has a `length` of 4.

```
myArray.length;
// 4
```

On the other hand, `childNodes` still has a `length` of 9.

```
var myUL = document.
  childNodes[1].
  childNodes[1].
  childNodes[1].
  childNodes[3];
myUL.childNodes.length;
// 9
```

Verify your work in this section with Figure 7–8.

Figure 7–8. Converting a NodeList to an array

So, initially `myArray` and `childNodes` had nine arrows on the stack pointing to nine values on the heap. In other words, there were eighteen arrows on the stack and nine values on the heap. You then deleted five arrows from the stack with `splice()`. Doing so left two arrows per Element node but one arrow per Text node.

Remember from Chapter 5 that values on the heap are manipulated by way of arrows on the stack. With this in mind, you can now manipulate the four `<li>` elements via their arrows in `myArray`, while being able to manipulate `myArray` with array methods like `splice()` or `pop()`. In turn, the code runs faster too since you are working with an array now rather than a live `NodeList`.

Converting a NodeList to an Array for Internet Explorer

One of the many failings Internet Explorer has in regard to DOM is that `NodeList` objects are not JavaScript objects (they are COM objects). Therefore, you cannot pass a `NodeList` as the first parameter to `Function.call()` in Internet Explorer because doing so will return an error since that parameter must be a JavaScript object. But don't worry. By rewriting the `NodeList` to array conversion with a `try catch` statement, which is covered in Chapter 4, you can accommodate Internet Explorer, too. So click Clear in both Firebug panels, and then enter and run the following cross-browser `NodeList` to array conversion.

```
var myArray, i, j, myNodeList = document.
  childNodes[1].
  childNodes[1].
  childNodes[1].
  childNodes[3].
  childNodes;
try {
  myArray = Array.prototype.slice.call(myNodeList, 0);
} catch (errorObject) {
  myArray = [];
  for (i = 0, j = myNodeList.length; i < j; i += 1) {
    myArray[i] = myNodeList[i];
  }
}
myArray instanceof Array;
// true
```

Verify your work with Figure 7–9.

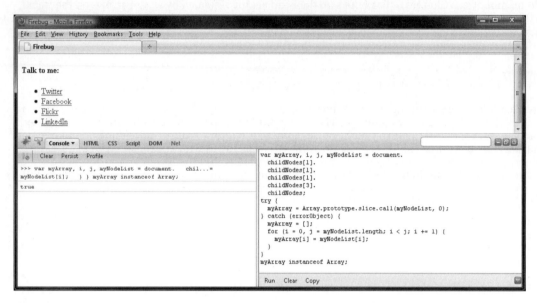

Figure 7–9. *Converting a* `NodeList` *to an array for Internet Explorer*

Firefox, Safari, and Opera convert the `NodeList` to an array by way of the `try` block, while Internet Explorer does so by way of the `catch` block, which JavaScript runs in the event that the `try` block throws an error.

Because you are running the code in Firefox, you need to make the `try` block throw an error in order to test the `catch` block. To do so, simply mistype the `myNodeList` identifier in the parameter list and then click Run:

```
var myArray, i, j, myNodeList = document.
  childNodes[1].
  childNodes[1].
  childNodes[1].
  childNodes[3].
  childNodes;
try {
  myArray = Array.prototype.slice.call(myNodes, 0);
} catch (errorObject) {
  myArray = [];
  for (i = 0, j = myNodeList.length; i < j; i += 1) {
    myArray[i] = myNodeList[i];
  }
}
myArray instanceof Array;
// true
```

Both our `try` path, which Firefox, Safari, and Opera will take, and our inelegant `catch` path, which only Internet Explorer will take, run fine. Note that, whenever you loop through a `NodeList` and do not add or delete nodes from it within the body of the loop, you can improve performance by saving the `length` member to a variable. Why would that be? `length`, like any other member in a `NodeList`, is a live

DOM query. So, by saving length to a variable named j in the previous sample, JavaScript queried DOM one time rather than nine.

■ **Note** Every object in the DOM tree is represented with a COM object rather than a JavaScript object in Internet Explorer. This failing will be a thorn in your side for DOM scripting.

Traversing the DOM without childNodes

childNodes is not really necessary because you can navigate to any node in the DOM tree by way of the firstChild, nextSibling, lastChild, previousSibling, and parentNode members. DOM traversal functions typically are implemented by way of those five members. So, click Clear in both Firebug panels, and let's write one of those ourselves:

```
function traverseTree(node, func) {
  func(node);
  node = node.firstChild;
  while (node !== null) {
    arguments.callee(node, func);
    node = node.nextSibling;
  }
}
```

traverseTree() works with two parameters. node is obviously a node from the DOM tree. func is a function to invoke on node. By way of recursion, which I covered in Chapter 6, of the firstChild and nextSibling members, traverseTree() descends the DOM tree and invokes func on every descendant of the first element you pass to it in node. So, save the <ul> element to a variable named root and have that be the starting point where traverseTree() descends from. Then pass in a function literal for func that will invoke toLowerCase() on the data member of any Text node you happen upon.

```
function traverseTree(node, func) {
  func(node);
  node = node.firstChild;
  while (node !== null) {
    arguments.callee(node, func);
    node = node.nextSibling;
  }
}
var root = document.
  childNodes[1].
  childNodes[1].
  childNodes[1].
  childNodes[3];
traverseTree(root, function(node) {
  if (node.nodeType === 3) {
    node.data = node.data.toLowerCase();
  }
});
```

Now click Run and verify your work with Figure 7–10.

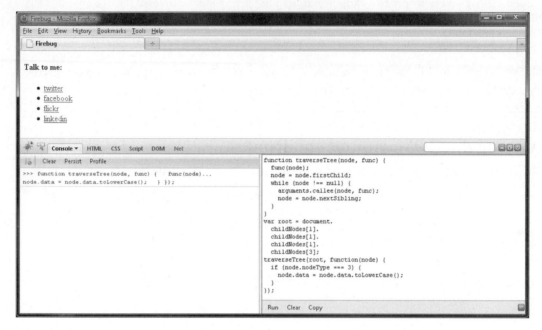

Figure 7–10. Using `traverseTree()` *to convert the text of our list items to lowercase*

One final note on `traverseTree()`: although you stepped through child nodes by way of `firstChild` and `nextSibling`, you could have done so with `lastChild` and `previousSibling`, too. Click the Refresh icon in Firefox to revert the text in the `<li>` elements to that from our markup, and then simply edit `traverseTree()`, changing `firstChild` to `lastChild` and `nextSibling` to `previousSibling`. Click Run to verify that `traverseTree()` works just as well traversing child nodes in reverse. More often than not, you will traverse child nodes moving forward with `nextSibling` rather than in reverse with `previousSibling`.

```
function traverseTree(node, func) {
  func(node);
  node = node.lastChild;
  while (node !== null) {
    arguments.callee(node, func);
    node = node.previousSibling;
  }
}
var root = document.
  childNodes[1].
  childNodes[1].
  childNodes[1].
  childNodes[3];
traverseTree(root, function(node) {
  if (node.nodeType === 3) {
    node.data = node.data.toLowerCase();
  }
});
```

Finding an Element by ID

Traversing the node tree is one way to find an element. But the most direct way is simply to pass `Document.getElementById()` the id of the element you want to work with. So, click Clear in both Firebug panels and Refresh in Firefox (to revert its display to the original markup). Then retrieve one of the `<li>` elements by its id:

```
var myLI = null;
myLI = document.getElementById("facebook");
// <li id="facebook" class="sprite">
```

Now that you have an element in `myLI`, let's do something to it.
Hmm.
Now let's see.
I know, why don't you change the text of its child `Text` node and then correspondingly update its id?

```
myLI.firstChild.firstChild.data = "Bebo";
myLI.firstChild.href = "http://www.bebo.com";
myLI.id = "bebo";
```

Now verify that Firefox updated its display, as in Figure 7–11.

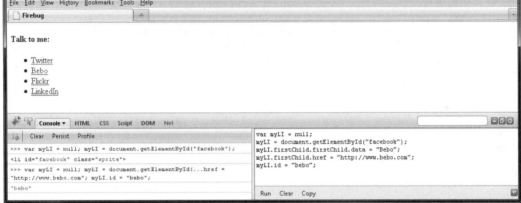

Figure 7–11. *Finding an element by its* `id`

Click Clear in both Firebug panels, and query `myLI` to verify that JavaScript changed the id to `"bebo"` from `"facebook"`:

```
myLI;
// <li id="bebo" class="sprite">
```

Then verify that the `href` attribute was updated, too:

```
myLI.firstChild;
// <a href="http://www.bebo.com">
```

Did everything work for you? Great! Now it's time for some notes on `Document.getElementById()`. First, type its identifier carefully. JavaScript is case sensitive, so `getElementByID` is not the same as

getElementById. Second, if no element in your markup has the desired id, then
Document.getElementById() returns null. This is what you ought to expect inasmuch as an Element node
is of the object datatype, which is to say its value is stored on the heap. Finally, in the event that more
than one element in your markup has the desired id, which is a markup error,
Document.getElementById() may return null, or it may randomly return one of the elements. Note that,
other than in Internet Explorer prior to version 8, the id parameter is case sensitive in all relevant
browsers. Therefore, for our <li> with an id of "twitter", passing Document.getElementById() the
parameter "Twitter" returns null in Firefox, Safari, Opera, and Internet Explorer 8+. On the other hand,
Internet Explorer 7 or older returns the <li> by mistake. With this in mind, do not give different elements
id attributes that vary only by case, such as "sprite" and "Sprite", since Internet Explorer may consider
those to be the same id.

Finding Elements by Their Tag Names

Oftentimes, you will want to do some stuff to elements with the same tag name. Say you want to turn
every <li> element with a class of "sprite" into a CSS sprite. Rather than traverse the DOM tree with a
function like traverseTree(), simply pass either Document.getElementsByTagName() or
Element.getElementsByTagName() a string indicating the tag name of the elements you want, and
JavaScript will return a NodeList containing those elements for your scripting pleasure. Take care to note
that it is Elements, plural, in getElementsByTagName(), but it's Element, singular, in getElementById().

So, you can call getElementsByTagName() on either an Element or a Document node. What's the
difference? If you want JavaScript to return all the elements in your markup that have the same tag
name, go with Document.getElementsByTagName(). On the other hand, if you just want descendants of a
certain element that have the same tag name, meaning you just want to work with a branch of the DOM
tree rather than the whole thing, then turn to Element.getElementsByTagName().

Click Refresh in Firefox (to revert the second <li> to "Facebook") and then click Clear in both
Firebug panels. Let's try Document.getElementsByTagName() first:

```
var myElements = document.getElementsByTagName("a");
myElements;
// [a www.twitter.com, a www.facebook.com, a www.flickr.com, a www.linkedin.com]
```

JavaScript returns a NodeList containing every <a> Element node from the DOM tree. myElements
contains four members. Now let's try Element.getElementsByTagName() on just a branch of the tree:

```
myElements = document.getElementById("twitter").getElementsByTagName("a");
// [a www.twitter.com]
```

Verify your work with Figure 7–12.

Figure 7–12. *Retrieving elements by their tag name from the DOM tree and from just a branch*

Here JavaScript returns every `<a>` element that is a descendant of the Twitter `<li>` element. So, `myElements` contains a `NodeList` with just one member, the Twitter `<a>`. Because `Element.getElementsByTagName()` searches for fish in a smaller pond than `Document.getElementsByTagName()` does, it is more efficient. Thus, favor `Element.getElementsByTagName()` whenever you can.

Finding Elements by Class

With `Document.getElementsByTagName()` or `Element.getElementsByTagName()`, you can find elements by their tag name. `Document.getElementById()` provides a way to find elements by the value of their `id` attribute. Is there a method, say `Document.getElementsByClass()`, that would enable you to find elements by the value of their class attribute? No, sorry. But you can write one with the help of the DOM traversal function `traverseTree()`.

Take a moment to remember where you put `traverseTree()`. Then click Clear in Firebug, and paste `traverseTree()` there. Or, if you forgot to save `traverseTree()` for later, just retype it like so:

```
function traverseTree(node, func) {
  func(node);
  node = node.firstChild;
  while (node !== null) {
    arguments.callee(node, func);
    node = node.nextSibling;
  }
}
```

Now define a function named `findClass()` that works with two arguments. `name` will contain the class to find, and `root` will contain a node to descend the DOM tree from. Note that `root` is optional and will default to the `<body>` element by way of the `||` operator, which I covered in Chapter 3. I'll present my code in a moment, but try writing the code yourself first and see how they compare at the end. Next, create an array named found, which will be the return value of findClass(). found will contain any elements of the class name that are descendants of root. Say that three times fast!

Now invoke traverseTree(), passing root as the first parameter and a function literal for the second parameter. Note that the first time that traverseTree() calls the anonymous function, it will pass root as the value of the argument node. Thereafter, traverseTree() will pass, one by one, every descendant of root.

So, the anonymous function will be passed every descendant of root in turn. Now what will it do with all those nodes? It will determine whether the node is an Element node with a class attribute other than the default "" empty string. You kill both of those birds with one stone with an if condition for the expression !! node.className. Of the 12 node types, only Element nodes have a className member. For the other 11, including those bothersome Text nodes representing markup formatting, node.className returns undefined. Remember from earlier in the book that the !! idiom converts a value of a datatype to a boolean and that undefined and "" convert to false. So, at the end of the day, JavaScript will run the if block only if node refers to an Element node that is a member of one or more classes.

Now className contains a string; therefore, you can manipulate its value with any of the wrapper methods that I covered in Chapter 2. In the event that the element is a member of two or more classes, those will be separated by whitespace. So, with those two things in mind, let's invoke String.split() on the className value and save the returned array to a names variable. Note that you declare names and the traditional loop variable i in the initialization part of a for loop. In this way, JavaScript creates the names array before taking the first roundabout of the for loop.

In the for block, you compare each member of names to the class you are trying to match, which is in the argument name. In the event you have a winner, you append the element in node to found by way of Array.push(), which I covered in Chapter 5. Then at the end of the day, findClass() returns the found array. Here's my finished code:

```
function traverseTree(node, func) {
  func(node);
  node = node.firstChild;
  while (node !== null) {
    arguments.callee(node, func);
    node = node.nextSibling;
  }
}
function findClass(name, root) {
  var found = [];
  root = root || document.body;
  traverseTree(root, function(node) {
    if (!! node.className) {
      for (var names = node.className.split(/\s+/), i = names.length; i --; ) {
        if (names[i] === name) {
          found.push(node);
        }
      }
    }
  });
  return found;
}
```

Now for the moment of truth. Pass "sprite" as the first parameter to findClass(), and let root default to <body>. Take a deep breath and click Run. Then verify your work with Figure 7–13.

```
function traverseTree(node, func) {
  func(node);
  node = node.firstChild;
```

```
  while (node !== null) {
    arguments.callee(node, func);
    node = node.nextSibling;
  }
}
function findClass(name, root) {
  var found = [];
  root = root || document.body;
  traverseTree(root, function(node) {
    if (!! node.className) {
      for (var names = node.className.split(/\s+/), i = names.length; i --; ) {
        if (names[i] === name) {
          found.push(node);
        }
      }
    }
  });
  return found;
}
findClass("sprite");
// [li#twitter.sprite, li#facebook.sprite, li#flickr.sprite, li#linkedin.sprite]
```

Did JavaScript return an array containing your four <li> elements? Good job. You're not a JavaScript bumpkin anymore!

Figure 7–13. Retrieving elements of the same class

Querying Attributes Like a Member

In addition to the members defined in the Node and Element interfaces, every Element node picks up id, className, title, lang, and dir members from HTMLElement and a style member from CSSStyleDeclaration. These members provide a way to query the tag attributes id, class, style, title, lang, and dir. Note that class is one of the reserved keywords in JavaScript, so the member is named className rather than class.

There are three ways to query attributes. The first and preferred way is with the . or [] operator. It's just like querying a Node member like nodeType or an Element member like tagName.

Click Clear in both Firebug panels, and let's query some members from HTMLElement:

```
var myElement = document.getElementById("twitter");
myElement.className;
// "sprite"
myElement.id;
// "twitter"
myElement.dir;
// ""
```

As you can see, if an attribute is set in your markup, JavaScript returns the value (as a string). Otherwise, it returns the default, "". You get a truthy string if the attribute is set and a falsy string if not, which provides a way to branch flow with an if condition.

Note that, like any member of an object, you may query an attribute with the . operator and an identifier. Or you can do so with the [] operator and a string, like so:

```
var myElement = document.getElementById("twitter");
myElement["className"];
// "sprite"
```

Generally, attributes contain a string. However, style is an exception. Rather than a string, style contains a CSSStyleDeclaration object, which I will cover in gory detail in Chapter 8. Note that CSSStyleDeclaration is an arraylike object. Remember that it has a length member but no array methods. Element.style.length returns an integer equal to the number of inline CSS declarations in your markup or added by script. So, style for the Twitter <li> refers to a CSSStyleDeclaration object with a length of 0:

```
var myElement = document.getElementById("twitter");
myElement.style;
// CSSStyleDeclaration length=0
```

Simple elements like <span> and <em> do not have any additional attributes other than id, class, style, title, lang, and dir, but the rest do. For those, there are myriad DOM interfaces that simply define members mirroring the additional tag attributes. For example, a <style> element picks up the disabled, media, and type members from a DOM interface named HTMLStyleElement. Note that essentially all of the additional element interfaces follow that naming convention: HTML and then the tag name in title case and then Element. For a <div> element, the DOM interface is named HTMLDivElement. For a <select> element, the DOM interface is named HTMLSelectElement, and so on. Keep that in mind whenever you refer to DOM documentation or a JavaScript tome, because doing so will save you some time.

Querying Attributes with Methods

Although I recommend that you query element attributes in the same way that you query other element members, which is to say with the . or [] operator, the Element interface defines 13 methods that work only with markup attributes. You can query id with them but not nodeType.

Now for some good news: of those 13 methods, I will cover just three. First, to read the value of an attribute, pass `Element.getAttribute()` the name of the attribute as a string. The method will then return the attribute value as a string. In the event that the attribute is not defined, `Element.getAttribute()` ought to return "". But most browsers return `null` by mistake. Because both "" and `null` are falsy and every string other than "" is truthy, this bug generally is not a problem. For example, an `if` condition with truthy and falsy paths will work regardless of whether the browser returns "" or `null` for an undefined attribute.

■ **Tip** To verify that `Element.getAttribute()` ought to return "" rather than null, visit www.w3.org/TR/DOM-Level-2-Core/core.html and scroll down to the `Element` interface. Or just take my word for it and be done.

Enough talk. Double-clear Firebug, and try querying an attribute or two with `Element.getAttribute()`:

```
var myElement = document.getElementById("twitter");
myElement.getAttribute("class");
// "sprite"
```

Note that, while you query the class member with the . or [] operator and the identifier `className`, you simply pass the string `"class"` to `Element.getAttribute()`. Now why would that be?
Hmm.
There are forbidden identifiers, class being one of them, but no forbidden strings.
Uh-huh.
Now then, let's see whether Firefox returns "" or `null` for an undefined attribute:

```
var myElement = document.getElementById("twitter");
myElement.getAttribute("dir");
// null
```

So, Firefox has the `null` bug, too. Bad Firefox, bad.
Now try to query a member, say `tagName`, that is not an attribute with `Element.getAttribute()`:

```
var myElement = document.getElementById("twitter");
myElement.getAttribute("tagName");
// null
```

On the other hand, querying `tagName` as a member with the . or [] operator returns `"LI"` rather than `null`:

```
var myElement = document.getElementById("twitter");
myElement.tagName;
// "LI"
```

Although you can query an attribute with either the . or [] operator or `Element.getAttribute()`, the same is not true for other members of an `Element` node.
Did you just have a eureka moment? Great. Now for `Element.getAttribute()`'s partner in crime, `Element.setAttribute()`, which writes the value of an attribute. `Element.setAttribute()` takes two string parameters, the name and value of the attribute.
Let's try writing an attribute with `Element.setAttribute()`. Maybe change class from `"sprite"` to `"sprout"` for the Twitter `<li>`:

```
var myElement = document.getElementById("twitter");
```

283

```
myElement.setAttribute("class", "sprout");
```

Then verify the change with `Element.getAttribute()`:

```
myElement.getAttribute("class");
// "sprout"
```

That worked. Note that, in the event the element does not have the attribute passed in the first parameter, JavaScript will add a new attribute to the element. It doesn't even have to be a standard one:

```
var myElement = document.getElementById("twitter");
myElement.setAttribute("verb", "tweet");
```

Then verify the addition with `Element.getAttribute()`:

```
myElement.getAttribute("verb");
// "tweet"
```

Let's try to query `myElement.verb` as a member with the `.` operator:

```
typeof myElement.verb;
// "undefined"
```

Where did the value for our custom attribute `verb` go? Nowhere, it is still there.

```
myElement.getAttribute("verb");
// "tweet"
```

In a nutshell, if you add a custom attribute to an element with `Element.setAttribute()` or directly in your XHTML markup, then you must query the attribute with `Element.getAttribute()`.

Conversely, if you add a member with the `.` or `[]` operators, it will become an attribute only if the DTD for your markup defines an attribute by that name. To illustrate this, try the following sample, verifying your work with Figure 7–14.

```
myElement.slogan = "What's happening?";
myElement.getAttribute("slogan");
// null
```

To JavaScript, predefined attributes like `href` or `id` are both attributes and members, while custom attributes like `verb` are attributes but not members. Conversely, predefined members like `tagName` and custom members like `slogan` are members but not attributes. At least, that's true in all browsers except for the one making mischief in its wolf suit. For Internet Explorer, custom attributes like `verb` are members, and custom members like `slogan` are attributes. That's just one more reason to query attributes like members with the `.` or `[]` operator.

Now for a couple more reasons. First, the `style` member, which I cover in Chapter 8, contains a `CSSStyleDeclaration` object, but the `style` attribute contains a string of text. Second, event listener members, which I cover in Chapter 9, contain a function, but event listener attributes contain a string of text—except in Internet Explorer. Prior to version 8, Internet Explorer returns a `CSSStyleDeclaration` object for both the style member and attribute and a function for event listener members and attributes.

With this mess in mind, only query custom attributes with DOM methods.

Figure 7–14. Custom members are not attributes.

■ **Note** If you are wondering whether an attribute is distinct from the member it maps to, it is. An attribute is represented by an `Attr` node, but its corresponding member is not.

Querying Attr Nodes

DOM provides a way to represent both HTML and XML markup. Whereas HTML attribute values may be fully represented with strings, this is not so for XML attributes. For this reason, DOM provides an `Attr` interface for representing attributes as nodes. Those are not part of the DOM tree. So, you will not bump into them while traversing the DOM.

Anyway, for HTML markup, `Attr` nodes have a single `Text` node child that you may query by way of the `value` member. On the other hand, XML `Attr` nodes may contain both a `Text` and `EntityReference` node, which is why XML attributes cannot be conveyed with just a string.

Click Clear in both Firebug panels, and let's try querying the members of the `Attr` node representing the class attribute for the Twitter `<li>`. First save the `Attr` node in a variable named `myAttrNode`. Note that you can query the `Attr` node with `Element.getAttributeNode()`. So, append `Node` to `Element.getAttribute()`, and you're good to go:

```
var myAttrNode = document.getElementById("twitter").getAttributeNode("class");
```

Now query some members from the Node interface. Remember to stop and click Run prior to each comment in order to verify the return value:

```
myAttrNode.nodeType;
// 11
myAttrNode.nodeName;
// "class"
myAttrNode.nodeValue;
// "sprite"
```

Now query some members the Attr node received by way of the Attr interface:

```
myAttrNode.name;
// "class"
myAttrNode.value;
// "sprite"
myAttrNode.value = "sprout";
myAttrNode.value;
// "sprout"
myAttrNode.specified;
// true
```

So for an Attr node, Node.nodeName and Attr.name contain the same value, a string indicating the name of the attribute. Similarly, both Node.nodeValue and Attr.value contain the value of the attribute as a string. So, the first two members, name and value, are redundant. On the other hand, Attr.specified contains a boolean: true if you explicitly set the attribute in your markup or by JavaScript and false if not. So, false means the attribute value is a default from the document's DTD. With those things in mind, querying Attr.specified will likely be the only time you work with an attribute through the Attr interface (as a node) rather than the Element interface (as a string).

Enumerating Attributes for an Element

For 11 of the 12 node types, the Node.attributes member simply contains null. But not for Element nodes. For those, Node.attributes contains a NamedNodeMap, which is an arraylike object. Remember that those contain numerically indexed members and a length member just like a genuine array but none of the handy array methods like Array.splice().

What does Node.attributes contain? For every attribute explicitly set in your markup or by script, Node.attributes contains a corresponding Attr node. So, no default Attr nodes in there.

Alrighty then, click Clear in both Firebug panels, and let's explore Node.attributes:

```
var arrayOfAttrNodes = document.getElementById("twitter").attributes;
arrayOfAttrNodes.length;
// 2
```

So two Attr nodes appear, one for id and one for class. But there are no default ones like style or dir. Now then, the numerical indexes in a NamedNodeMap are there just for enumeration purposes. That is to say, DOM does not specify whether those should be ordered relative to source code, alphabetically, or by any other pattern. So, browsers will vary in their numbering. For example, id appears first in the Twitter <li> but has an index of 1, not 0, in Firefox:

```
var arrayOfAttrNodes = document.getElementById("twitter").attributes;
arrayOfAttrNodes[1].name;
// "id"
```

But a `NamedNodeMap` is called a `NamedNodeMap` for a reason. You can, you know, query members by name, with an identifier and the `.` operator or with a string and the [ ] operator. Try both ways, verifying your work with Figure 7–15:

```
var arrayOfAttrNodes = document.getElementById("twitter").attributes;
arrayOfAttrNodes.id.value;
// "twitter"
var arrayOfAttrNodes = document.getElementById("twitter").attributes;
arrayOfAttrNodes["class"].value;
// "sprite"
```

Figure 7–15. *Querying attributes with refinement operators*

In regard to `Node.attributes`, Internet Explorer again says, "I'll be on my own side. By myself." Prior to version 8, Internet Explorer put every default attribute from the DTD in an element's attributes member. So, there might be like 100 in there. Yipes! Internet Explorer 8 does not have the bug.

Let's take a moment to sigh ruefully over this Internet Explorer bug. Then find a workaround for Internet Explorer 7 and earlier.

Hmm.

Why don't we...

No, that won't work.

I know, filter the `Attr` nodes in `attributes` by their `specified` member. Just throw away the ones with a value of `false`. Click Clear in both Firebug panels, and then define a helper function named `filterDefaultAttrNodes()` like so:

```
function filterDefaultAttrNodes(elem) {
  var filtered = [];
  for (var i = 0, j = elem.attributes.length; i < j; i ++) {
    if (elem.attributes[i].specified) {
      filtered.push(elem.attributes[i]);
    }
  }
  return filtered;
}
```

Note that the `NamedNodeMap` object in `Node.attributes` is a live DOM query just like a `NodeList` object is. To improve performance, you save the `length` member to a loop variable named j. In this way, you query the DOM one time for `length` rather than maybe 100 times for Internet Explorer.

Now pass the Twitter `<li>` as the parameter to `filterDefaultAttrNodes()`.

```
function filterDefaultAttrNodes(elem) {
  var filtered = [];
  for (var i = 0, j = elem.attributes.length; i < j; i ++) {
    if (elem.attributes[i].specified) {
      filtered.push(elem.attributes[i]);
    }
  }
  return filtered;
}
filterDefaultAttrNodes(document.getElementById("twitter"));
// [Attr, Attr]
```

Verify your work with Figure 7–16.

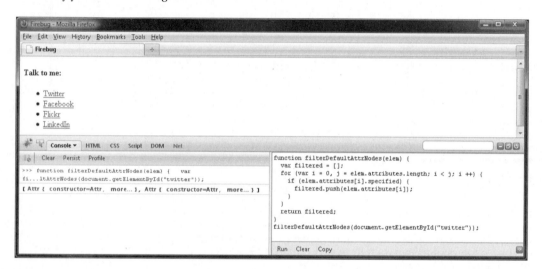

Figure 7–16. *Filtering maybe 100 default* `Attr` *nodes for Internet Explorer*

Two `Attr` nodes are in there. Note that, for Firefox, Safari, Opera, and Internet Explorer 8, `elem.attributes[i].specified` will always be `true`. So, this function does nothing for nonbuggy browsers. But for Internet Explorer 7 and older, it eliminates about 100 unwanted default `Attr` nodes. As an added benefit, the return value is a real array. Thus, unlike the arraylike `attributes` object, this one has all the array methods. You can manipulate the `Attr` nodes with those methods. Moreover, `Node.attributes` is a live DOM query and is memory intensive. On the other hand, the filtered array is not live, so it is very fast in comparison.

From an Internet Explorer lemon, we made lemonade!

Creating Element or Text Nodes

Oftentimes, you will want to create `Element` or `Text` nodes with JavaScript and then insert them into the DOM tree. Doing so is one way to dynamically add content to a web page.

One of the implications of DOM being defined with interfaces rather than classes is that you cannot, for example, create an `Element` node by writing something like this:

```
var myLI = new Element("li");
```

Rather than creating DOM nodes with constructor functions, you do so with factory methods from the `Document` interface. So let's try that. Click Clear in both Firebug panels, and create an `Element` node, say an `<li>`, with the factory method `Document.createElement()`:

```
var myLI = document.createElement("li");
```

That was pretty straightforward. Just pass `Document.createElement()` the tag name of the element as a string, and this factory method returns a new `Element` node to you. But it's blank; it has no attributes other than defaults from the DTD. It contains no child nodes either. So, you have some work to do before adding the `<li>` to the DOM tree. Let's tackle attributes first. You already know how—set `id` to "blog" and `class` to "sprite":

```
var myLI = document.createElement("li");
myLI.id = "bebo";
myLI.className = "sprite";
```

Now it's time for the children. The existing four `<li>` elements have a child `<a>` element with a child `Text` node. That's what you want this new `<li>` to have, too. Create the `<a>` first. Do it the same way as you did the `<li>`. Then add an `href` attribute with a value of "http://www.bebo.com".

```
var myLI = document.createElement("li"), myA = document.createElement("a");
myLI.id = "bebo";
myLI.className = "sprite";
myA.href = "http://www.bebo.com";
```

Now for the `Text` node. Like the element factory method, this one is defined by the `Document` interface, too. But be wary, unlike the element factory method, the identifier for this one ends with `Node`: `createTextNode`, not `createText`. `Document.createTextNode()` works with just one parameter, which is the string of text you want the node to represent.

```
var myLI = document.createElement("li"),
  myA = document.createElement("a"),
  myText = document.createTextNode("Bebo");
myLI.id = "bebo";
myLI.className = "sprite";
myA.href = "http://www.bebo.com";
```

Now you have two `Element` nodes and one `Text` node floating around in the ether. How do you insert those into the DOM tree? Well, every kind of node, yup all 12 of 'em, has three methods to do so:

```
Node.appendChild()
Node.insertBefore()
Node.replaceChild()
```

What do those do? The first one, `Node.appendChild()`, appends the node you pass to it to the end of the `childNodes` array of the node you invoke it upon. Invoke `Node.appendChild()` on myA, passing myText as the parameter:

```
var myLI = document.createElement("li"),
```

```
    myA = document.createElement("a"),
    myText = document.createTextNode("Bebo");
myLI.id = "bebo";
myLI.className = "sprite";
myA.href = "http://www.bebo.com";
myA.appendChild(myText);
```

So now you have the DOM representation of the following `<a>` tag floating around in memory:

```
<a href="http://www.bebo.com">Bebo</a>
```

Now let's try `Node.insertBefore()`. This one takes two parameters. First, it takes a node to insert, just like the parameter to `Node.appendChild()`. The second parameter is a node in the `childNodes` member of whatever node you call `insertBefore()` on. JavaScript inserts the node in the first parameter before the child node in the second parameter. So that's why the method is named `insertBefore()`. Uh-huh.

In the event that you pass `null` in as the second parameter, `Node.insertBefore()` does the same thing as `Node.appendChild()`. Take advantage of that feature so that you can call `Node.insertBefore()` on `myLI`, which does not have any child nodes for you to choose the second parameter from:

```
var myLI = document.createElement("li"),
    myA = document.createElement("a"),
    myText = document.createTextNode("Bebo");
myLI.id = "bebo";
myLI.className = "sprite";
myA.href = "http://www.bebo.com";
myA.appendChild(myText);
myLI.insertBefore(myA, null);
```

Great. Now you have an `<li>` element like the following floating around in memory, just waiting for you to insert it into the DOM tree:

```
<li id="bebo" class="sprite"><a href="http://www.bebo.com">Bebo</a></li>
```

So now for the moment of truth. By way of the third method, `Node.replaceChild()`, you will swap the Facebook `<li>` for the new Bebo `<li>`. `Node.replaceChild()` takes two parameters, a child node to insert and a child node to remove.

OK, so for the DOM tree, you want to call `Node.replaceChild()` on the `<ul>` element, passing `myLI` for the first parameter and the Facebook `<li>` for the second parameter:

```
var myLI = document.createElement("li"),
    myA = document.createElement("a"),
    myText = document.createTextNode("Bebo"),
    myUL = document.getElementsByTagName("ul")[0];
myLI.id = "bebo";
myLI.className = "sprite";
myA.href = "http://www.bebo.com";
myA.appendChild(myText);
myLI.insertBefore(myA, null);
myUL.replaceChild(myLI, document.getElementById("facebook"));
// <li id="facebook" class="sprite">
```

Click Run, and verify that Firefox updated its display like in Figure 7–17. Note that all three insertion methods have a return value that is a node. As Figure 7–17 shows, for `Node.replaceChild()`, the return value is the node you removed. So, that is why Firebug printed `<li id="facebook" class="sprite">`. For the other two, `Node.appendChild()` and `Node.insertBefore()`, it's the node you inserted.

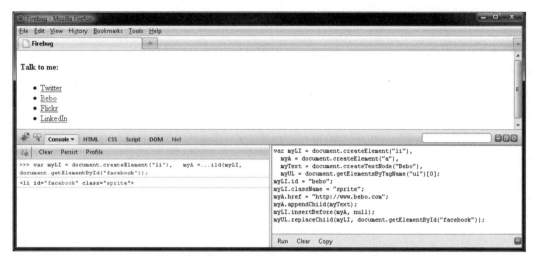

Figure 7–17. Replacing a node with `Node.replaceChild()`

Insofar as a node can be in only one place in the DOM tree at a time, the return value for `Node.appendChild()` and `Node.insertBefore()` is not very useful. On the other hand, you can reinsert the node returned by `Node.replaceChild()` somewhere else. So, click Refresh in Firefox to revert the display to our initial markup and then try reinserting the Facebook `<li>` like so:

```
var myLI = document.createElement("li"),
  myA = document.createElement("a"),
  myText = document.createTextNode("Bebo"),
  myUL = document.getElementsByTagName("ul")[0];
myLI.id = "bebo";
myLI.className = "sprite";
myA.href = "http://www.bebo.com";
myA.appendChild(myText);
myLI.insertBefore(myA, null);
myUL.appendChild(myUL.replaceChild(myLI, document.getElementById("facebook")));
// <li id="facebook" class="sprite">
```

As Figure 7–18 illustrates, JavaScript replaced the Facebook `<li>` with the new Bebo `<li>`. Then reinserted the Facebook `<li>` at the very end of the `NodeList` in `myUL.childNodes`. So, Firefox displays five `<li>` elements rather than four.

Figure 7–18. Reinserting the node removed by Node.replaceChild()

■ **Note** Content created with JavaScript does not have empty Text nodes representing formatting since there is none. That is to say, dynamically generated content is like markup where every opening tag is flush to the preceding element's closing tag.

Deleting Content

Now what if you simply want to delete some content without inserting any in its place? Doing so is straightforward. Just call Node.removeChild() on the parent of the node you want to delete. Pass Node.removeChild() the unwanted child node, and you're done. So, let's give the Flickr <li> the axe. But before doing so, click Clear in both Firebug panels and refresh Firefox so that it reverts its display to the original markup:

```
var myUL = document.getElementsByTagName("ul")[0];
myUL.removeChild(document.getElementById("flickr"));
```

Take a peek at Firefox's display. There are just three <li> elements now.

Since JavaScript printed <li id="flickr" class="sprite"> in the left panel of Firebug, does that mean Node.removeChild() returns the node it deleted? Yup.

It turns out you can use that return value to reinsert the deleted node elsewhere. Let's give that a try. But first click Refresh in Firefox so that you get the Flickr <li> back. Double-clear Firebug, too. Then enter and run the following:

```
var myUL = document.getElementsByTagName("ul")[0],
```

```
myLI = document.getElementById("facebook");
myUL.insertBefore(myUL.removeChild(document.getElementById("flickr")), myLI);
```

Now then, `Node.removeChild()` and `Node.insertBefore()` are called on the parent node of their parameters. With this in mind, you can call them on the `parentNode` member of the deleted or inserted node. In other words, you can be totally clueless about who the parent is. So, refresh Firefox; then rework the previous sample like so:

```
var myLI = document.getElementById("facebook");
myLI.parentNode.insertBefore(myLI.parentNode.removeChild(document.getElementById("flickr")),
  myLI);
```

Then click Run, and verify your cleverness with Figure 7–19. Note that this mystery parent trick works for `Node.appendChild()` and `Node.replaceChild()`, too. As long as you know the node you want to manipulate, you can call any of those four methods on its `parentNode` member, since `Element` and `Text` nodes always have a parent, even if they don't know their name.

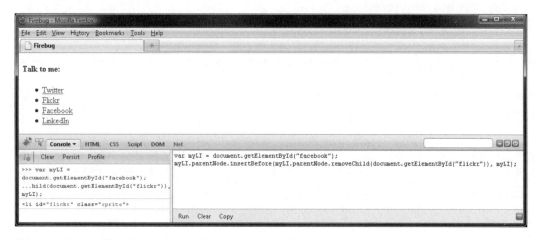

Figure 7–19. *It's OK to be totally clueless in regard to the parent node.*

Copying Content

Insofar as a node can be in only one place in the DOM tree at any given time, you may think that there is no way to duplicate content. But you would be wrong. If you want to copy a node with or without its descendants, just call its `cloneNode()` method. `Node.cloneNode()` takes a boolean parameter. Pass in `true` if you want to duplicate the node and its descendants (the whole branch of the DOM tree). Otherwise, pass in `false`, and JavaScript will duplicate the element as if it were empty. For `Text` nodes, which have no descendants, the parameter is moot. But pass in `false` to show you know what you're doing. Note that any event listener functions registered for an element, something you will learn how to do in Chapter 9, are not copied. This is stupid, but it is what it is. You have to redo any event binding for the duplicate element.

Alright, double-clear Firebug, refresh Firefox, and try duplicating the `<ul>` and its descendants. Then reinsert the duplicate branch in the DOM tree:

```
var myUL = document.getElementsByTagName("ul")[0];
myUL.parentNode.appendChild(myUL.cloneNode(true));
```

Note that, although `Node.cloneNode()` gives you the option to do a deep or shallow copy, `Node.appendChild()`, `Node.insertBefore()`, `Node.replaceChild()`, and `Node.removeChild()` do not. Those four manipulate a node with its descendants, no matter what.

Creating Elements with a Helper Function

Creating an element containing descendants with `Document.createElement()`, `Node.appendChild()`, and other methods can be mind-numbingly repetitive. Why not eliminate some drudgery by writing a helper function to create elements with?

No, I cannot think of any reason not to either. Let's get to it. But, before beginning, double-clear Firebug and refresh Firefox. Now define a function named `createElem()` that works with three parameters. First, `name` will contain the tag name as a string. Next, `members` will contain an object containing the names and values of any attributes you want the element to have. Finally, `children` will contain an array containing any child nodes you want the element to have. For a `Text` node child, you may put a `Text` node or a string in `children`.

```
function createElem(name, members, children) {
}
```

Now declare local variables named `elem` and `m`, initializing `elem` to the return value of `document.createElement(name)` and letting `m` default to `undefined`.

```
function createElem(name, members, children) {
  var elem = document.createElement(name), m;
}
```

Now you have a vanilla `Element` node with its `nodeName` and `tagName` members both set to `name`. Of course, JavaScript will also initialize any other default attributes or members for that particular tag. Let's go ahead and enumerate `members` with a `for in` loop. In the `for in` block, you will initialize attributes with the `[]` operator and the string in `m`. Remember from Chapter 4 that, during each roundabout of a `for in` loop, JavaScript assigns the name of a member to the loop variable as a string, regardless of whether it was named with a string or identifier in the object. But before you do, make sure that the `members` parameter really does contain an object. To do so, wrap the `for in` loop with an `if` condition:

```
function createElem(name, members, children) {
  var elem = document.createElement(name), m;
  if (members instanceof Object) {
    for (m in members) {
      elem[m] = members[m];
    }
  }
}
```

Moving right along, let's do something very similar with the `children` array. Insofar as `children` is an array, go with a `for` loop instead of a `for in` loop. Within the `for` block, you will pass `appendChild()` an expression cobbled together with the `?:` operator, which I covered in Chapter 3. In the event that `children[i]` is a node, which is to say an object, the `?:` expression will simply evaluate to the node. Otherwise, it will evaluate to passing the string in `children[i]` to `Document.createTextNode()`, which will in turn return a `Text` node. Either way, `appendChild()` will have a node to work with. So, it will be happy as a clam.

```
function createElem(name, members, children) {
  var elem = document.createElement(name), m;
  if (members instanceof Object) {
```

```
    for (m in members) {
      elem[m] = members[m];
    }
  }
  if (children instanceof Array) {
    for (i = 0; i < children.length; i ++ ) {
      elem.appendChild(
        typeof children[i] === "object" ? children[i] : document.createTextNode(children[i])
      );
    }
  }
}
```

Right now, createElem() returns undefined, so the element and its descendants cannot be inserted into the DOM tree. No, not good.

What do you do? Just return elem. That way, you can pass the return value of createElem() to a method like Node.appendChild(). To save your bacon, just amend createElem() like so:

```
function createElem(name, members, children) {
  var elem = document.createElement(name), m;
  if (members instanceof Object) {
    for (m in members) {
      elem[m] = members[m];
    }
  }
  if (children instanceof Array) {
    for (i = 0; i < children.length; i ++ ) {
      elem.appendChild(
        typeof children[i] === "object" ? children[i] : document.createTextNode(children[i])
      );
    }
  }
  return elem;
}
```

Now for the moment of truth. Earlier in the day, you laboriously created a Bebo <li> like so:

```
var myLI = document.createElement("li"),
  myA = document.createElement("a"),
  myText = document.createTextNode("Bebo");
myLI.id = "bebo";
myLI.className = "sprite";
myA.href = "http://www.bebo.com";
myA.appendChild(myText);
```

Now try to replace all that with a call to the createElem() function. Then you'll append the Bebo <li> element to your <ul>. Enter and run the following amended sample, before verifying your work with Figure 7–20.

```
function createElem(name, members, children) {
  var elem = document.createElement(name), m;
  if (members instanceof Object) {
    for (m in members) {
      elem[m] = members[m];
    }
```

```
  }
  if (children instanceof Array) {
    for (i = 0; i < children.length; i ++ ) {
      elem.appendChild(
        typeof children[i] === "object" ? children[i] : document.createTextNode(children[i])
      );
    }
  }
  return elem;
}
var child = createElem(
  "li",
  {id: "bebo", className: "sprite"},
  [createElem("a", {href: "http://www.bebo.com"}, ["Bebo"])]
);
document.getElementsByTagName("ul")[0].appendChild(child);
```

Did everything work for you? Good job. You're definitely well on your way from JavaScript dummy to expert.

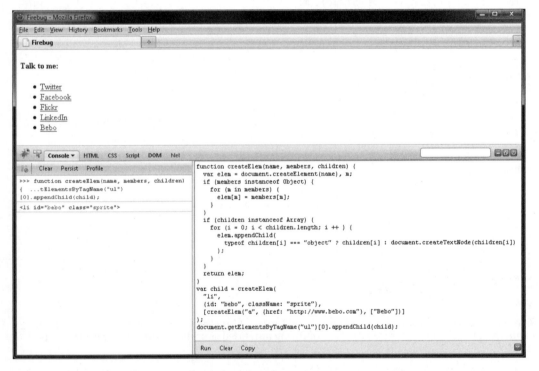

Figure 7–20. Creating elements with a helper function

Reordering Nested Lists

Let's try a final sample so that many of the features covered in this chapter take firm root in your noggin. You're going to write a function named orderUL that will alphabetically reorder any descendant <li> elements of a <ul> regardless of whether it contains nested <ul> elements.

First, download seven2.html (shown here) from the chapter downloads at www.apress.com. Then open it with Firefox and press F12 to enable Firebug. Note that seven2.html lists the 30 ice hockey teams in the NHL.

```
<!DOCTYPE html PUBLIC "-//W3C//DTD XHTML 1.0 Strict//EN"
"http://www.w3.org/TR/xhtml1/DTD/xhtml1-strict.dtd">
<html xmlns="http://www.w3.org/1999/xhtml">
<head>
<meta http-equiv="Content-Type" content="text/html; charset=utf-8" />
<title>Firebug</title>
</head>
<body>
<ul>
  <li><a href="#">Western Conference</a>
    <ul>
      <li><a href="http://blackhawks.nhl.com">Chicago Blackhawks</a></li>
      <li><a href="http://bluejackets.nhl.com">Columbus Blue Jackets</a></li>
      <li><a href="http://redwings.nhl.com">Detroit Red Wings</a></li>
      <li><a href="http://predators.nhl.com">Nashville Predators</a></li>
      <li><a href="http://blues.nhl.com">St Louis Blues</a></li>
      <li><a href="http://flames.nhl.com">Calgary Flames</a></li>
      <li><a href="http://avalanche.nhl.com">Colorado Avalanche</a></li>
      <li><a href="http://oilers.nhl.com">Edmonton Oilers</a></li>
      <li><a href="http://wild.nhl.com">Minnesota Wild</a></li>
      <li><a href="http://canucks.nhl.com">Vancouver Canucks</a></li>
      <li><a href="http://ducks.nhl.com">Anaheim Ducks</a></li>
      <li><a href="http://stars.nhl.com">Dallas Stars</a></li>
      <li><a href="http://kings.nhl.com">Los Angeles Kings</a></li>
      <li><a href="http://coyotes.nhl.com">Phoenix Coyotes</a></li>
      <li><a href="http://sharks.nhl.com">San Jose Sharks</a></li>
    </ul>
  </li>
  <li><a href="#">Eastern Conference</a>
    <ul>
      <li><a href="http://devils.nhl.com">New Jersey Devils</a></li>
      <li><a href="http://islanders.nhl.com">New York Islanders</a></li>
      <li><a href="http://rangers.nhl.com">New York Rangers</a></li>
      <li><a href="http://flyers.nhl.com">Philadelphia Flyers</a></li>
      <li><a href="http://penguins.nhl.com">Pittsburgh Penguins</a></li>
      <li><a href="http://bruins.nhl.com">Boston Bruins</a></li>
      <li><a href="http://sabres.nhl.com">Buffalo Sabres</a></li>
      <li><a href="http://canadiens.nhl.com">Montreal Canadiens</a></li>
      <li><a href="http://senators.nhl.com">Ottawa Senators</a></li>
      <li><a href="http://mapleleafs.nhl.com">Toronto Maple Leafs</a></li>
      <li><a href="http://thrashers.nhl.com">Atlanta Thrashers</a></li>
      <li><a href="http://hurricanes.nhl.com">Carolina Hurricanes</a></li>
      <li><a href="http://panthers.nhl.com">Florida Panthers</a></li>
      <li><a href="http://lightning.nhl.com">Tampa Bay Lightning</a></li>
      <li><a href="http://capitals.nhl.com">Washington Capitals</a></li>
```

```
      </ul>
    </li>
  </ul>
  </body>
</html>
```

Begin by saving the invocation expression, document.getElementsByTagName("ul"), to a variable named myElements. Then define a function named orderUL that works with an argument named root, which will refer to an ancestor of the <li> elements you want to reorder.

```
var myElements = document.getElementsByTagName("ul");
function orderUL(root) {
}
```

Note that root will typically be a <ul>, but any ancestor of the <li> elements you want to reorder will do. Even document will work fine. However, for your sample, pass myElements[0] to orderUL(). Of course, you have to write orderUL() before you can think of calling it. So let's get back to work.

Initialize a local variable named nodeList to root.getElementsByTagName("li"), which evaluates to a NodeList containing every descendant <li> of the parameter passed to orderUL(). Then create an empty array named helperArray to copy the <li> elements in nodeList to. Recall from earlier in the chapter that doing this will make orderUL() run faster since NodeList objects are live DOM queries. Finally, declare the traditional loop variable i:

```
var myElements = document.getElementsByTagName("ul");
function orderUL(root) {
  var nodeList = root.getElementsByTagName("li"), helperArray = [], i;
}
```

Now write a for loop to copy the <li> elements in nodeList to helperArray. Doing so will enable you to reorder the <li> elements with Array.sort(). Moreover, later you will loop through helperArray, removing and reinserting an <li> element during each roundabout. This is the kind of loop you should never use on a live NodeList. So, you definitely have reasons for the way you're doing things!

```
var myElements = document.getElementsByTagName("ul");
function orderUL(root) {
  var nodeList = root.getElementsByTagName("li"), helperArray = [], i;
  for (i = 0; i < nodeList.length; i ++) {
    helperArray.push(nodeList[i]);
  }
}
```

Recall from Chapter 5 that by default Array.sort() reorders strings and numbers relative to their character encoding. For example, "Zebra" would come before "antelope", and 450 would come before 9. Rarely will this default behavior be desirable. Obviously, it isn't here. Pass Array.sort() a function literal to reorder helperArray with. In this function literal, you determine whether to return -1, 1, or 0 relative to the lowercase versions of the strings the child Text nodes represent. However, remember that String.toLowerCase() does not lowercase the string that you call it on. Rather, it returns a lowercased copy of the string. So, save those to local variables named txt1 and txt2. Comparing those lowercased copies with the < and > operators takes care of the string and number bugs noted earlier. So feeling clever, you now have this:

```
var myElements = document.getElementsByTagName("ul");
function orderUL(root) {
  var nodeList = root.getElementsByTagName("li"), helperArray = [], i;
  for (i = 0; i < nodeList.length; i ++) {
    helperArray.push(nodeList[i]);
```

```
    }
    helperArray.sort(function(li1, li2) {
        var txt1 = li1.getElementsByTagName("a")[0].firstChild.nodeValue.toLowerCase();
        var txt2 = li2.getElementsByTagName("a")[0].firstChild.nodeValue.toLowerCase();
        if (txt1 < txt2) {
          return -1;
        } else if (txt1 > txt2) {
          return 1;
        } else {
          return 0;
        }
    });
}
```

Now here's the question: helperArray contains every descendant <li> of the element passed in the root parameter. That is to say, the <li> elements in helperArray may very well be from different <ul> elements. At this point, you have the <li> elements reordered as you want. Now you need to reinsert each <li> to the right <ul>. How do you do that?

Did you figure it out yet?

Take your time.

No hurry.

Remember, there are no stupid answers.

So, what do you think?

Good try, but that's not it.

Do you remember how every element has a parent? For example, parentNode is never null for an Element node. In this case, for every <li> element in the helperArray, parentNode refers to the <ul> it belongs to. Moreover, since nodes may be only one place in the DOM tree at a time, if you blindly call Node.appendChild() on the parentNode member of each <li>, JavaScript will remove the <li> from the childNodes member of its containing <ul>. Then reinsert it at the very end of the same <ul> element's childNodes member. So, do so one <li> at a time by way of a for loop:

```
var myElements = document.getElementsByTagName("ul");
function orderUL(root) {
  var nodeList = root.getElementsByTagName("li"), helperArray = [], i;
  for (i = 0; i < nodeList.length; i ++) {
    helperArray.push(nodeList[i]);
  }
  helperArray.sort(function(li1, li2) {
      var txt1 = li1.getElementsByTagName("a")[0].firstChild.nodeValue.toLowerCase();
      var txt2 = li2.getElementsByTagName("a")[0].firstChild.nodeValue.toLowerCase();
      if (txt1 < txt2) {
        return -1;
      } else if (txt1 > txt2) {
        return 1;
      } else {
        return 0;
      }
  });
  for (i = 0; i < helperArray.length; i ++) {
    helperArray[i].parentNode.appendChild(helperArray[i]);
  }
}
```

Taking the time to explore core DOM features is paying dividends. Now for the moment of truth: pass myElements[0] to orderUL(), cross your fingers, and click Run.

```
var myElements = document.getElementsByTagName("ul");
function orderUL(root) {
  var nodeList = root.getElementsByTagName("li"), helperArray = [], i;
  for (i = 0; i < nodeList.length; i ++) {
    helperArray.push(nodeList[i]);
  }
  helperArray.sort(function(li1, li2) {
      var txt1 = li1.getElementsByTagName("a")[0].firstChild.nodeValue.toLowerCase();
      var txt2 = li2.getElementsByTagName("a")[0].firstChild.nodeValue.toLowerCase();
      if (txt1 < txt2) {
        return -1;
      } else if (txt1 > txt2) {
        return 1;
      } else {
        return 0;
      }
    });
  for (i = 0; i < helperArray.length; i ++) {
    helperArray[i].parentNode.appendChild(helperArray[i]);
  }
}
orderUL(myElements[0]);
```

So as Figure 7–21 illustrates, JavaScript reordered the team and conference <li> elements. One last thing before I call this chapter a wrap. Remember those whitespace Text nodes representing markup formatting? Where do you think those were moved to?

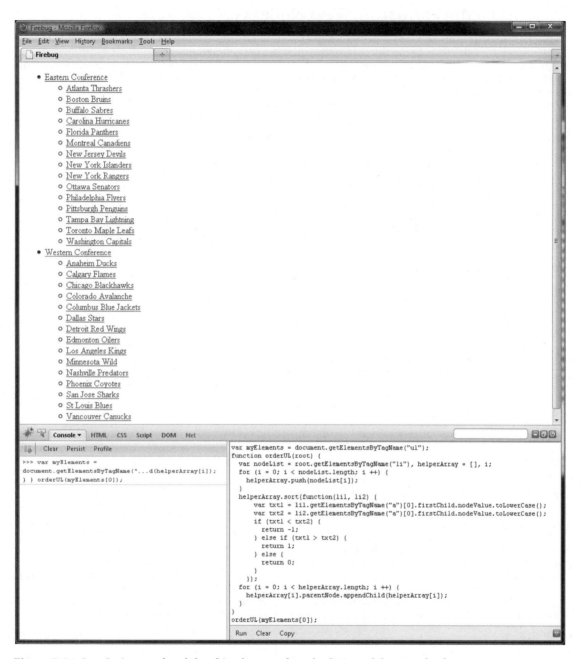

Figure 7–21. JavaScript reordered the `<li>` elements from both tiers of the nested `<ul>`.

Where Did the Formatting Text Nodes Go?

Now let's think this through. orderUL() plucked <li> elements from the DOM tree and reinserted them at the very end of the NodeList in the childNodes member of their parent <ul> element. Say that three times fast. Anyway, the formatting Text nodes were left alone. Therefore, after plucking an <li> from the tree, the formatting Text nodes that were on either side of the <li> wind up next to each other. By the time orderUL() finishes its work, the formatting Text nodes are bunched up at the beginning of the NodeList in the childNodes members of the <ul> elements.

Rather than take my word for it, refresh Firefox, and run the following amended sample:

```
var myElements = document.getElementsByTagName("ul");
function orderUL(root) {
  var nodeList = root.getElementsByTagName("li"), helperArray = [], i;
  for (i = 0; i < nodeList.length; i ++) {
    helperArray.push(nodeList[i]);
  }
  helperArray.sort(function(li1, li2) {
      var txt1 = li1.getElementsByTagName("a")[0].firstChild.nodeValue.toLowerCase();
      var txt2 = li2.getElementsByTagName("a")[0].firstChild.nodeValue.toLowerCase();
      if (txt1 < txt2) {
        return -1;
      } else if (txt1 > txt2) {
        return 1;
      } else {
        return 0;
      }
    });
  for (i = 0; i < helperArray.length; i ++) {
    helperArray[i].parentNode.appendChild(helperArray[i]);
  }
}
orderUL(myElements[0]);
myElements[1].childNodes;
```

JavaScript then prints the following in Firebug:

```
[<TextNode textContent="\n ">, <TextNode textContent="\n ">, <TextNode textContent="\n ">,
<TextNode textContent="\n ">, <TextNode textContent="\n ">, <TextNode textContent="\n ">,
<TextNode textContent="\n ">, <TextNode textContent="\n ">, <TextNode textContent="\n ">,
<TextNode textContent="\n ">, <TextNode textContent="\n ">, <TextNode textContent="\n ">,
<TextNode textContent="\n ">, <TextNode textContent="\n ">, <TextNode textContent="\n ">,
<TextNode textContent="\n ">, li, li, li, li, li, li, li, li, li, li, li, li, li, li, li]
```

So, although you initially had 17 formatting Text nodes interspersing 15 <li> Element nodes, now you have 17 formatting Text nodes followed by 15 <li> Element nodes. Having those formatting Text nodes bunched together does no harm. But if you want JavaScript to fold those 17 formatting Text nodes into one, call Node.normalize() on their parent or any other ancestor. JavaScript will then merge any adjacent Text nodes and delete any empty ones. Note that, by empty Text nodes, I mean those that do not even represent whitespace. As you might imagine, empty Text nodes are as rare as formatting Text nodes are prevalent.

Refresh Firefox; then run the following amended sample:

```
var myElements = document.getElementsByTagName("ul");
function orderUL(root) {
  var nodeList = root.getElementsByTagName("li"), helperArray = [], i;
```

```
  for (i = 0; i < nodeList.length; i ++) {
    helperArray.push(nodeList[i]);
  }
  helperArray.sort(function(li1, li2) {
      var txt1 = li1.getElementsByTagName("a")[0].firstChild.nodeValue.toLowerCase();
      var txt2 = li2.getElementsByTagName("a")[0].firstChild.nodeValue.toLowerCase();
      if (txt1 < txt2) {
        return -1;
      } else if (txt1 > txt2) {
        return 1;
      } else {
        return 0;
      }
  });
  for (i = 0; i < helperArray.length; i ++) {
    helperArray[i].parentNode.appendChild(helperArray[i]);
  }
}
orderUL(myElements[0]);
myElements[0].normalize();
myElements[1].childNodes;
```

JavaScript will then print the following in Firebug; as you can see, the 17 formatting Text nodes were folded into one:

```
[<TextNode textContent="\n \n \n \n \n \n \n \n \n \n \n \n \n \n \n \n ">, li, li, li, li,
li, li, li, li, li, li, li, li, li, li, li]
```

Now what if you don't want the giant whitespace Text node? Just delete it with `Node.removeChild()`, which we explored earlier. Refresh Firefox, and then run the amended sample, verifying your work with Figure 7–22:

```
var myElements = document.getElementsByTagName("ul");
function orderUL(root) {
  var nodeList = root.getElementsByTagName("li"), helperArray = [], i;
  for (i = 0; i < nodeList.length; i ++) {
    helperArray.push(nodeList[i]);
  }
  helperArray.sort(function(li1, li2) {
      var txt1 = li1.getElementsByTagName("a")[0].firstChild.nodeValue.toLowerCase();
      var txt2 = li2.getElementsByTagName("a")[0].firstChild.nodeValue.toLowerCase();
      if (txt1 < txt2) {
        return -1;
      } else if (txt1 > txt2) {
        return 1;
      } else {
        return 0;
      }
  });
  for (i = 0; i < helperArray.length; i ++) {
    helperArray[i].parentNode.appendChild(helperArray[i]);
  }
}
orderUL(myElements[0]);
myElements[0].normalize();
```

```
myElements[1].removeChild(myElements[1].firstChild);
myElements[1].childNodes;
// [li, li, li, li, li, li, li, li, li, li, li, li, li, li, li]
```

So now the Eastern Conference `<ul>` has just `<li>` children, just as if you had removed all formatting whitespace from the XHTML markup (or if Internet Explorer were representing it).

Figure 7–22. Eliminating formatting Text *nodes with* normalize() *and* removeChild()

Summary

In this chapter, we explored how to query, traverse, and modify the DOM tree representing your markup; in other words, you learned how to manipulate the content layer of a web page. To do so, you worked with features provided by several interfaces, which are just lists of methods and members that need to be implemented together. Element, Document, Text, and other node types implement several interfaces. But every kind of node has the features listed in the Node interface. One member from Node, nodeType, returns an integer between 1 and 12 that tells you what other interface the node accumulates features from. For example, 1 tells you the node has the methods and members listed in the Element interface, too. Therefore, knowing what feature lists, or interfaces, to consult is very important to effectively script DOM.

In the next chapter, we will explore how to manipulate the presentation layer via the CSS module provided by DOM. Then, in Chapter 9, we will explore how to add a behavior layer with the Events module. There's much to look forward to!

CHAPTER 8

■ ■ ■

Scripting CSS

Booming by a hilly golf course in a new pair of lime green Nike Lunar Elites, I observed some deer running through the deep snow that a blizzard referred to as "Snowmageddon" had dumped on Pittsburgh. Though I love to run in fresh powder, 3 feet could be too much. But the deer did just fine. Besides, in those lime green shoes, I felt invincible. So, off the road and into the snow I went.

Probably ten minutes later, my heart thumping forcefully enough to burst, I glanced down at my run timer. Ugh. Still 70 minutes left. I was going to drop dead before it beeps, I thought. So, after cresting the highest hilltop, raising my fists, and rasping "Drago!" a few times, I turned tail and made for the road to finish my run.

But midway through the downhill, the snow depth suddenly increased, sending me airborne less one lime green shoe. Landing in a snow drift, I flailed about for a while trying to right myself. Eventually I had to more or less swim to shallower snow. Finding my missing shoe, I then continued to the road without further mishap and finished my run. Passersby certainly gave me some odd looks, dusty with snow as I was from head to toe!

Now then, deer with their four spindly legs and hooves are better designed for deep-snow running than we are with our two bulkier legs and feet. In the same way, Firefox, Safari, and Opera are better designed to script CSS with DOM than Internet Explorer is. So in this chapter, we will have to dumb things down for Internet Explorer. That is to say, we'll put some snow shoes on our DOM dummy so that it can keep up!

DOM Interfaces for Working with CSS

In Chapter 7, we explored some DOM interfaces for querying markup. So as you might guess, in this chapter, we will explore those for querying CSS. We won't explore all of them, just some essential ones:

```
CSSStyleDeclaration
CSS2Properties
StyleSheet
CSSStyleSheet
CSSRuleList
CSSRule
CSSStyleRule
CSSImportRule
ElementCSSInlineStyle
ViewCSS
DocumentStyle
StyleSheetList
```

Remember from Chapter 7 that an interface is a feature list for an object. That is, an interface tells you what methods and members an object contains for your scripting pleasure. So, those are the names to look under on the Web or in a printed DOM reference when you inevitably forget what I tell you here!

Clarifying Some CSS Jargon

Before we get rolling, let's go over some CSS jargon. Consider the following:

```
img {display:block;border:0;}
```

The whole enchilada, `img {display:block;border:0;}`, is referred to as a *rule*. Rules have two parts. First there is a selector indicating what part of the document to which to apply the rule. In our sample rule, `img` is the selector. So, the rule is for any `img` element in the document. The second part of a rule is the declaration block. They contain one or more declarations. In our sample rule, `{display:block;border:0;}` is the declaration block. `display:block;` is a declaration. `border:0;` is too. A declaration pairs a property with a value. That means in our rule, the `display` property is paired with the `block` value. And the `border` property is paired with the `0` value.

How Does JavaScript Represent a Rule?

You can't query a CSS rule unless you know what to query. JavaScript represents a CSS rule like `img {display:block;border:0;}` with a `CSSStyleRule` object. They receive the following two members from `CSSStyleRule`:

```
selectorText
style
```

Then they receive four more from `CSSRule`:

```
cssText
parentRule
parentStyleSheet
type
```

That is, they do in Firefox, Safari, and Opera. Internet Explorer implements `CSSStyleRule` but not `CSSRule`. So, we will dumb things down for Internet Explorer and work with just `selectorText` and `style`.

■ **Note** `CSSStyleRule` objects have the members listed in both the `CSSStyleRule` and `CSSRule` interfaces. So, there are two lists of features for this kind of DOM object.

Moving right along, here's a question for you: for our sample rule, `img {display:block;border:0;}`, what do you think `CSSStyleRule.selectorText` would contain?

Yup, `"img"`. So, `selectorText` contains the rule's selector as a string. Who'd have thought?

The other member, `CSSStyleRule.style`, is not so simple. JavaScript represents a declaration block like `{display:block;border:0;}` with a `CSSStyleDeclaration` object, which is what the `style` member contains.

Now then, a `CSSStyleDeclaration` object has the following features listed in the `CSSStyleDeclaration` interface:

```
cssText
length
parentRule
getPropertyCSSValue()
getPropertyPriority()
getPropertyValue()
item()
removeProperty()
setProperty()
```

Now for the bad news—the Internet Explorer news. Other than cssText, Internet Explorer does not implement any methods or members from CSSStyleDeclaration. We will have to pretend cssText is the only CSSStyleDeclaration member. Even though this is not true for Firefox, Safari, and Opera, it is for dummy Internet Explorer. Sigh and move forward. It is what it is.

On the bright side, pretending CSSStyleDeclaration has one member means I can only give you a one-question test: for our sample declaration block, {display:block;border:0;}, what would CSSStyleDeclaration.cssText contain?

Here's a hint: some CSS text.

Hmm. cssText contains CSS text.

That much was obvious. Sorry.

OK, what do you think?

Close, but not quite. Though cssText does contain the CSS code of the declaration block, it doesn't contain the curly braces. For a CSS rule like {display:block;border:0;}, cssText would contain "display:block;border:0;", not {display:block;border:0;}.

Internet Explorer failing to implement any of the CSSStyleDeclaration methods for querying property values would seem to be a disaster. I mean if Internet Explorer is totally illiterate, which is to say it cannot read or write CSS properties, how do we script CSS cross-browser?

Don't panic.

To simplify querying the property-value pairings within a declaration block, JavaScript extends CSSStyleDeclaration with an optional interface named CSS2Properties that Internet Explorer, Firefox, Safari, and Opera all implement. CSS2Properties adds one member for every CSS property in the CSS2 standard to a CSSStyleDeclaration object. So for any CSS property, reading a CSS2Properties member is equivalent to invoking CSSStyleDeclaration.getPropertyValue(). Conversely, writing a CSS2Properties member is equivalent to invoking CSSStyleDeclaration.setProperty().

In other words, CSSStyleDeclaration.getProperty() and CSSStyleDeclaration.setProperty() are redundant, so it's no big deal that Internet Explorer fails to implement them.

Just as a reminder, insofar as CSS2Properties members are named with an identifier, you may query those with the . operator and an identifier or with the [ ] operator and a string, typically in the form of a variable or parameter. If you are foggy on how those operators work, flip back to Chapter 3. I'll wait for you to return. Promise.

One-word CSS properties such as display or left have identically named CSS2Properties members. But JavaScript identifiers cannot have dashes. But you know that from Chapter 1. So, any CSS property containing dashes has a CSS2Properties member that is named in camel case rather than in dash case. For example, margin-bottom is named marginBottom. Finally, float is a JavaScript reserved word. So, float is represented by a member named cssFloat in Firefox, Safari, and Opera. For whatever reason, Internet Explorer deviates from DOM and names its member styleFloat instead...just roll your eyes.

CSS2Properties members are named with camel case identifiers. What about their values? Those are always strings. Yup, always. Even if you want to set a property like left or border to 0, you have to assign "0".

Whenever we want to script declarations, remember those are property-value pairings, we will query either CSS2Properties members or the CSSStyleDeclaration member, cssText, since those are the only features that dummy Explorer knows about. So if we had a variable named myDeclarations containing a CSSStyleDeclaration object, it would contain an object equivalent to the following:

```
var myDeclarations = {
  display: "block",
  border: "0",
  cssText: "display:block;border:0;"
}
```

I did that one. Now it's your turn. Create an object literal equivalent to the CSSStyleRule representing our sample rule, img {display:block;border:0;}. Save it to a variable named myRule.

Here's a hint: one of the members might just contain my object literal.

One more minute.

Time is up.

Did you create an object literal like the following? Give yourself a pat on the back.

```
var myRule = {
  selectorText: "img",
  style: {
    display: "block",
    border: "0",
    cssText: "display:block;border:0;"
  }
}
```

Two Other Declaration Blobs

CSSStyleDeclaration and CSS2Properties provide a way for you to query the declarations in a rule. Additionally, those enable you to work with two other kinds of declaration blobs that we'll explore later in the day. First, the cumulative declarations from the CSS cascade that target an element (however, note that those declarations are read-only), and second, the declarations in an element's style attribute. These declarations are represented by ElementCSSInlineStyle.style and, like the declarations in a rule, are read-write. Therefore, you can change CSS property values in a rule or style attribute, but not the cumulative ones from the cascade.

■ **Note** For any tag in your markup lacking a style attribute, the element representing the tag will still have a style member containing a CSSStyleDeclaration object, which may have some default members from the DTD.

Downloading the Sample Files

Download or code the following markup, eight.html, from this book's web site:

```
<!DOCTYPE html PUBLIC "-//W3C//DTD XHTML 1.0 Strict//EN"
"http://www.w3.org/TR/xhtml1/DTD/xhtml1-strict.dtd">
<html xmlns="http://www.w3.org/1999/xhtml">
<head>
<meta http-equiv="Content-Type" content="text/html; charset=utf-8" />
<title>Scripting CSS</title>
<link rel="stylesheet" type="text/css" href="eight.css" id="spriteStyles" />
</head>
<body>
```

```
<div id="running">
  <h4>Running</h4>
  <ul class="blue">
    <li><a id="adidas" href="http://www.adidas.com">adidas</a></li>
    <li><a id="asics" href="http://www.asics.com">ASICS</a></li>
    <li><a id="brooks" href="http://www.brooksrunning.com">Brooks</a></li>
    <li><a id="newBalance" href="http://www.newbalance.com">New Balance</a></li>
    <li><a id="nike" href="http://www.nike.com">Nike</a></li>
    <li><a id="saucony" href="http://www.saucony.com">Saucony</a></li>
  </ul>
</div>
</body>
</html>
```

Additionally, download or code the following CSS file, eight.css. Put it in the same folder with eight.html.

```
* {
  margin:0;
  padding:0;
  border:0;
}
body {
  background:rgb(255,255,255);
  color:rgb(0,0,0);
  font:11px Verdana, Arial, Helvetica, sans-serif;
}
div#running {
  position:absolute;
  left:40px;
  top:40px;
  width:120px;
  height:243px;
  background:url(images/container.gif) 0 0 no-repeat;
}
div#running h4 {
  position:absolute;
  left:0px;
  top:0px;
  width:63px;
  height:25px;
  text-indent:-9999px;
  text-decoration:none;
  overflow:hidden;
}
div#running li {
  display:inline;
}
div#running li a {
  position:absolute;
  left:10px;
  width:100px;
  height:28px;
  color:rgb(0,0,0);
```

```
    text-indent:-9999px;
    text-decoration:none;
    overflow:hidden;
}
ul.blue a {
    background-image:url(images/blue.gif);
}
ul.fuchsia a {
    background-image:url(images/fuchsia.gif);
}
ul.green a {
    background-image:url(images/green.gif);
}
a#adidas {
    top:30px;
    background-position:0 0;
}
a#asics {
    top:65px;
    background-position:0 -27px;
}
a#brooks {
    top:100px;
    background-position:0 -54px;
}
a#newBalance {
    top:135px;
    background-position:0 -81px;
}
a#nike {
    top:170px;
    background-position:0 -108px;
}
a#saucony {
    top:205px;
    background-position:0 -135px;
}
```

Finally, download the sprite images: blue.gif, fuchsia.gif, and green.gif. Download the background image, container.gif, too. Put those four images in a folder aptly named images within the folder you put eight.html and eight.css in. If you are unfamiliar with sprites, they work by sliding an image to different coordinates by way of the CSS property background-position. As Figure 8–1 illustrates, this enables us to combine all 12 link images into a single image, which improves load time.

Figure 8–1. *The blue sprite contains all 12 button images.*

Querying a Style Attribute

Open eight.html in Firefox, and then press F12 to enable Firebug. If you're just joining us, flip back to the preface for details on how to do this.

Now let's try querying the style attribute for the Nike link. Insofar as its markup tag does not contain a style attribute, ElementCSSInlineStyle.style will contain a bunch of "" empty strings. That makes this a pretty dull read. Nevertheless, take a peek at some CSS properties:

```
var myStyle = document.getElementById("nike").style;
myStyle.backgroundPosition;
// ""
myStyle.backgroundImage;
// ""
myStyle.left;
// ""
myStyle.top;
// ""
```

As Figure 8–2 displays, JavaScript returns one "" empty string after another. If you abide by the separation of markup content from CSS presentation credo, this will be the case for every Element node in the DOM tree—at least initially.

Figure 8–2. Just one "" empty string after another

Let's see what I mean by that cryptic comment. Go ahead and write the members from the previous sample like so, and click Run, verifying your work with Figure 8–3:

```
var myStyle = document.getElementById("nike").style;
myStyle.backgroundPosition = "-99px -108px";
myStyle.backgroundImage = "url(images/fuchsia.gif)";
myStyle.left = "200px";
myStyle.top = "30px";
```

Figure 8–3. *Writing some inline styles*

We replaced the blue sprite with the fuchsia one, slid the sprite to the left in order to reveal the down button, and moved the link entirely out of the container. It's pretty draconian, but it illustrates the power of writing an element's style member: scripted declarations in `ElementCSSInlineStyle.style` override those from anywhere else in the CSS cascade.

One more thing: take another peek at `ElementCSSInlineStyle.style` for the Nike link. There's something there other than one `""` empty string after another now:

```
var myStyle = document.getElementById("nike").style;
myStyle.backgroundPosition;
// "-99px -108px"
myStyle.left;
// "200px"
```

So, our writing four CSS properties by way of `ElementCSSInlineStyle.style` was equivalent to doing so by way of the following markup:

```
<a style="background-position:-99px -108px;background-
image:url(images/fuchsia.gif);left:200px;top:30px" id="nike"
href="http://www.nike.com">Nike</a>
```

In turn, this is why our scripted styles override those from elsewhere in the cascade, in other words, from `eight.css`.

We're good with querying CSS2Properties members. Now let's take a peek at CSSStyleDeclaration.cssText. Clear both Firebug panels, but do not refresh Firefox. This leaves our scripted styles in place so cssText has something for us to read other than an "" empty string. Enter and run the following, verifying your work with Figure 8–4:

```
myStyle.cssText;
// "background-position: -99px -108px; background-image: url("images/fuchsia.gif"); left:
200px; top: 30px;"
```

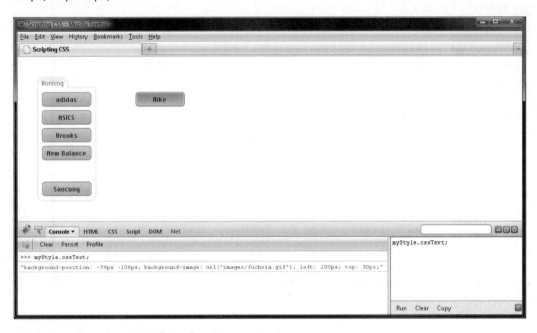

Figure 8–4. *Querying* CSSStyleDeclaration.cssText

cssText contains the CSS text of the style attribute. Imagine that. Now take a peek at cssText for the adidas link:

```
document.getElementById("adidas").style.cssText;
// ""
```

It's just a dull "" empty string. If you fully separate CSS from markup, reading cssText will be as mind-numbing as reading CSS2Properties members—unless you have a thing for "" empty strings. On the other hand, writing cssText provides a way to change several CSS properties in one fell swoop. Want to try doing that? Me too. Refresh Firefox, clear Firebug, and then enter and run the following sample. Note that the second statement wraps to two lines in this book but should be keyed in as one line in Firebug:

```
var myStyle = document.getElementById("brooks").style;
myStyle.cssText = "background-image:url(images/fuchsia.gif);left:210px;top:0;padding-
left:99px;height:55px";
```

That did in one assignment statement what would have taken five with CSS2Properties members. Now for the tricky part: writing cssText wipes away any previous inline style declarations. With this in mind, click Clear in Firebug, but do not refresh Firefox, and then enter the following assignment; however, before clicking Run, take a guess at what will happen. You get a Smiley Cookie if you get it right.

```
myStyle.cssText = "background-image:url(images/fuchsia.gif)";
```

■ **Note** Smiley Cookies are a Pittsburgh institution. If you want to try them, visit www.eatnpark.com, and click the Create your own Smiley Cookies! link. Trust me, you'll love them.

Does your guess correspond to Figure 8–5?

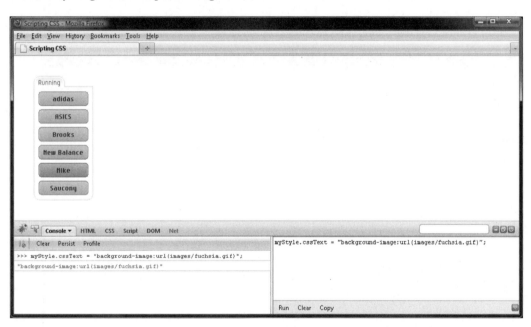

Figure 8–5. Any declarations you write to cssText totally overwrite those already in there.

Don't feel bad. I didn't think you'd get that one right. What's going on here? Any declarations you write to cssText totally overwrite those already in there. So, our declarations for left, top, padding-left, and height disappeared. This in turn means that the declarations for those properties in eight.css now shine through. Therefore, other than swapping the blue sprite for the fuchsia one, our brooks link is styled the same as when the page initially loaded. This is equivalent to the following markup:

```
<a style="background-image:url(images/fuchsia.gif);" id="brooks"
href="http://www.brooksrunning.com">Brooks</a>
```

Note that when you write the value of cssText, property names are dash case, not camel case—just like in the CSS standard.

Scripting Classes

Writing CSS2Properties members or cssText provides a way to restyle one element, but what if you want to do so for several elements? One way is to script className, typically of an ancestor element. Remember that for any element, the className member represents the class attribute.

In our included style sheet, eight.css, we have a rule for a blue class and a fuchsia class. The latter is dormant. That is to say, no element in our markup is a member of the fuchsia class. So, refresh Firefox, clear Firebug, and let's change the className member for the <ul> element from blue to fuchsia. Doing so, as Figure 8–6 illustrates, swaps the sprite for all six links in one fell swoop:

```
document.getElementsByTagName("ul")[0].className = "fuchsia";
```

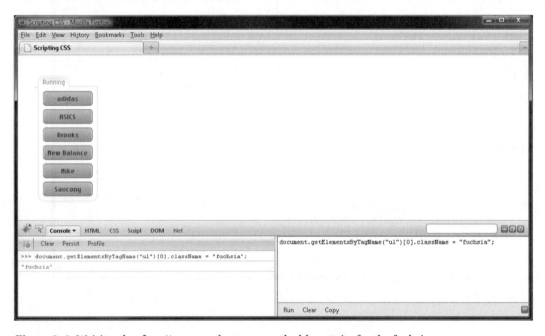

Figure 8–6. Writing the className member to swap the blue sprite for the fuchsia one

Totally overwriting className like that is fine if the element is a member of just one class that you want to replace. But an element can be a member of two or more classes. So, is there a less draconian way to go about scripting className?

Of course. Why else would I even bring it up? Scripting className is something you will do quite often. With this in mind, let's write a function to do the job for us. Maybe name it swapClass. Then refresh Firefox, clear Firebug, and enter the following:

```
function swapClass(element, oldClass, newClass) {
  var re = new RegExp("\\b" + oldClass + "\\b", "g");
  element.className = element.className.replace(re, newClass);
}
```

swapClass() works with three parameters. element is an Element node that you want to change className for. newClass is the name of the class you want to replace oldClass with. Note that both oldClass and newClass are strings.

swapClass() does its work in just two statements. First, we save a regular expression to a local variable named re. This will match a word boundary, followed by the value of oldClass, followed by another word boundary. So, re will match "blue" but not "blueberry". In the next statement, we call String.replace() on className, passing re for the first parameter and newClass for the second. Doing so swaps oldClass for newClass.

■ **Note** String.replace() and other wrapper methods for strings were covered in Chapter 2.

There it is. Now let's try swapping "blue" for "fuchsia" for the <ul> element with the help of swapClass(). Verify your work with Figure 8–7:

```
function swapClass(element, oldClass, newClass) {
  var re = new RegExp("\\b" + oldClass + "\\b", "g");
  element.className = element.className.replace(re, newClass);
}
swapClass(document.getElementsByTagName("ul")[0], "blue", "fuchsia");
```

Figure 8–7. Testing swapClass() on the <ul> element

Scripting Rules

In addition to scripting className, another way to change the appearance of several elements is to script a rule that targets them. Rather than swapping className from "blue" for "fuchsia" for the <ul>, we could just as well change the rule for the blue class in eight.css.

Now that we have our marching orders, refresh Firefox, and clear Firebug. JavaScript represents a style sheet like eight.css with a CSSStyleSheet object. Those implement the members listed in two DOM interfaces, StyleSheet and CSSStyleSheet. The following seven members come from StyleSheet:

```
disabled
href
media
ownerNode
parentStyleSheet
title
type
```

Additionally, four CSS-only members come from the `CSSStyleSheet` interface:

```
cssRules
ownerRule
deleteRule()
insertRule()
```

Internet Explorer, of course, deviates from the DOM standard but not by much for `StyleSheet`. Internet Explorer renames `ownerNode`, which refers to the `<link>` or `<style>` element for the style sheet, as `owningElement`. For the other `StyleSheet` members, Internet Explorer abides by the DOM names.

On the other hand, Internet Explorer does not implement any members from `CSSStyleSheet`. But don't worry. There are Internet Explorer–only members that will enable us to muddle through. The ones we will explore are as follows:

```
rules
imports
addRule()
addImport()
removeRule()
removeImport()
cssText
```

Things could be worse, you know. Internet Explorer deviating from DOM makes scripting style sheets tough. But the proprietary workarounds make it doable. So, rather than feel sorry for ourselves, let's start moving forward in small steps.

Before we can query a rule, we need to get at the style sheet that contains the rule. One way is to query the `sheet` member of a `<link>` or `<style>` element in Firefox, Safari, and Opera. Internet Explorer deviates from DOM, no surprise, and implements a proprietary `styleSheet` member instead. With this in mind, our first steps will be the following:

```
var myStyleSheet = document.getElementsByTagName("link")[0];
myStyleSheet = myStyleSheet.sheet || myStyleSheet.styleSheet;
```

Another, less reliable way to query a style sheet is by way of `document.styleSheets`, which contains an array-like object with one member for every `<style>` or `<link>` element having a `rel` attribute value set to `"stylesheet"`. Internet Explorer and Opera also add one member for every `<style>` or `<link>` element having a `rel` attribute value set to `"alternate stylesheet"`. No browser adds imported style sheets to `document.styleSheets`—just those included with a `<link>` or embedded in a `<style>`. Anyway, we could rewrite the previous sample like so:

```
var myStyleSheet = document.styleSheets[0];
```

■ **Note** `document.styleSheets` is provided by the `DocumentStyle` interface. In turn, `styleSheets` contains an array-like object provided by the `StyleSheetList` interface. Members contained by a `StyleSheetList` are objects that have the features listed in the `StyleSheet` and `CSSStyleSheet` interfaces. So, there are four interfaces for you to consult in a DOM reference.

Now `myStyleSheet` contains an object representing `eight.css`. Let's find the rule for the `blue` class. Where would that be? It's in a `cssRules` member for Firefox, Safari, and Opera, but in a `rules` member for

Explorer. Those are both `CSSRuleList` objects. Those are array-like objects, which is to say their members are elements. Moreover, `cssRules.length` or `rules.length` contains the number of members.

cssRules contains both styling rules and @ directives like `@import`. On the other hand, `rules` contains only styling rules. In other words, it contains the ones comprised of a selector and declaration block. So if a style sheet contains @ directives, `cssRules.length` will be greater than `rules.length`. In Internet Explorer, `@import` directives are nowhere to be found, but any `@page` directives are in an array-like object named `pages`. Note that although `@import` directives are missing in Internet Explorer, scripting imported style sheets remains doable by way of `imports`, `addImport()`, and `removeImport()`. Later in the day, we will explore those features. Note that Internet Explorer splits grouped selectors into more than one rule. Therefore, for the following rule, Internet Explorer would add two members to `rules`, while Firefox, Safari, and Opera would add one member to `cssRules`:

```
div#mast form, div#mast h1 {
  display:inline;
}
```

In other words, Internet Explorer separates the previous rule into two like so:

```
div#mast form {
  display:inline;
}
  div#mast h1 {
  display:inline;
}
```

With all those variations between `cssRules` and `rules` in mind, obviously do not hard-code the index of a rule, because it is apt to be wrong in Internet Explorer or in Firefox, Safari, and Opera.

Now, with `length` and either `cssRules` or `rules`, we can loop through the styling rules in `eight.css`. Note that in any browser, rules are numerically indexed in source code order. Say we want to find the rule with the selector `"ul.blue a"` in order to change the sprite to fuchsia; a for loop like the following would work cross-browser:

```
var myStyleSheet = document.getElementsByTagName("link")[0];
myStyleSheet = myStyleSheet.sheet || myStyleSheet.styleSheet;
var myRules = myStyleSheet.cssRules || myStyleSheet.rules;
for (var i = myRules.length - 1; i > -1; i --) {
  if (myRules[i].selectorText && myRules[i].selectorText.toLowerCase() === "ul.blue a") {
    myRules[i].style.backgroundImage = "url(images/fuchsia.gif)";
    break;
  }
}
```

Three things in the for loop bear explaining. Thought I'd leave you in the lurch, didn't you?

- First, we loop through the rules in reverse order. Now why would we do that? CSS precedence: in the event that more than one rule in the style sheet has the selector we are looking for, we want to change the last one.

- Second, `@import` and other @ rules do not define a `selectorText` or style member. Calling `String.toLowerCase()` on undefined returns an error. So, we use the `&&` operator to skip any rules that do not define `selectorText`.

- Third, the string in `selectorText` may or may not match the CSS selector. For this reason, we lowercase `selectorText` prior to comparing it with `===`.

■ **Note** If you have forgotten how the && and === operators work, flip back to Chapter 3.

Now let's see whether everything goes according to plan. Refresh Firefox to revert the sprite to blue. Then click Run in Firebug, and verify your work with Figure 8–8.

Figure 8–8. Manually finding a rule by its selector

Finding a rule certainly takes some doing. And it's something we're likely to do often. So, maybe we ought to write a helper function to simplify things. Yup, that's what we'll do. Refresh Firefox, clear Firebug, and then declare a function named findRule() that takes two parameters. element will contain the <link> or <style> element, and selector will contain the selector for the rule we want to find.

```
function findRule(element, selector) {
}
```

So, an Element node and selector string will go in one end of findRule(), and then a CSSStyleRule object will pop out of the other. Great. Now let's make it happen.

First, compensate for Internet Explorer deviating from DOM by renaming sheet and cssRules. To do so, create a couple local variables like so. Then lowercase the string in the selector argument. This will save your bacon in the event you forget to pass in the selector in lowercase to begin with.

```
function findRule(element, selector) {
  var sheet = element.sheet || element.styleSheet;
  var rules = sheet.cssRules || sheet.rules;
  selector = selector.toLowerCase()
}
```

Now findRules() has the values necessary to find the desired rule. Let's tweak the for loop from the previous sample; the body of the loop just needs to return the matching CSSStyleRule object. In case there are none, return null following the for loop. Recall from earlier in the book that a function that typically returns an object ought to return null (which conveys no object) on failure rather than undefined (which conveys no string, number, or boolean).

With those brave words, our work is done:

```
function findRule(element, selector) {
  var sheet = element.sheet || element.styleSheet;
  var rules = sheet.cssRules || sheet.rules;
  selector = selector.toLowerCase()
  for (var i = rules.length - 1; i > -1; i --) {
    if (rules[i].selectorText && rules[i].selectorText.toLowerCase() === selector) {
      return rules[i];
    }
  }
  return null;
}
```

Now let's see whether findRule() works as planned. Refresh Firefox to revert the sprite to blue. Then in Firebug, swap the blue sprite for the fuchsia sprite with the help of findRule(), verifying your work with Figure 8–9.

```
function findRule(element, selector) {
  var sheet = element.sheet || element.styleSheet;
  var rules = sheet.cssRules || sheet.rules;
  selector = selector.toLowerCase()
  for (var i = rules.length - 1; i > -1; i --) {
    if (rules[i].selectorText && rules[i].selectorText.toLowerCase() === selector) {
      return rules[i];
    }
  }
  return null;
}
var myRule = findRule(document.getElementsByTagName("link")[0], "ul.blue a");
if (myRule !== null) {
  myRule.style.backgroundImage = "url(images/fuchsia.gif)";
}
```

Figure 8–9. *Swapping the blue sprite for the fuchsia one with* `findRule()`

Remember from earlier in the chapter that `CSSStyleRule.style` contains an object with the members listed in the `CSSStyleDeclaration` and `CSS2Properties` interfaces. We just wrote `CSS2Properties.backgroundImage`. Now by way of `CSSStyleDeclaration.cssText`, let's change the sprite from blue to green for the Saucony link and slide it to the down position. To do so, refresh Firefox, and rework the previous sample like so. Then click Run.

```
function findRule(element, selector) {
  var sheet = element.sheet || element.styleSheet;
  var rules = sheet.cssRules || sheet.rules;
  selector = selector.toLowerCase()
  for (var i = rules.length - 1; i > -1; i --) {
    if (rules[i].selectorText && rules[i].selectorText.toLowerCase() === selector) {
      return rules[i];
    }
  }
  return null;
}
var myRule = findRule(document.getElementsByTagName("link")[0], "a#saucony");
if (myRule !== null) {
  myRule.style.cssText = "background:url(images/green.gif) -99px -135px; top:205px";
}
```

One thing to note or reiterate is that changing cssText is draconian, obliterating any declarations in there. This is why we had to reset top to 205px in the previous sample. Another, more general thing to note is that a style sheet differs from a <link> or <style>. The latter is markup, while the former is CSS. In other words, a style sheet is the CSS code in the file included by a <link> element or contained by a <style> element. So, you cannot, for example, retrieve a style sheet by its id member, since it does not have one. However, you can and probably should retrieve the corresponding <link> or <style> element by its id. Doing so ensures that your script continues to work in the event that CSS designers add more <link> or <style> tags. It's also the case if you add more tags dynamically by script, which we will cover not far down the road.

For example, rather than hoping that the first <link> element continues to be the one we want to script in the future, we ought to modify the previous sample like so:

```
function findRule(element, selector) {
  var sheet = element.sheet || element.styleSheet;
  var rules = sheet.cssRules || sheet.rules;
  selector = selector.toLowerCase()
  for (var i = rules.length - 1; i > -1; i --) {
    if (rules[i].selectorText && rules[i].selectorText.toLowerCase() === selector) {
      return rules[i];
    }
  }
  return null;
}
var myRule = findRule(document.getElementById("spriteStyles"), "a#saucony");
if (myRule !== null) {
  myRule.style.cssText = "background:url(images/green.gif) -99px -135px; top:205px";
}
```

Scripting Imported Style Sheets

Now then, what if you want to script an imported style sheet? In other words, say you want to script one included with an @import directive. First, save eight.html as running_copy.html; then, replace the <link> element with a <style> element that imports eight.css like so:

```
<!DOCTYPE html PUBLIC "-//W3C//DTD XHTML 1.0 Strict//EN"
"http://www.w3.org/TR/xhtml1/DTD/xhtml1-strict.dtd">
<html xmlns="http://www.w3.org/1999/xhtml">
<head>
<meta http-equiv="Content-Type" content="text/html; charset=utf-8" />
<title>Scripting CSS</title>
<style type="text/css">
@import url(eight.css);
</style>
</head>
<body>
<div id="running">
  <h4>Running</h4>
  <ul class="blue">
    <li><a id="adidas" href="http://www.adidas.com">adidas</a></li>
    <li><a id="asics" href="http://www.asics.com">ASICS</a></li>
    <li><a id="brooks" href="http://www.brooksrunning.com">Brooks</a></li>
    <li><a id="newBalance" href="http://www.newbalance.com">New Balance</a></li>
    <li><a id="nike" href="http://www.nike.com">Nike</a></li>
```

```
      <li><a id="saucony" href="http://www.saucony.com">Saucony</a></li>
    </ul>
  </div>
</body>
</html>
```

As noted earlier in the day, an @import rule does not have a selectorText or style member. The reason for this is that an @import rule does not implement the CSSStyleRule interface but instead implements CSSImportRule. This interface provides three members:

```
href
media
styleSheet
```

StyleSheet refers the imported style sheet. So if we want to change left to 500px for the running <div>, we can do so by entering and running the following in Firebug:

```
document.getElementsByTagName("style")[0].sheet.cssRules[0].styleSheet.cssRules[2].style.left
= "500px";
```

This works for Firefox, Safari, and Opera. But it doesn't work for Internet Explorer, which does not implement CSSImportRule. Rather, for a <style> or <link> element, styleSheet.imports contains a collection of imported style sheets. So, we would rework the previous sample like so:

```
document.getElementsByTagName("style")[0].styleSheet.imports[0].rules[2].style.left = "500px";
```

Adding or Deleting a Rule

Now then, what if you want to dynamically determine the numeric index of a rule cross-browser? Can it be done? Yup. But why would you want to know a rule's index? A couple reasons: to add a rule or delete one. So, before we try explore those operations, let's figure out how to determine the numeric index of a rule regardless of the visitor's browser.

Insofar as this is something we will want to frequently do, you probably know what I am going to say. Right, let's code a helper function. So, delete running_copy.html and reload eight.html in Firebug. Then key in the following function, which differs from findRule() in just two ways:

- First, it returns the loop variable i rather than a CSSStyleRule object. i will be the index of the desired rule. That was painless.

- Second, to convey failure in the event no rule in the style sheet has the selector we gave findIndex() to work with, the return value will be undefined rather than null. Why? findIndex() ought to return a number. Those are stored on the stack, and undefined conveys no value on the stack. On the other hand, findRule() ought to return a object. Those are stored on the heap, and null conveys no value on the heap. You forgot about all that, didn't you?

```
function findIndex(element, selector) {
  var sheet = element.sheet || element.styleSheet;
  var rules = sheet.cssRules || sheet.rules;
  selector = selector.toLowerCase()
  for (var i = rules.length - 1; i > -1; i --) {
    if (rules[i].selectorText && rules[i].selectorText.toLowerCase() === selector) {
      return i;
    }
  }
}
```

}

Let's see whether findIndex() works as planned. Refresh Firefox to revert the sprite to blue. Then pass in "a#adidas" for selector, and click Run. Since that is the tenth rule in eight.css, the return value ought to be 9 because JavaScript numbers them beginning with 0. Verify your work with Figure 8–10.

```
function findIndex(element, selector) {
  var sheet = element.sheet || element.styleSheet;
  var rules = sheet.cssRules || sheet.rules;
  selector = selector.toLowerCase()
  for (var i = rules.length - 1; i > -1; i --) {
    if (rules[i].selectorText && rules[i].selectorText.toLowerCase() === selector) {
      return i;
    }
  }
}
findIndex(document.getElementById("spriteStyles"), "a#adidas");
// 9
```

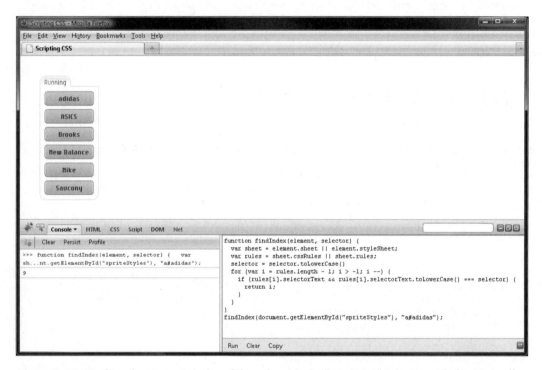

Figure 8–10. Finding the numeric index of the rule with the "a#adidas" selector with findIndex()

Adding a Rule to a Style Sheet

Now that we have a helper function to provide us with the numeric index of a rule, we can explore how to insert a rule into a style sheet. Of course, there is a DOM way and an Internet Explorer way. Let's write another helper function to compensate for Internet Explorer's skullduggery.

Clear Firebug, but do not refresh Firefox because we want `findIndex()` to remain in memory. Name the helper function `insertRule`. This one will work with four parameters:

- `element` will be a `<link>` or `<style>` Element node.

- `selector` will be the text of the selector for the new rule, in other words, a string like `"div#running li"`.

- `declarations` will be the text of the declaration block, minus the curly braces, such as a string like `"top:135px; background-position:0 -81px"`. Note that property names are dash case. It's just like in your CSS code or in `CSSStyleDeclaration.cssText`.

- `index` contains the text of the selector for the rule you want to insert the new rule before. So, that's the selector string we will pass to `findIndex()`, which will then return a numeric index, or `undefined` if we are out of luck.

```
function insertRule(element, selector, declarations, index) {
}
```

Now let's move on to the body of our helper function. Assign either the DOM or Internet Explorer member that contains the `CSSStyleSheet` object to a local variable named `sheet`. Similarly, assign the DOM or Internet Explorer member that contains the `CSSRuleList` array-like object to one named `rules`. It's just like we did in `findIndex()`.

Now let's make the `index` parameter optional by way of a couple `if` statements. JavaScript will run the block of the first `if` statement in the event that we did pass a selector string for the value of index. Otherwise, JavaScript will run the block of the second `if` statement, like if we invoked `insertRule()` with just three parameters rather than four. In this case, `index` defaults to `undefined`. Let's overwrite that value with `rules.length`, which contains a number one greater than the total number of rules in the style sheet. Later, this numeric index will enable us to append the new rule to the very end of the style sheet. Thus far we have this:

```
function insertRule(element, selector, declarations, index) {
  var sheet = element.sheet || element.styleSheet;
  var rules = sheet.cssRules || sheet.rules;
  if (typeof index === "string") {
    index = findIndex(element, index);
  }
  if (typeof index !== "number") {
    index = rules.length;
  }
}
```

Now `sheet` will contain either a DOM method named `insertRule()` or an Internet Explorer method named `addRule()`. Let's figure out which one is available by way of the `else if` idiom. In the event that Firefox, Safari, or Opera is running our function, `insertRule()` will be defined. This method takes two parameters:

- The full text of the rule, curly braces and all. So, we will cobble that together with the + operator.

- The numeric index of the new rule. We have that number on hand in the index, so just pass that in, and we're done.

Now let's code a path for Internet Explorer to run. Its method, `addRule()`, takes three parameters: the text for the selector, the text for the declarations, and the numeric index for where to insert the rule. Simply pass in the values of `selector`, `declarations`, and `index`. It's simple as can be:

```
function insertRule(element, selector, declarations, index) {
  var sheet = element.sheet || element.styleSheet;
  var rules = sheet.cssRules || sheet.rules;
  if (typeof index === "string") {
    index = findIndex(element, index);
  }
  if (typeof index !== "number") {
    index = rules.length;
  }
  if (sheet.insertRule) {
    sheet.insertRule(selector + "{" + declarations + "}", index);
  } else if (sheet.addRule) {
    sheet.addRule(selector, declarations, index);
  }
}
```

Between the rules with the selectors `"ul.blue a"` and `"ul.fuchsia a"`, let's insert a new one to swap the sprite from blue to fuchsia by calling `insertRule()` like so. Verify your work with Figure 8–11.

```
function insertRule(element, selector, declarations, index) {
  var sheet = element.sheet || element.styleSheet;
  var rules = sheet.cssRules || sheet.rules;
  if (typeof index === "string") {
    index = findIndex(element, index);
  }
  if (typeof index !== "number") {
    index = rules.length;
  }
  if (sheet.insertRule) {
    sheet.insertRule(selector + "{" + declarations + "}", index);
  } else if (sheet.addRule) {
    sheet.addRule(selector, declarations, index);
  }
}
insertRule(document.getElementById("spriteStyles"), "ul.blue a",
  "background-image:url(images/fuchsia.gif)", "ul.fuchsia a");
```

Figure 8–11. Inserting a rule with our helper functions, findIndex() and insertRule()

Of course, since the final rule in a style sheet clobbers any similar ones appearing earlier, we could just as well omitted the fourth parameter. Our function will then append our new rule to the very end of the rule collection. Take advantage of that feature to swap the sprite from fuchsia to green like so:

```
function insertRule(element, selector, declarations, index) {
  var sheet = element.sheet || element.styleSheet;
  var rules = sheet.cssRules || sheet.rules;
  if (typeof index === "string") {
    index = findIndex(element, index);
  }
  if (typeof index !== "number") {
    index = rules.length;
  }
  if (sheet.insertRule) {
    sheet.insertRule(selector + "{" + declarations + "}", index);
  } else if (sheet.addRule) {
    sheet.addRule(selector, declarations, index);
  }
}
```

```
insertRule(document.getElementById("spriteStyles"), "ul.blue a",
  "background-image:url(images/green.gif)");
```

Deleting a Rule from a Style Sheet

Now then, let's draft a helper function to delete a rule from a style sheet. Just as with adding a rule, Internet Explorer implements a proprietary method instead of the one from the DOM standard. Our game plan for this helper function will be similar to the one for adding a rule. In other words, we will have Firefox, Safari, and Opera invoke the DOM method, deleteRule(), and Internet Explorer will invoke its proprietary one, removeRule(). There will be one path for standard savvy browsers and one path for dummy Internet Explorer.

Clear Firebug, but do not refresh Firefox because we want to keep findIndex() in memory. Name the helper function deleteRule. It's the same identifier as for the DOM method. Now why do those identifiers not collide?

Take your time.

This is one you ought to know.

By the way, we named the helper function for adding a rule with the identifier for the DOM method, insertRule. Those didn't collide either.

What do you think?

Yup, different namespaces. The helper functions insertRule() and deleteRule() are methods of window. On the other hand, the DOM functions insertRule() and deleteRule() are methods of a CSSStyleSheet object. They're in different folders, so to speak.

Where were we? Hmm. OK, now define two named arguments:

- The first one, element, will be a <link> or <style> Element node.

- The second one, selector, will be the text of the selector for the rule to delete.

Insofar as the DOM and Internet Explorer functions for deleting a rule are methods of a CSSStyleSheet object, we need to save a reference to the one containing the rule to delete. Put that in a local variable named sheet. Then save the return value of passing element and selector to findIndex() to another local variable named index. If findIndex() has no luck with those parameters and has to return undefined instead of a number, we cannot delete a rule—not unless we want to do so randomly! So, write an if statement to abort deleteRule() in the event we have no numeric index to work with.

Thus far we have this:

```
function deleteRule(element, selector) {
  var sheet = element.sheet || element.styleSheet;
  var index = findIndex(element, selector);
  if (typeof index !== "number") {
    return;
  }
}
```

Now for the mojo. Both the DOM and Internet Explorer methods work with one parameter, the numeric index of the rule to delete. Just as a reminder, indexes are integers beginning with 0. So, code two paths with the if else idiom. Firefox, Safari, and Opera go down the first path, and Internet Explorer goes down the second. We're done:

```
function deleteRule(element, selector) {
  var sheet = element.sheet || element.styleSheet;
  var index = findIndex(element, selector);
  if (typeof index !== "number") {
    return;
```

```
  }
  if (sheet.deleteRule) {
    sheet.deleteRule(index);
  } else if (sheet.removeRule) {
    sheet.removeRule(index);
  }
}
```

Now let's try to delete a couple rules, such as the two we just added with insertRule(). Those both have a selector of "ul.blue a". The first time we pass "ul.blue a" to deleteRule(), the sprite turns from green to fuchsia, and the second time, it turns from fuchsia to blue. So, run the following twice in Firebug, verifying your work with Figure 8–12:

```
function deleteRule(element, selector) {
  var sheet = element.sheet || element.styleSheet;
  var index = findIndex(element, selector);
  if (typeof index !== "number") {
    return;
  }
  if (sheet.deleteRule) {
    sheet.deleteRule(index);
  } else if (sheet.removeRule) {
    sheet.removeRule(index);
  }
}
deleteRule(document.getElementById("spriteStyles"), "ul.blue a");
```

Figure 8–12. Deleting the two newly inserted rules with `deleteRule()` *swaps the sprite from green to fuchsia to blue.*

Querying Overall Styles from the Cascade

Now then, what if you want to query the overall styles from the CSS cascade for an element? In other words, you want to know the declarations that have the highest precedence. Those form one humongous declaration block, which, like the declaration block for a rule, JavaScript represents with a `CSSStyleDeclaration` object. You already know how to query those cumulative declarations—the `.` operator and a `CSS2Properties` member. Remember they are camel case, not dash case. On the other hand, `CSSStyleDeclaration.cssText` contains the declarations block, minus the curly braces, as a string. However, this string is oftentimes too lengthy to bother with.

The cumulative declaration block from the cascade differs from that of a rule in a style sheet in a few ways:

- It is read-only. Try to assign a new value to a property from the cascade, and JavaScript calls you a dummy by way of an error.

- Any relative values are converted to absolute values. Typically this means converting the value to pixels.

- Any property that sets several properties in one fell swoop, such as a margin or border, may contain undefined, while their corresponding fully expanded properties, such as marginLeft or borderRightStyle, will always contain a value. As a rule of thumb, do not query rollup values from the cascade. Query their fully expanded equivalents instead.

Refresh Firefox, clear Firebug, and let's cobble together a helper function named queryCascade() that works with two parameters:

- element will contain an Element node for the DOM tree.

- property will contain the name of the CSS property as a camel case string. That is to say, don't pass a dash case string or a camel case identifier.

Now let's send Firefox, Safari, and Opera down one path and Internet Explorer down another by way of an if statement and the else if idiom. First let's test for the DOM function getComputedStyle() by way of the typeof operator. If typeof returns "function" rather than "undefined", invoke with two parameters, element and null. getComputedStyle() will then return a CSSStyleDeclaration object containing the cumulative declarations from the cascade, as well as those implicitly calculated by the browser, for element. Then query property by way of the [] operator.

```
function queryCascade(element, property) {
  if (typeof getComputedStyle === "function") {
    return getComputedStyle(element, null)[property];
  }
}
```

Do you remember why doing so with the . operator will not work?
Come on, you know this one.
I'm not telling you the answer.
Maybe I'll go reorganize the Penske file while you think it through.

■ **Note** George reorganized the Penske file in the *Seinfeld* episode "The Barber."

What do you think? Right, the . operator works with a hard-coded identifier. On the other hand, [] works with a string or any expression that evaluates to a string, most notably a variable or parameter.

■ **Note** The if statement and else if idiom were covered in Chapter 4, while the typeof and refinement operators were covered in Chapter 3. So if you have forgotten how those work, take a moment to flip back and refresh your memory. I'll wait for you to return before continuing. Promise!

Why do we use null for the second parameter? This can be a pseudo-element as a string, for example, ":before" or ":after". However, Internet Explorer's proprietary alternative to getComputedStyle() does not support pseudo-elements. Therefore, pass null to make things work cross-browser.

Now for our DOM dummy, Internet Explorer, which does not implement the ViewCSS interface that provides getComputedStyle(). Internet Explorer's way is simple: an Element node has not only a style member for inline styles but also a currentStyle member for cascade styles. Both style and currentStyle contain a CSSStyleDeclaration object. The Internet Explorer path is straightforward, and we're done coding queryCascade().

```
function queryCascade(element, property) {
  if (typeof getComputedStyle === "function") {
    return getComputedStyle(element, null)[property];
  } else if (element.currentStyle) {
    return element.currentStyle[property];
  }
}
```

Now let's query a CSS property from the cascade. Then we have a couple that were calculated behind the scenes by Firefox:

```
function queryCascade(element, property) {
  if (typeof getComputedStyle === "function") {
    return getComputedStyle(element, null)[property];
  } else if (element.currentStyle) {
    return element.currentStyle[property];
  }
}
queryCascade(document.getElementById("adidas"), "width");
// "100px"
queryCascade(document.getElementsByTagName("ul")[0], "width");
// "120px"
queryCascade(document.getElementsByTagName("ul")[0], "height");
// "0px"
```

For the Adidas <a> element, queryCascade() returned the value from an explicit declaration in eight.css. On the other hand, the values for the <ul> element were calculated behind the scenes for us by Firefox. Note that insofar as the <ul> is a block element, its width is set to that of the containing <div>, which we set to "120px". On the other hand, since the <a> elements within the <ul> are absolutely positioned relative to the <div> and the <li> has a display value of inline, the <ul> collapses to a height of "0px".

Here is the situation. Nowadays, CSS presentation and markup content are in separate files. Initially, the CSSStyleDeclaration object in the style member for an Element node will be irrelevant, with just scores of "" empty strings and other default values. On the other hand, the CSSStyleDeclaration object representing cascade declarations is totally relevant but read-only. So if you do not know what rule or style sheet contains the declaration with the highest precedence, then what do you do? Typically, scripters read the cascade and write the inline style attribute. That is to say, they query two separate CSSStyleDeclaration objects. Obviously, if you know where to find the rule, then you simply read and write the CSSStyleDeclaration object representing the rule's declaration block, like we did earlier in the day. But more often than not, you won't have that option.

Making the computed styles from the cascade read-only is a DOM failing. But to be fair, the standard predates the notion of putting markup, CSS, and JavaScript in separate layers by five years. Maybe someday the flaw will be fixed. But that day is far off and may never come at all. So, let's give the "read the cascade, write the attribute" thing a try.

Clear Firebug, but do not refresh Firefox because we want queryCascade() to remain available in memory. Then save the <div> to a variable named myDIV. Pass myDIV and "left" to queryCascade(), which will then return "40px". Convert that string to the number 40 by way of parseInt(), and then add 10. Next, convert the sum of 50 to the string "50", and append "px". Finally, write that string, "50px", to the style attribute. Click Run repeatedly until left is set to "700px". JavaScript will move our running shoe menu to the right by 10 pixels each time you click Run.

■ **Note** If you have forgotten how parseInt() works, flip back to Chapter 2. Datatype conversion is covered there, too.

```
function queryCascade(element, property) {
  if (typeof getComputedStyle === "function") {
    return getComputedStyle(element, null)[property];
  } else if (element.currentStyle) {
    return element.currentStyle[property];
  }
}
var myDIV = document.getElementById("running");
myDIV.style.left = parseInt(queryCascade(myDIV, "left")) + 10 + "px";
```

Verify your work with Figure 8–13.

Figure 8–13. Moving the interface to the right in 10-pixel increments with the help of queryCascade( )

JavaScript animations typically work in this way – that is to say, by writing the style attribute at regular intervals. Later in the book, we will do just that.

Enabling and Disabling Style Sheets

Now then, sometimes you will want to turn a style sheet on or off. Maybe you'll want to change the skin for an interface, for example. Doing so is straightforward and even works in our DOM dummy, Internet Explorer. Every style sheet embedded in a <style> element or included by a <link> element has a disabled member (which comes from the CSSStyleSheet interface, by the way).

Now do you remember the JavaScript datatype to convey on or off?

It's the same as the one that conveys yes or no.

Come on, you know this one.

Right, the booleans, true and false. The only tricky thing with the disabled member is that it isn't named enabled. In other words, true means the style sheet is off, and false means that the style sheet is on. Trust me, you will get this mixed up from time to time.

Refresh Firefox, and clear Firebug. Then disable eight.css, entering and running the following helper function and verifying your work with Figure 8–14:

```
function toggleSheet(element) {
  var sheet = element.sheet || element.styleSheet;
  sheet.disabled = ! sheet.disabled;
}
toggleSheet(document.getElementById("spriteStyles"));
```

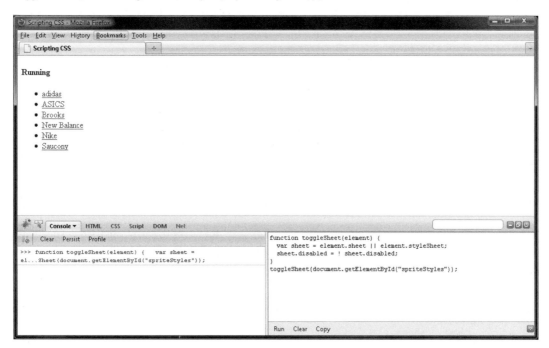

Figure 8–14. *Disabling a style sheet by setting its disabled member to* `true`

Our markup is totally unstyled now. No, I don't like it either. Click Run again to have Firefox reapply `eight.css`.

Including or Importing Style Sheets

At this point, there's no `disabled` attribute in the markup for a `<link>` or `<style>` tag. `disabled` is a member of an `Element` node but not an attribute. Note that we covered difference between a member and an attribute in Chapter 7; flip back to that chapter if you have forgotten.

Inasmuch as `disabled` is not a markup attribute, we can set its value to `true` only with JavaScript. If JavaScript is not available, we cannot turn off a style sheet by calling `toggleSheet()`. But what if we want a style sheet to be applied to a document only when JavaScript is available? Simple. We create and insert a new `<link>` or `<style>` Element node. However, like everything else with scripting CSS, there are Internet Explorer pitfalls. So, let's code a helper function to do the job.

Refresh Firefox, and clear Firebug. Then name the helper function `addSheet`, defining two arguments:

- `tag` will contain the string `"link"` or `"style"`.

- `url` will contain the URL of the style sheet.

Next, pass `tag` to `document.createElement()`, saving the return value to a local variable named `element`. Regardless of whether `element` now contains a `<link>` or `<style>`, the type attributes will be `"text/css"`. Thus far, we have this:

```
function addSheet(tag, url) {
  var element = document.createElement(tag);
  element.type = "text/css";
}
```

Now append `element` to `childNodes` for `<head>` by way of `appendChild()`, which we covered in Chapter 7. We have to do this now for the remainder of the function to work cross-browser.

```
function addSheet(tag, url) {
  var element = document.createElement(tag);
  element.type = "text/css";
  document.getElementsByTagName("head")[0].appendChild(element);
}
```

In the event we passed `"link"` for `tag`, set `rel` to `"stylesheet"` and `href` to the string in `url`. The browser will then apply the style sheet to the document. So for a `<link>`, we're done.

```
function addSheet(tag, url) {
  var element = document.createElement(tag);
  element.type = "text/css";
  document.getElementsByTagName("head")[0].appendChild(element);
  if (tag === "link") {
    element.rel = "stylesheet";
    element.href = url;
  }
}
```

Things are trickier if `tag` contains `"style"`. For Firefox, Safari, and Opera, we just cobble together an `@import` directive and pass that to `insertRule()`. For Internet Explorer, you might think to insert the directive with `addRule()`. But you would be wrong. Internet Explorer has a separate method named `addImport()` for inserting `@import` directives. `addImport()` works with two parameters:

- The URL of the style sheet to import. Just pass in the URL for the first parameter; there's no need to cobble together an `@import` directive.

- The second parameter, which is optional, is the numeric index for where to insert the directive in `imports`. Remember from earlier in the chapter that `imports` is where Explorer puts `@import` directives. That is to say, those are kept separate from the rule sets in `rules`.

Let's code these two paths by way of a `try catch` statement. The `try` block will work in Firefox, Safari, and Opera but will generate an error in Internet Explorer, which will then go down the `catch` path, merrily as can be. Our final code for `addSheet()` is as follows:

```
function addSheet(tag, url) {
  var element = document.createElement(tag);
  element.type = "text/css";
```

```
  document.getElementsByTagName("head")[0].appendChild(element);
  if (tag === "link") {
    element.rel = "stylesheet";
    element.href = url;
  } else if (tag === "style") {
    try {
      element.sheet.insertRule("@import url(" + url + ")", 0);
    } catch (whyNot) {
      element.styleSheet.addImport(url);
    }
  }
}
```

So that we can tangibly test addSheet(), let's first delete the <link> that includes eight.css. Remember how to do so from the previous chapter? Yup, with removeChild(). Just invoke removeChild() on the <head> element and pass in the <link>, and Firefox will redisplay our document as unstyled markup, as Figure 8–15 illustrates.

```
function addSheet(tag, url) {
  var element = document.createElement(tag);
  element.type = "text/css";
  document.getElementsByTagName("head")[0].appendChild(element);
  if (tag === "link") {
    element.rel = "stylesheet";
    element.href = url;
  } else if (tag === "style") {
    try {
      element.sheet.insertRule("@import url(" + url + ")", 0);
    } catch (whyNot) {
      element.styleSheet.addImport(url);
    }
  }
}
document.getElementsByTagName("head")[0].
  removeChild(document.getElementsByTagName("link")[0]);
```

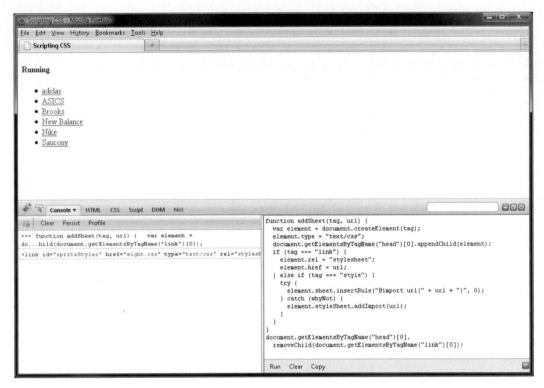

Figure 8–15. *Delete the <link> element with removeChild(), and Firefox redisplays the document as unstyled markup.*

By the way, even though it may be obvious, note that passing a <link> or <style> to removeChild() does the inverse of what addSheet() does. So, removing a style sheet is simpler than adding one.

Now that our document is totally unstyled, we can tangibly test addSheet(). Let's first try to include eight.css with a new <link>. Go ahead and delete the removeChild() invocation. Then call addSheet() like so, verifying your work with Figure 8–16.

```
function addSheet(tag, url) {
  var element = document.createElement(tag);
  element.type = "text/css";
  document.getElementsByTagName("head")[0].appendChild(element);
  if (tag === "link") {
    element.rel = "stylesheet";
    element.href = url;
  } else if (tag === "style") {
    try {
      element.sheet.insertRule("@import url(" + url + ")", 0);
    } catch (whyNot) {
      element.styleSheet.addImport(url);
    }
```

```
   }
}
addSheet("link", "eight.css");
```

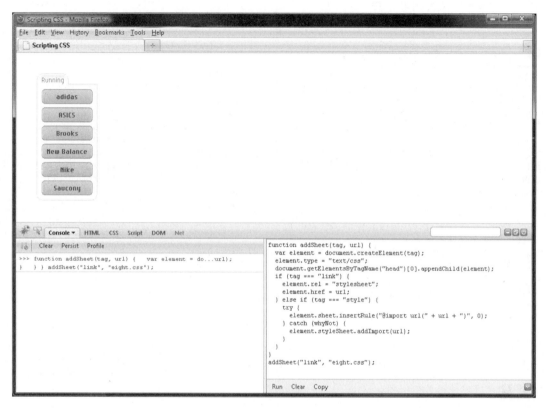

Figure 8–16. Dynamically including eight.css with addSheet()

Did Firefox restyle your document with the blue sprite? Great. Now let's again remove the `<link>` with removeChild(). Then insert a `<style>` with an @import directive with the help of addSheet(). Doing so restyles the document, too.

```
function addSheet(tag, url) {
  var element = document.createElement(tag);
  element.type = "text/css";
  document.getElementsByTagName("head")[0].appendChild(element);
  if (tag === "link") {
    element.rel = "stylesheet";
    element.href = url;
  } else if (tag === "style") {
    try {
      element.sheet.insertRule("@import url(" + url + ")", 0);
    } catch (whyNot) {
      element.styleSheet.addImport(url);
```

```
      }
    }
  }
document.getElementsByTagName("head")[0].
  removeChild(document.getElementsByTagName("link")[0]);addSheet("style", "eight.css");
```

Embedding a Style Sheet

Sometimes you may want to embed a style sheet in a new <style> element rather than including or importing one. Insofar as the newly minted <style> is empty, the simplest way to embed a style sheet is to create a Text node containing all the rules and then insert it into the <style> with appendChild(). It works fine for Firefox, Safari, and Opera, but not for Internet Explorer. There's a workaround, though. In Internet Explorer, styleSheet has a cssText member. Rather than create a Text node from our string of CSS rules, we will simply assign the string to cssText. With those brave words, let's code a helper function named embedSheet(). This one works with one parameter, a string of CSS rules. The fork in the road where Firefox, Safari, and Opera and Internet Explorer part company will be formed from a try catch statement:

```
function embedSheet(text) {
  var element = document.createElement("style");
  element.type = "text/css";
  document.getElementsByTagName("head")[0].appendChild(element);
  text = document.createTextNode(text);
  try {
    element.appendChild(text);
  } catch (whyNot) {
    element.styleSheet.cssText = text.data;
  }
}
```

Now let's test embedSheet() by passing in a couple of rules that will change the sprite from blue to fuchsia and move the interface to the right. Enter and run the following, and then verify your work with Figure 8–17:

```
function embedSheet(text) {
  var element = document.createElement("style");
  element.type = "text/css";
  document.getElementsByTagName("head")[0].appendChild(element);
  text = document.createTextNode(text);
  try {
    element.appendChild(text);
  } catch (whyNot) {
    element.styleSheet.cssText = text.data;
  }
}
embedSheet("ul.blue a {background-image:url(images/fuchsia.gif);} div#running {left:500px;}");
```

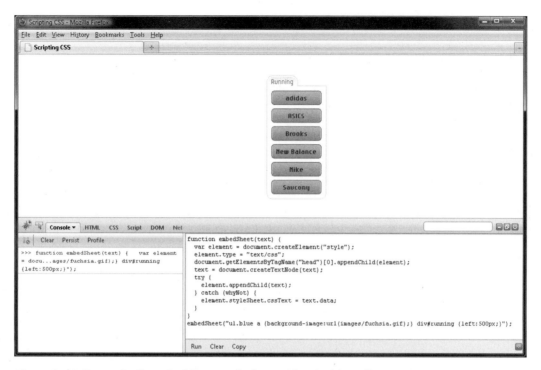

Figure 8–17. Dynamically embedding a style sheet with embedSheet()

Summary

In this chapter, we explored a number of DOM interfaces for scripting CSS, while in Chapter 7 we explored the interfaces for scripting markup. Now you know how to do what JavaScript behaviors do. You can change the presentation or content of a document. Controlling when those changes occur is the topic of the next chapter. There we will explore event interfaces provided by DOM and Internet Explorer. See you there!

CHAPTER 9

Listening for Events

Twenty-five hundred years ago in 490 BC, a Greek herald named Pheidippides ran several dispatches totaling 240 km (150 miles) during the final two days of the Battle of Marathon. The distance of his final run from Marathon to Athens to deliver news of the Greek victory over the Persians with the word Νενικήκαμεν (we have won) is the basis for the marathon race being 42 km (26.2 miles). Insofar as Pheidippides ran those dispatches over mountainous terrain in hot weather and would have been 40 (born in 530 BC), it is not surprising that he collapsed and died moments later.

Nowadays, dying from running a marathon is rare, but developing rigor mortis, referred to as hitting the wall, is not. Typically this happens in the final fourth of the marathon when, because of glycogen depletion, muscle fibers lock up, effectively turning a runner into a staggering corpse. So to run a fast marathon time, you must not hit the wall. During the race, this more or less comes down to making good decisions about how to respond to events as they unfold—stuff like whether to speed up or slow down relative to the display on a split clock or whether to follow a surging runner or remain in the chase pack.

In the same way, you have to be smart about how JavaScript behaviors respond to events, with things such as visitors moving their mouse or the page loading in order to prevent the browser from developing rigor mortis. Why would JavaScript freeze the browser anyway? For one, whenever some JavaScript code is running, the browser cannot do any repaints, reflows, or any other UI updates. So, a button clicked while JavaScript is executing may never look like it was clicked. For another, while a JavaScript file is downloading, a browser cannot download any other kind of file. Therefore, CSS and image downloads are temporarily blocked, both while a JavaScript file downloads and executes, typically causing a blank white page.

But not to worry—we will explore not only how to respond to events but also how to be quick about it. Insofar as JavaScript responds to events by running functions, referred to as *event listeners*, this typically means coding snappy functions. Some techniques for doing so, such as optimizing loops, are already in your bailiwick. Others, such as advance conditional loading, are new but well within your grasp.

Working with the Event Object

A couple of notes before start coding: first, to respond to an event, you have to tell JavaScript to listen for it as it traverses the DOM tree. In Internet Explorer 9, Firefox, Safari, Chrome, and Opera, you can tell JavaScript to listen while an event either descends (capturing phase) or ascends (bubbling phase) the DOM tree. In Internet Explorer 8 or earlier, JavaScript can listen only during the bubbling phase.

How do you know the who, what, when, where, and how of an event? Those details are provided by the members of an event object that Internet Explorer 9, Firefox, Safari, Chrome, and Opera pass as the sole parameter to an event listener function. Internet Explorer 8 or earlier, on the other hand, saves its event object to the global variable, event, that is, to `window.event`. As you might imagine, `window.event` is constantly being overwritten by Internet Explorer. However, even though this is a bit of a kludge, it works for the reason that no two events ever take place at the same moment in time. Note that

INTERNET EXPLORER 9 and Opera save an event object to `window.event` in addition to passing it to an event listener function.

Now then, to tell JavaScript to listen for an event in Internet Explorer 9, Firefox, Safari, Chrome, and Opera, you invoke the DOM method `addEventListener()` on an `Element` or `Document` node. `addEventListener()` works with three parameters:

- The first one is the name of the event to listen for. This can be a string literal or expression, such as a variable.

- The second parameter is an event listener function for JavaScript to call when the event from the first parameter takes place on the node or one of its descendents. It is in this event listener function that we deal with the event that has happened. This parameter may be either a function literal or an expression, such as an identifier naming a function. So, it consists of the same two options, literal or expression, as with the first parameter.

- The third parameter is simpler. It's just a boolean, `false` or `true`. `false` means call the event listener function during the bubbling phase. On the other hand, `true` means call the event listener function during the capturing phase. Because Internet Explorer does not implement capturing, you will nearly always pass `false` for the third parameter.

Internet Explorer does not implement `addEventListener()` or any other feature from the DOM events module. But it does have a proprietary way to tell JavaScript to listen for events (just during the bubbling phase, however). In Internet Explorer, `Element` and `Document` nodes have a proprietary method named `attachEvent()` that works with two parameters:

- The first one is the name of the event to listen for as a string literal or expression. Note that this differs from the first parameter to `addEventListener()` in that you must prefix event names with on—for example, `onclick` instead of `click`.

- The second parameter is the same as for `addEventListener()`—the event listener function as a literal or expression, such as an identifier naming a function. Because Internet Explorer can listen for events only during the bubbling phase, `attachEvent()` does not take a boolean indicating whether to listen during capturing or bubbling. So, there's just two parameters.

Downloading Project Files

It's time to code some snappy event listeners. However, doing so in Firebug is a bit impractical. We're going to do so with whatever plain-text editor you code your XHTML and CSS with. The only difference is that you save a JavaScript file with a `.js` extension rather than an `.html` or `.css` extension. With this in mind, create a plain-text file named `nine.js`. Then download the supporting XHTML, CSS, and image files from www.apress.com. Put the images in a subfolder (named `images`) of the one you put the XHTML, CSS, and JavaScript files in.

Let's take a peek at what we have in there. In `nine.html`, we have the following structural markup. Note that we link in `nine.js` just before the closing tag for the `<body>` element. Remember why from Chapter 1? Uh-huh, it's to prevent an initially blank page.

```
<!DOCTYPE html PUBLIC "-//W3C//DTD XHTML 1.0 Strict//EN"
"http://www.w3.org/TR/xhtml1/DTD/xhtml1-strict.dtd">
<html xmlns="http://www.w3.org/1999/xhtml">
<head>
<meta http-equiv="Content-Type" content="text/html; charset=utf-8" />
```

```
<title>JavaScript for Absolute Beginners</title>
<link rel="stylesheet" type="text/css" href="nine.css" />
<link rel="stylesheet" type="text/css" href="blue.css" id="skin" />
</head>
<body>
<div id="running">
  <h4 class="drag">Running</h4>
  <ul>
    <li><a class="sprite" id="adidas" href="http://www.adidas.com">adidas</a></li>
    <li><a class="sprite" id="asics" href="http://www.asics.com">ASICS</a></li>
    <li><a class="sprite" id="brooks" href="http://www.brooksrunning.com">Brooks</a></li>
    <li><a class="sprite" id="newBalance" href="http://www.newbalance.com">New
Balance</a></li>
    <li><a class="sprite" id="nike" href="http://www.nike.com">Nike</a></li>
    <li><a class="sprite" id="saucony" href="http://www.saucony.com">Saucony</a></li>
  </ul>
</div>
<script src="nine.js" type="text/javascript"></script>
</body>
</html>
```

Now the lion's share of the CSS presentation is in nine.css. It's pretty straightforward, as you can see:

```
* {
  margin:0;
  padding:0;
  border:0;
}
body {
  background:rgb(255,255,255);
  color:rgb(0,0,0);
  font:11px Verdana, Arial, Helvetica, sans-serif;
}
div#running {
  position:absolute;
  left:40px;
  top:40px;
  width:120px;
  height:243px;
  background:url(images/container.gif) 0 0 no-repeat;
}
div#running h4 {
  position:absolute;
  left:0px;
  top:0px;
  width:63px;
  height:25px;
  text-indent:-9999px;
  text-decoration:none;
  overflow:hidden;
}
div#running li {
  display:inline;
```

```
}
div#running li a {
  position:absolute;
  left:10px;
  width:100px;
  height:28px;
  color:rgb(0,0,0);
  text-indent:-9999px;
  text-decoration:none;
  overflow:hidden;
}
a#adidas {
  top:30px;
  background-position:0 0;
}
a#asics {
  top:65px;
  background-position:0 -27px;
}
a#brooks {
  top:100px;
  background-position:0 -54px;
}
a#newBalance {
  top:135px;
  background-position:0 -81px;
}
a#nike {
  top:170px;
  background-position:0 -108px;
}
a#saucony {
  top:205px;
  background-position:0 -135px;
}
```

Styles just for the blue, fuchsia, and green skins, which we will write a behavior to swap by key, are in the aptly named files blue.css, fuchsia.css, and green.css. Those are pretty simple for our project—just one rule each. For a full-blown web app, there would of course be many more. So in blue.css, we have this:

```
.sprite {
  background-image:url(images/blue.gif);
}
```

Then in fuchsia.css, just the name of the GIF differs:

```
.sprite {
  background-image:url(images/fuchsia.gif);
}
```

The same goes for green.css:

```
.sprite {
  background-image:url(images/green.gif);
}
```

Then there are the blue, fuchsia, and green sprites. Those go in the images subfolder of the one you put the XHTML, CSS, and JavaScript files in. Because this is a black-and-white book, I'm just going to reproduce the blue sprite in Figure 9–1.

Figure 9–1. An example sprite from this chapter's application

Regardless of whether the skin is blue, fuchsia, or green, the image for the tabbed container, shown in Figure 9–2, will be the same: `container.gif`. Note that we will write a behavior so that we can grab the menu by the Running tab and then drag and drop it elsewhere on the page.

Figure 9–2. Download tabbed container that all three skins share.

With those supporting project files in tow, let's begin by coding four helper functions to make working with events a little bit easier.

Advance Conditional Loading

The DOM and Internet Explorer methods for telling JavaScript to listen for events are similar enough that we can replace those with a helper function. In our nine.js JavaScript file, let's create a variable named addListener and then assign one of two function literals to it with the ?: conditional operator (one for Internet Explorer and one for all the other browsers). Remember from earlier in the book that JavaScript converts the first operand of the ?: operator to a boolean and that a function converts to true. So if the first operand to ?: is document.addEventListener, JavaScript converts that to true in Internet Explorer 9, Firefox, Safari, Chrome, and Opera but to false in Internet Explorer 8 or earlier, which do not implement document.addEventListener. As a result, JavaScript assigns the second operand for ?: to addListener for Internet Explorer 9, Firefox, Safari, Chrome, and Opera, but the third operand for Internet Explorer 8 or earlier, where these operands are function literals.

Since we are doing the feature testing with the ?: conditional operator prior to defining an appropriate function, this technique, which we covered in Chapter 6, is referred to as advance conditional loading. This is much snappier than running the feature test over and over every time the function is called.

Thus far, we have the following skeleton. Note that to prevent errors deriving from JavaScript's automatic semicolon insertion feature, we break lines after the ? and : tokens of the ?: operator. So, the = assignment statement is currently spread over five lines.

```
var addListener = (document.addEventListener) ?
  function() {
  } :
  function() {
  } ;
```

Let's define four parameters for the function literal intended for Internet Explorer 9, Firefox, Safari, Chrome, and Opera:

- First, node will refer to an Element or Document node from the DOM tree.

- In turn, type is the name of the event node should listen for.

- listener will refer to the event listener function to run whenever the event in type occurs on node or one of its descendents.

- phase will contain true for capturing and false or undefined for bubbling. That is to say, for bubbling, there is no need to explicitly pass false since undefined, the default value for a parameter, will do the same thing.

Now we have this:

```
var addListener = (document.addEventListener) ?
  function(node, type, listener, phase) {
  } :
  function() {
  } ;
```

Having defined the parameters for the DOM-savvy function, let's move on to the block. Just one statement in there; invoke addEventListener() as a method of the node parameter, passing in type and listener the way we found them. On the other hand, let's convert phase to a boolean with the !! idiom. Doing so converts undefined to false, which is why phase is optional. So, we're done with the first function literal:

```
var addListener = (document.addEventListener) ?
  function(node, type, listener, phase) {
```

```
    node.addEventListener(type, listener, !! phase);
  } :
  function() {
  } ;
```

■ **Note** Both the !! idiom and ! operator were covered in Chapter 3.

Now for the Internet Explorer 8 or earlier function literal. It's just three parameters, though. Internet Explorer 8 or earlier just implements bubbling, so there's no need to define a phase parameter. It's just node, type, and listener:

```
var addListener = (document.addEventListener) ?
  function(node, type, listener, phase) {
    node.addEventListener(type, listener, !! phase);
  } :
  function(node, type, listener) {
  } ;
```

Now in the block, invoke attachEvent() on the Element or Document node in the node parameter. Prefix the name of the event in type with on, but pass listener as is. Here it is. Note that Internet Explorer 9 and Opera implement both addEventListener() and attachEvent().

```
var addListener = (document.addEventListener) ?
  function(node, type, listener, phase) {
    node.addEventListener(type, listener, !! phase);
  } :
  function(node, type, listener) {
    node.attachEvent("on" + type, listener);
  } ;
```

Telling JavaScript to Stop Listening for an Event

Now and then you will want to tell JavaScript to stop listening for an event. In Internet Explorer 9, Firefox, Safari, Chrome, and Opera, you do so with removeEventListener(). In Internet Explorer 8 or earlier, you do so with detachEvent(). Note that Internet Explorer 9 and Opera implement both removeEventListener() and detachEvent().

Insofar as those both delete a previously added event listener, you have to pass them the same parameters you added the event listener with. Therefore, we can tweak addListener() to create a helper function to delete event listeners with.

Just cut and paste addListener, renaming the copy removeListener. Next, change addEventListener to removeEventListener in the boolean expression and first function literal. Finally, change attachEvent to detachEvent in the second function literal. Those four edits are in bold here:

```
var removeListener = (document.removeEventListener) ?
  function(node, type, listener, phase) {
    node.removeEventListener(type, listener, !! phase);
  } :
  function(node, type, listener) {
    node.detachEvent("on" + type, listener);
  } ;
```

`removeListener()` will come in handy when we code our drag-and-drop behavior.

Preventing Default Actions from Taking Place

Some event types have a default action associated with them. For example, if a click event occurs on an `<a>` element, JavaScript loads a new URL. Oftentimes you will want to cancel this default action. Say you want to load the new content with Ajax rather than by loading a new URL. To do so for Internet Explorer 9, Firefox, Safari, Chrome, and Opera, you would call `preventDefault()` on the event object for the click. For IE 8 or earlier, you would assign `false` to `returnValue`. Note that Internet Explorer 9 and Opera implement both `preventDefault()` and `returnValue`.

So, depending on the browser, we want to either call a method or write a member of an event object. Let's write a helper function named `thwart()` to do the job. Preventing a default action is not typically something JavaScript has to do right away as a page loads, so let's define `thwart()` by the lazy loading technique, which we explored in Chapter 6.

Now the only value `thwart()` needs to do its job is an event object. Traditionally, a parameter for an event object is named `e`, so let's not rock the boat:

```
function thwart(e) {
}
```

That's fine and dandy. Now let's write our path for Internet Explorer 9, Firefox, Safari, Chrome, and Opera with an `if` statement. In the event that referring to `e.preventDefault` does not return `undefined`, we will overwrite `thwart` with a function literal that calls `preventDefault()` on the event object:

```
function thwart(e) {
  if (e.preventDefault) {
    thwart = function(e) {
      e.preventDefault();
    };
  }
}
```

Referring to `e.preventDefault` in Internet Explorer 8 or earlier will return `undefined`, so those Internet Explorer versions will follow the `else` path. Yup, I know we don't have one yet. Let's fix that by overwriting `thwart` with a function literal that changes `returnValue` to `false` from `true`, its default value.

```
function thwart(e) {
  if (e.preventDefault) {
    thwart = function(e) {
      e.preventDefault();
    };
  } else {
    thwart = function(e) {
      e.returnValue = false;
    };
  }
}
```

So far, so good. The only problem with this is that the first time we call `thwart()`, it overwrites itself without canceling the default action (because we assign a new function to the `thwart` identifier but don't actually call the new function). Good grief!

To fix this, we need for the initial version of `thwart()` to call the new version of `thwart()`, passing the event object in:

```
function thwart(e) {
  if (e.preventDefault) {
    thwart = function(e) {
      e.preventDefault();
    };
  } else {
    thwart = function(e) {
      e.returnValue = false;
    };
  }
  thwart(e);
}
```

The first time `thwart()` runs, it does a lot of work. But thereafter, `thwart()` runs snappily since its block contains but one statement. In Internet Explorer 9, Firefox, Safari, Chrome, and Opera, that would be `e.preventDefault()`, and in Internet Explorer or earlier that would be `e.returnValue = false`.

Preventing an Event from Traversing the DOM Tree

Now then, in Internet Explorer 9, Firefox, Safari, Chrome, and Opera, an event object descends the DOM tree to the element an event happened on. Then turns tail and ascends the DOM tree. So, the event object passes by any ancestor of the target of the event two times. On the other hand, in Internet Explorer 8 or earlier, the event object passes by any ancestor one time, that is, while bubbling upward through the DOM tree. Therefore, if you register event listeners for a certain kind of event, say a click, on nodes that are on different tiers of the DOM tree, all of those could potentially run when a click event occurs.

There ought to be a way to prevent an event object from traversing any further through the DOM tree to avoid triggering additional event listeners, right? And there is. Just as with preventing default actions, you do so by calling a method for Internet Explorer 9, Firefox, Safari, Chrome, and Opera and by writing a member for Internet Explorer 8 or earlier. The DOM method is named `stopPropagation()`, and the Internet Explorer 8 or earlier member is named `cancelBubble`. Note that Internet Explorer 9 and Opera implement both `stopPropagation()` and `cancelBubble`. With this in mind, we can write a lazy loader to do the job by changing some identifiers in `thwart()`.

Now cut and paste `thwart()`. Then change the identifier thwart to burst in four places:

```
function burst(e) {
  if (e.preventDefault) {
    burst = function(e) {
      e.preventDefault();
    };
  } else {
    burst = function(e) {
      e.returnValue = false;
    };
  }
  burst(e);
}
```

Next, change the identifier for the DOM method from `preventDefault` to `stopPropagation` in two places:

```
function burst(e) {
  if (e.stopPropagation) {
```

```
      burst = function(e) {
        e.stopPropagation();
      };
   } else {
      burst = function(e) {
        e.returnValue = false;
      };
   }
   burst(e);
}
```

Now change the identifier for the proprietary Internet Explorer member from `returnValue` to `cancelBubble`. However, `cancelBubble` has to be set to `true` to prevent an event object from bubbling further. Change `false` to `true`, and we're done:

```
function burst(e) {
   if (e.stopPropagation) {
      burst = function(e) {
        e.stopPropagation();
      };
   } else {
      burst = function(e) {
        e.cancelBubble = true;
      };
   }
   burst(e);
}
```

We're done coding helper functions for working with events. This is the final code for them:

```
var addListener = (document.addEventListener) ?
   function(node, type, listener, phase) {
      node.addEventListener(type, listener, !! phase);
   } :
   function(node, type, listener) {
      node.attachEvent("on" + type, listener);
   } ;
var removeListener = (document.removeEventListener) ?
   function(node, type, listener, phase) {
      node.removeEventListener(type, listener, !! phase);
   } :
   function(node, type, listener) {
      node.detachEvent("on" + type, listener);
   } ;
function thwart(e) {
   if (e.preventDefault) {
      thwart = function(e) {
        e.preventDefault();
      };
   } else {
      thwart = function(e) {
        e.returnValue = false;
      };
   }
   thwart(e);
}
```

```
}
function burst(e) {
  if (e.stopPropagation) {
    burst = function(e) {
      e.stopPropagation();
    };
  } else {
    burst = function(e) {
      e.cancelBubble = true;
    };
  }
  burst(e);
}
```

Writing Helper Functions

Now that you have seen advance conditional loading, let's rework a few helper functions from the past two chapters with it. This will improve their performance immensely and make sure we're using the best technique in each case.

Crawling the DOM Tree

In Chapter 7, we wrote a helper function named traverseTree() to crawl the DOM tree, which we'll have to do again in this chapter. The code for traverseTree() appears here:

```
function traverseTree(node, func) {
  func(node);
  node = node.firstChild;
  while (node !== null) {
    arguments.callee(node, func);
    node = node.nextSibling;
  }
}
```

Coding traverseTree() to crawl the DOM by way of firstChild and nextSibling rather than iterating over childNodes is more than 100 times faster in Internet Explorer. So, our take on traverseTree() is already optimized relative to that Internet Explorer bug. Note that Firefox, Safari, and Opera crawl the DOM just as fast by iterating over childNodes.

However, in Internet Explorer 9, Firefox, Safari, Chrome, and Opera,, traverseTree() has to crawl through Text nodes representing formatting whitespace in our XHTML markup. So if we could eliminate that ridiculous bit of work, traverseTree() would be much snappier in Internet Explorer 9, Firefox, Safari, Chrome, and Opera.

DOM 3 defines an ElementTraversal interface that enables us to do just that. ElementTraversal provides the following members that we can use in place of firstChild, lastChild, previousSibling, nextSibling, and childNodes.length:

```
firstElementChild
lastElementChild
previousElementSibling
nextElementSibling
childElementCount
```

As its name implies, ElementTraversal is designed for traversing Element nodes. So, firstElementChild, lastElementChild, previousElementSibling, and nextElementSibling will contain an Element node or null (and never a Text, Comment, or any other kind of node). Note that childElementCount differs from childNodes.length in that it contains just the number of child Element nodes rather than the overall number of child nodes.

Therefore, for Internet Explorer 9, Firefox, Safari, Chrome, and Opera, we can rework traverseTree() with firstElementChild and nextElementSibling to replace firstChild and nextSibling. The two function literals in the ?: expression differ only by those identifiers:

```
var traverseTree = document.documentElement.firstElementChild ?
  function traverseTree (node, func) {
    func(node);
    node = node.firstElementChild;
    while (node !== null) {
      traverseTree(node, func);
      node = node.nextElementSibling;
    }
  } :
  function traverseTree (node, func) {
    func(node);
    node = node.firstChild;
    while (node !== null) {
      traverseTree(node, func);
      node = node.nextSibling;
    }
  } ;
```

Note that the boolean expression, document.documentElement.firstElementChild, queries firstElementChild for the <html> Element node. That would be the <head> Element node.

Why not simply query the firstElementChild of the Document node? We could see whether document.firstElementChild refers to the <html> Element node. That's a bad idea: ElementTraversal is implemented only by Element nodes. So although all 12 node types have a firstChild member, only an Element node has a firstElementChild member, too.

Hmm. If it were up to me, a Document node would implement ElementTraversal, too. But I do not write the standards, just about them.

■ **Note** If you want to wade through the details of the ElementTraversal interface, visit

www.w3.org/TR/ElementTraversal/.

Finding an Element by Class

The next helper function we want to rework is findClass(), which we wrote in Chapter 7 to help us find an Element node by its class attribute. DOM 3 adds a NodeSelector interface that defines two methods, querySelectorAll() and querySelector(). Those provide a way to query Element nodes with CSS selectors. That is to say, querySelectorAll() and querySelector() enable you to query elements in the same way that you would target them in a CSS rule. So for example, to query the <h4> element in our markup, we could invoke querySelectorAll() in any of the following ways in Firebug:

```
document.querySelectorAll("h4.drag")[0];
// <h4 class="drag">
document.querySelectorAll("div#running h4")[0];
// <h4 class="drag">
document.getElementById("running").querySelectorAll("h4")[0];
// <h4 class="drag">
```

As the previous samples illustrate, NodeSelector is implemented by both Document and Element nodes. So you may query the whole DOM tree or just a branch, just like with getElementsByTagName().

■ **Note** DocumentFragment nodes also implement NodeSelector.

Like getElementsByTagName(), querySelectorAll() returns a NodeList. But unlike getElementsByTagName(), querySelectorAll() does not return a live DOM query, just a copy of the matching Element nodes. This is a terrific feature as far as script speed is concerned. It's sort of like optimizing some code by copying the Element nodes returned by getElementsByTagName() into an array so that you can work solely in ECMAScript.

By the way, querySelector() returns the first Element node in the DOM tree matching a CSS selector. Since this is totally dependent on XHTML content, which is always being updated, I'd discourage you from using querySelector(). If the element you want is no longer the first one in source code order months down the road, your script won't work.

Just after the var statement for traverseTree, write one for findClass. The first operand to the ?: operator will be document.querySelectorAll, which will convert to true in Internet Explorer 8, Firefox 3.5, Safari 3.1, Chrome 4, and Opera 10. So, those versions or later will assign the first function literal to findClass. This one takes two parameters:

- name is the name of the class to find.

- root is where we begin descending the DOM tree from. root may be a Document or Element node. However, root is optional. In the event that root is undefined, we will simply assign document.documentElement to the parameter, which is the <html> element.

```
var findClass = document.querySelectorAll ?
  function (name, root) {
    root = root || document.documentElement;
  } :
  function() {
  } ;
```

Next, call querySelectorAll() on the root parameter. Insofar as querySelectorAll() works with a CSS selector, we need to prefix a . on the class string in name. Let's do so and then return the value of calling querySelectorAll():

```
var findClass = document.querySelectorAll ?
  function (name, root) {
    root = root || document.documentElement;
    return root.querySelectorAll("." + name);
  } :
  function() {
  } ;
```

The second function literal, the one for older browsers, is just the `findClass()` function we wrote in Chapter 7 but as a function literal. Remember that function literals are values, so those can be an operand to an operator like `?:`. Our completed advance conditional loader for `findClass` looks as follows. Just be sure to remember the `?` and `:` tokens and the terminating semicolon.

```
var findClass = document.querySelectorAll ?
  function (name, root) {
    root = root || document.documentElement;
    return root.querySelectorAll("." + name);
  } :
  function (name, root) {
    var found = [];
    root = root || document.documentElement;
    traverseTree(root, function(node) {
      if (!! node.className) {
        for (var names = node.className.split(/\s+/), i = names.length; i --; ) {
          if (names[i] === name) {
            found.push(node);
          }
        }
      }
    });
    return found;
  } ;
```

Testing for getElementsByClassName()

As of this writing, the fourth working draft of HTML 5 defines a `getElementsByClassName()` method for `Document` and `Element` nodes to query elements by their `class` attribute. Even though HTML 5 is not yet a W3C recommendation, Explorer 9, Firefox 3, Safari 3.1, Chrome 4, and Opera 9.62 already implement `getElementsByClassName()`.

`getElementsByClassName()` works with one parameter, a string of one or more class names separated by spaces, just like the `class` attribute for an XHTML tag. The return value is a `NodeList` containing any matching `Element` nodes. However, this `NodeList` differs from the one returned by `querySelectorAll()` in that it is a live DOM query.

Now let's rework our advanced conditional loader for `findClass()` so that `getElementsByClassName()` is the preferred option. Rather than nest `?:` expressions, let's go with the `else if` idiom. This is a little more readable for a three-option advance conditional loader.

Because an `if` statement cannot be the right operand to an `=` operator (only an expression or literal can be an operand), we are going to have to put the var statement before the `if`. Then in the `if` statement, we will assign one of three function literals to `findClass`. Reworking our previous take on `findClass()`, we have the following:

```
var findClass;
if () {
} else if (document.querySelectorAll) {
  findClass = function (name, root) {
    root = root || document.documentElement;
    return root.querySelectorAll("." + name);
  };
} else {
  findClass = function (name, root) {
    var found = [];
```

```
    root = root || document.documentElement;
    traverseTree(root, function(node) {
      if (!! node.className) {
        for (var names = node.className.split(/\s+/), i = names.length; i --; ) {
          if (names[i] === name) {
            found.push(node);
          }
        }
      }
    });
    return found;
  };
}
```

Now put document.getElementsByClassName in the empty () following the if keyword. This will return either a function, which converts to true, or undefined, which converts to false:

```
var findClass;
if (document.getElementsByClassName) {
} else if (document.querySelectorAll) {
  findClass = function (name, root) {
    root = root || document.documentElement;
    return root.querySelectorAll("." + name);
  };
} else {
  findClass = function (name, root) {
    var found = [];
    root = root || document.documentElement;
    traverseTree(root, function(node) {
      if (!! node.className) {
        for (var names = node.className.split(/\s+/), i = names.length; i --; ) {
          if (names[i] === name) {
            found.push(node);
          }
        }
      }
    });
    return found;
  };
}
```

Now for the empty if block. Just as with the other two blocks, we want to assign a function literal to findClass there, since at the moment findClass contains undefined. This one is almost identical to the one for querySelectorAll(). Just change the identifier to getElementsByClassName and pass in name as is.

```
var findClass;
if (document.getElementsByClassName) {
  findClass = function (name, root) {
    root = root || document.documentElement;
    return root.getElementsByClassName(name);
  };
} else if (document.querySelectorAll) {
  findClass = function (name, root) {
    root = root || document.documentElement;
    return root.querySelectorAll("." + name);
```

```
    };
  } else {
    findClass = function (name, root) {
      var found = [];
      root = root || document.documentElement;
      traverseTree(root, function(node) {
        if (!! node.className) {
          for (var names = node.className.split(/\s+/), i = names.length; i --; ) {
            if (names[i] === name) {
              found.push(node);
            }
          }
        }
      });
      return found;
    };
  }
```

So there it is. `findClass` will be one of three function literals that return elements of the same class from the overall DOM tree or a branch of it. Note that native browser functions such as `getElementsByClassName()` or `querySelectorAll()` are compiled not interpreted. This is why they are snappier than ones you write yourself.

■ **Note** If you want to view W3 documentation on `querySelectorAll()` or `querySelector()`, visit:

`www.w3.org/TR/selectors-api/`

If you want to view W3 documentation on `getElementsByClassName()` or HTML 5, visit:

`www.w3.org/TR/html5/`

Querying the Cascade

In Chapter 8, we wrote the following function to query CSS values from the cascade by either the DOM `getComputedStyle()` method or the Internet Explorer `currentStyle` property.

```
function queryCascade(element, property) {
  if (typeof getComputedStyle === "function") {
    return getComputedStyle(element, null)[property];
  } else if (element.currentStyle) {
    return element.currentStyle[property];
  }
}
```

Regardless of whether JavaScript queries the CSS cascade in the DOM or Internet Explorer way, doing so is quite a speed bump. With this in mind, let's at least eliminate the redundant feature testing by recoding queryCascade() as an advance conditional loader. Note that we will still have to try to avoid querying the cascade, which remains slow as a turtle.

The first thing we need to do is declare queryCascade with a var statement, rather than a function statement:

```
var queryCascade;
```

Next, initialize queryCascade to a ?: expression that returns one of two function literals. The boolean expression prior to the ? token can be the one from the if else shown earlier, typeof getComputedStyle === "function". Or more simply, it can be window.getComputedStyle:

```
var queryCascade = window.getComputedStyle ?
  function() {
  } :
  function() {
  } ;
```

Now between the ? and : tokens, code a function literal to do the job of the if clause shown previously. That is to say, just cut and paste the return statement. But remember to define the element and property parameters:

```
var queryCascade = window.getComputedStyle ?
  function(element, property) {
    return getComputedStyle(element, null)[property];
  } :
  function() {
  } ;
```

Finally, between the : and ; tokens, code a function literal containing the return statement from the else clause shown previously. Yup, cut and paste. And again, don't forget the element and property parameters:

```
var queryCascade = window.getComputedStyle ?
  function(element, property) {
    return getComputedStyle(element, null)[property];
  } :
  function(element, property) {
    return element.currentStyle[property];
  } ;
```

So there it is. In Explorer 9, Firefox, Safari, Chrome, and Opera, JavaScript assigns the first function literal to queryCascade, and in Internet Explorer 8 or earlier, it assigns the second one. There's no feature testing to do whenever JavaScript calls queryCascade(). Not even the first time!

We're done reworking our helper functions for working with markup and CSS, so our JavaScript file now looks like so:

```
var addListener = document.addEventListener ?
  function(node, type, listener, phase) {
    node.addEventListener(type, listener, !! phase);
  } :
  function(node, type, listener) {
    node.attachEvent("on" + type, listener);
  } ;
var removeListener = document.removeEventListener ?
  function(node, type, listener, phase) {
    node.removeEventListener(type, listener, !! phase);
  } :
  function(node, type, listener) {
    node.detachEvent("on" + type, listener);
  } ;
function thwart(e) {
```

```
      if (e.preventDefault) {
        thwart = function(e) {
          e.preventDefault();
        };
      } else {
        thwart = function(e) {
          e.returnValue = false;
        };
      }
      thwart(e);
    }
    function burst(e) {
      if (e.stopPropagation) {
        burst = function(e) {
          e.stopPropagation();
        };
      } else {
        burst = function(e) {
          e.cancelBubble = true;
        };
      }
      burst(e);
    }
    var traverseTree = document.documentElement.firstElementChild ?
      function traverseTree (node, func) {
        func(node);
        node = node.firstElementChild;
        while (node !== null) {
          traverseTree(node, func);
          node = node.nextElementSibling;
        }
      } :
      function traverseTree (node, func) {
        func(node);
        node = node.firstChild;
        while (node !== null) {
          traverseTree(node, func);
          node = node.nextSibling;
        }
      } ;

    var findClass;
    if (document.getElementsByClassName) {
      findClass = function (name, root) {
        root = root || document.documentElement;
        return root.getElementsByClassName(name);
      };
    } else if (document.querySelectorAll) {
      findClass = function (name, root) {
        root = root || document.documentElement;
        return root.querySelectorAll("." + name);
      };
    } else {
      findClass = function (name, root) {
```

```
      var found = [];
      root = root || document.documentElement;
      traverseTree(root, function(node) {
        if (!! node.className) {
          for (var names = node.className.split(/\s+/), i = names.length; i --; ) {
            if (names[i] === name) {
              found.push(node);
            }
          }
        }
      });
      return found;
    };
  }
  var queryCascade = window.getComputedStyle ?
    function(element, property) {
      return getComputedStyle(element, null)[property];
    } :
    function(element, property) {
      return element.currentStyle[property];
    } ;
```

Sliding Sprites

Now for the first of our behaviors. This one will slide a sprite whenever a visitor rolls their mouse over or off an element of the sprite class. JavaScript will be listening for mouseover and mouseout events.

The rough skeleton for our sprite behavior will have an event listener function named slideSprite() nested within a preparatory function named prepSprites(). Doing so means the event listener function may query the call object of prepSprites() even though prepSprites() will be invoked just one time, shortly after the page loads. Thus far we have this:

```
function prepSprites() {
  function slideSprite() {
  }
}
```

Preparing the Ground

What are these secret variables we want slideSprite() to be able to query even after prepSprites() has returned? The first one, elements, will contain the return value of passing "sprite" to our helper function, findClass(). So, any elements of the sprite class will be in there. The second one, sprites, will for now contain an empty object but later will contain details of each sprite. We'll add members to sprites in a moment. Note that creating an object with literal notation is snappier than doing so with new and the Object() constructor. Therefore, {} it is:

```
function prepSprites() {
  var elements = findClass("sprite"), sprites = {};
  function slideSprite() {
  }
}
```

Now let's iterate over the `Element` nodes in `elements`. Remember from Chapter 4 that looping in reverse is snappier in that we can test and update the loop variable i in a single expression. Note too that we want to initialize i to `elements.length` so that we don't slow things down by querying `elements.length` every roundabout of the loop. Finally, initialize a variable named `offsets` to `null` since it will later contain an array of offsets identifying where the sprites are:

```
function prepSprites() {
  var elements = findClass("sprite"), sprites = {};
  for (var i = elements.length, offsets = null; i --; ) {
  }
  function slideSprite() {
  }
}
```

Now for every `Element` node in `elements`, we want to name a member in `sprites` with the value of its id attribute. So, relative to our XHTML markup, sprites will contain members named `"adidas"`, `"asics"`, `"brooks"`, and so on. Those will initially contain an empty array, which we will create with array literal notation, since that is snappier than doing so with `new` and `Array()`:

```
function prepSprites() {
  var elements = findClass("sprite"), sprites = {};
  for (var i = elements.length, offsets = null; i --; ) {
    sprites[elements[i].id] = [];
  }
  function slideSprite() {
  }
}
```

Now we have to work around some Internet Explorer 8 or earlier skullduggery. Querying `currentStyle.backgroundPosition` for an element returns undefined even though querying `style.backgroundPosition` for the very same element returns the horizontal and vertical offsets of the background image. I know, that's preposterous.

Are those offsets simply missing in `currentStyle`?

No, they're just in a different drawer. Internet Explorer 8 or earlier separates them into members named `backgroundPositionX` and `backgroundPositionY`. We will have to code one path for Explorer 9, Firefox, Safari, Chrome, and Opera and another for Internet Explorer 8 or earlier. Let's do the former first. Test for the DOM method `getComputedStyle()`, and then query `backgroundPosition`, saving that to `sprites[elements[i].id][0]`. So for example, `sprites.saucony[0]` will contain `"0px -135px"`, which is the off position for the sprite (the position when the mouse is off the sprite).

Now we need to separate the horizontal and vertical offsets. To do so, call `String.split()` on the off position that we just saved to `elements[i].id][0]`. Remember from Chapter 2 that `String.split()` returns an array of smaller strings created by separating the larger string relative to its parameter. So if we divide the off string based on whitespace, we get an array with two elements. So for the Saucony sprite, the array would be as follows:

```
["0px", "-135px"]
```

Save that to the `offsets` variable that we initialized to `null` a moment ago. So we now have this:

```
function prepSprites() {
  var elements = findClass("sprite"), sprites = {};
  for (var i = elements.length, offsets = null; i --; ) {
    sprites[elements[i].id] = [];
    if (typeof getComputedStyle === "function") {
      sprites[elements[i].id][0] = queryCascade(elements[i], "backgroundPosition");
      offsets = sprites[elements[i].id][0].split(/\s+/);
```

```
    }
  }
  function slideSprite() {
  }
}
```

Now for the else clause for Internet Explorer 8 or earlier. Insofar as its offsets are already separated, we will do things in reverse. Create the offsets array from backgroundPositionX and backgroundPositionY. Then call Array.join() on offsets, passing " " as the parameter, and save the return value to sprites[elements[i].id][0]. For example, sprites.nike would now contain "0px -108px":

```
function prepSprites() {
  var elements = findClass("sprite"), sprites = {};
  for (var i = elements.length, offsets = null; i --; ) {
    sprites[elements[i].id] = [];
    if (typeof getComputedStyle === "function") {
      sprites[elements[i].id][0] = queryCascade(elements[i], "backgroundPosition");
      offsets = sprites[elements[i].id][0].split(/\s+/);
    } else {
      offsets = [
        queryCascade(elements[i], "backgroundPositionX"),
        queryCascade(elements[i], "backgroundPositionY")
      ];
      sprites[elements[i].id][0] = offsets.join(" ");
    }
  }
  function slideSprite() {
  }
}
```

Now that sprites[elements[i].id][0] and offsets have the same values in Firefox, Safari, Chrome, Opera, and Internet Explorer, we can calculate the over position by subtracting the width of the element from 1 and concatenating that to "px " and the vertical offset, which remains the same in the over position (the over position being for when the mouse is over the button). Internet Explorer doesn't make up a different name for width, so we can simply call queryCascade() this time. However, we need to remove the "px" from the width value with parseInt() before subtracting it from 1:

```
function prepSprites() {
  var elements = findClass("sprite"), sprites = {};
  for (var i = elements.length, offsets = null; i --; ) {
    sprites[elements[i].id] = [];
    if (typeof getComputedStyle === "function") {
      sprites[elements[i].id][0] = queryCascade(elements[i], "backgroundPosition");
      offsets = sprites[elements[i].id][0].split(/\s+/);
    } else {
      offsets = [
        queryCascade(elements[i], "backgroundPositionX"),
        queryCascade(elements[i], "backgroundPositionY")
      ];
      sprites[elements[i].id][0] = offsets.join(" ");
    }
    sprites[elements[i].id][1] = 1 - parseInt(queryCascade(elements[i], "width")) + "px " +
      offsets[1];
```

```
  }
  function slideSprite() {
  }
}
```

Now JavaScript has created the following object that our nested event listener function, slideSprite(), can query even after prepSprites() returns:

```
var sprites = {
  "adidas": ["0px 0px", "-99px 0px"],
  "asics": ["0px -27px", "-99px -27px"],
  "brooks": ["0px -54px", "-99px -54px"],
  "newBalance": ["0px -81px", "-99px -81px"],
  "nike": ["0px -108px", "-99px -108px"],
  "saucony": ["0px -135px", "-99px -135px"]
}
```

Now we want to tell JavaScript to run slideSprite() whenever mouseover and mouseout events occur on the <a> in elements[i]. This is where our helper function, addListener(), earns its keep. Note that only the second parameter differs in our two calls to addListener(). Feel free to cut and paste:

```
function prepSprites() {
  var elements = findClass("sprite"), sprites = {};
  for (var i = elements.length, offsets = null; i --; ) {
    sprites[elements[i].id] = [];
    if (typeof getComputedStyle === "function") {
      sprites[elements[i].id][0] = queryCascade(elements[i], "backgroundPosition");
      offsets = sprites[elements[i].id][0].split(/\s+/);
    } else {
      offsets = [
        queryCascade(elements[i], "backgroundPositionX"),
        queryCascade(elements[i], "backgroundPositionY")
      ];
      sprites[elements[i].id][0] = offsets.join(" ");
    }
    sprites[elements[i].id][1] = 1 - parseInt(queryCascade(elements[i], "width")) + "px " +
      offsets[1];
    addListener(elements[i], "mouseover", slideSprite);
    addListener(elements[i], "mouseout", slideSprite);
  }
  function slideSprite() {
  }
}
```

That ends the for loop, and prepSprites() would now return. Note that only our nested event listener function, slideSprite(), can query the offsets in sprites, which lives on in a closure. With this in mind, let's go ahead and fill in slideSprite().

Moving the Sprites

The first thing we need to do is define a parameter for the event object that Internet Explorer 9, Firefox, Safari, Chrome, and Opera will pass to slideSprite() whenever a mouseover or mouseout event takes place on our sprites. By convention, this parameter is named e. It doesn't have to be. We could name it brownCow if we wanted. But let's not rock the boat.

Internet Explorer 8 or earlier does not pass an event object to event listener functions. Rather, it continually overwrites the global variable, event, with the latest event object. Insofar as only one event can ever take place at a time, this works. It's a bit of a kludge, but it works. Note that for interoperability, Internet Explorer 9 and Opera implement window.event, too.

Anyway, if e contains undefined, as it would in Internet Explorer 8 or earlier, let's overwrite that value with window.event:

```
function prepSprites() {
  var elements = findClass("sprite"), sprites = {};
  for (var i = elements.length, offsets = null; i --; ) {
    sprites[elements[i].id] = [];
    if (typeof getComputedStyle === "function") {
      sprites[elements[i].id][0] = queryCascade(elements[i], "backgroundPosition");
      offsets = sprites[elements[i].id][0].split(/\s+/);
    } else {
      offsets = [
        queryCascade(elements[i], "backgroundPositionX"),
        queryCascade(elements[i], "backgroundPositionY")
      ];
      sprites[elements[i].id][0] = offsets.join(" ");
    }
    sprites[elements[i].id][1] = 1 - parseInt(queryCascade(elements[i], "width")) + "px " +
      offsets[1];
    addListener(elements[i], "mouseover", slideSprite);
    addListener(elements[i], "mouseout", slideSprite);
  }
  function slideSprite(e) {
    if (!e) e = window.event;
  }
}
```

e now contains an object with members that detail what the visitor did. One of those members refers to the node in the DOM tree that the event took place on. For Internet Explorer 9, Firefox, Safari, Chrome, and Opera, the member is named target. For Internet Explorer 8 or earlier, the member is named srcElement. Note that Internet Explorer 9 and Opera implement both target and srcElement.

Anyway, if e does not have a target member, referring to e.target returns undefined. In that case, we want to add a target member to e that refers to window.event.srcElement:

```
function prepSprites() {
  var elements = findClass("sprite"), sprites = {};
  for (var i = elements.length, offsets = null; i --; ) {
    sprites[elements[i].id] = [];
    if (typeof getComputedStyle === "function") {
      sprites[elements[i].id][0] = queryCascade(elements[i], "backgroundPosition");
      offsets = sprites[elements[i].id][0].split(/\s+/);
    } else {
      offsets = [
        queryCascade(elements[i], "backgroundPositionX"),
        queryCascade(elements[i], "backgroundPositionY")
      ];
      sprites[elements[i].id][0] = offsets.join(" ");
    }
    sprites[elements[i].id][1] = 1 - parseInt(queryCascade(elements[i], "width")) + "px " +
      offsets[1];
    addListener(elements[i], "mouseover", slideSprite);
```

```
      addListener(elements[i], "mouseout", slideSprite);
    }
    function slideSprite(e) {
      if (!e) e = window.event;
      if (!e.target) e.target = e.srcElement;
    }
  }
```

To know whether to slide the sprite to the over or off position, we need to know whether a mouseover or mouseout event took place. The answer to our query is in e.type. Even in Internet Explorer 8 or earlier! So if e.type contains "mouseover", we want to slide the sprite to sprites[e.target.id][1]. Otherwise, we want to slide it to sprites[e.target.id][0]. That sounds like a job for an if else statement:

```
function prepSprites() {
  var elements = findClass("sprite"), sprites = {};
  for (var i = elements.length, offsets = null; i --; ) {
    sprites[elements[i].id] = [];
    if (typeof getComputedStyle === "function") {
      sprites[elements[i].id][0] = queryCascade(elements[i], "backgroundPosition");
      offsets = sprites[elements[i].id][0].split(/\s+/);
    } else {
      offsets = [
        queryCascade(elements[i], "backgroundPositionX"),
        queryCascade(elements[i], "backgroundPositionY")
      ];
      sprites[elements[i].id][0] = offsets.join(" ");
    }
    sprites[elements[i].id][1] = 1 - parseInt(queryCascade(elements[i], "width")) + "px " +
      offsets[1];
    addListener(elements[i], "mouseover", slideSprite);
    addListener(elements[i], "mouseout", slideSprite);
  }
  function slideSprite(e) {
    if (!e) e = window.event;
    if (!e.target) e.target = e.srcElement;
    if (e.type == "mouseover") {
      e.target.style.backgroundPosition = sprites[e.target.id][1];
    } else {
      e.target.style.backgroundPosition = sprites[e.target.id][0];
    }
  }
}
```

So there it is. Now to verify that this all works as planned, load nine.html in Firefox, enable Firebug, and then call prepSprites():

```
prepSprites();
```

Now roll your mouse over and off the sprites to test the swaps. In Figure 9–3, I rolled my mouse over the New Balance sprite, which has the shading at the top now, rather than at the bottom:

Figure 9–3. Testing the sprites by manually calling prepSprites() with the Firebug console

Snappier Sprites

So prepSprites() and slideSprite() are written to work for Internet Explorer 9, Firefox, Safari, Chrome, and Opera or for Internet Explorer 8 or earlier. Even though lumping DOM-savvy and DOM-dummy paths together in event listener functions is commonplace (most scripts you maintain will do so), all that feature testing makes them run slower. With this in mind, let's rework prepSprites() and slideSprite() as advance conditional loaders so that our sprites are snappier for visitors.

First, we want to define prepSprites with a var statement rather than a function statement. Then, we initialize its value to one of two function literals relative to whether getComputedStyle() is defined:

```
var prepSprites = window.getComputedStyle ?
  function () {
  } :
  function () {
  } ;
```

Now let's fill in the function literal for Internet Explorer 9, Firefox, Safari, Chrome, and Opera by eliminating all the workarounds for Internet Explorer 8 or earlier:

```
var prepSprites = window.getComputedStyle ?
  function () {
    var elements = findClass("sprite"), sprites = {};
    for (var i = elements.length, offsets = null; i --; ) {
      sprites[elements[i].id] = [];
      sprites[elements[i].id][0] = queryCascade(elements[i], "backgroundPosition");
      offsets = sprites[elements[i].id][0].split(/\s+/);
      sprites[elements[i].id][1] = 1 - parseInt(queryCascade(elements[i], "width")) +
        "px " + offsets[1];
      addListener(elements[i], "mouseover", slideSprite);
      addListener(elements[i], "mouseout", slideSprite);
    }
    function slideSprite(e) {
      if (e.type == "mouseover") {
        e.target.style.backgroundPosition = sprites[e.target.id][1];
      } else {
        e.target.style.backgroundPosition = sprites[e.target.id][0];
      }
    }
  } :
  function () {
  } ;
```

Now for the one that Internet Explorer 8 or earlier can palate. Just remove the code intelligible only to Internet Explorer 9, Firefox, Safari, Chrome, and Opera. Note that in slideSprite(), we save window.event to a local variable e. Caching any global variable that you query more than one time in a function to a local variable makes the lookup snappier. Remember from earlier in the book that global variables reside on the very last variable object in a function's execution context. So, caching the global variable to a local one prevents JavaScript from fruitlessly querying activation objects for a global variable.

With those things in mind, let's fill in the block of the function literal for Internet Explorer 8 or earlier like so:

```
var prepSprites = window.getComputedStyle ?
  function () {
    var elements = findClass("sprite"), sprites = {};
    for (var i = elements.length, offsets = null; i --; ) {
      sprites[elements[i].id] = [];
      sprites[elements[i].id][0] = queryCascade(elements[i], "backgroundPosition");
      offsets = sprites[elements[i].id][0].split(/\s+/);
      sprites[elements[i].id][1] = 1 - parseInt(queryCascade(elements[i], "width")) +
        "px " + offsets[1];
      addListener(elements[i], "mouseover", slideSprite);
      addListener(elements[i], "mouseout", slideSprite);
    }
    function slideSprite(e) {
      if (e.type == "mouseover") {
        e.target.style.backgroundPosition = sprites[e.target.id][1];
      } else {
        e.target.style.backgroundPosition = sprites[e.target.id][0];
      }
```

```
      }
    } :
    function () {
      var elements = findClass("sprite"), sprites = {};
      for (var i = elements.length, offsets = null; i --; ) {
        sprites[elements[i].id] = [];
        offsets = [queryCascade(elements[i], "backgroundPositionX"),
          queryCascade(elements[i], "backgroundPositionY")];
        sprites[elements[i].id][0] = offsets.join(" ");
        sprites[elements[i].id][1] = 1 - parseInt(queryCascade(elements[i], "width")) +
          "px " + offsets[1];
        addListener(elements[i], "mouseover", slideSprite);
        addListener(elements[i], "mouseout", slideSprite);
      }
      function slideSprite() {
        var e = window.event;
        if (e.type == "mouseover") {
          e.srcElement.style.backgroundPosition = sprites[e.srcElement.id][1];
        } else {
          e.srcElement.style.backgroundPosition = sprites[e.srcElement.id][0];
        }
      }
    }
  } ;
```

So there it is. Neither Internet Explorer 9, Firefox, Safari, Chrome, and Opera nor Internet Explorer 8 or earlier have to do any feature testing whenever prepSprites() or slideSprite() run. Not even the first time. All in all, JavaScript has less work to do, and our visitors get snappier sprites.

Before moving on to the drag-and-drop behavior, verify your work by refreshing Firefox and calling prepSprites() via Firebug:

```
prepSprites();
```

Then roll your mouse over and off the sprites to test the swaps.

Does it work for you, too? Great. But if not, verify that your script is just like the rest of ours:

```
var addListener = document.addEventListener ?
  function(node, type, listener, phase) {
    node.addEventListener(type, listener, !! phase);
  } :
  function(node, type, listener) {
    node.attachEvent("on" + type, listener);
  } ;

var removeListener = document.removeEventListener ?
  function(node, type, listener, phase) {
    node.removeEventListener(type, listener, !! phase);
  } :
  function(node, type, listener) {
    node.detachEvent("on" + type, listener);
  } ;

function thwart(e) {
  if (e.preventDefault) {
    thwart = function(e) {
```

```
      e.preventDefault();
    };
  } else {
    thwart = function(e) {
      e.returnValue = false;
    };
  }
  thwart(e);
}

function burst(e) {
  if (e.stopPropagation) {
    burst = function(e) {
      e.stopPropagation();
    };
  } else {
    burst = function(e) {
      e.cancelBubble = true;
    };
  }
  burst(e);
}

var traverseTree = document.documentElement.firstElementChild ?
  function traverseTree (node, func) {
    func(node);
    node = node.firstElementChild;
    while (node !== null) {
      traverseTree(node, func);
      node = node.nextElementSibling;
    }
  } :
  function traverseTree (node, func) {
    func(node);
    node = node.firstChild;
    while (node !== null) {
      traverseTree(node, func);
      node = node.nextSibling;
    }
  } ;

var findClass;

if (document.getElementsByClassName) {
  findClass = function (name, root) {
    root = root || document.documentElement;
    return root.getElementsByClassName(name);
  };
} else if (document.querySelectorAll) {
  findClass = function (name, root) {
    root = root || document.documentElement;
    return root.querySelectorAll("." + name);
  };
} else {
```

```
  findClass = function (name, root) {
    var found = [];
    root = root || document.documentElement;
    traverseTree(root, function(node) {
      if (!! node.className) {
        for (var names = node.className.split(/\s+/), i = names.length; i --; ) {
          if (names[i] === name) {
            found.push(node);
          }
        }
      }
    });
    return found;
  };
}

var queryCascade = window.getComputedStyle ?
  function(element, property) {
    return getComputedStyle(element, null)[property];
  } :
  function(element, property) {
    return element.currentStyle[property];
  } ;

var doZ = function() {
  var z = 400;
  return function() {
    return z ++;
  };
}();

// sprite swaps

var prepSprites = window.getComputedStyle ?
  function () {
    var elements = findClass("sprite"), sprites = {};
    for (var i = elements.length, offsets = null; i --; ) {
      sprites[elements[i].id] = [];
      sprites[elements[i].id][0] = queryCascade(elements[i], "backgroundPosition");
      offsets = sprites[elements[i].id][0].split(/\s+/);
      sprites[elements[i].id][1] = 1 - parseInt(queryCascade(elements[i], "width")) +
        "px " + offsets[1];
      addListener(elements[i], "mouseover", slideSprite);
      addListener(elements[i], "mouseout", slideSprite);
    }
    function slideSprite(e) {
      if (e.type == "mouseover") {
        e.target.style.backgroundPosition = sprites[e.target.id][1];
      } else {
        e.target.style.backgroundPosition = sprites[e.target.id][0];
      }
    }
  } :
  function () {
```

```
      var elements = findClass("sprite"), sprites = {};
      for (var i = elements.length, offsets = null; i --; ) {
        sprites[elements[i].id] = [];
        offsets = [queryCascade(elements[i], "backgroundPositionX"),
          queryCascade(elements[i], "backgroundPositionY")];
        sprites[elements[i].id][0] = offsets.join(" ");
        sprites[elements[i].id][1] = 1 - parseInt(queryCascade(elements[i], "width")) +
          "px " + offsets[1];
        addListener(elements[i], "mouseover", slideSprite);
        addListener(elements[i], "mouseout", slideSprite);
      }
      function slideSprite() {
        var e = window.event;
        if (e.type == "mouseover") {
          e.srcElement.style.backgroundPosition = sprites[e.srcElement.id][1];
        } else {
          e.srcElement.style.backgroundPosition = sprites[e.srcElement.id][0];
        }
      }
    }
  } ;
```

Drag-and-Drop Behavior

Now it's time for the drag-and-drop behavior, where we can move the panel of buttons around the page. For this one to work, we need to have JavaScript listen for mousedown, mousemove, and mouseup events. Those occur whenever a visitor presses down on their mouse button, moves their mouse, and releases their mouse button. Who'd have thought?

Writing the Mousedown Event Listener

The rough skeleton will be a mousedown event listener named drag() containing the mousemove and mouseup event listeners, named move() and drop(). Those two nested functions can then query the call object for drag(), which is where we will store several coordinates for later (the position of the moveable panel and the position of the mouse when the event occurs). Note that all three event listeners define an e parameter for the event object that Internet Explorer 9, Firefox, Safari, Chrome, and Opera send their way. Then assign window.event to e if it contains undefined, if the browser is Internet Explorer 8 or earlier. Thus far we have the following:

```
function drag(e) {
  if (!e) e = window.event;
  function move(e) {
    if (!e) e = window.event;
  }
  function drop(e) {
    if (!e) e = window.event;
  }
}
```

Now let's fill in the block for drag(). This is the only one of the three event listeners that needs to query e.target, because we can then use the results of this query elsewhere. Remember that e.target is the node the event happened to. For drag(), that would a mousedown event on an element of the drag class. Taking a peek at our markup, that would be the <h4> element. So fine, if e does not have a target member, add one that refers to srcElement for Internet Explorer 8 or earlier:

```
function drag(e) {
  if (!e) e = window.event;
  if (!e.target) e.target = e.srcElement;
  function move(e) {
    if (!e) e = window.event;
  }
  function drop(e) {
    if (!e) e = window.event;
  }
}
```

By the way, if you are wondering whether we will be recoding this as an advance conditional loader, don't. Other than redefining e and its members, there's no workarounds for Internet Explorer 8 or earlier. So our first cut will be our final one.

Where were we? Right. Now we don't want to move the running tab, which is to say the <h4> element. Rather, we want to move the <div> wrapping the whole shebang, which is e.target.parentNode. We'll save that to a local variable aptly named wrapper. That way, both move() and drop() can manipulate the <div> later. But one thing we need to do straightaway is make sure wrapper displays in front of any other content in the document so the user can always see it when dragging. To do so, set its z-index to the return value of doZ(), a helper function we will write later (remind me if I forget). We now have this:

```
function drag(e) {
  if (!e) e = window.event;
  if (!e.target) e.target = e.srcElement;
  var wrapper = e.target.parentNode;
  wrapper.style.zIndex = doZ();
  function move(e) {
    if (!e) e = window.event;
  }
  function drop(e) {
    if (!e) e = window.event;
  }
}
```

We just need to jot down some coordinates for move() to do calculations with later. First, we want to save CSS values for left and top (stripped of their units of measure) to local variables named, well, left and top, which we will use later to recalculate the new position of the panel. Then we want to save clientX and clientY for the mousedown event to local variables named, you guessed it, clientX and clientY. The clientX and clientY members of the event object provide those coordinates in pixels. However, those are numbers, not strings. So, no "px" suffix to strip away with parseInt(). Note that clientX and clientY are not in document coordinates because CSS values for left and top would need to be when we reposition wrapper (in other words, clientX and clientY are the coordinates on the current window rather than the position in the document). Still, we need clientX and clientY to calculate left and top as well as to keep the visitors mouse pinned to the same spot on the Running tab (you'll see the actual calculations in the next section). We now have this:

```
function drag(e) {
  if (!e) e = window.event;
  if (!e.target) e.target = e.srcElement;
  var wrapper = e.target.parentNode;
  var left = parseInt(queryCascade(wrapper, "left"));
```

```
  var top = parseInt(queryCascade(wrapper, "top"));
  var clientX = e.clientX;
  var clientY = e.clientY;
  wrapper.style.zIndex = doZ();
  function move(e) {
    if (!e) e = window.event;
  }
  function drop(e) {
    if (!e) e = window.event;
  }
}
```

Observant readers will notice that we put those last four var statements before the wrapper.style.zIndex = doZ() statement. Any ideas as to why?

Right. It's good programming practice to put all local variable declarations at the top of their function's block. Smiley cookie for remembering.

Now we want to have document listen for every mousemove event. Why do we want to run an event listener function for every mousemove event? Why not just listen for those that happen on the <h4> element?

It turns out a visitor can move their mouse faster than an event listener on just the <h4> can respond to them. So, if we just run move() for mousemove events on the <h4>, the visitor's mouse will leave its confines. Consequently, after an initial nudge, the <div> will not follow their mouse. Sort of like a stubborn mule.

Not wanting that to be the case, let's bind move() to document rather than the <h4>. And to improve performance in Internet Explorer 9, Firefox, Safari, Chrome, and Opera, let's do so for the capture phase. Note that in Internet Explorer 8 or earlier, document will listen during the bubble phase instead. So, pass true as the optional fourth parameter to addListener():

```
function drag(e) {
  if (!e) e = window.event;
  if (!e.target) e.target = e.srcElement;
  var wrapper = e.target.parentNode;
  var left = parseInt(queryCascade(wrapper, "left"));
  var top = parseInt(queryCascade(wrapper, "top"));
  var clientX = e.clientX;
  var clientY = e.clientY;
  wrapper.style.zIndex = doZ();
  addListener(document, "mousemove", move, true);
  function move(e) {
    if (!e) e = window.event;
  }
  function drop(e) {
    if (!e) e = window.event;
  }
}
```

Just as we registered move() on document in order to keep up with the visitor's mouse, we also want to register drop() on document so as not to miss the mouseup event, which tells us where to drop the Running <div>, that is, where the visitor wanted to drag it to.

Could you tell me what would happen if we did miss that vital mouseup event?

This one is worth a couple Smiley cookies.

What do you think?

Sort of. If the visitor stopped moving their mouse, the <div> would drop pretty much where they wanted it to. However, whenever they started moving their mouse again, say from the <h4> tab down to the Brooks `<a>`, the `<div>` would follow their mouse. They'd never be able to click the Brooks `<a>`—or any other link on the page. Great googly moogly, we can't have that!

Let's register drop() on document, too. Pass true for the fourth parameter again to improve performance in Internet Explorer 9, Firefox, Safari, Chrome, and Opera. Rather than wait for the mouseup event to descend and ascend the DOM tree, just nip it in the bud:

```
function drag(e) {
  if (!e) e = window.event;
  if (!e.target) e.target = e.srcElement;
  var wrapper = e.target.parentNode;
  var left = parseInt(queryCascade(wrapper, "left"));
  var top = parseInt(queryCascade(wrapper, "top"));
  var clientX = e.clientX;
  var clientY = e.clientY;
  wrapper.style.zIndex = doZ();
  addListener(document, "mousemove", move, true);
  addListener(document, "mouseup", drop, true);
  function move(e) {
    if (!e) e = window.event;
  }
  function drop(e) {
    if (!e) e = window.event;
  }
}
```

Now call burst() and thwart(), remembering to pass in e, which contains the mousedown event object. Doing so prevents any mousedown event listeners bound to ancestors of the `<h4>` from running and a context menu from appearing for Mac visitors:

```
function drag(e) {
  if (!e) e = window.event;
  if (!e.target) e.target = e.srcElement;
  var wrapper = e.target.parentNode;
  var left = parseInt(queryCascade(wrapper, "left"));
  var top = parseInt(queryCascade(wrapper, "top"));
  var clientX = e.clientX;
  var clientY = e.clientY;
  wrapper.style.zIndex = doZ();
  addListener(document, "mousemove", move, true);
  addListener(document, "mouseup", drop, true);
  burst(e);
  thwart(e);
  function move(e) {
    if (!e) e = window.event;
  }
  function drop(e) {
    if (!e) e = window.event;
  }
}
```

We're done with the mousedown event listener. Now let's move on to move(), mousemove event listener. Sorry for the pun.

Writing the Mousemove Event Listener

One note of caution for those who are bad at math. There is some possibility that your head will explode trying to comprehend how move() calculates left and top during the drag. So, maybe cover your ears and close your eyes while we work on move(). Someone will give you a poke when we're done to let you know it's safe to follow along again.

Now even though drag() will have returned prior to JavaScript ever calling move(), which it will do rapid-fire during a drag, wrapper continues to refer to the Running <div> by way of a closure. Therefore, we can reposition the <div> by changing wrapper.style.left and wrapper.style.top.

This is where things get tricky. Even though the clientX and clientY members of an event object are in window coordinates, but CSS values for left and top are in document coordinates, we can use the former to calculate the latter for the reason that the document does not scroll during the drag, while move() is running.

With this in mind, we can calculate the CSS value for wrapper.style.left by adding the X coordinate of the mousemove event in e.clientX to the local variable left and then subtracting the X coordinate of the mousedown event. Finally, we concatenate "px" to that number:

```
function drag(e) {
  if (!e) e = window.event;
  if (!e.target) e.target = e.srcElement;
  var wrapper = e.target.parentNode;
  var left = parseInt(queryCascade(wrapper, "left"));
  var top = parseInt(queryCascade(wrapper, "top"));
  var clientX = e.clientX;
  var clientY = e.clientY;
  wrapper.style.zIndex = doZ();
  addListener(document, "mousemove", move, true);
  addListener(document, "mouseup", drop, true);
  burst(e);
  thwart(e);
  function move(e) {
    if (!e) e = window.event;
    wrapper.style.left = left + e.clientX - clientX + "px";
  }
  function drop(e) {
    if (!e) e = window.event;
  }
}
```

In the same way, we can calculate the CSS value for wrapper.style.top by adding the Y coordinate of the mousemove event in e.clientY to the local variable top and then subtracting the Y coordinate of the mousedown event. Finally, we concatenate "px" to that number:

```
function drag(e) {
  if (!e) e = window.event;
  if (!e.target) e.target = e.srcElement;
  var wrapper = e.target.parentNode;
  var left = parseInt(queryCascade(wrapper, "left"));
  var top = parseInt(queryCascade(wrapper, "top"));
  var clientX = e.clientX;
  var clientY = e.clientY;
  wrapper.style.zIndex = doZ();
  addListener(document, "mousemove", move, true);
  addListener(document, "mouseup", drop, true);
```

```
  burst(e);
  thwart(e);
  function move(e) {
    if (!e) e = window.event;
    wrapper.style.left = left + e.clientX - clientX + "px";
    wrapper.style.top = top + e.clientY - clientY + "px";
  }
  function drop(e) {
    if (!e) e = window.event;
  }
}
```

Now to prevent the mousemove event object from traversing the DOM tree any further, pass e to burst(). Note that this is just for Internet Explorer 9, Firefox, Safari, Chrome, and Opera since in Internet Explorer 8 or earlier the mousemove event has already ended its journey by bubbling up to document. Note too that there would be no point in passing e to thwart() inasmuch as there is no default action for a mousemove event.

And with that, we're done coding move(). So if any one next to you has their ears covered and eyes closed, give them a poke. Then have them cut and paste our code for move(), which appears here:

```
function drag(e) {
  if (!e) e = window.event;
  if (!e.target) e.target = e.srcElement;
  var wrapper = e.target.parentNode;
  var left = parseInt(queryCascade(wrapper, "left"));
  var top = parseInt(queryCascade(wrapper, "top"));
  var clientX = e.clientX;
  var clientY = e.clientY;
  wrapper.style.zIndex = doZ();
  addListener(document, "mousemove", move, true);
  addListener(document, "mouseup", drop, true);
  burst(e);
  thwart(e);
  function move(e) {
    if (!e) e = window.event;
    wrapper.style.left = left + e.clientX - clientX + "px";
    wrapper.style.top = top + e.clientY - clientY + "px";
    burst(e);
  }
  function drop(e) {
    if (!e) e = window.event;
  }
}
```

Writing the Mouseup Event Listener

Now for the mouseup event listener, drop(). First, we want to tell JavaScript not to listen for mousemove or mouseup events on document. This is where our helper function removeListener() earns its keep. Remember that to remove an event listener with removeEventListener() or detachEvent(), you must pass the same parameters that you added the event listener with. With this in mind, let's cut and paste our addListener calls within drag(). Then just change addListener to removeListener:

```
function drag(e) {
  if (!e) e = window.event;
  if (!e.target) e.target = e.srcElement;
  var wrapper = e.target.parentNode;
  var left = parseInt(queryCascade(wrapper, "left"));
  var top = parseInt(queryCascade(wrapper, "top"));
  var clientX = e.clientX;
  var clientY = e.clientY;
  wrapper.style.zIndex = doZ();
  addListener(document, "mousemove", move, true);
  addListener(document, "mouseup", drop, true);
  burst(e);
  thwart(e);
  function move(e) {
    if (!e) e = window.event;
    wrapper.style.left = left + e.clientX - clientX + "px";
    wrapper.style.top = top + e.clientY - clientY + "px";
    burst(e);
  }
  function drop(e) {
    if (!e) e = window.event;
    removeListener(document, "mousemove", move, true);
    removeListener(document, "mouseup", drop, true);
  }
}
```

Now then, if an element has negative `left` or `top` CSS values, browsers do not render scrollbars to make the element accessible to visitors. For this reason, if a visitor drags and drops the Running `<div>` beyond the browser window to the left or top, there will be no way for them to view the `<div>`. It's sort of like dropping the `<div>` down a black hole.

What to do? Well, simply query `left` and `top`, and if their values are negative, change them to 0, which will snap the `<div>` back into view, flush to edge of the window:

```
function drag(e) {
  if (!e) e = window.event;
  if (!e.target) e.target = e.srcElement;
  var wrapper = e.target.parentNode;
  var left = parseInt(queryCascade(wrapper, "left"));
  var top = parseInt(queryCascade(wrapper, "top"));
  var clientX = e.clientX;
  var clientY = e.clientY;
  wrapper.style.zIndex = doZ();
  addListener(document, "mousemove", move, true);
  addListener(document, "mouseup", drop, true);
  burst(e);
  thwart(e);
  function move(e) {
    if (!e) e = window.event;
    wrapper.style.left = left + e.clientX - clientX + "px";
    wrapper.style.top = top + e.clientY - clientY + "px";
    burst(e);
  }
  function drop(e) {
    if (!e) e = window.event;
```

```
      removeListener(document, "mousemove", move, true);
      removeListener(document, "mouseup", drop, true);
      if (parseInt(wrapper.style.left) < 0) wrapper.style.left = "0px";
      if (parseInt(wrapper.style.top) < 0) wrapper.style.top = "0px";
  }
}
```

Finally, pass the mouseup event object in e to burst() and thwart(), and we're done:

```
function drag(e) {
  if (!e) e = window.event;
  if (!e.target) e.target = e.srcElement;
  var wrapper = e.target.parentNode;
  var left = parseInt(queryCascade(wrapper, "left"));
  var top = parseInt(queryCascade(wrapper, "top"));
  var clientX = e.clientX;
  var clientY = e.clientY;
  wrapper.style.zIndex = doZ();
  addListener(document, "mousemove", move, true);
  addListener(document, "mouseup", drop, true);
  burst(e);
  thwart(e);
  function move(e) {
    if (!e) e = window.event;
    wrapper.style.left = left + e.clientX - clientX + "px";
    wrapper.style.top = top + e.clientY - clientY + "px";
    burst(e);
  }
  function drop(e) {
    if (!e) e = window.event;
    removeListener(document, "mousemove", move, true);
    removeListener(document, "mouseup", drop, true);
    if (parseInt(wrapper.style.left) < 0) wrapper.style.left = "0px";
    if (parseInt(wrapper.style.top) < 0) wrapper.style.top = "0px";
    burst(e);
    thwart(e);
  }
}
```

The doZ() Helper Function

Now for doZ()—thanks for reminding me. This helper function will always return the next highest integer after the one it last returned. So if we set the z-index of the element the visitor is dragging to the return value of doZ(), we can be sure they will never drag it underneath another element. Yup, good idea.

Declare a variable doZ containing the return value of a self-invoking function literal. This will create a closure to save the z-index within from one doZ() call to the next:

```
var doZ = function() {
}();
```

Now initialize a private variable z to an integer greater than any z-index on your page. I dun no, say 400:

```
var doZ = function() {
```

```
  var z = 400;
}();
```

Right now, doZ evaluates to undefined since the self-invoking function literal does not explicitly return a value. We have some work to do; return a function literal for JavaScript to initialize doZ to, that is, the helper function we want doZ to refer to.

```
var doZ = function() {
  var z = 400;
  return function() {
  };
}();
```

Now return the unincremented value of the private z variable. Then increment z to the value doZ() ought to return the next time we call it. To do so, place the ++ operator in the post-increment position. So the first call of doZ() returns 400 and saves 401 to z, the second call of doZ() returns 401 and saves 402 to z, the third call of doZ() returns 402 and saves 403 to z, and so on. doZ() returns z from the closure and then remembers what to return the next time.

> **Note** The ++ operator and the pre- and post-increment positions were covered in Chapter 3.

```
var doZ = function() {
  var z = 400;
  return function() {
    return z ++;
  };
}();
```

Before moving on, let's put doZ() up with the other helper functions, say right before prepSprites(). Yup, cut and paste.

Prepping the Drag

Now we want to tell JavaScript to listen for mousedown events on any element of the drag class. We'll do so within a function named prepDrag(), which as you might imagine will prep the drag-and-drop behavior:

```
function prepDrag() {
}
```

Now in a local variable elements, let's save any element in our markup that is a member of the drag class by passing "drag" to our findClass() helper function:

```
function prepDrag() {
  var elements = findClass("drag");
}
```

Then write an optimized for loop to iterate over elements. During each roundabout of the for loop, tell JavaScript to listen for mousedown events on elements[i], that is, every element that is a member of the drag class. To do so, pass our helper function addListener() the DOM node that elements[i] refers to, the string "mousedown", and the identifier for our drag() function.

■ **Caution** It bears repeating that the third parameter to addListener() is an identifier naming a function, not a function invocation expression. That is to say, we are telling JavaScript the name of a function to run rather than running the function by appending the () operator.

With those words of caution, we're done:

```
function prepDrag() {
  var elements = findClass("drag");
  for (var i = elements.length; i --; ) {
    addListener(elements[i], "mousedown", drag);
  }
}
```

Now let's put our drag-and-drop behavior through the wringer. Save our JavaScript file. Then refresh Firefox, and call prepDrag() from the Firebug console. Optionally, call prepSprites() again, too; refreshing Firefox KO'd the sprite event listeners.

```
prepSprites();
prepDrag();
```

Now grab the Running tab with your mouse, and drag and drop the menu to a different spot on the page. Figure 9–4 the Running menu after I moved it from its usual starting position. Note that as you drag, your mouse stays pinned to wherever you grabbed hold of the tab.

Figure 9–4. Grabbing the menu by the tab and dragging it elsewhere on the page

Now drag the menu beyond the bounds of the Firefox window, either to the left or top. Once it has disappeared from view, drop it and watch JavaScript snap it flush to the edge of the Firefox window. Figure 9–5 illustrates where I dragged the Running menu to and where JavaScript snapped it back into view.

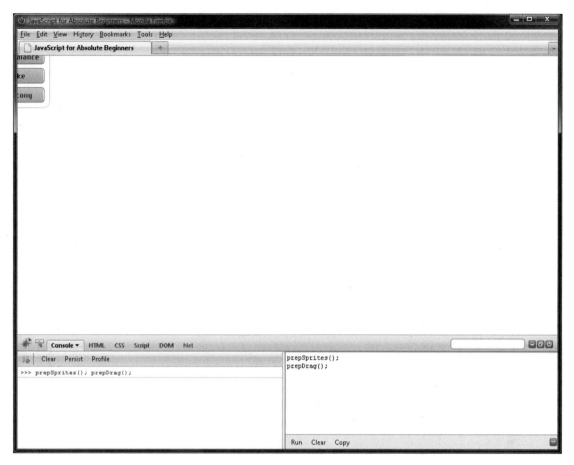

Figure 9–5. Dragging the Running menu beyond the bounds of the Firefox window.

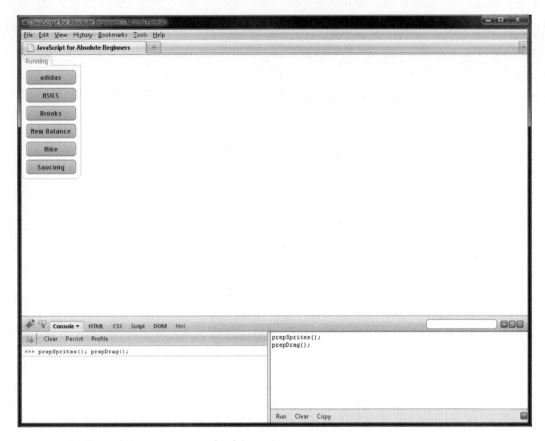

Figure 9–6. The Running menu snaps back into view

How did it go? I hope you're smiling like a butcher's dog. But if not, carefully compare your script to that of your fearless leader:

```
var addListener = document.addEventListener ?
  function(node, type, listener, phase) {
    node.addEventListener(type, listener, !! phase);
  } :
  function(node, type, listener) {
    node.attachEvent("on" + type, listener);
  } ;

var removeListener = document.removeEventListener ?
  function(node, type, listener, phase) {
    node.removeEventListener(type, listener, !! phase);
  } :
  function(node, type, listener) {
    node.detachEvent("on" + type, listener);
  } ;
```

```
function thwart(e) {
  if (e.preventDefault) {
    thwart = function(e) {
      e.preventDefault();
    };
  } else {
    thwart = function(e) {
      e.returnValue = false;
    };
  }
  thwart(e);
}

function burst(e) {
  if (e.stopPropagation) {
    burst = function(e) {
      e.stopPropagation();
    };
  } else {
    burst = function(e) {
      e.cancelBubble = true;
    };
  }
  burst(e);
}

var traverseTree = document.documentElement.firstElementChild ?
  function traverseTree (node, func) {
    func(node);
    node = node.firstElementChild;
    while (node !== null) {
      traverseTree(node, func);
      node = node.nextElementSibling;
    }
  } :
  function traverseTree (node, func) {
    func(node);
    node = node.firstChild;
    while (node !== null) {
      traverseTree(node, func);
      node = node.nextSibling;
    }
  } ;

var findClass;

if (document.getElementsByClassName) {
  findClass = function (name, root) {
    root = root || document.documentElement;
    return root.getElementsByClassName(name);
  };
} else if (document.querySelectorAll) {
  findClass = function (name, root) {
    root = root || document.documentElement;
```

```
      return root.querySelectorAll("." + name);
    };
  } else {
    findClass = function (name, root) {
      var found = [];
      root = root || document.documentElement;
      traverseTree(root, function(node) {
        if (!! node.className) {
          for (var names = node.className.split(/\s+/), i = names.length; i --; ) {
            if (names[i] === name) {
              found.push(node);
            }
          }
        }
      });
      return found;
    };
  }

  var queryCascade = window.getComputedStyle ?
    function(element, property) {
      return getComputedStyle(element, null)[property];
    } :
    function(element, property) {
      return element.currentStyle[property];
    } ;

  var doZ = function() {
    var z = 400;
    return function() {
      return z ++;
    };
  }();

  // sprite swaps

  var prepSprites = window.getComputedStyle ?
    function () {
      var elements = findClass("sprite"), sprites = {};
      for (var i = elements.length, offsets = null; i --; ) {
        sprites[elements[i].id] = [];
        sprites[elements[i].id][0] = queryCascade(elements[i], "backgroundPosition");
        offsets = sprites[elements[i].id][0].split(/\s+/);
        sprites[elements[i].id][1] = 1 - parseInt(queryCascade(elements[i], "width")) +
          "px " + offsets[1];
        addListener(elements[i], "mouseover", slideSprite);
        addListener(elements[i], "mouseout", slideSprite);
      }
      function slideSprite(e) {
        if (e.type == "mouseover") {
          e.target.style.backgroundPosition = sprites[e.target.id][1];
        } else {
          e.target.style.backgroundPosition = sprites[e.target.id][0];
        }
```

```
      }
  } :
  function () {
    var elements = findClass("sprite"), sprites = {};
    for (var i = elements.length, offsets = null; i --; ) {
      sprites[elements[i].id] = [];
      offsets = [queryCascade(elements[i], "backgroundPositionX"),
        queryCascade(elements[i], "backgroundPositionY")];
      sprites[elements[i].id][0] = offsets.join(" ");
      sprites[elements[i].id][1] = 1 - parseInt(queryCascade(elements[i], "width")) +
        "px " + offsets[1];
      addListener(elements[i], "mouseover", slideSprite);
      addListener(elements[i], "mouseout", slideSprite);
    }
    function slideSprite() {
      var e = window.event;
      if (e.type == "mouseover") {
        e.srcElement.style.backgroundPosition = sprites[e.srcElement.id][1];
      } else {
        e.srcElement.style.backgroundPosition = sprites[e.srcElement.id][0];
      }
    }
  }
} ;

// drag and drop

function drag(e) {
  if (!e) e = window.event;
  if (!e.target) e.target = e.srcElement;
  var wrapper = e.target.parentNode;
  var left = parseInt(queryCascade(wrapper, "left"));
  var top = parseInt(queryCascade(wrapper, "top"));
  var clientX = e.clientX;
  var clientY = e.clientY;
  wrapper.style.zIndex = doZ();
  addListener(document, "mousemove", move, true);
  addListener(document, "mouseup", drop, true);
  burst(e);
  thwart(e);

  function move(e) {
    if (!e) e = window.event;
    wrapper.style.left = left + e.clientX - clientX + "px";
    wrapper.style.top = top + e.clientY - clientY + "px";
    burst(e);
  }

  function drop(e) {
    if (!e) e = window.event;
    removeListener(document, "mousemove", move, true);
    removeListener(document, "mouseup", drop, true);
    if (parseInt(wrapper.style.left) < 0) wrapper.style.left = "0px";
    if (parseInt(wrapper.style.top) < 0) wrapper.style.top = "0px";
    burst(e);
```

```
      thwart(e);
  }
}

function prepDrag() {
  var elements = findClass("drag");
  for (var i = elements.length; i --; ) {
    addListener(elements[i], "mousedown", drag);
  }
}
```

Swapping Skins by Key

Now for a skin-swapping behavior. This one will swap the skin to fuchsia if the visitor presses f on their keyboard, to green if they press g, and back to blue if they press b. Note that case does not matter. So for example, f or F will swap the skin to fuchsia. To implement this behavior, we want to have JavaScript listen for keypress events. They can tell you the character that would normally print in response to pressing a key or combination of keys. That is to say, a keypress event can differentiate between an r and an R even though they share the same key on a typical keyboard.

Insofar as we want to respond to every keypress event, we will bind the skin-swapping event listener to document, which as you know is omniscient. For Internet Explorer 9, Firefox, Safari, Chrome, and Opera, JavaScript will nip the keypress in the bud by listening during the capturing phase. On the other hand, Internet Explorer 8 or earlier will listen during the bubbling phase. So, Internet Explorer 8 or earlier will have to wait for the event to traverse the DOM tree, but Internet Explorer 9, Firefox, Safari, Chrome, and Opera will not.

The rough framework for this behavior will be a keypress event listener named swapSkinByKey() nested inside a preparatory function named prepSkinKeys(). In this way, swapSkinByKey() can query the local variables of prepSkinKeys() even after prepSkinKeys() has returned. Note that prepSkinKeys() defines no parameters, but swapSkinByKey() defines e for the keypress event object. Thus far we have this:

```
function prepSkinKeys() {
  function swapSkinByKey(e) {
  }
}
```

Now declare a local variable named sheet referring to the skin style sheet— the one containing the CSS rules that vary among the blue, fuchsia, and green skins. swapSkinByKey() may then query sheet even after prepSkinKeys() has returned. That's a good thing, since prepSkinKeys() will only run one time, right after the page loads:

```
function prepSkinKeys() {
  var   sheet = document.getElementById("skin");
  function swapSkinByKey(e) {
  }
}
```

On to the nested event listener swapSkinByKey(). Begin with a couple of statements to ensure e refers to the keypress event object and that e.target refers to the DOM node the keypress took place on:

```
function prepSkinKeys() {
  var   sheet = document.getElementById("skin");
  function swapSkinByKey(e) {
    if (!e) e = window.event;
```

```
        if (!e.target) e.target = e.srcElement;
    }
}
```

Since we do not want to swap skins if the visitor is typing some text in a form (wouldn't that be bizarre!), let's terminate `swapSkinByKey()` if `e.target` is an `<input>` or `<textarea>` element:

```
function prepSkinKeys() {
    var    sheet = document.getElementById("skin");
    function swapSkinByKey(e) {
        if (!e) e = window.event;
        if (!e.target) e.target = e.srcElement;
        if (e.target.nodeName.toLowerCase() === "input" ||
            e.target.nodeName.toLowerCase() === "textarea") return;
    }
}
```

If JavaScript gets this far, we really do want to swap skins. To do so, we will convert the ASCII value of the key the visitor pressed to a string by way of `String.fromCharCode()`. In turn, we will then convert that string to lowercase with `String.toLowerCase()`. Flip back to Chapter 2 if you have forgotten how those two methods work.

Like me, you probably do not know the ASCII values for b, f, g, B, F, and G off hand. Table 9–1 contains the lowdown.

Table 9–1. ASCII Values for b, f, g, B, F, and G

ASCII Value	Printable Character
66	B
70	F
71	G
98	b
102	f
103	g

Now we just need to query the keypress event object for the ASCII value of the key the visitor pressed. It's in `e.charCode` for Firefox and Safari but `e.keyCode` for Internet Explorer, Opera, and Safari, so either one will do for Safari! On the other hand, `e.keyCode` will be 0 in Firefox while `e.charCode` will be undefined in Internet Explorer and Opera. Since 0 and undefined are both falsy, we can grock the ASCII value of the keypress cross-browser with the expression `e.charCode || e.keyCode`. We will get the ASCII value from charCode in Firefox and Safari, but from keyCode in Internet Explorer and Opera. As to why things have to be so muddled, I have no idea.

Let's add a letter member to the keypress event object. Then save the converted ASCII value to `e.letter`:

```
function prepSkinKeys() {
    var    sheet = document.getElementById("skin");
    function swapSkinByKey(e) {
        if (!e) e = window.event;
        if (!e.target) e.target = e.srcElement;
```

```
      if (e.target.nodeName.toLowerCase() === "input" ||
        e.target.nodeName.toLowerCase() === "textarea") return;
      e.letter = String.fromCharCode(e.charCode || e.keyCode).toLowerCase();
  }
}
```

Now we want to swap skins (or do nothing) relative to the string in e.letter. Let's go with the else if idiom for the job. Insofar as the initial skin is blue, let's optimize things by making b the third choice. Don't want to make it the default, though. Otherwise, every key other than f or g would be a shortcut for the blue skin!

I dun no, of the other two, fuchsia probably would be more popular. So, let's put that before green. Then in the event the visitor did not press f, g, or b, we want to do nothing. To do so, put a naked return in an else clause or omit the else clause entirely. Let's go with the former to make our intentions clear:

```
function prepSkinKeys() {
  var   sheet = document.getElementById("skin");
  function swapSkinByKey(e) {
    if (!e) e = window.event;
    if (!e.target) e.target = e.srcElement;
    if (e.target.nodeName.toLowerCase() === "input" ||
      e.target.nodeName.toLowerCase() === "textarea") return;
    e.letter = String.fromCharCode(e.charCode || e.keyCode).toLowerCase();
    if (e.letter === "f") {
      sheet.href = "fuchsia.css";
    } else if (e.letter === "g") {
      sheet.href = "green.css";
    } else if (e.letter === "b") {
      sheet.href = "blue.css";
    } else {
      return;
    }
  }
}
```

We're done with swapSkinByKey(). Now we want to tell JavaScript to run it whenever a keypress occurs:

```
function prepSkinKeys() {
  var   sheet = document.getElementById("skin");
  function swapSkinByKey(e) {
    if (!e) e = window.event;
    if (!e.target) e.target = e.srcElement;
    if (e.target.nodeName.toLowerCase() === "input" ||
      e.target.nodeName.toLowerCase() === "textarea") return;
    e.letter = String.fromCharCode(e.charCode || e.keyCode).toLowerCase();
    if (e.letter === "f") {
      sheet.href = "fuchsia.css";
    } else if (e.letter === "g") {
      sheet.href = "green.css";
    } else if (e.letter === "b") {
      sheet.href = "blue.css";
    } else {
      return;
    }
```

```
    }
    addListener(document, "keypress", swapSkinByKey, true);
}
```

Insofar as a skin swap requires a repaint and possibly a reflow, optimizing swapSkinByKey() as either a lazy loader or advance conditional loader is not worthwhile. Compared to the time a browser takes to reflow the render tree and repaint the page, the time JavaScript takes to run swapSkinByKey() is insignificant. Let's leave swapSkinByKey() the way it is and move on to testing.

You know what to do. Refresh Firefox, and then use the Firebug console to run the three prepatory functions like so:

```
prepSprites();
prepDrag();
prepSkinKeys();
```

Now click somewhere within the Firefox window (so that you do not continuing typing in the Firebug console), and press f or F to swap the skin from blue to fuchsia, verifying your work with Figure 9–7. Then press g or G to change the skin to green and b or B to revert to the initial blue skin.

Figure 9–7. *Pressing f or F swaps the skin from blue to fuchsia (this may not be so obvious in a black-and-white book, but take my word for it).*

In the unlikely event that things did not go according to plan, take a deep breath, and verify your script with that of the fella next to you.

Initiating Behaviors When the DOM Tree Is Available

To load our behaviors, we want JavaScript to run prepSprites(), prepDrag(), and prepSkinKeys(). However, to prevent errors, we don't want to run these functions until the DOM tree is fully available. How do we know when that is?

Simple, window will be the target of a load event when the DOM tree is fully available. Moreover, when that load event takes place, you know that the browser has loaded and parsed all markup, CSS, JavaScript, and images.

Insofar as the load event listener for window will simply invoke prepSprites(), prepDrag(), and prepSkinKeys(), a function literal will do. So in our JavaScript file, let's call addListener() like so:

```
addListener(window, "load", function() {
    prepSprites();
    prepDrag();
    prepSkinKeys();
});
```

Save our JavaScript file, and then refresh Firefox. This time around there's no need manually call prepSprites(), prepDrag(), and prepSkinKeys() from the Firebug console.

Fighting Global Evil

One final touch to wrap things up. Rather than risk that another script will overwrite our functions, or vice versa, let's paste our script (yup, the whole enchilada) into the body of a self-invoking function literal that is wrapped with parentheses. Doing so creates a module, a global abatement technique covered in Chapter 6. Pretty simple to do, too. Just take a look at the first and last lines, which are in bold, of the final code for our script below.

Then save our JavaScript file, refresh Firefox, and test the behaviors one last time.

```
(function() {
var addListener = document.addEventListener ?
  ...

var removeListener = document.removeEventListener ?
  ...

function thwart(e) {
  ...
}
function burst(e) {
  ...
}

var traverseTree = document.documentElement.firstElementChild ?
  ...

var findClass;
if (document.getElementsByClassName) {
```

```
...
} else if (document.querySelectorAll) {
  ...
} else {
  ...
}

var queryCascade = window.getComputedStyle ?
  ...

var doZ = function() {
  ...
}();

// sprite swaps
var prepSprites = window.getComputedStyle ?
  ...

// drag and drop
function drag(e) {
  ...
}
function prepDrag() {
  ...
}

// swap skins by key
function prepSkinKeys() {
  ...
}

// load behaviors when the DOM tree is fully available
addListener(window, "load", function() {
    prepSprites();
    prepDrag();
    prepSkinKeys();
  });
})();
```

Summary

In this chapter, we explored how to have JavaScript listen for an event that occurs on an element or its ancestors and in turn respond by running a function referred to as an event listener. Moreover, we covered a couple of techniques to make an event listener or its supporting functions snappier. Those that would run straightaway when a page loads were rewritten as advance conditional loaders, while those that run later in time were rewritten as lazy loaders.

In the next chapter, we will add some BOM features to this script—things like timers for animations and Ajax for dynamic content. It's going to be a real hootenanny!

CHAPTER 10

■ ■ ■

Scripting BOM

A while ago, I worked a scene in the Russell Crowe and Liam Neeson film *The Next Three Days*. Probably the thing that surprised me most was how dynamic things were on set. Paul Haggis, who won two Oscars for *Crash*, kept reworking the content of the scene, especially the timing; he must have had Jason Beghe (Detective Quinn) run out of every single door in the precinct and say, "We found his son!" each time. Oftentimes Haggis would tell us what to do just moments before filming another take. Needless to say, having a good short-term memory was vital.

Now in JavaScript, those things (dynamic content, timing, short-term memory) are the purview of the Browser Object Model (BOM). For dynamic content, there's XMLHttpRequest, an object for loading data at runtime without having to refresh the page, a technique called Ajax. Then for timing things like animations, BOM provides four timer functions: `setTimeout()`, `setInterval()`, `clearTimeout()`, and `clearInterval()`. Finally, in order to give a browser a memory, BOM provides cookies. You might have heard of those.

In this chapter, Ajax, timers, and cookies are on the docket. These are pretty disparate features, but that's the way with BOM, which isn't a standard, but rather a hodgepodge of initially proprietary features that are now implemented by Internet Explorer, Firefox, Safari, and Opera. For example, XMLHttpRequest began life as a proprietary Internet Explorer feature.

Downloading the Project Files

Prior to rolling up our sleeves and coding, download the project files from www.apress.com. There are quite a few of them this time. Let's take a peek at the markup in ten.html, displayed here. Later in the chapter, we will turn the branch of the DOM tree beginning with `<div class="scroller" id="s1">` into an animated gallery. Then we'll dynamically add additional galleries by way of Ajax.

```
<!DOCTYPE html PUBLIC "-//W3C//DTD XHTML 1.0 Strict//EN"
"http://www.w3.org/TR/xhtml1/DTD/xhtml1-strict.dtd">
<html xmlns="http://www.w3.org/1999/xhtml">
<head>
<meta http-equiv="Content-Type" content="text/html; charset=utf-8" />
<title>Getting StartED with JavaScript</title>
<link rel="stylesheet" type="text/css" href="ten.css" />
<link rel="stylesheet" type="text/css" href="blue.css" id="skin" />
</head>
<body>
<div id="running">
  <h4 class="drag">Running</h4>
  <ul>
    <li><a class="sprite" id="adidas" href="http://www.adidas.com">adidas</a></li>
    <li><a class="sprite" id="asics" href="http://www.asics.com">ASICS</a></li>
    <li><a class="sprite" id="brooks" href="http://www.brooksrunning.com">Brooks</a></li>
```

```html
        <li><a class="sprite" id="newBalance" href="http://www.newbalance.com">New
Balance</a></li>
        <li><a class="sprite" id="nike" href="http://www.nike.com">Nike</a></li>
        <li><a class="sprite" id="saucony" href="http://www.saucony.com">Saucony</a></li>
    </ul>
</div>
<div class="scroller" id="s1">
  <div class="wrapper">
    <ul class="slide">
        <li><a href="ten.html"><img alt="Nike LunaRacer" src="images/lunaracer.jpg" /></a></li>
        <li><a href="ten.html"><img alt="Nike Lunar Glide, Boston" src="images/glide_bos.jpg"
/></a></li>
        <li><a href="ten.html"><img alt="Nike Lunar Glide, NYC" src="images/glide_nyc.jpg"
/></a></li>
        <li><a href="ten.html"><img alt="Nike Mariah" src="images/mariah.jpg" /></a></li>
        <li><a href="ten.html"><img alt="Nike Lunar Fly, Orange" src="images/fly_org.jpg"
/></a></li>
        <li><a href="ten.html"><img alt="Nike Lunar Fly, Black" src="images/fly_blk.jpg"
/></a></li>
        <li><a href="ten.html"><img alt="Nike Lunar Elite" src="images/elite.jpg" /></a></li>
        <li><a href="ten.html"><img alt="Nike Zoom Vomero" src="images/vomero.jpg" /></a></li>
        <li><a href="ten.html"><img alt="Nike Air Max" src="images/max.jpg" /></a></li>
    </ul>
  </div>
  <div class="left arrow sprite"></div>
  <div class="right arrow sprite"></div>
</div>
<script src="ten.js" type="text/javascript"></script>
</body>
</html>
```

Note that the three sprites now have four arrows (as displayed in Figure 10–1). We'll need those to scroll the galleries.

Figure 10–1. *The blue, fuchsia, and green sprites now have four arrows.*

Remembering Visitor Data with Cookies

In Chapter 9, we wrote a skin-swapping behavior. However, if you click Refresh in Firefox to reload `ten.html`, JavaScript totally forgets which skin you preferred. Similarly, if you close Firefox, the next time you open `ten.html`, the skin reverts to blue, which is the default.

So, we need to find a way to give JavaScript a memory. For this, BOM provides cookies. Our goal will be to save a visitor's skin preference to a cookie. That way, we can preset the skin to their favorite skin. We ought to make them feel welcome. However, working with cookies is not entirely straightforward.

On the one hand, writing a cookie is simple. Just assign name value pairs, separated by semicolons, to `document.cookie`, and you're done. Here are a couple of name-value pairs:

```
name=john;preference=blue
```

On the other hand, reading a cookie is a nightmare. JavaScript returns the name-value pair of every cookie, joined by semicolons, in one long string. It's sort of like the ticker tapes that stock exchanges used to work with. You have to search through all those cookies for the one you want. That's ridiculous, of course. But with BOM, ridiculous is the status quo.

With this in mind, it makes sense to write a helper function to read the value of a cookie. There's no need to write a second one to write the value of a cookie, since that is simple enough.

Getting the User's Preference

Open `ten.js`, which right now is just the final code for `nine.js`, in your preferred text editor. Scroll down to just past `doZ()`, the last helper function we coded in Chapter 9, and insert a new helper function named `getCookie()`. Then define a `name` parameter, which will contain the name of the cookie to clip from the ticker-tape string in `document.cookie`:

```
function getCookie(name) {
}
```

Now define some local variables:

- `batch` will contain the ticker-tape string in `document.cookie`.

- `i` will contain the return value of passing `name` concatenated to `=` to `String.indexOf()`. Remember from Chapter 2 that this wrapper method returns the offset from the beginning of the string or -1 to convey failure. `i` will enable us to clip our cookie from `batch`.

- Just let `firstCut` and `secondCut` default to undefined for now.

Thus far we have this:

```
function getCookie(name) {
  var batch = document.cookie, i, firstCut, secondCut;
  i = batch.indexOf(name + "=");
}
```

So if JavaScript can find our cookie in `batch`, `i` will not contain -1. Let's write an if conditional for `i` `!==` -1 before we go any further:

```
function getCookie(name) {
  var batch = document.cookie, i, firstCut, secondCut;
  i = batch.indexOf(name + "=");
```

```
    if (i !== -1) {
    }
}
```

Now that we are sure there is a cookie named with the string in the `name` parameter, we want to clip its value from the ticker tape. That cut will begin at the index equivalent to `i`, plus the character length of the string in `name`, plus 1 for the `=` sign. Remember from Chapter 2 that `String.length` contains the number of characters comprising a string. So, for a cookie named `skin`, that would be 4. Let's assign the value of the expression indicating the offset where the value of our cookie begins to `firstCut`:

```
function getCookie(name) {
  var batch = document.cookie, i, firstCut, secondCut;
  i = batch.indexOf(name + "=");
  if (i !== -1) {
    firstCut = i + name.length + 1;
  }
}
```

As you might imagine, `secondCut` will be the offset in the `document.cookie` ticker tape where the value of our cookie ends. That will either be the first semicolon after `firstCut` or the end of the string of cookies. So to find the semicolon, we would again call `indexOf()` on `batch`. But this time, we would pass `firstCut` as the optional second parameter, which tells JavaScript where to begin its search. Note that `i` would work here, too. However, passing `secondCut` results in a quicker match since it's closer to the semicolon than `i`:

```
function getCookie(name) {
  var batch = document.cookie, i, firstCut, secondCut;
  i = batch.indexOf(name + "=");
  if (i !== -1) {
    firstCut = i + name.length + 1;
    secondCut = batch.indexOf(";", firstCut);
  }
}
```

In the event that our cookie is the last one in `batch`, `secondCut` will contain -1. If that's the case, we want to overwrite -1 with the length of the string of cookies. That is to say, we want to overwrite it with `batch.length`:

```
function getCookie(name) {
  var batch = document.cookie, i, firstCut, secondCut;
  i = batch.indexOf(name + "=");
  if (i !== -1) {
    firstCut = i + name.length + 1;
    secondCut = batch.indexOf(";", firstCut);
    if (secondCut === -1) secondCut = batch.length;
  }
}
```

Now for the moment of truth. Clip the value of our cookie from `batch` by passing `String.substring()` the offsets in `firstCut` and `secondCut`. However, to decode any whitespace, commas, or semicolons in the cookie value, be sure to pass the return value of `substring()` to `decodeURIComponent()`. Note that cookie values may not contain any whitespace, commas, or semicolons, so it's always best to clean them out just in case. I'll remind you of that in a bit when we write the value of our cookie.

Anyway, `getCookie()` has done its job at this point, so let's return the cookie value like so:

```
function getCookie(name) {
  var batch = document.cookie, i, firstCut, secondCut;
  i = batch.indexOf(name + "=");
  if (i !== -1) {
    firstCut = i + name.length + 1;
    secondCut = batch.indexOf(";", firstCut);
    if (secondCut === -1) secondCut = batch.length;
    return decodeURIComponent(batch.substring(firstCut, secondCut));
  }
}
```

Finally, if getCookie() cannot find a cookie named name, let's convey failure by appending an else clause that returns false. In just a moment, we will check for false prior to presetting the skin relative to a visitor's preference. The final code for getCookie() would be as follows:

```
function getCookie(name) {
  var batch = document.cookie, i, firstCut, secondCut;
  i = batch.indexOf(name + "=");
  if (i !== -1) {
    firstCut = i + name.length + 1;
    secondCut = batch.indexOf(";", firstCut);
    if (secondCut === -1) secondCut = batch.length;
    return decodeURIComponent(batch.substring(firstCut, secondCut));
  } else {
    return false;
  }
}
```

Setting the User's Skin Preference

Now for a function to preset the skin to blue, fuchsia, or green depending on the visitor's preference. Hmm. Let's cleverly name it presetSkin(). In its block, declare a local variable named pref, and assign to it the return value of passing "skin" to getCookie():

```
function presetSkin() {
  var pref = getCookie("skin");
}
```

So, pref will contain "blue", "fuchsia", or "green" if the visitor set their preference during a previous visit. Otherwise, pref will contain false. Note that if cookies are disabled, pref will contain false as well. With this in mind, let's make sure pref does not contain false before we do anything else. An if condition and the !== operator will do the job:

```
function presetSkin() {
  var pref = getCookie("skin");
  if (pref !== false) {
  }
}
```

Fine and dandy. Now if JavaScript runs the if block, we have a skin to set. Just set the href member of the skin style sheet to "blue.css", "fuchsia.css", or "green.css" by concatenating pref to ".css":

```
function presetSkin() {
  var pref = getCookie("skin");
```

```
  if (pref !== false) {
    document.getElementById("skin").href = pref + ".css";
  }
}
```

We're done with presetSkin(). The final code for that and our getCookie() helper would be as follows:

```
function getCookie(name) {
  var batch = document.cookie, i, firstCut, secondCut;
  i = batch.indexOf(name + "=");
  if (i !== -1) {
    firstCut = i + name.length + 1;
    secondCut = batch.indexOf(";", firstCut);
    if (secondCut === -1) secondCut = batch.length;
    return decodeURIComponent(batch.substring(firstCut, secondCut));
  } else {
    return false;
  }
}
// some intervening code
function presetSkin() {
  var pref = getCookie("skin");
  if (pref !== false) {
    document.getElementById("skin").href = pref + ".css";
  }
}
```

Setting the User's Preference

We can now read the skin cookie whenever the visitor returns. But it's not very useful unless we create the skin cookie elsewhere in our script. Let's do so by rewriting swapSkinByKey(), the keypress event listener we cobbled together in Chapter 9. That's nested in prepSkinKeys(). Right now we have this:

```
function prepSkinKeys() {
  var   sheet = document.getElementById("skin");
  function swapSkinByKey(e) {
    if (!e) e = window.event;
    if (!e.target) e.target = e.srcElement;
    if (e.target.nodeName.toLowerCase() === "input" || e.target.nodeName.toLowerCase() ===
"textarea") return;
    e.letter = String.fromCharCode(e.charCode || e.keyCode).toLowerCase();
    if (e.letter === "f") {
      sheet.href = "fuchsia.css";
    } else if (e.letter === "g") {
      sheet.href = "green.css";
    } else if (e.letter === "b") {
      sheet.href = "blue.css";
    } else {
      return;
    }
  }
  addListener(document, "keypress", swapSkinByKey, true);
}
```

First declare a local variable named `pref` prior to the `if` statement. Then replace the three `href` assignment statements with `pref` ones:

```
function prepSkinKeys() {
  var   sheet = document.getElementById("skin");
  function swapSkinByKey(e) {
    if (!e) e = window.event;
    if (!e.target) e.target = e.srcElement;
    if (e.target.nodeName.toLowerCase() === "input" || e.target.nodeName.toLowerCase() ===
"textarea") return;
    e.letter = String.fromCharCode(e.charCode || e.keyCode).toLowerCase();
    var pref;
    if (e.letter === "f") {
      pref = "fuchsia";
    } else if (e.letter === "g") {
      pref = "green";
    } else if (e.letter === "b") {
      pref = "blue";
    } else {
      return;
    }
  }
  addListener(document, "keypress", swapSkinByKey, true);
}
```

Following the `else` clause, reinsert the `href` assignment. However, we can now do so in one fell swoop by concatenating `pref` to `".css"`:

```
function prepSkinKeys() {
  var   sheet = document.getElementById("skin");
  function swapSkinByKey(e) {
    if (!e) e = window.event;
    if (!e.target) e.target = e.srcElement;
    if (e.target.nodeName.toLowerCase() === "input" || e.target.nodeName.toLowerCase() ===
"textarea") return;
    e.letter = String.fromCharCode(e.charCode || e.keyCode).toLowerCase();
    var pref;
    if (e.letter === "f") {
      pref = "fuchsia";
    } else if (e.letter === "g") {
      pref = "green";
    } else if (e.letter === "b") {
      pref = "blue";
    } else {
      return;
    }
    sheet.href = pref + ".css";
  }
  addListener(document, "keypress", swapSkinByKey, true);
}
```

Now for the reason why we gutted `swapSkinByKey()` in the first place. Yup, it's time to create or write the `skin` cookie. Both of those operations work the same way. Just cobble together a string to assign to `document.cookie`. Note that this does not overwrite any cookies already in there. I know, it's not very intuitive. Such is the sad state of BOM. Anyway, just concatenate `"skin="` to `pref`:

```
function prepSkinKeys() {
  var   sheet = document.getElementById("skin");
  function swapSkinByKey(e) {
    if (!e) e = window.event;
    if (!e.target) e.target = e.srcElement;
    if (e.target.nodeName.toLowerCase() === "input" || e.target.nodeName.toLowerCase() ===
"textarea") return;
    e.letter = String.fromCharCode(e.charCode || e.keyCode).toLowerCase();
    var pref;
    if (e.letter === "f") {
      pref = "fuchsia";
    } else if (e.letter === "g") {
      pref = "green";
    } else if (e.letter === "b") {
      pref = "blue";
    } else {
      return;
    }
    sheet.href = pref + ".css";
    document.cookie = "skin=" + pref;
  }
  addListener(document, "keypress", swapSkinByKey, true);
}
```

There's one problem with what we did. Although our cookie would survive a refresh, it would be deleted when the visitor closes their browser. That's because we created a session cookie, meaning one with no sell by date.

Let's fix that by setting the optional max-age attribute, the value for which is the life span of the cookie in seconds. Like me, you probably do not know off-hand the number of seconds in a week, month, year, and so forth. Therefore, let's let JavaScript do the math for us. Say for a 30-day cookie, we would write this:

```
function prepSkinKeys() {
  var   sheet = document.getElementById("skin");
  function swapSkinByKey(e) {
    if (!e) e = window.event;
    if (!e.target) e.target = e.srcElement;
    if (e.target.nodeName.toLowerCase() === "input" || e.target.nodeName.toLowerCase() ===
"textarea") return;
    e.letter = String.fromCharCode(e.charCode || e.keyCode).toLowerCase();
    var pref;
    if (e.letter === "f") {
      pref = "fuchsia";
    } else if (e.letter === "g") {
      pref = "green";
    } else if (e.letter === "b") {
      pref = "blue";
    } else {
      return;
    }
    sheet.href = pref + ".css";
    document.cookie = "skin=" + pref + "; max-age=" + (60*60*24*30);
  }
  addListener(document, "keypress", swapSkinByKey, true);
```

```
}
```

As it is right now, `presetSkin()` will never run. To fix that, simply call `presetSkin()` first thing in the load event listener:

```
addListener(window, "load", function() {
    presetSkin();
    prepSprites();
    prepDrag();
    prepSkinKeys();
});
```

Now let's test this in Firefox. Save `ten.js`, and then open `ten.html` with Firefox. Press f or F to swap the skin to fuchsia, and then click Refresh to make sure the skin remains fuchsia.

Now exit Firefox to end your browsing session. Then reopen `ten.html` to see whether our sell by date worked as planned. Skin still green?

Great. There you have it—a script with a memory!

Animating with Timers

Timers are the next BOM feature we will explore. Those are the cornerstone JavaScript animations. Scrollers are one kind of animated behavior. Let's add one of those to our script so that visitors can scroll right or left through an image gallery of running shoes. But before we do, download `ten.html`, `ten.css`, and `images` folder from www.apress.com (and refer to the listing of `ten.html` at the start of this chapter for the layout of the elements we're going to work with in this section, particularly the wrapper and scroller parts). In addition to images for the gallery, revised blue, fuchsia, and green sprites are in the `images` folder, too. There's no need to download `ten.js`, though, since we are coding that over the course of this chapter.

Preparing the Scrollers

Beneath `prepSkinKeys()`, add a function named `prepScrollers()`. Then assign to a local variable named `elements` the return value of passing `"scroller"` to the helper function, `findClass()`. There will be one element per scrolling gallery in there.

```
function prepScrollers() {
  var elements = findClass("scroller");
}
```

Now iterate over `elements` with a `for` loop. To make that snappier (remember, the browser is frozen while JavaScript is doing something), we will query `elements.length` just one time, saving that to the venerable loop variable `i`. Then we will decrement `i` in the test expression. That is to say, we will loop through `elements` in reverse and omit the third expression, which is traditionally where `i` would be incremented. Just remember to put a semicolon following `i --` in order to prevent a syntax error.

```
function prepScrollers() {
  var elements = findClass("scroller");
  for (var i = elements.length; i --; ) {
  }
}
```

During each roundabout of the `for` loop, we'll pass `elements[i]` to a function literal that defines a `scroller` argument, which is the `div` that contains the scroller panel. But we cannot call it until it is defined. So, wrap the function literal in parentheses, like so:

```
function prepScrollers() {
  var elements = findClass("scroller");
  for (var i = elements.length; i --; ) {
    (function (scroller) {
    })(elements[i]);
  }
}
```

Now we are going to save some local variables to the call object of the function literal. Closure will make those persistent and private to some nested functions we will code in a moment or two.

The first private variable, `wrapper`, will contain the descendent of `scroller` that is of the `wrapper` class. Similarly, `slide` will contain the descendent of `scroller` that is of the `slide` class. So in both cases, we pass `scroller` as the value of the root parameter to `findClass()`. However, its return value is an array, so grab the first and only element by passing 0 to the [ ] operator:

```
function prepScrollers() {
  var elements = findClass("scroller");
  for (var i = elements.length; i --; ) {
    (function (scroller) {
      var wrapper = findClass("wrapper", scroller)[0];
      var slide = findClass("slide", scroller)[0];
    })(elements[i]);
  }
}
```

Querying computed styles from the CSS cascade forces the browser to flush its rendering queue and do any pending reflow or repaint. That's not something you want to do very often, unless of course you like to torment visitors by freezing their browser. So, let's save the width of `wrapper` and `slide`, which are values we will need to query every 15 milliseconds as the gallery is animating, to private variables named `w1` and `w2`. Note that JavaScript can look up tersely named variables like `w1` faster than more readable ones like `wrapperWidth`. Finally, let's clip off the `"px"` from `w1` and `w2` with `parseInt()` while we are here:

```
function prepScrollers() {
  var elements = findClass("scroller");
  for (var i = elements.length; i --; ) {
    (function (scroller) {
      var wrapper = findClass("wrapper", scroller)[0];
      var slide = findClass("slide", scroller)[0];
      var w1 = parseInt(queryCascade(wrapper, "width"));
      var w2 = parseInt(queryCascade(slide, "width"));
    })(elements[i]);
  }
}
```

Now initialize a `timer` variable to `null`. This will later contain a timer ID that we will need in the event we want to defuse a timer before it goes off. Just picture a timer ID as the trigger code some bomb-squad guy tries frantically to crack in a movie.

```
function prepScrollers() {
  var elements = findClass("scroller");
  for (var i = elements.length; i --; ) {
    (function (scroller) {
```

```
        var wrapper = findClass("wrapper", scroller)[0];
        var slide = findClass("slide", scroller)[0];
        var w1 = parseInt(queryCascade(wrapper, "width"));
        var w2 = parseInt(queryCascade(slide, "width"));
        var timer = null;
      })(elements[i]);
    }
  }
}
```

To animate our gallery, we will increment or decrement slide.style.left. Its value is "" right now, so at some point we will have to query the CSS cascade for the computed value of left. Rather than cause an initial lurch by waiting until the beginning of an animation to query the cascade, let's do so now. Querying the cascade takes time, you know.

By the way, during the course of an animation, JavaScript will read and write slide.style.left every 15 milliseconds. Bet you couldn't do that—or anything else in .015 seconds! Don't feel bad, though. JavaScript would struggle to query left from the cascade that fast, which is why we saved it locally to slide.style.left in this step:

```
function prepScrollers() {
  var elements = findClass("scroller");
  for (var i = elements.length; i --; ) {
    (function (scroller) {
      var wrapper = findClass("wrapper", scroller)[0];
      var slide = findClass("slide", scroller)[0];
      var w1 = parseInt(queryCascade(wrapper, "width"));
      var w2 = parseInt(queryCascade(slide, "width"));
      var timer = null;
      slide.style.left = queryCascade(slide, "left");
    })(elements[i]);
  }
}
```

Now we want to bind a mousedown event listener named press(), which we haven't written yet, to the arrows. So, initialize a variable named arrows to the findClass("arrow", scroller) invocation expression. Initialize the loop variable i to arrows.length and re to a regular expression for the word "right", too. We have three loop variables initialized with one var statement:

```
function prepScrollers() {
  var elements = findClass("scroller");
  for (var i = elements.length; i --; ) {
    (function (scroller) {
      var wrapper = findClass("wrapper", scroller)[0];
      var slide = findClass("slide", scroller)[0];
      var w1 = parseInt(queryCascade(wrapper, "width"));
      var w2 = parseInt(queryCascade(slide, "width"));
      var timer = null;
      slide.style.left = queryCascade(slide, "left");
      for (var arrows = findClass("arrow", scroller), i = arrows.length, re = /\bright\b/; i -
-; ) {
        addListener(arrows[i], "mousedown", press);
      }
    })(elements[i]);
  }
}
```

In addition to binding press() for the mousedown event, we want to add a jump member to both `<div>` elements. For the one of the right class, jump will contain -10. On the other hand, jump will be 10 for the `<div>` of the left class. During an animation, JavaScript will add jump to slide.style.left. That is to say, pressing down on the right arrow will decrement left for slide by 10 pixels, while pressing down on the left arrow will increment left for slide by 10 pixels. That happens in just 15 milliseconds, mind you.

Anyway, this is where re earns its keep. Remember from Chapter 2 that RegExp.test() returns true if the regular expression matches the string parameter and false if not. If we pass re.test() the value of the class attribute for both arrows, it will return true for the right arrow and false for the left arrow. With this in mind, we can initialize jump to the appropriate value by making the call to RegExp.test() the boolean expression prior to the ? token of the conditional operator:

```
function prepScrollers() {
  var elements = findClass("scroller");
  for (var i = elements.length; i --; ) {
    (function (scroller) {
      var wrapper = findClass("wrapper", scroller)[0];
      var slide = findClass("slide", scroller)[0];
      var w1 = parseInt(queryCascade(wrapper, "width"));
      var w2 = parseInt(queryCascade(slide, "width"));
      var timer = null;
      slide.style.left = queryCascade(slide, "left");
      for (var arrows = findClass("arrow", scroller), i = arrows.length, re = /\bright\b/; i -
-; ) {
        addListener(arrows[i], "mousedown", press);
        arrows[i].jump = (re.test(arrows[i].className)) ? -10 : 10;
      }
    })(elements[i]);
  }
}
```

Adding the Press Event Listener

Now on to the event listener press(), which will execute whenever a mousedown event fires on an arrow `<div>`. Define an e parameter for the DOM event object. Then if JavaScript defaults e to undefined, assign window.event to e. Remember, window.event is where Internet Explorer will save details about the mousedown event. One of those tidbits, window.event.srcElement, will refer to the left or right arrow `<div>`. DOM-savvy browsers call that member target. So in Internet Explorer, initialize a new window.event.target member that refers to window.event.srcElement. That way, e.target refers to an arrow `<div>` cross-browser:

```
function prepScrollers() {
  var elements = findClass("scroller");
  for (var i = elements.length; i --; ) {
    (function (scroller) {
      var wrapper = findClass("wrapper", scroller)[0];
      var slide = findClass("slide", scroller)[0];
      var w1 = parseInt(queryCascade(wrapper, "width"));
      var w2 = parseInt(queryCascade(slide, "width"));
      var timer = null;
      slide.style.left = queryCascade(slide, "left");
      for (var arrows = findClass("arrow", scroller), i = arrows.length, re = /\bright\b/; i -
-; ) {
```

```
      addListener(arrows[i], "mousedown", press);
      arrows[i].jump = (re.test(arrows[i].className)) ? -10 : 10;
    }

    function press(e) {
      if (!e) e = window.event;
      if (!e.target) e.target = e.srcElement;
    }
  })(elements[i]);
  }
}
```

Now then, the `<div>` that `e.target` refers to has a `jump` member containing 10 or -10. Inasmuch as JavaScript can look up a local variable faster than a nested object member, save `e.target.jump` to a local variable `jump`. While animating our particular gallery, JavaScript may need to query `jump` 143 times. So, saving `e.target.jump` to a local variable is certainly worthwhile.

Now call `animate()`, a function we will nest in `press()` in a moment. Note that `animate()` can query `jump` from the call object on `press()`. That's a good thing, because it will do so every 15 milliseconds! Before we code `animate()`, though, pass the mousedown event object to both `burst()` and `thwart()` to prevent the event from bubbling any further and a context menu from pestering Mac visitors:

```
function prepScrollers() {
  var elements = findClass("scroller");
  for (var i = elements.length; i --; ) {
    (function (scroller) {
      var wrapper = findClass("wrapper", scroller)[0];
      var slide = findClass("slide", scroller)[0];
      var w1 = parseInt(queryCascade(wrapper, "width"));
      var w2 = parseInt(queryCascade(slide, "width"));
      var timer = null;
      slide.style.left = queryCascade(slide, "left");
      for (var arrows = findClass("arrow", scroller), i = arrows.length, re = /\bright\b/; i -
-; ) {
        addListener(arrows[i], "mousedown", press);
        arrows[i].jump = (re.test(arrows[i].className)) ? -10 : 10;
      }

      function press(e) {
        if (!e) e = window.event;
        if (!e.target) e.target = e.srcElement;
        var jump = e.target.jump;
        animate();
        burst(e);
        thwart(e);
      }
    })(elements[i]);
  }
}
```

Writing the Animation Function

Now nest animate() in press() so that it can query jump from the call object for press(). Note that animate() can (and will) query slide, w1, w2, and timer from the call object of the function literal press() is nested within.

```
function prepScrollers() {
  var elements = findClass("scroller");
  for (var i = elements.length; i --; ) {
    (function (scroller) {
      var wrapper = findClass("wrapper", scroller)[0];
      var slide = findClass("slide", scroller)[0];
      var w1 = parseInt(queryCascade(wrapper, "width"));
      var w2 = parseInt(queryCascade(slide, "width"));
      var timer = null;
      slide.style.left = queryCascade(slide, "left");
      for (var arrows = findClass("arrow", scroller), i = arrows.length, re = /\bright\b/; i -
-; ) {
        addListener(arrows[i], "mousedown", press);
        arrows[i].jump = (re.test(arrows[i].className)) ? -10 : 10;
      }

      function press(e) {
        if (!e) e = window.event;
        if (!e.target) e.target = e.srcElement;
        var jump = e.target.jump;
        animate();
        burst(e);
        thwart(e);

        function animate() {
        }
      }
    })(elements[i]);
  }
}
```

First convert slide.style.left to a number by passing it to parseInt(). Then add jump, which will be either 10 or -10, to that number, saving the sum to a variable named x. Now we want to determine whether x is in bounds, that is, no less than w1 - w2 and no greater than 0. For our gallery that would mean an integer between -1424 and 0 inclusive. If x falls within those bounds, we want to concatenate "px" to x, which converts it to a string—remember CSS values are all of the string datatype—then assign that to slide.style.left.

```
function prepScrollers() {
  var elements = findClass("scroller");
  for (var i = elements.length; i --; ) {
    (function (scroller) {
      var wrapper = findClass("wrapper", scroller)[0];
      var slide = findClass("slide", scroller)[0];
      var w1 = parseInt(queryCascade(wrapper, "width"));
      var w2 = parseInt(queryCascade(slide, "width"));
      var timer = null;
      slide.style.left = queryCascade(slide, "left");
```

```
      for (var arrows = findClass("arrow", scroller), i = arrows.length, re = /\bright\b/; i -
-; ) {
         addListener(arrows[i], "mousedown", press);
         arrows[i].jump = (re.test(arrows[i].className)) ? -10 : 10;
      }

      function press(e) {
         if (!e) e = window.event;
         if (!e.target) e.target = e.srcElement;
         var jump = e.target.jump;
         animate();
         burst(e);
         thwart(e);

         function animate() {
            var x = parseInt(slide.style.left) + jump;
            if (x >= w1 - w2 && x <= 0) {
               slide.style.left = x + "px";
            }
         }
      }
   })(elements[i]);
   }
}
```

But what if x is too negative, which is to say less than -1424, or at all positive? In the former case, we want to assign "-1424px" to slide.style.left, and in the latter case we want to assign "0px". Let's make that happen by way of the else if idiom, which we explored in Chapter 4.

```
function prepScrollers() {
  var elements = findClass("scroller");
  for (var i = elements.length; i --; ) {
    (function (scroller) {
       var wrapper = findClass("wrapper", scroller)[0];
       var slide = findClass("slide", scroller)[0];
       var w1 = parseInt(queryCascade(wrapper, "width"));
       var w2 = parseInt(queryCascade(slide, "width"));
       var timer = null;
       slide.style.left = queryCascade(slide, "left");
       for (var arrows = findClass("arrow", scroller), i = arrows.length, re = /\bright\b/; i -
-; ) {
          addListener(arrows[i], "mousedown", press);
          arrows[i].jump = (re.test(arrows[i].className)) ? -10 : 10;
       }

       function press(e) {
          if (!e) e = window.event;
          if (!e.target) e.target = e.srcElement;
          var jump = e.target.jump;
          animate();
          burst(e);
          thwart(e);

          function animate() {
```

413

```
                var x = parseInt(slide.style.left) + jump;
                if (x >= w1 - w2 && x <= 0) {
                    slide.style.left = x + "px";
                } else if (x < w1 - w2) {
                    slide.style.left = w1 - w2 + "px";
                } else {
                    slide.style.left = "0px";
                }
            }
        }
    })(elements[i]);
    }
}
```

Using the Gallery

Now let's put the gallery through the wringer. To do so, scroll down and add `prepScrollers()` to the load event listener:

```
addListener(window, "load", function() {
    presetSkin();
    prepSprites();
    prepDrag();
    prepSkinKeys();
    prepScrollers();
});
```

Then save ten.js, refresh Firefox, and press the right arrow.

Hmm. It just nudges the gallery by 10 pixels. We'd have to press and release the right arrow 143 times to scroll to the end!

Maybe you didn't notice, but when we pressed on the right arrow, it swapped to the down version of the left arrow. And when we let go, it swapped to the up version of the left arrow. But if you press and release the left arrow, its sprite remains correct. Great googly-moogly, what's going on?

Well, the two arrow <div> elements do not have an ID, which our sprite-swapping behavior relies on. Actually, that's not entirely true. The arrow <div> elements both have an ID of "", which is the empty string is the default value for the ID. Moreover, you can name an object member with any string, including "". So when `prepSprites()` ran, it first added a member named "" to the sprites object with offsets for the right arrow. Then it overwrote "" with offsets for the left arrow. So in the `slideSprite()` event listener function, `sprites[e.target.id]` refers to `sprites[""]` for both arrow <div> elements. The code is shown here for your reference:

```
var prepSprites = window.getComputedStyle ?
    function () {
        var elements = findClass("sprite"), sprites = {};
        for (var i = elements.length, offsets = null; i --; ) {
            sprites[elements[i].id] = [];
            sprites[elements[i].id][0] = queryCascade(elements[i], "backgroundPosition");
            offsets = sprites[elements[i].id][0].split(/\s+/);
            sprites[elements[i].id][1] = 1 - parseInt(queryCascade(elements[i], "width")) + "px " +
offsets[1];
            addListener(elements[i], "mouseover", slideSprite);
            addListener(elements[i], "mouseout", slideSprite);
```

```
      }
    function slideSprite(e) {
        if (e.type == "mouseover") {
          e.target.style.backgroundPosition = sprites[e.target.id][1];
        } else {
          e.target.style.backgroundPosition = sprites[e.target.id][0];
        }
      }
    }
  } :
  function () {
    var elements = findClass("sprite"), sprites = {};
    for (var i = elements.length, offsets = null; i --; ) {
      sprites[elements[i].id] = [];
      offsets = [queryCascade(elements[i], "backgroundPositionX"), queryCascade(elements[i],
"backgroundPositionY")];
      sprites[elements[i].id][0] = offsets.join(" ");
      sprites[elements[i].id][1] = 1 - parseInt(queryCascade(elements[i], "width")) + "px " +
offsets[1];
      addListener(elements[i], "mouseover", slideSprite);
      addListener(elements[i], "mouseout", slideSprite);
    }
    function slideSprite() {
      var e = window.event;
      if (e.type == "mouseover") {
        e.srcElement.style.backgroundPosition = sprites[e.srcElement.id][1];
      } else {
        e.srcElement.style.backgroundPosition = sprites[e.srcElement.id][0];
      }
    }
  }
} ;
```

So, we have two issues to fix. First, we want JavaScript to animate rather than nudge the gallery. Second, we want the arrow sprites to swap correctly.

Animating the Gallery

To eliminate the nudging bugaboo, we'll add a timer to move the animation along. BOM provides two kinds: window.setTimeout() runs a function after a certain number of milliseconds have elapsed, and window.setInterval() runs a function in intervals of a certain number of milliseconds. Regardless of which timer you go with, the parameters are the same. The first one is the function to run, and the second is the number of milliseconds to wait.

I tend to favor setTimeout() over setInterval() for the reason that JavaScript will not honor the call to setInterval() in the event that the last task setInterval() added to the UI queue is still in there. This behavior can result in jerky animations.

So setTimeout() it is. If x is within bounds, we will tell JavaScript to run animate() again in 15 milliseconds. It is always preferable to recurse by way of arguments.callee, which refers to the function that is running, than to do so with an identifier like animate. With this in mind, let's modify animate() like so:

```
function prepScrollers() {
  var elements = findClass("scroller");
  for (var i = elements.length; i --; ) {
    (function (scroller) {
```

415

```
        var wrapper = findClass("wrapper", scroller)[0];
        var slide = findClass("slide", scroller)[0];
        var w1 = parseInt(queryCascade(wrapper, "width"));
        var w2 = parseInt(queryCascade(slide, "width"));
        var timer = null;
        slide.style.left = queryCascade(slide, "left");
        for (var arrows = findClass("arrow", scroller), i = arrows.length, re = /\bright\b/; i -
-; ) {
          addListener(arrows[i], "mousedown", press);
          arrows[i].jump = (re.test(arrows[i].className)) ? -10 : 10;
        }

        function press(e) {
          if (!e) e = window.event;
          if (!e.target) e.target = e.srcElement;
          var jump = e.target.jump;
          animate();
          burst(e);
          thwart(e);

          function animate() {
            var x = parseInt(slide.style.left) + jump;
            if (x >= w1 - w2 && x <= 0) {
              slide.style.left = x + "px";
              setTimeout(arguments.callee, 15);
            } else if (x < w1 - w2) {
              slide.style.left = w1 - w2 + "px";
            } else {
              slide.style.left = "0px";
            }
          }
        }
      })(elements[i]);
    }
}
```

Save ten.js, and then refresh ten.html in Firefox. Press down on the right arrow until a few images have scrolled by, and then let go.

Did the gallery keep right on rolling like a runaway train? It did so for me, too. Try the left arrow. It has the same problem.

So, we need to tell JavaScript to stop scrolling the gallery whenever a visitor releases one of the arrows. That, and we still need to fix the screwy sprites. Sigh.

OK, the sprites will have to wait. To fix the runaway gallery thingy, we need to employ the services of window.clearTimeout(). If we pass that the return value of setTimeout(), it will call off the hounds.

So, the first thing we have to do is save the return value of setTimeout() to timer, the variable we saved to the call object of the function literal that press() and in turn animate() are nested within.

```
function prepScrollers() {
  var elements = findClass("scroller");
  for (var i = elements.length; i --; ) {
    (function (scroller) {
      var wrapper = findClass("wrapper", scroller)[0];
      var slide = findClass("slide", scroller)[0];
      var w1 = parseInt(queryCascade(wrapper, "width"));
```

```
      var w2 = parseInt(queryCascade(slide, "width"));
      var timer = null;
      slide.style.left = queryCascade(slide, "left");
      for (var arrows = findClass("arrow", scroller), i = arrows.length, re = /\bright\b/; i -
-; ) {
        addListener(arrows[i], "mousedown", press);
        arrows[i].jump = (re.test(arrows[i].className)) ? -10 : 10;
      }

    function press(e) {
      if (!e) e = window.event;
      if (!e.target) e.target = e.srcElement;
      var jump = e.target.jump;
      animate();
      burst(e);
      thwart(e);

      function animate() {
        var x = parseInt(slide.style.left) + jump;
        if (x >= w1 - w2 && x <= 0) {
          slide.style.left = x + "px";
          timer = setTimeout(arguments.callee, 15);
        } else if (x < w1 - w2) {
          slide.style.left = w1 - w2 + "px";
        } else {
          slide.style.left = "0px";
        }
      }
    }
  })(elements[i]);
  }
}
```

If you are curious as to what the return value of setTimeout() is, don't be. It's an opaque value referred to as a timer ID. Typically this will be a number, but there's no standard saying what it should be. Anything goes. Note that you snuff out a setInterval() timer in a similar way by passing its return value to window.clearInterval(). So, BOM provides two pairs of timer functions—four in all. Don't mix and match, or you'll come to grief.

Now where were we? Right, call off the timer to fix the runaway train bug. But where? In a function named release() that we will temporarily bind to document whenever press() is called. So that the release identifier resolves faster, let's nest release() in press(). That way, it'll be on the first variable object in the scope chain.

release() will do two things. First, it will call off the hounds by passing timer to clearTimeout(). Second, it will resign its position. In other words, it will remove the mouseup event listener from document. Note that we bind the mouseup event listener to document so that if the visitor's mouse drifts off the arrow before they let go, the animation will still stop. Passing true as the optional fourth parameter puts the brakes on sooner in DOM savvy browsers. Note too that once we stop the animation, we don't want document running release() whenever subsequent mouseup events take place elsewhere on the page. This is why we have release() resign after calling clearTimeout():

```
function prepScrollers() {
  var elements = findClass("scroller");
  for (var i = elements.length; i --; ) {
    (function (scroller) {
```

```
        var wrapper = findClass("wrapper", scroller)[0];
        var slide = findClass("slide", scroller)[0];
        var w1 = parseInt(queryCascade(wrapper, "width"));
        var w2 = parseInt(queryCascade(slide, "width"));
        var timer = null;
        slide.style.left = queryCascade(slide, "left");
        for (var arrows = findClass("arrow", scroller), i = arrows.length, re = /\bright\b/; i -
-; ) {
            addListener(arrows[i], "mousedown", press);
            arrows[i].jump = (re.test(arrows[i].className)) ? -10 : 10;
        }

        function press(e) {
            if (!e) e = window.event;
            if (!e.target) e.target = e.srcElement;
            addListener(document, "mouseup", release, true);
            var jump = e.target.jump;
            animate();
            burst(e);
            thwart(e);

            function animate() {
                var x = parseInt(slide.style.left) + jump;
                if (x >= w1 - w2 && x <= 0) {
                    slide.style.left = x + "px";
                    timer = setTimeout(arguments.callee, 15);
                } else if (x < w1 - w2) {
                    slide.style.left = w1 - w2 + "px";
                } else {
                    slide.style.left = "0px";
                }
            }

            function release(e) {
                clearTimeout(timer);
                removeListener(document, "mouseup", release, true);
            }
        }
    })(elements[i]);
    }
}
```

Now let's test our revision. Save ten.js, refresh ten.html in Firefox, and press down on the right arrow until a few images scroll by. Then let go. Did the gallery stop on a dime? Great.

Now press down again on the right arrow, move your mouse off of the arrow, and let go. Did it work that way too?

This is pretty good as it is. But it won't take but a moment for us to have the gallery stop scrolling whenever a visitor moves their mouse off the arrow without previously letting up on their mouse. Just duplicate the addListener() and removeListener() calls, changing just the second parameter from "mouseup" to "mouseout" like so:

```
function prepScrollers() {
    var elements = findClass("scroller");
    for (var i = elements.length; i --; ) {
```

```
(function (scroller) {
  var wrapper = findClass("wrapper", scroller)[0];
  var slide = findClass("slide", scroller)[0];
  var w1 = parseInt(queryCascade(wrapper, "width"));
  var w2 = parseInt(queryCascade(slide, "width"));
  var timer = null;
  slide.style.left = queryCascade(slide, "left");
  for (var arrows = findClass("arrow", scroller), i = arrows.length, re = /\bright\b/; i -
-; ) {
    addListener(arrows[i], "mousedown", press);
    arrows[i].jump = (re.test(arrows[i].className)) ? -10 : 10;
  }

  function press(e) {
    if (!e) e = window.event;
    if (!e.target) e.target = e.srcElement;
    addListener(document, "mouseup", release, true);
    addListener(document, "mouseout", release, true);
    var jump = e.target.jump;
    animate();
    burst(e);
    thwart(e);

    function animate() {
      var x = parseInt(slide.style.left) + jump;
      if (x >= w1 - w2 && x <= 0) {
        slide.style.left = x + "px";
        timer = setTimeout(arguments.callee, 15);
      } else if (x < w1 - w2) {
        slide.style.left = w1 - w2 + "px";
      } else {
        slide.style.left = "0px";
      }
    }

    function release(e) {
      clearTimeout(timer);
      removeListener(document, "mouseup", release, true);
      removeListener(document, "mouseout", release, true);
    }
  }
})(elements[i]);
  }
}
```

Now save ten.js, refresh ten.html in Firefox, and press on the right arrow. Then after a few images scroll by, move your mouse off the right arrow without letting go of your mouse button. Did the animation halt nonetheless, just like we wanted? For me, too.

The gallery is good to go. Now let's fix those screwy sprites.

Swapping Sprites by ID or Class

Oftentimes a number of elements will share the same parts of a sprite. In an e-commerce site, for example, every Add to Cart link would share the same off and over image. If you have several JavaScript scrollers on a page, the same thing goes for the arrow sprites.

One way to fix this would be to give each element a unique ID, say add_to_cart_01 through add_to_cart_72. In addition to being error prone and inefficient, that would be fairly ridiculous.

Numbering ID values won't do. However, swapping sprites by class would be quite elegant. Identically styled elements typically are of the same class. So, swapping their sprites by class makes a good deal of sense.

That's what we'll do then. It's pretty simple to modify prepSprites() and swapSprites(). In the var bit of the for loop, declare a member variable. Then in the beginning of the for block, initialize member to id or className by way of the || operator. If id contains "", which is falsey, the || returns the value of the class attribute, which is a string. For our arrows, that would be "left arrow sprite" or "right arrow sprite". Insofar as an object member may be named with any string, including "", we'll next name a member in sprites with one of those two class strings, but only if sprites does not already have a member member. In that event, we'll calculate offsets just like in Chapter 9 except that we need to replace sprites[elements[i].id] with sprites[member] inasmuch as members are not necessarily named by ID anymore. So, there are four replacements in the DOM version and three in the Internet Explorer version:

```
var prepSprites = window.getComputedStyle ?
  function () {
    var elements = findClass("sprite"), sprites = {};
    for (var i = elements.length, offsets = null, member; i --; ) {
      member = elements[i].id || elements[i].className;
      if (! sprites[member]) {
        sprites[member] = [];
        sprites[member][0] = queryCascade(elements[i], "backgroundPosition");
        offsets = sprites[member][0].split(/\s+/);

        sprites[member][1] = 1 - parseInt(queryCascade(elements[i], "width")) + "px " +
offsets[1];

      }
      addListener(elements[i], "mouseover", slideSprite);
      addListener(elements[i], "mouseout", slideSprite);
    }
    function slideSprite(e) {
      if (e.type == "mouseover") {
        e.target.style.backgroundPosition = sprites[e.target.id][1];
      } else {
        e.target.style.backgroundPosition = sprites[e.target.id][0];
      }
    }
  } :
  function () {
    var elements = findClass("sprite"), sprites = {};
    for (var i = elements.length, offsets = null, member; i --; ) {
      member = elements[i].id || elements[i].className;
      if (! sprites[member]) {
        sprites[member] = [];

        offsets = [queryCascade(elements[i], "backgroundPositionX"), queryCascade(elements[i],
"backgroundPositionY")];
```

```
          sprites[member][0] = offsets.join(" ");
          sprites[member][1] = 1 - parseInt(queryCascade(elements[i], "width")) + "px " +
offsets[1];
        }
      addListener(elements[i], "mouseover", slideSprite);
      addListener(elements[i], "mouseout", slideSprite);
    }
    function slideSprite() {
      var e = window.event;
      if (e.type == "mouseover") {
        e.srcElement.style.backgroundPosition = sprites[e.srcElement.id][1];
      } else {
        e.srcElement.style.backgroundPosition = sprites[e.srcElement.id][0];
      }
    }
  } ;
```

Why didn't we put the addListener() invocations in the if block, too? Regardless of whether we save off and over offsets for a sprite, we still want it to have a sprite-swapping behavior. For example, if you have three scrollers on a page, as we will by the end of the day, you want all three left arrows to run slideSprite() for mouseover and mouseout events. However, if we were to put the addListener() invocations in the if block, only one pair of arrows would run slideSprite() for mouseover and mouseout events.

Hmm. I don't like the sound of that either.

Now in the DOM version of slideSprite(), replace e.target.id with e.target.id || e.target.className in two places. That way, if id contains "", then JavaScript will query sprites by the string in className. Similarly renovate the Internet Explorer version, replacing e.srcElement.id with e.srcElement.id || e.srcElement.className, and you're done:

```
var prepSprites = window.getComputedStyle ?
  function () {
    var elements = findClass("sprite"), sprites = {};
    for (var i = elements.length, offsets = null, member; i --; ) {
      member = elements[i].id || elements[i].className;
      if (! sprites[member]) {
        sprites[member] = [];
        sprites[member][0] = queryCascade(elements[i], "backgroundPosition");
        offsets = sprites[member][0].split(/\s+/);
        sprites[member][1] = 1 - parseInt(queryCascade(elements[i], "width")) + "px " +
offsets[1];
      }
      addListener(elements[i], "mouseover", slideSprite);
      addListener(elements[i], "mouseout", slideSprite);
    }
    function slideSprite(e) {
      if (e.type == "mouseover") {

        e.target.style.backgroundPosition = sprites[e.target.id || e.target.className][1];

      } else {
        e.target.style.backgroundPosition = sprites[e.target.id || e.target.className][0];
      }
    }
```

```
  } :
  function () {
    var elements = findClass("sprite"), sprites = {};
    for (var i = elements.length, offsets = null, member; i --; ) {
      member = elements[i].id || elements[i].className;
      if (! sprites[member]) {
        sprites[member] = [];
        offsets = [queryCascade(elements[i], "backgroundPositionX"), queryCascade(elements[i],
"backgroundPositionY")];
        sprites[member][0] = offsets.join(" ");
        sprites[member][1] = 1 - parseInt(queryCascade(elements[i], "width")) + "px " +
offsets[1];
      }
      addListener(elements[i], "mouseover", slideSprite);
      addListener(elements[i], "mouseout", slideSprite);
    }
    function slideSprite() {
      var e = window.event;
      if (e.type == "mouseover") {
        e.srcElement.style.backgroundPosition = sprites[e.srcElement.id ||
e.srcElement.className][1];
      } else {
        e.srcElement.style.backgroundPosition = sprites[e.srcElement.id ||
e.srcElement.className][0];
      }
    }
  } ;
```

Save ten.js, refresh ten.html in Firefox, and put the arrows, which are swapped by class, and the running links, which are swapped by ID, through the wringer. Verify your work with Figure 10–2.

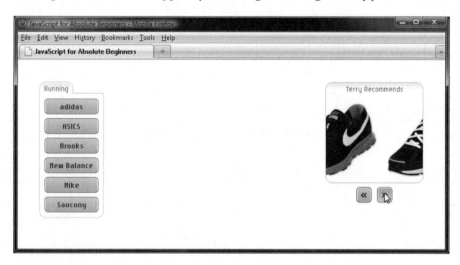

Figure 10–2. The scroller works fine, now.

Everything work fine now? Great, now on to scripting HTTP.

Writing Dynamic Pages Using Ajax

Now we come to Asynchronous JavaScript and XML (Ajax), which has had a lot of prominence over the last few years. It's a great way to add dynamic features to your web pages to make them more responsive and user friendly. Traditionally, web pages were a static lump of HTML that was delivered from the web server to the web browser; when a user interacted with the UI in any way, details of their action was sent back to the server, and a new lump of HTML was returned, even if that meant there was only a small change to make to the web page (just consider all that data and time spent waiting for not very much).

You can already see how JavaScript can help here, because actions such as button clicks and mouse over events can be handled by the browser without it having to contact the web server. In other words, user interaction can be captured by the browser without having to involve the server at all (just recall all the examples where we displayed new text on a web page without a web server being involved). However, this isn't always quite what we want. Sometimes we want to get data from a web server in response to the user's actions and display it using the JavaScript techniques we've already learned, without disturbing any content that doesn't need to change. This can certainly make a web page much more responsive and user-friendly, because there is no page refresh needed and only the data we need to send is sent.

This in essence is Ajax: updating a web page following an event, without waiting for the server to send a lump of HTML to replace the entire web page. The user can continue to view the page while JavaScript and the web server are passing data around in the background (that's the asynchronous bit in Ajax). The XML bit of Ajax is the data exchange format; it's not always XML as we'll see here, but XML is commonly used. The secret ingredient to all this is the XMLHttpRequest (XHR) object in BOM. It handles all the behind-the-scenes calls to the web server and passes any data returned to your JavaScript.

So, let's get on with it. Open ten.html in your text editor, the one you are coding ten.js in, and then delete the `<div class="scroller" id="s1">` element and all its descendents. Don't worry, we'll be adding some new scrollers with Ajax. Now our markup looks like so:

```
<!DOCTYPE html PUBLIC "-//W3C//DTD XHTML 1.0 Strict//EN"
"http://www.w3.org/TR/xhtml1/DTD/xhtml1-strict.dtd">
<html xmlns="http://www.w3.org/1999/xhtml">
<head>
<meta http-equiv="Content-Type" content="text/html; charset=utf-8" />
<title>Getting StartED with JavaScript</title>
<link rel="stylesheet" type="text/css" href="ten.css" />
<link rel="stylesheet" type="text/css" href="blue.css" id="skin" />
</head>
<body>
<div id="running">
  <h4 class="drag">Running</h4>
  <ul>
    <li><a class="sprite" id="adidas" href="http://www.adidas.com">adidas</a></li>
    <li><a class="sprite" id="asics" href="http://www.asics.com">ASICS</a></li>
    <li><a class="sprite" id="brooks" href="http://www.brooksrunning.com">Brooks</a></li>
    <li><a class="sprite" id="newBalance" href="http://www.newbalance.com">New
Balance</a></li>
    <li><a class="sprite" id="nike" href="http://www.nike.com">Nike</a></li>
    <li><a class="sprite" id="saucony" href="http://www.saucony.com">Saucony</a></li>
  </ul>
</div>
<script src="ten.js" type="text/javascript"></script>
</body>
</html>
```

Testing XMLHttpRequest from Your Local File System

One very important thing to note before we begin scripting HTTP with an XMLHttpRequest object is that it works with the HTTP protocol. So, file URLs must begin with `http://`, not `file://`. This means you must test an Ajax script on a web server, not your local file system, which is to say your computer. In Internet Explorer, anyway. On the other hand, Firefox, Safari, and Opera relax this restriction and let you load URLs with either the `http://` or `file://` protocol.

What this means is that you can test the Ajax part of this script on your computer in Firefox, Safari, and Opera, but not in Internet Explorer. Of course, on a web server you can test the script in Internet Explorer, Firefox, Safari, and Opera.

Creating Tree Branches with createElem()

One helper function we'll need for the job is `createElem()`, which we wrote in Chapter 7 to simplify creating branches of the DOM tree. The code for `createElem()` is listed here. Put it with the other helper functions in `ten.js`.

```
function createElem(name, members, children) {
  var elem = document.createElement(name), m;
  if (members instanceof Object) {
    for (m in members) {
      elem[m] = members[m];
    }
  }
  if (children instanceof Array) {
    for (i = 0; i < children.length; i ++ ) {
      elem.appendChild(typeof children[i] === "object" ? children[i] :
document.createTextNode(children[i]));
    }
  }
  return elem;
}
```

Now we're going to conditionally define a helper function named `createXHR()`, which will create an XMLHttpRequest object by way of the `XMLHttpRequest()` constructor in Firefox, Safari, Opera, and Internet Explorer 7 or greater, and by way of the `ActiveXObject()` constructor in Internet Explorer 5 or 6. Note that the XMLHttpRequest object returned by `XMLHttpRequest()` and `ActiveXObject()` works the same.

Okeydokey, declare `createXHR`, initializing its value to `null`. Recall from Chapter 1 that `null` is preferable to `undefined` for representing no value on the heap, which is where function values are saved. So, right beneath `createElem()`, we write the following:

```
var createXHR = null;
```

Now if the identifier `XMLHttpRequest` is defined, we'll overwrite `null` with a function literal that creates an XMLHttpRequest object with the `XMLHttpRequest()` constructor. Because Internet Explorer and Safari return `"object"` for `typeof XMLHttpRequest`, but Firefox and Opera return `"function"`, we'll avoid their disagreement like so:

```
var createXHR = null;
if (typeof XMLHttpRequest !== "undefined") {
  createXHR = function() {
    return new XMLHttpRequest();
  };
}
```

Now the waters muddy considerably. To create an XMLHttpRequest object in Internet Explorer 5 or 6, we have to pass a program id to the ActiveXObject() constructor. During the ten years Internet Explorer 5 and 6 were in active development, Microsoft released several of those. So in an array named versions, let's save four of the most common, ordered newest to oldest:

```
var createXHR = null;
if (typeof XMLHttpRequest !== "undefined") {
  createXHR = function() {
    return new XMLHttpRequest();
  };
} else if (typeof ActiveXObject !== "undefined") {
  var versions = ["MSXML2.XMLHTTP.6.0", "MSXML2.XMLHTTP.3.0", "MSXML2.XMLHTTP",
"Microsoft.XMLHTTP"];
}
```

To figure out the newest program ID a visitor's copy of Internet Explorer supports, we'll loop through versions. Within a try block, we'll then attempt to create an XMLHttpRequest object with the program ID in versions[i]. In the event doing so does not throw an error, we'll save that program ID to version, which we initialized to "" prior to the first roundabout, and then terminate the for loop with a break statement.

Note that the empty catch block prevents an error from propagating to the nearest containing catch block. So by analogy, JavaScript errors bubble upward through a script just like events bubble upward through the DOM. Therefore, a catch clause squishes an error object in the same way that burst() squishes an event object. Note too that try must be followed by a catch or finally clause. So, our empty catch block prevents a syntax error, too.

```
var createXHR = null;
if (typeof XMLHttpRequest !== "undefined") {
  createXHR = function() {
    return new XMLHttpRequest();
  };
} else if (typeof ActiveXObject !== "undefined") {
  var versions = ["MSXML2.XMLHTTP.6.0", "MSXML2.XMLHTTP.3.0", "MSXML2.XMLHTTP",
"Microsoft.XMLHTTP"];

  for (var i = 0, j = versions.length, version = ""; i < j; i ++) {

    try {
      new ActiveXObject(versions[i]);
      version = versions[i];
      break;
    }
    catch(e) {
    }
  }
}
```

If version does not contain its initial value (the "" empty string), then overwrite null with a function literal that returns an XMLHttpRequest object by passing the program ID in version to ActiveXObject(). So final code for the createXHR() advance conditional loader would be:

```
var createXHR = null;
if (typeof XMLHttpRequest !== "undefined") {
  createXHR = function() {
    return new XMLHttpRequest();
  };
} else if (typeof ActiveXObject !== "undefined") {
  var versions = ["MSXML2.XMLHTTP.6.0", "MSXML2.XMLHTTP.3.0", "MSXML2.XMLHTTP",
"Microsoft.XMLHTTP"];
  for (var i = 0, j = versions.length, version = ""; i < j; i ++) {
    try {
      new ActiveXObject(versions[i]);
      version = versions[i];
      break;
    }
    catch(e) {
    }
  }
  if (version !== "") {
    createXHR = function() {
      return new ActiveXObject(version);
    };
  }
}
```

Asynchronously Requesting Data

Now that we can create an XMLHttpRequest object with the XMLHttpRequest() or ActiveXObject() constructor, we'll write a helper function named getData() to asynchronously request (GET) any kind of data with. Typically, an XMLHttpRequest object is used to fetch JSON or XML. Occasionally, you will want to fetch XHTML or plain text, too. Regardless, getData() can do the job.

getData() works with two parameters:

- url is the URL of the data to fetch.

- callback is a function to pass the XMLHttpRequest object containing the data to.

```
function getData(url, callback) {
}
```

Now we want to ensure createXHR was conditionally defined; that is, it does not still contain null, which would indicate the visitor has a browser from the Pleistocene epoch—a dark time predating any version of Firefox, Safari, or Opera, and version 5 or greater of Internet Explorer.

```
function getData(url, callback) {
  if (createXHR !== null) {
  }
}
```

Now we need to do four things. First, create an XMLHttpRequest object. Just call createXHR(), saving the return value to a local variable named req:

```
function getData(url, callback) {
  if (createXHR !== null) {
    var req = createXHR();
```

```
  }
}
```

Second, define a readystatechange event listener for JavaScript to call whenever the number in XMLHttpRequest.readyState changes from 0 to 1 to 2 to 3 and finally to 4. More what those numbers mean in a bit.

Our readystatechange event listener will do nothing, which is to say simply return undefined, whenever readyState changes to 1, 2, or 3. But when it changes to 4, which indicates the GET request is done, we'll pass the XMLHttpRequest object to the callback function. Note that 4 means the GET request is done but not that we have the data in url. For example, if we mistyped url, the server returns a 404 "File not found" HTTP status code. But that's for the callback function to worry about. Our readystatechange event listener looks like so:

```
function getData(url, callback) {
  if (createXHR !== null) {
    var req = createXHR();
    req.onreadystatechange = function() {
      if (req.readyState === 4) {
        callback(req);
      }
    }
  }
}
```

Note that unlike event listeners bound to nodes in the DOM tree, a readystatechange event listener does not work with an event object. There's no e parameter. Note too that we bind the listener to XMLHttpRequest.onreadystatechange instead of doing so by calling our helper function addListener(). This is the DOM 0 way of binding events. Note that DOM 0, like BOM, is not a standard, which is why we did not explore binding events this way in Chapter 9. Since you are a clean slate, I didn't want to encourage bad habits. However, for binding a readystatechange event cross-browser, we have to resign ourselves to DOM 0. Just don't be doing this for DOM tree events, or I'd be most unhappy.

The third thing we need to do is clue JavaScript in to the details of the GET request. To do so, we'll pass the XMLHttpRequest.open() method three parameters:

- The first one is a string for the type of HTTP request, typically GET or POST, to do.

- The second one is a string for the URL to request. Note that the URL is relative to the page (ten.html in our case) making the request.

- The third parameter is a boolean indicating whether to do an asynchronous request (true) or a synchronous request (false). More plainly, true means do not freeze the browser until the HTTP request is done, and false means go right ahead and freeze the browser. Note that the default is true.

```
function getData(url, callback) {
  if (createXHR !== null) {
    var req = createXHR();
    req.onreadystatechange = function() {
      if (req.readyState === 4) {
        callback(req);
      }
    }
    req.open("GET", url, true);
  }
}
```

Calling open() prepares an HTTP request to be sent but doesn't send it. So, there's a fourth step to do—call XMLHttpRequest.send(). This method takes one parameter: null for a GET request and a query string like "sport=running&brand=Nike&shoe=LunaRacer" for a POST request. Note that for a synchronous request, JavaScript blocks until send() returns. So, this is why asynchronous requests are preferred. We don't want to freeze the visitor's browser, right?

Anyway, we're done coding getData(), which looks like so:

```
function getData(url, callback) {
  if (createXHR !== null) {
    var req = createXHR();
    req.onreadystatechange = function() {
      if (req.readyState === 4) {
        callback(req);
      }
    }
    req.open("GET", url, true);
    req.send(null);
  }
}
```

Before moving on, let's recap what the readyState numbers mean, since the details are now comprehensible to you:

- 0—A new XMLHttpRequest object has been created by calling XMLHttpRequest() or ActiveXObject(). Insofar as 0 is the initial value for readyState, the readystatechange event listener is not invoked.

- 1—XMLHttpRequest.open() has been called.

- 2—XMLHttpRequest.send() has been called. For things to work cross-browser, you need to bind the readystatechange event listener prior to calling open() and send().

- 3—HTTP response headers have been received and the body is beginning to load. Note that if the XHR was created by passing "MSXML2.XMLHTTP.3.0", "MSXML2.XMLHTTP", or "Microsoft.XMLHTTP" to ActiveXObject(), the readystatechange event listener is not invoked.

- 4—The response is complete, so if the HTTP status code is 200 "OK" or 304 "Not modified," there's data for the callback to add to the page.

Parsing an HTML Response

The first callback function will parse the HTML markup in data/s2.html, shown here. It contains the slide <ul>:

```
<ul class="slide">
  <li><a href="ten.html"><img alt="Nike LunaRacer" src="images/lunaracer.jpg" /></a></li>
  <li><a href="ten.html"><img alt="Nike Lunar Glide, Boston" src="images/glide_bos.jpg"
/></a></li>
  <li><a href="ten.html"><img alt="Nike Lunar Glide, NYC" src="images/glide_nyc.jpg"
/></a></li>
  <li><a href="ten.html"><img alt="Nike Mariah" src="images/mariah.jpg" /></a></li>
  <li><a href="ten.html"><img alt="Nike Lunar Fly, Orange" src="images/fly_org.jpg"
/></a></li>
```

```
    <li><a href="ten.html"><img alt="Nike Lunar Fly, Black" src="images/fly_blk.jpg" /></a></li>
    <li><a href="ten.html"><img alt="Nike Lunar Elite" src="images/elite.jpg" /></a></li>
    <li><a href="ten.html"><img alt="Nike Zoom Vomero" src="images/vomero.jpg" /></a></li>
    <li><a href="ten.html"><img alt="Nike Air Max" src="images/max.jpg" /></a></li>
</ul>
```

However, we receive this as a string:

```
"<ul class="slide">
    <li><a href="ten.html"><img alt="Nike LunaRacer" src="images/lunaracer.jpg" /></a></li>
    <li><a href="ten.html"><img alt="Nike Lunar Glide, Boston" src="images/glide_bos.jpg"
/></a></li>
    <li><a href="ten.html"><img alt="Nike Lunar Glide, NYC" src="images/glide_nyc.jpg"
/></a></li>
    <li><a href="ten.html"><img alt="Nike Mariah" src="images/mariah.jpg" /></a></li>
    <li><a href="ten.html"><img alt="Nike Lunar Fly, Orange" src="images/fly_org.jpg"
/></a></li>
    <li><a href="ten.html"><img alt="Nike Lunar Fly, Black" src="images/fly_blk.jpg" /></a></li>
    <li><a href="ten.html"><img alt="Nike Lunar Elite" src="images/elite.jpg" /></a></li>
    <li><a href="ten.html"><img alt="Nike Zoom Vomero" src="images/vomero.jpg" /></a></li>
    <li><a href="ten.html"><img alt="Nike Air Max" src="images/max.jpg" /></a></li>
</ul>"
```

So, we're going to have to write a function to search through the string and create the `<ul>`, `<li>`, `<a>`, and `<img>` Element nodes before we can place them on the page, making sure of course to get the nesting right.

Because this is the final chapter in the book, you probably can roll a helper function to do the job by yourself. So I'll leave that, as they say, as an exercise for the reader.

Just kidding. You'd likely gnaw off a finger or two in frustration trying to code that.

It'd be pretty dull to explain, too. Turns out, I won't have to.

Internet Explorer 4 gave every `Element` node a proprietary `innerHTML` member. If you assign a string to `innerHTML`, JavaScript parses it into HTML and then replaces all descendents of the `Element` node with that DOM branch. That may be draconian, but it's practical, too. It's so much so that Firefox, Safari, and Opera have always implemented `innerHTML`, even though it's not part of any DOM standard.

Anyway, `innerHTML` is totally perfect for parsing an HTML response, quietly converting it from a string value to a branch of the DOM tree. I guess we'll use it then.

Here's how: `XMLHttpRequest.responseText` contains the string equivalent of the HTML in `data/s2.html`. `parseHTML()` will assign that to `innerHTML` for `<div class="wrapper">`. However, we're going to need to create that and the other elements of the scroller first with our helper function, `createElem()`—but only if we received `data/s2.html` all right from the server or browser cache. To make sure of that we test whether `XMLHttpRequest.status` is 200 (received `data/s2.html` from the server) or 304 (received `data/s2.html` from the cache).

With all those details spilling out of mind, let's begin coding `parseHTML()` like so. Note that the `req` parameter will contain the `XMLHttpRequest` object passed in by `getData()` when `XMLHttpRequest.readyState` changes to 4:

```
function parseHTML(req) {
  if (req.status === 200 || req.status === 304) {
  }
}
```

Note that if you are testing this script on your computer, which is to say loading URLs with the `file://` protocol, there obviously will not be an `http://` status code. So, `XMLHttpRequest.status` will always be 0, no matter what. With this in mind, if you are testing the script on your computer, you must replace 200 or 304 with 0. Otherwise, the `if` block will never run!

```
function parseHTML(req) {
  if (req.status === 0 || req.status === 304) {
  }
}
```

Within the block of the if conditional, we then want to create the HTML for the scroller, less <ul class="slide">, by calling createElem() like so.

```
function parseHTML(req) {
  if (req.status === 200 || req.status === 304) {
    var div = createElem("div", {className: "scroller", id: "s2"}, [
      createElem("div", {className: "wrapper"}),
      createElem("div", {className: "left arrow sprite"}),

      createElem("div", {className: "right arrow sprite"})]);

  }
}
```

Doing so creates the following DOM branch in memory:

```
<div class="scroller" id="s2">
  <div class="wrapper">
  </div>
  <div class="left arrow sprite"></div>
  <div class="right arrow sprite"></div>
</div>
```

Now we want to parse the string of text in XMLHttpRequest.responseText into HTML. Then attach that branch to the DOM tree limb, <div class="wrapper">, which we refer to as div.firstChild. One simple assignment to innerHTML does that all in one fell swoop:

```
function parseHTML(req) {
  if (req.status === 200 || req.status === 304) {
    var div = createElem("div", {className: "scroller", id: "s2"}, [
      createElem("div", {className: "wrapper"}),
      createElem("div", {className: "left arrow sprite"}),
      createElem("div", {className: "right arrow sprite"})]);
    div.firstChild.innerHTML = req.responseText;
  }
}
```

I've given Internet Explorer some grief in this book. Deservedly so, too. However, innerHTML is a good idea. I wish it were added to the DOM standard.

Enough with the compliments. The local variable <div> now contains the following HTML:

```
<div class="scroller" id="s2">
  <div class="wrapper">
    <ul class="slide">
      <li><a href="ten.html"><img alt="Nike LunaRacer" src="images/lunaracer.jpg" /></a></li>
      <li><a href="ten.html"><img alt="Nike Lunar Glide, Boston" src="images/glide_bos.jpg"
/></a></li>
      <li><a href="ten.html"><img alt="Nike Lunar Glide, NYC" src="images/glide_nyc.jpg"
/></a></li>
      <li><a href="ten.html"><img alt="Nike Mariah" src="images/mariah.jpg" /></a></li>
      <li><a href="ten.html"><img alt="Nike Lunar Fly, Orange" src="images/fly_org.jpg"
/></a></li>
```

```
        <li><a href="ten.html"><img alt="Nike Lunar Fly, Black" src="images/fly_blk.jpg"
/></a></li>
        <li><a href="ten.html"><img alt="Nike Lunar Elite" src="images/elite.jpg" /></a></li>
        <li><a href="ten.html"><img alt="Nike Zoom Vomero" src="images/vomero.jpg" /></a></li>
        <li><a href="ten.html"><img alt="Nike Air Max" src="images/max.jpg" /></a></li>
      </ul>
    </div>
  <div class="left arrow sprite"></div>
  <div class="right arrow sprite"></div>
</div>
```

The only problem is it's floating around in memory, totally invisible to visitors. So, we want to insert it into the DOM tree with appendChild(), a method we covered in Chapter 7:

```
function parseHTML(req) {
  if (req.status === 200 || req.status === 304) {
    var div = createElem("div", {className: "scroller", id: "s2"}, [
      createElem("div", {className: "wrapper"}),
      createElem("div", {className: "left arrow sprite"}),
      createElem("div", {className: "right arrow sprite"})]);
    div.firstChild.innerHTML = req.responseText;
    document.body.appendChild(div);
  }
}
```

Regardless of the HTTP status code for our GET request for data/s2.html, we want to call a function named prep(), which will replace the function literal we currently have for the load event. That way, if we get an undesirable status code, say a 404 "Not found" for mistyping the URL, prep() will still run, adding the drag and drop, sprite, and other behaviors elements on our page.

```
function parseHTML(req) {
  if (req.status === 200 || req.status === 304) {
    var div = createElem("div", {className: "scroller", id: "s2"}, [
      createElem("div", {className: "wrapper"}),
      createElem("div", {className: "left arrow sprite"}),
      createElem("div", {className: "right arrow sprite"})]);
    div.firstChild.innerHTML = req.responseText;
    document.body.appendChild(div);
  }
  prep();
}
```

Underneath parseHTML(), define a function named prep(). In its body, call prepSprites(), prepDrag(), prepSkinKeys(), and prepScrollers(). Finally, in the body of the load event listener, which now contains just a call to presetSkin(), append a call to getData() to fetch data/s2.html. Our script now ends like so:

```
function prep() {
  prepSprites();
  prepDrag();
  prepSkinKeys();
  prepScrollers();
}
addListener(window, "load", function(e) {
    presetSkin();
    getData("data/s2.html", parseHTML);
```

```
});
```

Why bother making those changes? Wouldn't adding a call to getData() to the old load event listener, say like in the following code, work just as well?

```
addListener(window, "load", function(e) {
    presetSkin();
    getData("data/s2.html", parseHTML);
    prepSprites();
    prepDrag();
    prepSkinKeys();
    prepScrollers();
});
```

Well no, it wouldn't. Because we requested data/s2.html asynchronously, JavaScript does not block until data/s2.html has loaded. That is to say, prepSprites() and prepScrollers() would very likely run before parseHTML() added the new scroller to the page. Therefore, pressing on the arrows for the new scroller would do nothing whatsoever.

That would be bad, so let's add the prep() function, save ten.js, and reload ten.html in Firefox. Put the new scroller through the wringer, verifying you work with Figure 10–3.

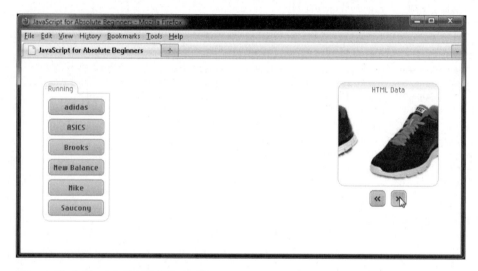

Figure 10–3. Testing the HTML scroller

Parsing an XML Response

For the first few years, XML was the preferred data exchange format for Ajax. Although JSON (which we will cover in a bit) has overtaken XML in popularity, you will likely need to work with XML for years to come.

With this in mind, let's write a function named parseXML() to parse the contents of the XML file, data/s3.xml, code for which appears in this section. This is the data from the original ten.html, marked up as data:

```
<?xml version="1.0" encoding="utf-8"?>
<gallery>
```

```
   <shoe>
     <href>ten.html</href>
     <src>images/lunaracer.jpg</src>
     <alt>Nike LunaRacer</alt>
   </shoe>
   <shoe>
     <href>ten.html</href>
     <src>images/glide_bos.jpg</src>
     <alt>Nike Lunar Glide, Boston</alt>
   </shoe>
   <shoe>
     <href>ten.html</href>
     <src>images/glide_nyc.jpg</src>
     <alt>Nike Lunar Gllide, NYC</alt>
   </shoe>
   <shoe>
     <href>ten.html</href>
     <src>images/mariah.jpg</src>
     <alt>Nike Mariah</alt>
   </shoe>
   <shoe>
     <href>ten.html</href>
     <src>images/fly_org.jpg</src>
     <alt>Nike Lunar Fly, Orange</alt>
   </shoe>
   <shoe>
     <href>ten.html</href>
     <src>images/fly_blk.jpg</src>
     <alt>Nike Lunar Fly, Black</alt>
   </shoe>
   <shoe>
     <href>ten.html</href>
     <src>images/elite.jpg</src>
     <alt>Nike Lunar Elite</alt>
   </shoe>
   <shoe>
     <href>ten.html</href>
     <src>images/vomero.jpg</src>
     <alt>Nike Zoom Vomero</alt>
   </shoe>
   <shoe>
     <href>ten.html</href>
     <src>images/max.jpg</src>
     <alt>Nike Air Max</alt>
   </shoe>
</gallery>
```

We'll use this data in a second scroller below the one we created in the previous example. The first thing we need to do is move the prep() invocation from parseHTML() to parseXML(), replacing it with a call to getData() for data/s3.xml. Doing so ensures the two new scrollers are in the DOM tree prior to JavaScript running prepSprites() and prepScrollers().

```
function parseHTML(req) {
  if (req.status === 200 || req.status === 304) {
```

```
    var div = createElem("div", {className: "scroller", id: "s2"}, [
      createElem("div", {className: "wrapper"}),
      createElem("div", {className: "left arrow sprite"}),
      createElem("div", {className: "right arrow sprite"})]);
    div.firstChild.innerHTML = req.responseText;
    document.body.appendChild(div);
  }
  getData("data/s3.xml", parseXML);
}
function parseXML(req) {
  prep();
}
```

An XML response differs from an HTML one in that it is a `Document` node containing `Element` and `Text` nodes rather than a string of plain text. So you query XML data the same way as a DOM tree. Yup, with the methods we covered in Chapter 7.

So as you might guess, the DOM tree representing `data/s3.xml` isn't in `XMLHttpRequest.responseText`. That value is a string not an object. Rather, the DOM tree for our XML is in `XMLHttpRequest.responseXML`. So after we make sure `XMLHttpRequest.status` is either 200 or 304, same as we did for HTML, we'll save the DOM tree for our XML to a local variable named `domTree`.

```
function parseXML(req) {
  if (req.status === 200 || req.status === 304) {
    var domTree = req.responseXML;
  }
  prep();
}
```

Note that if you are testing this script on your computer, which is to say loading URLs with the `file://` protocol, there obviously will not be an `http://` status code. So `XMLHttpRequest.status` will always be 0, no matter what. With this in mind, if you are testing the script on your computer, you must replace 200 or 304 with 0. Otherwise, the `if` block will never run!

```
function parseXML(req) {
  if (req.status === 0 || req.status === 304) {
    var domTree = req.responseXML;
  }
  prep();
}
```

Now we want to save the nine `<shoe>` `Element` nodes to a local variable named `elements`. Fetch those as if they were `<div>` or `<li>` elements—with `Document.getElementsByTagName()`, which we covered in Chapter 7:

```
function parseXML(req) {
  if (req.status === 200 || req.status === 304) {
    var domTree = req.responseXML;
    var elements = domTree.getElementsByTagName("shoe");
  }
  prep();
}
```

Now for any of those `<shoe>` elements, we can query the `Text` node in a child `<href>` like so:

```
elements[i].getElementsByTagName("href")[0].firstChild.data
```

Same thing works for a child <src> or <alt>:

```
elements[i].getElementsByTagName("src")[0].firstChild.data
elements[i].getElementsByTagName("alt")[0].firstChild.data
```

With this in mind, we can cobble together a scroller with our helper function, createElem(), like so:

```
function parseXML(req) {
  if (req.status === 200 || req.status === 304) {
    var domTree = req.responseXML;
    var elements = domTree.getElementsByTagName("shoe");
    var div, ul = createElem("ul", {className: "slide"}), li;
    for (var i = 0, j = elements.length; i < j; i ++) {
      li = createElem("li", null, [
        createElem("a", {href: elements[i].getElementsByTagName("href")[0].firstChild.data}, [
        createElem("img", {src: elements[i].getElementsByTagName("src")[0].firstChild.data,
          alt: elements[i].getElementsByTagName("alt")[0].firstChild.data})])]);
      ul.appendChild(li);
    }
    div = createElem("div", {className: "scroller", id: "s3"}, [
      createElem("div", {className: "wrapper"}, [ul]),
      createElem("div", {className: "left arrow sprite"}),
      createElem("div", {className: "right arrow sprite"})]);
  }
  prep();
}
```

Now the local variable <div> contains the following DOM branch:

```
<div class="scroller" id="s3">
  <div class="wrapper">
    <ul class="slide">
      <li><a href="ten.html"><img alt="Nike LunaRacer" src="images/lunaracer.jpg" /></a></li>
      <li><a href="ten.html"><img alt="Nike Lunar Glide, Boston" src="images/glide_bos.jpg"
/></a></li>
      <li><a href="ten.html"><img alt="Nike Lunar Glide, NYC" src="images/glide_nyc.jpg"
/></a></li>
      <li><a href="ten.html"><img alt="Nike Mariah" src="images/mariah.jpg" /></a></li>
      <li><a href="ten.html"><img alt="Nike Lunar Fly, Orange" src="images/fly_org.jpg"
/></a></li>
      <li><a href="ten.html"><img alt="Nike Lunar Fly, Black" src="images/fly_blk.jpg"
/></a></li>
      <li><a href="ten.html"><img alt="Nike Lunar Elite" src="images/elite.jpg" /></a></li>
      <li><a href="ten.html"><img alt="Nike Zoom Vomero" src="images/vomero.jpg" /></a></li>
      <li><a href="ten.html"><img alt="Nike Air Max" src="images/max.jpg" /></a></li>
    </ul>
  </div>
  <div class="left arrow sprite"></div>
  <div class="right arrow sprite"></div>
</div>
```

But it's floating around in memory invisible to visitors. So, we need attach the DOM branch to the tree, the same way we did in parseHTML():

```
function parseXML(req) {
```

```
if (req.status === 200 || req.status === 304) {
  var domTree = req.responseXML;
  var elements = domTree.getElementsByTagName("shoe");
  var div, ul = createElem("ul", {className: "slide"}), li;
  for (var i = 0, j = elements.length; i < j; i ++) {
    li = createElem("li", null, [
      createElem("a", {href: elements[i].getElementsByTagName("href")[0].firstChild.data}, [
        createElem("img", {src: elements[i].getElementsByTagName("src")[0].firstChild.data,
          alt: elements[i].getElementsByTagName("alt")[0].firstChild.data})])]);
    ul.appendChild(li);
  }
  div = createElem("div", {className: "scroller", id: "s3"}, [
    createElem("div", {className: "wrapper"}, [ul]),
    createElem("div", {className: "left arrow sprite"}),
    createElem("div", {className: "right arrow sprite"})]);
  document.body.appendChild(div);
}
prep();
}
```

Okeydokey, save ten.js, and reload ten.html in Firefox, comparing its display to Figure 10–4:

Figure 10–4. Testing the XML scroller

Parsing Simple XML

Like HTML, XML is fairly bloated. That is to say, the ratio of data to structure (tags) is quite low. For this reason, encoding data in XML tag attributes has gained favor over doing so with child nodes. Take a peek at the XML file data/s4.xml to see what I mean by that. Compare its code, displayed here, to that of data/s3.xml. We'll put this into a third scroller.

```
<?xml version="1.0" encoding="utf-8"?>
<gallery>
  <shoe href="ten.html" src ="images/lunaracer.jpg" alt="Nike LunaRacer"></shoe>
  <shoe href="ten.html" src ="images/glide_bos.jpg" alt="Nike Lunar Glide, Boston"></shoe>
  <shoe href="ten.html" src ="images/glide_nyc.jpg" alt="Nike Lunar Glide, NYC"></shoe>
  <shoe href="ten.html" src ="images/mariah.jpg" alt="Nike Mariah"></shoe>
  <shoe href="ten.html" src ="images/fly_org.jpg" alt="Nike Lunar Fly, Orange"></shoe>
  <shoe href="ten.html" src ="images/fly_blk.jpg" alt="Nike Lunar Fly, Black"></shoe>
  <shoe href="ten.html" src ="images/elite.jpg" alt="Nike Lunar Elite"></shoe>
  <shoe href="ten.html" src ="images/vomero.jpg" alt="Nike Zoom Vomero"></shoe>
  <shoe href="ten.html" src ="images/max.jpg" alt="Nike  Air Max"></shoe>
</gallery>
```

Because XML encoded this way is referred to as Simple XML, let's name the function that will parse data/s4.xml, parseSimpleXML(). Like before, the first thing we want to do is move the prep() invocation from parseXML() to parseSimpleXML(), replacing it with a call to getData() for data/s4.xml. You know, so that the three new scrollers are in the DOM tree prior to JavaScript running prepSprites() and prepScrollers():

```
function parseXML(req) {
  if (req.status === 200 || req.status === 304) {
    var domTree = req.responseXML;
    var elements = domTree.getElementsByTagName("shoe");
    var div, ul = createElem("ul", {className: "slide"}), li;
    for (var i = 0, j = elements.length; i < j; i ++) {
      li = createElem("li", null, [
        createElem("a", {href: elements[i].getElementsByTagName("href")[0].firstChild.data}, [
          createElem("img", {src: elements[i].getElementsByTagName("src")[0].firstChild.data,
            alt: elements[i].getElementsByTagName("alt")[0].firstChild.data})])]);
      ul.appendChild(li);
    }
    div = createElem("div", {className: "scroller", id: "s3"}, [
      createElem("div", {className: "wrapper"}, [ul]),
      createElem("div", {className: "left arrow sprite"}),
      createElem("div", {className: "right arrow sprite"})]);
    document.body.appendChild(div);
  }

  getData("data/s4.xml", parseSimpleXML);

}
function parseSimpleXML(req) {
  prep();
}
```

Now what would you do next in parseSimpleXML()?

Make sure XMLHttpRequest.status is either 200 or 304, the same as we did for parseHTML() and parseXML().

```
function parseSimpleXML(req) {
  if (req.status === 200 || req.status === 304) {
  }
  prep();
}
```

Next?

Right again. Save the DOM tree for our XML to a local variable named domTree, just like we did in parseXML().

```
function parseSimpleXML(req) {
  if (req.status === 200 || req.status === 304) {
    var domTree = req.responseXML;
  }
  prep();
}
```

And now?

Yup, save the nine <shoe> elements to a local variable, the same as for parseXML().

```
function parseSimpleXML(req) {
  if (req.status === 200 || req.status === 304) {
    var domTree = req.responseXML;
    var elements = domTree.getElementsByTagName("shoe");
  }
  prep();
}
```

Note that if you are testing this script on your computer, which is to say loading URLs with the file:// protocol, there obviously will not be an http:// status code. XMLHttpRequest.status will always be 0, no matter what. With this in mind, if you are testing the script on your computer, you must replace 200 or 304 with 0. Otherwise, the if block will never run!

```
function parseSimpleXML(req) {
  if (req.status === 0 || req.status === 304) {
    var domTree = req.responseXML;
    var elements = domTree.getElementsByTagName("shoe");
  }
  prep();
}
```

Do you remember how to query a custom attribute for an element?

We can't use the . or [] operators. Rather, we need to call Element.getAttribute(), a method defined by each <shoe> element. For example, to query the href attribute, we'd write this:

```
elements[i].getAttribute("href")
```

The same thing goes for the src and alt attributes:

```
elements[i].getAttribute("src")
elements[i].getAttribute("alt")
```

Even that is less verbose than for traditional XML. Anyway, with this in mind, we can cobble together a scroller with our helper function, createElem(), like so:

```
function parseSimpleXML(req) {
  if (req.status === 200 || req.status === 304) {
    var domTree = req.responseXML;
```

```
  var elements = domTree.getElementsByTagName("shoe");
  var div, ul = createElem("ul", {className: "slide"}), li;
  for (var i = 0, j = elements.length; i < j; i ++) {
    li = createElem("li", null, [
      createElem("a", {href: elements[i].getAttribute("href")}, [
      createElem("img", {src: elements[i].getAttribute("src"), alt:
elements[i].getAttribute("alt")})])]);
    ul.appendChild(li);
  }

  div = createElem("div", {className: "scroller", id: "s4"}, [

    createElem("div", {className: "wrapper"}, [ul]),
    createElem("div", {className: "left arrow sprite"}),
    createElem("div", {className: "right arrow sprite"})]);
  }
  prep();
}
```

Now the local variable <div> contains the following DOM branch:

```
<div class="scroller" id="s4">
  <div class="wrapper">
    <ul class="slide">
      <li><a href="ten.html"><img alt="Nike LunaRacer" src="images/lunaracer.jpg" /></a></li>
      <li><a href="ten.html"><img alt="Nike Lunar Glide, Boston" src="images/glide_bos.jpg"
/></a></li>
      <li><a href="ten.html"><img alt="Nike Lunar Glide, NYC" src="images/glide_nyc.jpg"
/></a></li>
      <li><a href="ten.html"><img alt="Nike Mariah" src="images/mariah.jpg" /></a></li>
      <li><a href="ten.html"><img alt="Nike Lunar Fly, Orange" src="images/fly_org.jpg"
/></a></li>
      <li><a href="ten.html"><img alt="Nike Lunar Fly, Black" src="images/fly_blk.jpg"
/></a></li>
      <li><a href="ten.html"><img alt="Nike Lunar Elite" src="images/elite.jpg" /></a></li>
      <li><a href="ten.html"><img alt="Nike Zoom Vomero" src="images/vomero.jpg" /></a></li>
      <li><a href="ten.html"><img alt="Nike Air Max" src="images/max.jpg" /></a></li>
    </ul>
  </div>
  <div class="left arrow sprite"></div>
  <div class="right arrow sprite"></div>
</div>
```

But it's in memory, invisible to visitors. How would you fix that?
Yep, put the DOM branch on the tree:

```
function parseSimpleXML(req) {
  if (req.status === 200 || req.status === 304) {
    var domTree = req.responseXML;
    var elements = domTree.getElementsByTagName("shoe");
    var div, ul = createElem("ul", {className: "slide"}), li;
    for (var i = 0, j = elements.length; i < j; i ++) {
      li = createElem("li", null, [
```

```
            createElem("a", {href: elements[i].getAttribute("href")}, [
            createElem("img", {src: elements[i].getAttribute("src"), alt:
elements[i].getAttribute("alt")})])]);
        ul.appendChild(li);
    }
    div = createElem("div", {className: "scroller", id: "s4"}, [
        createElem("div", {className: "wrapper"}, [ul]),
        createElem("div", {className: "left arrow sprite"}),
        createElem("div", {className: "right arrow sprite"})]);
    document.body.appendChild(div);
  }
  prep();
}
```

It's time to give parseSimpleXML() a whirl. So, save ten.js and reload ten.html in Firefox, comparing its display to Figure 10–5:

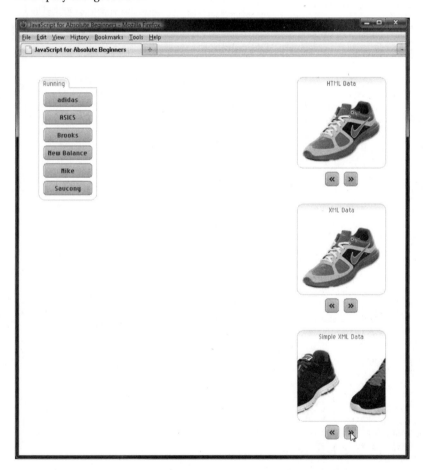

Figure 10–5. *Testing the Simple XML scroller*

Parsing JSON

More and more, XML is being supplanted by JSON, a data exchange format derived from JavaScript object and array literal syntax. JSON downloads snappy and is simple to parse. Just pass JSON data to `window.eval()`, and you have a JavaScript array or object. However, passing third-party JSON data, which may be malformed or malicious, to `eval()` is a horrible idea.

■ **Caution** The `eval()` method is a powerful and dangerous tool. You should not pass any third-party data to it, because that third-party data could well contain malicious code for your users' browsers to run. This could lead to all sorts of attacks and discomforts.

For this reason, Internet Explorer 8, Firefox 3.5, and Safari 4 define a method, `JSON.parse()`, for you to use instead of `eval()`. For other versions and browsers, download the free JSON parser maintained by Douglas Crockford, JSON's creator, from `http://json.org/json2.js`. Delete the first line:

```
alert('IMPORTANT: Remove this line from json2.js before deployment.');
```

Save the file as `json2.js` to the same directory as your other JavaScript files. Then link it in to your XHTML page. `json2.js` will define `window.JSON` only if it is missing. So for `ten.html`, we would link in `json2.js` like so:

```
<!DOCTYPE html PUBLIC "-//W3C//DTD XHTML 1.0 Strict//EN"
"http://www.w3.org/TR/xhtml1/DTD/xhtml1-strict.dtd">
<html xmlns="http://www.w3.org/1999/xhtml">
<head>
<meta http-equiv="Content-Type" content="text/html; charset=utf-8" />
<title>Getting StartED with JavaScript</title>
<link rel="stylesheet" type="text/css" href="ten.css" />
<link rel="stylesheet" type="text/css" href="blue.css" id="skin" />
</head>
<body>
<div id="running">
  <h4 class="drag">Running</h4>
  <ul>
    <li><a class="sprite" id="adidas" href="http://www.adidas.com">adidas</a></li>
    <li><a class="sprite" id="asics" href="http://www.asics.com">ASICS</a></li>
    <li><a class="sprite" id="brooks" href="http://www.brooksrunning.com">Brooks</a></li>
    <li><a class="sprite" id="newBalance" href="http://www.newbalance.com">New
Balance</a></li>
    <li><a class="sprite" id="nike" href="http://www.nike.com">Nike</a></li>
    <li><a class="sprite" id="saucony" href="http://www.saucony.com">Saucony</a></li>
  </ul>
</div>
<script src="ten.js" type="text/javascript"></script>

<script src="json2.js" type="text/javascript"></script>

</body>
</html>
```

Note that http://json.org/json2.js is the very same JSON parser that Internet Explorer 8, Firefox 3.5, Safari 4, and Opera 10.5 natively define. The only difference is that the native version is compiled rather than interpreted. So, it runs faster.

JSON in a Nutshell

Okeydokey, JSON differs from JavaScript object and array literals in a few ways. First, JSON object members may only be named with strings. So no identifiers. Second, JSON does not permit values to be functions or undefined. That is to say, a JSON value may be a string, number, boolean, null, object literal, or array literal.

Pretty simple, don't you think?

We're going to be doing exactly the same as we did in the previous examples, except we're using JSON to pass the data, rather than HTML or XML. We'll add another scroller to the page, using the JSON data. To encode data for a scroller with JSON, we would write the following, which is what data/s5.js contains:

```
[
  {
    "href": "ten.html",
    "src": "images/lunaracer.jpg",
    "alt": "Nike LunaRacer"
  },
  {
    "href": "ten.html",
    "src": "images/glide_bos.jpg",
    "alt": "Nike Lunar Glide, Boston"
  },
  {
    "href": "ten.html",
    "src": "images/glide_nyc.jpg",
    "alt": "Nike Lunar Glide, NYC"
  },
  {
    "href": "ten.html",
    "src": "images/mariah.jpg",
    "alt": "Nike Mariah"
  },
  {
    "href": "ten.html",
    "src": "images/fly_org.jpg",
    "alt": "Nike Lunar Fly, Orange"
  },
  {
    "href": "ten.html",
    "src": "images/fly_blk.jpg",
    "alt": "Nike Lunar Fly, Black"
  },
  {
    "href": "ten.html",
    "src": "images/elite.jpg",
    "alt": "Nike Lunar Elite"
  },
  {
```

```
    "href": "ten.html",
    "src": "images/vomero.jpg",
    "alt": "Nike Zoom Vomero"
  },
   {
    "href": "ten.html",
    "src": "images/max.jpg",
    "alt": "Nike Air Max"
  }
]
```

With JSON data and parser in hand, let's create a new scroller. The function to do so will, oddly enough, be named parseJSON(). But before I forget, relocate prep() and have getData() go GET the JSON data. Hmm. I've seen this fish before!

```
function parseSimpleXML(req) {
  if (req.status === 200 || req.status === 304) {
    var domTree = req.responseXML;
    var elements = domTree.getElementsByTagName("shoe");
    var div, ul = createElem("ul", {className: "slide"}), li;
    for (var i = 0, j = elements.length; i < j; i ++) {
      li = createElem("li", null, [
        createElem("a", {href: elements[i].getAttribute("href")}, [
        createElem("img", {src: elements[i].getAttribute("src"), alt:
elements[i].getAttribute("alt")})])]);
      ul.appendChild(li);
    }
    div = createElem("div", {className: "scroller", id: "s4"}, [
      createElem("div", {className: "wrapper"}, [ul]),
      createElem("div", {className: "left arrow sprite"}),
      createElem("div", {className: "right arrow sprite"})]);
    document.body.appendChild(div);
  }
  getData("data/s5.js", parseJSON);
}
function parseJSON(req) {
  prep();
}
```

Now then, eval() and JSON.parse() work with a string. Moreover, an XMLHttpRequest has but two hiding places for data, XMLHttpRequest.responseText or XMLHttpRequest.responseXML.

So, where would our JSON data be?

Right, XMLHttpRequest.responseText. I'd have fallen into despair had you missed that one.

After making sure the HTTP request did not fail, create a local variable named data containing the return value of passing XMLHttpRequest.responseText to JSON.parse(). Remember, that'll be a compiled or interpreted version of Crockford's JSON parser. So no worries; this works perfectly cross-browser.

```
function parseJSON(req) {
  if (req.status === 200 || req.status === 304) {

    var data = JSON.parse(req.responseText);

  }
  prep();
}
```

Note that if you are testing this script on your computer, which is to say loading URLs with the file:// protocol, there obviously will not be an http:// status code. XMLHttpRequest.status will always be 0, no matter what. With this in mind, if you are testing the script on your computer, you must replace 200 or 304 with 0. Otherwise, the if block will never run!

```
function parseJSON(req) {
  if (req.status === 0 || req.status === 304) {
    var data = JSON.parse(req.responseText);
  }
  prep();
}
```

The local variable data now contains an array of objects, just like if we had written this:

```
function parseJSON(req) {
  if (req.status === 200 || req.status === 304) {
    var data = [
      {
        "href": "ten.html",
        "src": "images/lunaracer.jpg",
        "alt": "Nike LunaRacer"
      },
      {
        "href": "ten.html",
        "src": "images/glide_bos.jpg",
        "alt": "Nike Lunar Glide, Boston"
      },
      {
        "href": "ten.html",
        "src": "images/glide_nyc.jpg",
        "alt": "Nike Lunar Glide, NYC"
      },
      {
        "href": "ten.html",
        "src": "images/mariah.jpg",
        "alt": "Nike Mariah"
      },
      {
        "href": "ten.html",
        "src": "images/fly_org.jpg",
        "alt": "Nike Lunar Fly, Orange"
      },
      {
        "href": "ten.html",
        "src": "images/fly_blk.jpg",
        "alt": "Nike Lunar Fly, Black"
      },
      {
        "href": "ten.html",
        "src": "images/elite.jpg",
        "alt": "Nike Lunar Elite"
      },
      {
        "href": "ten.html",
        "src": "images/vomero.jpg",
```

```
      "alt": "Nike Zoom Vomero"
    },
    {
      "href": "ten.html",
      "src": "images/max.jpg",
      "alt": "Nike Air Max"
    }
  ];
}
prep();
}
```

To query say the `src` member of the third element in data, we would write one of the following:

```
data[2].src
data[2]["src"]
```

Those would both return the string, `images/glide_nyc.jpg`. Remember from Chapter 5 you may query a member named with a string with an identifier so long as the string, `src` in our case, is a valid identifier.

With this in mind, we can create a new scroller from our JSON data and `createElem()` helper function like so:

```
function parseJSON(req) {
  if (req.status === 200 || req.status === 304) {
    var data = JSON.parse(req.responseText);

    var div, ul = createElem("ul", {className: "slide"}), li;

    for (var i = 0, j = data.length; i < j; i ++) {
      li = createElem("li", null, [
        createElem("a", {href: data[i].href}, [
        createElem("img", {src: data[i].src, alt: data[i].alt})])]);
      ul.appendChild(li);
    }
    div = createElem("div", {className: "scroller", id: "s5"}, [
      createElem("div", {className: "wrapper"}, [ul]),
      createElem("div", {className: "left arrow sprite"}),

      createElem("div", {className: "right arrow sprite"})]);

  }
  prep();
}
```

Then add the DOM branch to the tree. Note that displaying our new scroller to the visitor is a UI update. Just like rendering the down image for a sprite. Remember that if the UI thread is running JavaScript at the time, those have to take a number and wait in the UI queue. I'm just trying to reinforce why it's vital to write JavaScript that runs snappy. UI rigor mortis is unpleasant for the visitor.

```
function parseJSON(req) {
  if (req.status === 200 || req.status === 304) {
    var data = JSON.parse(req.responseText);
    var div, ul = createElem("ul", {className: "slide"}), li;
    for (var i = 0, j = data.length; i < j; i ++) {
      li = createElem("li", null, [
```

```
        createElem("a", {href: data[i].href}, [
          createElem("img", {src: data[i].src, alt: data[i].alt})])]);
      ul.appendChild(li);
    }
    div = createElem("div", {className: "scroller", id: "s5"}, [
      createElem("div", {className: "wrapper"}, [ul]),
      createElem("div", {className: "left arrow sprite"}),
      createElem("div", {className: "right arrow sprite"})]);
    document.body.appendChild(div);
  }
  prep();
}
```

Now let's throw parseJSON() into the pool and see whether it sinks or swims; save ten.js and reload ten.html in Firefox, comparing its display to Figure 10–6.

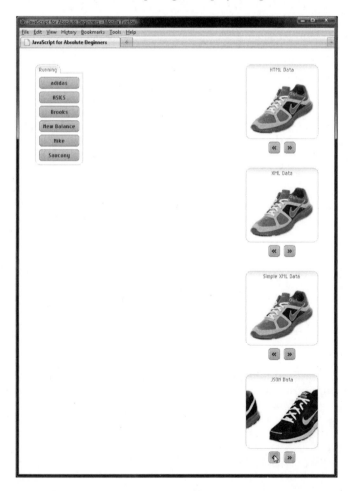

Figure 10–6. Testing the JSON scroller

Padding JSON

Since JSON is valid JavaScript, you do not need an XMLHttpRequest object to retrieve JSON data. This is referred to as JSON-P, JSON with Padding.

JSON-P works like this:

- The JSON data created by a PHP or some other server-side script is wrapped in a callback function. So in data/s6.js, displayed next, the JSON array from the previous gallery is wrapped in a callback function named padJSON(), which we'll define in a bit.

- A <script> element with an src set to the URL of the JSON-P file is dynamically inserted into the page, into ten.html in our case. Note that for cross-browser compatibility, the <script> has to go into the <head>, not the <body>. The browser then executes the JSON-P data file like any other JavaScript file. So, the JSON array gets passed to the callback function it is wrapped in.

```
padJSON([
    {
    "href": "ten.html",
    "src": "images/lunaracer.jpg",
    "alt": "Nike LunaRacer"
    },
    {
    "href": "ten.html",
    "src": "images/glide_bos.jpg",
    "alt": "Nike Lunar Glide, Boston"
    },
    {
    "href": "ten.html",
    "src": "images/glide_nyc.jpg",
    "alt": "Nike Lunar Glide, NYC"
    },
    {
    "href": "ten.html",
    "src": "images/mariah.jpg",
    "alt": "Nike Mariah"
    },
    {
    "href": "ten.html",
    "src": "images/fly_org.jpg",
    "alt": "Nike Lunar Fly, Orange"
    },
    {
    "href": "ten.html",
    "src": "images/fly_blk.jpg",
    "alt": "Nike Lunar Fly, Black"
    },
    {
    "href": "ten.html",
    "src": "images/elite.jpg",
    "alt": "Nike Lunar Elite"
    },
```

```
    {
      "href": "ten.html",
      "src": "images/vomero.jpg",
      "alt": "Nike Zoom Vomero"
    },
    {
      "href": "ten.html",
      "src": "images/max.jpg",
      "alt": "Nike Air Max"
    }
]);
```

Let's define a function named parseJSONP. Insofar as we're not making an parseJSONP request, let's name the parameter data, not req. As we've done several times before, move prep() from parseJSON() to parseJSONP(). However, rather than call getData() for data/s6.js, simply call parseJSONP() instead. Remember, we're bypassing XMLHttpRequest entirely.

```
function parseJSON(req) {
  if (req.status === 200 || req.status === 304) {
    var data = JSON.parse(req.responseText);
    var div, ul = createElem("ul", {className: "slide"}), li;
    for (var i = 0, j = data.length; i < j; i ++) {
      li = createElem("li", null, [
        createElem("a", {href: data[i].href}, [
          createElem("img", {src: data[i].src, alt: data[i].alt})])]);
      ul.appendChild(li);
    }
    div = createElem("div", {className: "scroller", id: "s5"}, [
      createElem("div", {className: "wrapper"}, [ul]),
      createElem("div", {className: "left arrow sprite"}),
      createElem("div", {className: "right arrow sprite"})]);
    document.body.appendChild(div);
  }

  parseJSONP();

}

function parseJSONP(data) {
  prep();
}
```

Now when parseJSON() calls parseJSONP(), data will be undefined. In that event, we want to define padJSON(), the JSON-P callback function. But it has to be global so that it is callable from data/s6.js. Remember, none of the functions in ten.js is global. They're all saved to the call object of the self-invoking function wrapping the script.

So by way of a closure, we'll make parseJSONP() callable from the global scope like so. Remember from Chapter 6 that arguments.callee refers to the function that is running—parseJSONP().

```
function parseJSONP(data) {

  if (typeof data === "undefined") {
    var f = arguments.callee;
    window.padJSON = function(d) {
        f(d);
      };
```

```
}
  prep();
}
```

Now we'll dynamically insert a <script> with an src of data/s6.js, the URL of our JSON-P file. Then return to terminate parseJSONP(). This is when the <script> element is added to the DOM tree. Our JSON array then gets passed to padJSON(), which in turn passes it on to parseJSONP(). The second time parseJSONP() is called, data contains the JSON array not undefined. But a JSON array is a valid JavaScript array, too. So, we can create a new scroller from data just like we did in parseJSON():

```
function parseJSONP(data) {
  if (typeof data === "undefined") {
    var f = arguments.callee;
    window.padJSON = function(d) {
        f(d);
    };

    var script = document.createElement("script");
    script.src = "data/s6.js";
    document.getElementsByTagName("head")[0].appendChild(script);
    return;
  }
  var div, ul = createElem("ul", {className: "slide"}), li;
  for (var i = 0, j = data.length; i < j; i ++) {
    li = createElem("li", null, [
      createElem("a", {href: data[i].href}, [
      createElem("img", {src: data[i].src, alt: data[i].alt})])]);
    ul.appendChild(li);
  }
  div = createElem("div", {className: "scroller", id: "s6"}, [
    createElem("div", {className: "wrapper"}, [ul]),
    createElem("div", {className: "left arrow sprite"}),
    createElem("div", {className: "right arrow sprite"})]);

  prep();
}
```

Finally, it's time to put the branch on the DOM tree. You know what to do:

```
function parseJSONP(data) {
  if (typeof data === "undefined") {
    var f = arguments.callee;
    window.padJSON = function(d) {
        f(d);
    };
    var script = document.createElement("script");
    script.src = "data/s6.js";
    document.getElementsByTagName("head")[0].appendChild(script);
    return;
  }
  var div, ul = createElem("ul", {className: "slide"}), li;
  for (var i = 0, j = data.length; i < j; i ++) {
    li = createElem("li", null, [
      createElem("a", {href: data[i].href}, [
```

```
      createElem("img", {src: data[i].src, alt: data[i].alt})])]);
    ul.appendChild(li);
  }
  div = createElem("div", {className: "scroller", id: "s6"}, [
    createElem("div", {className: "wrapper"}, [ul]),
    createElem("div", {className: "left arrow sprite"}),
    createElem("div", {className: "right arrow sprite"})]);

  document.body.appendChild(div);

  prep();
}
```

Now let's test parseJSONP(); save ten.js, and reload ten.html in Firefox, comparing its display to Figure 10–7.

Figure 10–7. *Testing the JSON-P scroller*

Yielding with Timers

In addition to animations, one other use for timers is to yield control of the UI thread so that the browser can update its display. Doing so prevents browser rigormortis.

At the moment, JavaScript blocks while `prep()` is running. So, until `prepSprites()`, `prepDrag()`, `prepSkinKeys()`, and `prepScrollers()` have all returned, a visitor's browser will be frozen.

To fix that, we'll create an array named `mojo` containing those four functions. Then yield the UI thread for 30 milliseconds, long enough for most UI updates, between each call:

```
function prep() {
  var mojo = [prepSprites, prepDrag, prepSkinKeys, prepScrollers];
  setTimeout(function() {
    (mojo.shift())();
    if (mojo.length !== 0) {
      setTimeout(arguments.callee, 30);
    }
  }, 30);
}
```

Converting function declarations to expressions

Other than the conditional advance loaders, the functions in our script are defined by way of declarations rather than expressions. Doing so is helpful while initially coding a script insofar as you can invoke declared functions prior to defining them. So you can be bit messy while you are trying to get things working if you code your functions with declarations. Moreover, a debugger like Firebug can use a declared function's nonstandard name member as an indicator to convey errors with.

However, function expressions are preferred over declarations insofar as function expressions require you to use functions as values, which is the key to unlocking the power of JavaScript. Moreover, function expressions require you to define a function prior to invoking it, which is good programming practice. This is why we explored functions with expressions rather than declarations in Chapter 6.

With this in mind, let's now go through and recode our function declarations as expressions. Doing so is fairly simple for the most part. Just declare a variable named with the identifier from the declaration and then assign an unnamed function expression to it. The body of the expression is the identical to the body of the declaration. So we're pretty much just moving the identifier. Finally, follow the `}` curly brace at the end of the function body with a `;` semicolon to end the var statement.

Except for the nested functions, we were careful not to invoke functions prior to their declaration. So in addition to converting the nested function declarations to expressions, we will need to move them higher in their parent function's body so that we are invoking a function rather than `undefined`.

Furthermore, let's rework our conditional advance loaders for `createXHR()` and `findClass()` with the `?:` operator rather than with an `if else` statement. In this way, our script will contain 24 function expressions followed by 1 invocation expression (of `addListener()`). Yup, pretty elegant.

ECMAScript 5 adds a strict mode that tells a JavaScript interpreter to throw errors if you try to use deprecated features such as `argument.callee`. To trigger strict mode, simply put `"use strict";` on the very first line of a script. Internet Explorer 9, Firefox 4, and other ECMAScript 5 compliant browsers will then parse our script in strict mode, while older browsers will simply ignore the string literal, which is not saved to any variable. So let's insert `"use strict";` on the very first line of our script.

Now for the final moment of truth. Save `ten.js`, and then reload `ten.html` in Firefox. Put all the behaviors we coded in Chapters 9 and 10 through the wringer.

Final code for `ten.js` appears here. Note that in the downloads for this chapter at `www.apress.com`; this is `tenFinal.js`:

```
"use strict";
(function () {

var addListener = document.addEventListener ?
  function (node, type, listener, phase) {
    node.addEventListener(type, listener, !! phase);
  } :
  function (node, type, listener) {
    node.attachEvent("on" + type, listener);
  } ;

var removeListener = document.removeEventListener ?
  function (node, type, listener, phase) {
    node.removeEventListener(type, listener, !! phase);
  } :
  function (node, type, listener) {
    node.detachEvent("on" + type, listener);
  } ;

var thwart = function (e) {
  if (e.preventDefault) {
    thwart = function (e) {
      e.preventDefault();
    };
  } else {
    thwart = function (e) {
      e.returnValue = false;
    };
  }
  thwart(e);
};

var burst = function (e) {
  if (e.stopPropagation) {
    burst = function (e) {
      e.stopPropagation();
    };
  } else {
    burst = function (e) {
      e.cancelBubble = true;
    };
  }
  burst(e);
};

var traverseTree = document.documentElement.firstElementChild ?
  function traverseTree (node, func) {
    func(node);
    node = node.firstElementChild;
    while (node !== null) {
      traverseTree(node, func);
      node = node.nextElementSibling;
    }
  } :
```

```
function traverseTree (node, func) {
  func(node);
  node = node.firstChild;
  while (node !== null) {
    traverseTree(node, func);
    node = node.nextSibling;
  }
} ;

var findClass = document.getElementsByClassName ?
  function (name, root) {
    root = root || document.documentElement;
    return root.getElementsByClassName(name);
  } :
  document.querySelectorAll ?
  function (name, root) {
    root = root || document.documentElement;
    return root.querySelectorAll("." + name);
  } :
  function (name, root) {
    var found = [];
    root = root || document.documentElement;
    traverseTree(root, function (node) {
      if (!! node.className) {
        for (var names = node.className.split(/\s+/), i = names.length; i --; ) {
          if (names[i] === name) {
            found.push(node);
          }
        }
      }
    });
    return found;
  } ;

var queryCascade = window.getComputedStyle ?
  function (element, property) {
    return getComputedStyle(element, null)[property];
  } :
  function (element, property) {
    return element.currentStyle[property];
  } ;

var doZ = function () {
  var z = 400;
  return function () {
    return z ++;
  };
}();

var getCookie = function (name) {
  var batch = document.cookie, i, firstCut, secondCut;
  i = batch.indexOf(name + "=");
  if (i !== -1) {
    firstCut = i + name.length + 1;
```

```
      secondCut = batch.indexOf(";", firstCut);
      if (secondCut === -1) secondCut = batch.length;
      return decodeURIComponent(batch.substring(firstCut, secondCut));
    } else {
      return false;
    }
  };

  var createElem = function (name, members, children) {
    var elem = document.createElement(name), m;
    if (members instanceof Object) {
      for (m in members) {
        elem[m] = members[m];
      }
    }
    if (children instanceof Array) {
      for (i = 0; i < children.length; i ++ ) {
        elem.appendChild(typeof children[i] === "object" ?
          children[i] : document.createTextNode(children[i]));
      }
    }
    return elem;
  };

  var createXHR = typeof XMLHttpRequest !== "undefined" ?
    function () {
      return new XMLHttpRequest();
    } :
    typeof ActiveXObject !== "undefined" ?
    function () {
      var versions = ["MSXML2.XMLHTTP.6.0", "MSXML2.XMLHTTP.3.0",
        "MSXML2.XMLHTTP", "Microsoft.XMLHTTP"];
      for (var i = 0, j = versions.length, version = ""; i < j; i ++) {
        try {
          new ActiveXObject(versions[i]);
          version = versions[i];
          break;
        }
        catch(e) {
        }
      }
      if (version !== "") {
        return function () {
          return new ActiveXObject(version);
        };
      } else {
        return null;
      }
    }() :
    null ;

  var getData = function (url, callback) {
    if (createXHR !== null) {
      var req = createXHR();
```

```
      req.onreadystatechange = function () {
        if (req.readyState === 4) {
          callback(req);
        }
      }
      req.open("GET", url, true);
      req.send(null);
    }
};

var prepSprites = window.getComputedStyle ?
  function () {
    var elements = findClass("sprite"), sprites = {};
    var slideSprite = function (e) {
      if (e.type == "mouseover") {
        e.target.style.backgroundPosition =
          sprites[e.target.id || e.target.className][1];
      } else {
        e.target.style.backgroundPosition =
          sprites[e.target.id || e.target.className][0];
      }
    };
    for (var i = elements.length, offsets = null, member; i --; ) {
      member = elements[i].id || elements[i].className;
      if (! sprites[member]) {
        sprites[member] = [];
        sprites[member][0] = queryCascade(elements[i], "backgroundPosition");
        offsets = sprites[member][0].split(/\s+/);
        sprites[member][1] = 1 - parseInt(queryCascade(elements[i], "width")) +
          "px " + offsets[1];
      }
      addListener(elements[i], "mouseover", slideSprite);
      addListener(elements[i], "mouseout", slideSprite);
    }
  } :
  function () {
    var elements = findClass("sprite"), sprites = {};
    for (var i = elements.length, offsets = null, member; i --; ) {
      member = elements[i].id || elements[i].className;
      if (! sprites[member]) {
        sprites[member] = [];
        offsets = [queryCascade(elements[i], "backgroundPositionX"),
          queryCascade(elements[i], "backgroundPositionY")];
        sprites[member][0] = offsets.join(" ");
        sprites[member][1] = 1 - parseInt(queryCascade(elements[i], "width")) +
          "px " + offsets[1];
      }
      addListener(elements[i], "mouseover", slideSprite);
      addListener(elements[i], "mouseout", slideSprite);
    }
    var slideSprite = function () {
      var e = window.event;
      if (e.type == "mouseover") {
        e.srcElement.style.backgroundPosition =
```

```
                sprites[e.srcElement.id || e.srcElement.className][1];
          } else {
            e.srcElement.style.backgroundPosition =
                sprites[e.srcElement.id || e.srcElement.className][0];
          }
        };
      } ;

  var drag = function (e) {
    if (!e) e = window.event;
    if (!e.target) e.target = e.srcElement;
    var wrapper = e.target.parentNode;
    var left = parseInt(queryCascade(wrapper, "left"));
    var top = parseInt(queryCascade(wrapper, "top"));
    var clientX = e.clientX;
    var clientY = e.clientY;
    wrapper.style.zIndex = doZ();
    var move = function (e) {
      if (!e) e = window.event;
      wrapper.style.left = left + e.clientX - clientX + "px";
      wrapper.style.top = top + e.clientY - clientY + "px";
      burst(e);
    };
    var drop = function (e) {
      if (!e) e = window.event;
      removeListener(document, "mousemove", move, true);
      removeListener(document, "mouseup", drop, true);
      if (parseInt(wrapper.style.left) < 0) wrapper.style.left = "0px";
      if (parseInt(wrapper.style.top) < 0) wrapper.style.top = "0px";
      burst(e);
      thwart(e);
    };
    addListener(document, "mousemove", move, true);
    addListener(document, "mouseup", drop, true);
    burst(e);
    thwart(e);
  };

  var prepDrag = function () {
    var elements = findClass("drag");
    for (var i = elements.length; i --; ) {
      addListener(elements[i], "mousedown", drag);
    }
  };

  var presetSkin = function () {
    var pref = getCookie("skin");
    if (pref !== false) {
      document.getElementById("skin").href = pref + ".css";
    }
  };

  var prepSkinKeys = function () {
    var sheet = document.getElementById("skin");
```

```
  var swapSkinByKey = function (e) {
    if (!e) e = window.event;
    if (!e.target) e.target = e.srcElement;
    if (e.target.nodeName.toLowerCase() === "input" ||
      e.target.nodeName.toLowerCase() === "textarea") return;
    e.letter = String.fromCharCode(e.charCode ||
      e.keyCode).toLowerCase();
    var pref;
    if (e.letter === "f") {
      pref = "fuchsia";
    } else if (e.letter === "g") {
      pref = "green";
    } else if (e.letter === "b") {
      pref = "blue";
    } else {
      return;
    }
    sheet.href = pref + ".css";
    document.cookie = "skin=" + pref + "; max-age=" + (60*60*24*30);
  };
  addListener(document, "keypress", swapSkinByKey, true);
};

var prepScrollers = function () {
  var elements = findClass("scroller");
  for (var i = elements.length; i --; ) {
    (function (scroller) {
      var wrapper = findClass("wrapper", scroller)[0];
      var slide = findClass("slide", scroller)[0];
      var w1 = parseInt(queryCascade(wrapper, "width"));
      var w2 = parseInt(queryCascade(slide, "width"));
      var timer = null;
      slide.style.left = queryCascade(slide, "left");

      var press = function (e) {
        if (!e) e = window.event;
        if (!e.target) e.target = e.srcElement;
        var jump = e.target.jump;

        var animate = function animate () {
          var x = parseInt(slide.style.left) + jump;
          if (x >= w1 - w2 && x <= 0) {
            slide.style.left = x + "px";
            timer = setTimeout(animate, 15);
          } else if (x < w1 - w2) {
            slide.style.left = w1 - w2 + "px";
          } else {
            slide.style.left = "0px";
          }
        };

        var release = function (e) {
          clearTimeout(timer);
          removeListener(document, "mouseup", release, true);
```

457

```
                removeListener(document, "mouseout", release, true);
            };
            addListener(document, "mouseup", release, true);
            addListener(document, "mouseout", release, true);
            animate();
            burst(e);
            thwart(e);
        };
        for (var arrows = findClass("arrow", scroller),
          i = arrows.length, re = /\bright\b/; i --; ) {
            addListener(arrows[i], "mousedown", press);
            arrows[i].jump = (re.test(arrows[i].className)) ? -10 : 10;
        }
    })(elements[i]);
  }
};

var parseHTML = function (req) {
  if (req.status === 200 || req.status === 304) {
    var div = createElem("div", {className: "scroller", id: "s2"}, [
      createElem("div", {className: "wrapper"}),
      createElem("div", {className: "left arrow sprite"}),
      createElem("div", {className: "right arrow sprite"})]);
    div.firstChild.innerHTML = req.responseText;
    document.body.appendChild(div);
  }
  getData("data/s3.xml", parseXML);
};

var parseXML = function (req) {
  if (req.status === 200 || req.status === 304) {
    var domTree = req.responseXML,
      m = "getElementsByTagName";
    var elements = domTree[m]("shoe");
    var div, ul = createElem("ul", {className: "slide"}), li;
    for (var i = 0, j = elements.length; i < j; i ++) {
      li = createElem("li", null, [
        createElem("a", {href: elements[i][m]("href")[0].firstChild.data}, [
        createElem("img", {src: elements[i][m]("src")[0].firstChild.data,
        alt: elements[i][m]("alt")[0].firstChild.data})])]);
      ul.appendChild(li);
    }
    div = createElem("div", {className: "scroller", id: "s3"}, [
      createElem("div", {className: "wrapper"}, [ul]),
      createElem("div", {className: "left arrow sprite"}),
      createElem("div", {className: "right arrow sprite"})]);
    document.body.appendChild(div);
  }
  getData("data/s4.xml", parseSimpleXML);
};

var parseSimpleXML = function (req) {
  if (req.status === 200 || req.status === 304) {
    var domTree = req.responseXML;
```

```
    var elements = domTree.getElementsByTagName("shoe");
    var div, ul = createElem("ul", {className: "slide"}), li;
    for (var i = 0, j = elements.length; i < j; i ++) {
      li = createElem("li", null, [
        createElem("a", {href: elements[i].getAttribute("href")}, [
        createElem("img", {src: elements[i].getAttribute("src"),
        alt: elements[i].getAttribute("alt")})])]);
      ul.appendChild(li);
    }
    div = createElem("div", {className: "scroller", id: "s4"}, [
      createElem("div", {className: "wrapper"}, [ul]),
      createElem("div", {className: "left arrow sprite"}),
      createElem("div", {className: "right arrow sprite"})]);
    document.body.appendChild(div);
  }
  getData("data/s5.js", parseJSON);
};

var parseJSON = function (req) {
  if (req.status === 200 || req.status === 304) {
    var data = JSON.parse(req.responseText);
    var div, ul = createElem("ul", {className: "slide"}), li;
    for (var i = 0, j = data.length; i < j; ++) {
      li = createElem("li", null, [
        createElem("a", {href: data[i].href}, [
        createElem("img", {src: data[i].src, alt: data[i].alt})])]);
      ul.appendChild(li);
    }
    div = createElem("div", {className: "scroller", id: "s5"}, [
      createElem("div", {className: "wrapper"}, [ul]),
      createElem("div", {className: "left arrow sprite"}),
      createElem("div", {className: "right arrow sprite"})]);
    document.body.appendChild(div);
  }
  parseJSONP();
};

var parseJSONP = function parseJSONP (data) {
  if (typeof data === "undefined") {
    var f = parseJSONP;
    window.padJSON = function (d) {
        f(d);
      };
    var script = document.createElement("script");
    script.src = "data/s6.js";
    document.getElementsByTagName("head")[0].appendChild(script);
    return;
  }
  var div, ul = createElem("ul", {className: "slide"}), li;
  for (var i = 0, j = data.length; i < j; i ++) {
    li = createElem("li", null, [
      createElem("a", {href: data[i].href}, [
      createElem("img", {src: data[i].src, alt: data[i].alt})])]);
    ul.appendChild(li);
```

```
    }
    div = createElem("div", {className: "scroller", id: "s6"}, [
      createElem("div", {className: "wrapper"}, [ul]),
      createElem("div", {className: "left arrow sprite"}),
      createElem("div", {className: "right arrow sprite"})]);
    document.body.appendChild(div);
    prep();
  };

  var prep = function () {
    var mojo = [prepSprites, prepDrag, prepSkinKeys, prepScrollers];
    setTimeout(function yield () {
      (mojo.shift())();
      if (mojo.length !== 0) {
        setTimeout(yield, 30);
      }
    }, 30);
  };

  addListener(window, "load", function (e) {
      presetSkin();
      getData("data/s2.html", parseHTML);
  });

})();
```

Summary

In this chapter we explored how to save visitor data in a cookie in order to remember their preference for a blue, fuchsia, or green skin, animate part of the DOM tree and yield the UI thread with timers, and dynamically add content with Ajax or JSON-P. Finally, we explored how to recode our function declarations as function expressions and to have JavaScript interpret our script in strict mode, which is new in ECMAScript 5.

Though function declarations are simpler to work with while writing and debugging a script, function expressions are preferred insofar as those require you to use functions as values. Doing so is the key to unlocking the power of JavaScript and to your becoming a JavaScript wizard.

Index

■ ■ ■